A Day for Very Great Things

The Lives of
Howard Colby and Mabel Rice-Wray Ives

A Day for Very Great Things

The Lives of
Howard Colby and Mabel Rice-Wray Ives

Earl Redman and Erica Toussaint

GEORGE RONALD
OXFORD

George Ronald, Publisher
Oxford
www.grbooks.com

© Earl Redman and Erica Toussaint 2023
All Rights Reserved

A catalogue record for this book is available from the British Library

ISBN 978-0-85398-661-4

Cover design Steiner Graphics

*This book is dedicated to
the many generations of spiritual offspring
of Howard and Mabel Ives:
Hands of the Cause of God, Knights of Bahá'u'lláh,
members of National, Regional and Local Spiritual Assemblies,
Auxiliary Board members, pioneers, travel teachers
and simply dedicated Bahá'ís,
whose lives of service and devotion
have been enriched by their example*

Contents

Foreword ix
Acknowledgements xvii

1	Introduction	1
2	Howard Colby Ives, the Early Years	7
3	Howard Meets the Master and Is Transformed	18
4	Finding His Way	40
5	Mabel Rice-Wray, the Early Years	55
6	Howard and Mabel Get Married	79
7	A New Plan of Action and the Beginnings of a Life of Sacrifice: 1920–1925	88
8	Spiritual Struggles and Tests	107
9	Race Unity Work: 1926–1931	123
10	Howard Breaks Down	136
11	Early 1932	143
12	Howard's Weekly 'Hakouk' Letters: January–March 1932	153
13	Travel Teaching and a Boarding House	168
14	Howard Discovers His Writing Skills	184
15	Howard Writes *Portals to Freedom*	204
16	The Song Celestial	220
17	Howard's Other Literary Work	236
18	Opening the Seven Year Plan: 1936–1937	256
19	Moncton, New Brunswick, Canada: 1937	285
20	Scranton, Pennsylvania, and Chicago: 1938	297
21	Back in Canada: 1938–1939	311

22	Memphis and Howard's Declining Health	331
23	Further Afield in the American South: 1940–1941	352
24	The End of Howard's Physical Road: 1941	372
25	Mabel Soldiers on in the South: 1941–1943	397
26	Mabel Joins Howard	416
Epilogue: Lives Well Lived		442

Appendices
  1 Two Talks by Howard Colby Ives   435
  2 Two Talks by Mabel Rice-Wray Ives   451

Bibliography   461
Notes and References   467
Index

Foreword
by Erica Toussaint

During the 1950s and 60s, when my two younger siblings and I were growing up in Northwest Oregon, our family comprised the only Bahá'í community in the county. Despite our relative isolation, our family culture was rich with deep devotion to the Cause of Bahá'u'lláh, and His teachings informed our thoughts and actions. Our mother, Barbara Ives Reich Kochmann, was a wonderful storyteller in her own right, after our grandmother, Muriel Ives Barrow Newhall, who seems to have inherited her father's ability as a writer and story-teller. Stories of my illustrious great-grandfather were often woven with other tales of the heroism and sacrifice of the early believers in America. My mother and grandmother both told these stories so frequently as we were growing up that some of my earliest memories are of hearing about 'Great Uncle Grandaddy' (my mother had called him, 'Uncle Grandaddy' as a child, and the term of endearment just stuck).

One story in particular that stands out clearly for being told many times over the years was of an incident that can be found in his book, *Portals to Freedom*. 'Abdu'l-Bahá had invited Howard to accompany him on His daily walk, during which Howard raised a theological question. 'Abdu'l-Bahá replied to the question, but based on his training in theology, Howard didn't agree with 'Abdu'l-Bahá's view, and marshalled back a rebuttal. 'Abdu'l-Bahá just looked at him and said, 'Meester Ives, you try your way and I will try mine.' Their telling of the story always ended with a description of how Howard's face would turn beet red in embarrassment whenever he shared that story because it was inconceivable to him thereafter that he could have even considered arguing with 'Abdu'l-Bahá!

Both my mother and my grandmother were women who deeply studied the writings of the Bahá'í Faith, and had been profoundly influenced by Howard. His constant study of the Writings of Bahá'u'lláh, 'Abdu'l-Bahá and Shoghi Effendi resulted in many compilations on topics he was exploring. My grandmother followed the same practice, and we have a stack of her compilation notebooks in the family libraries.

My mother also followed suit – diving deep into the Ocean of Bahá'u'lláh's Revelation, seeking to understand the intended meaning of the Manifestation of God and His designated successors. This passion resulted in the Words of Bahá'u'lláh and of 'Abdu'l-Bahá frequently being quoted in our everyday life at home. For example, when sibling rivalry erupted in the household, and we sought mother's intervention, she would quote: 'Conflict and contention are categorically forbidden in the Book,' reminding us that 'Every aggressor deprives himself of God's grace'. As a child I often felt impatient when hearing these words, wishing that she would just solve the issue (and hopefully take my side). As an adult, I realize the priceless legacy of hearing the words of Bahá'u'lláh quoted so often in practical application to everyday life.

'Abdu'l-Bahá's profound impact on Howard Colby Ives, and Howard's faithful study and application of the guidance found in the Writings of the Bahá'í Faith, not only influenced the generations of our immediate and extended family, but can be traced through many generations of his spiritual progeny throughout the world.

One can recognize a kind of discipline in reading and studying the Writings used by Howard that has communicated itself to this present day. As I look back over the course of years with the many who came to our home to learn about and study the Bahá'í Faith, my childhood memories are rich with the common sight of Bahá'í books open, stacked on one another on the kitchen table; a conversation about the Faith unfolding.

It was common to see my mother leaping up to grab a copy of *Gleanings*, turning to a well-known page and reading a relevant passage from Bahá'u'lláh that addressed a question raised. Like her grandfather, she found herself impatient with her own opinions, and always sought the holy grail of having the Writings define themselves. It was a glorious moment when she would happen upon phrases like 'by this is meant', or would come upon a clear explanation of a meaning. For example, when looking at the short obligatory prayer, the beginning of the prayer reads, 'I bear witness O my God, that thou hast created me to know Thee . . .' when mother read 'Abdu'l-Bahá's explanation of the knowledge of God in *Some Answered Questions* she was ecstatic: 'Knowing God, therefore, means the comprehension and the knowledge of His attributes, and not of His Reality.'

In this book, you'll find Howard's instructions to one of his spiritual children, Nancy Phillips, about how to study the Writings, which illustrates his disciplined approach. Nancy has, like so many others who were taught the Faith and then deepened their knowledge by aid of Howard's methods, shared this same approach with those whom they themselves introduced to and taught the Faith of Bahá'u'lláh. And it has served them well.

Coming from this family experience, you can imagine how it felt to receive an email in 2007 out of the blue from Roger Dahl, the archivist of the US Bahá'í National Archives, informing me that my great-grandfather's papers were now catalogued and available for research – and there were 13 boxes in all! This was my first knowledge that Howard Colby Ives papers even existed. And to think that there were 13 boxes of them was dizzying! At the time, as I was serving on the National Spiritual Assembly of the Bahá'ís of the United States, I regularly travelled to Wilmette, Illinois every month and could easily arrange an appointment to take a look at the collection.

When I opened the first box, inside the first folder I found the translation of 'Abdu'l-Bahá's first Tablet to Howard Colby Ives! Written on 12 August 1912, while 'Abdu'l-Bahá was still in America, I read the opening lines in the flowing handwriting of the translator on what was now ageing, yellowed lined paper:

> To his honor Doctor Ives
> Upon him be Baha-o-llah El Abha
> He is God

Holding this actual piece of history in my hand, I knew at that moment that I MUST explore the contents of these precious boxes and that a biography could be written about this man who is beloved by the generations of Bahá'ís touched by *Portals to Freedom*. For the next few years, it was commonly possible to come in a day early for the meetings of the National Spiritual Assembly to continue to explore and scan hundreds of documents in this treasure trove of his life's work.

The first few boxes contained the original translations and copies of the letters exchanged between Howard Colby Ives and 'Abdu'l-Bahá, and later with the Guardian of the Bahá'í Faith, Shoghi Effendi. I was thrilled to see that Howard had kept copies of his letters to them – and realized that never before had the letters that prompted the well-known responses of 'Abdu'l-Bahá been seen!

Howard's communications with the Centre of the Covenant were deeply passionate, personal, and filled with expressions of deep loyalty and love. After the passing of 'Abdu'l-Bahá, Howard turned to Shoghi Effendi, writing 41 letters between 1926 and 1940. Those letters are from a spiritual soldier in the field writing to the General – reporting his activities, sharing insights, asking for greater understanding, and above all swearing his fealty to the appointed Centre of the Covenant. Every one of the 21 responses from Shoghi Effendi bore a personal note of encouragement at the end.

Stunned by all that lay in this treasure trove, I was not prepared for what I found next as I began to explore the forty folders of letters between Howard and his dear Riswanea (Mabel). Most readers of *Portals to Freedom,* and that includes my generation of descendants of Howard's family, know little of their personal relationship. The family stories that I had heard as a child didn't include much about them – the focus was on 'Abdu'l-Bahá – Howard was always the secondary character.

What unfolds in these precious letters is the deeply loving relationship between them; they are letters spilling over with expressions of their deep, tender love for each other.

Reading the letters, the reason why there are so many letters becomes clear: much of their married life they were teaching and serving apart from one another. They were both powerful Bahá'í teachers and were frequently sent to different goal areas by the National Teaching Committee. Although they missed each other terribly they never refused these requests.

The many letters include details of their teaching efforts, the sweet encouragement and advice they offered one another, and their homey conversations about money, their living situations, and expressions of hope for the next time they would be together. Woven brightly throughout this personal correspondence between husband and wife is the humility of their service, their utter devotion to the Cause they strove to serve with every breath, their commitment to continually growing spiritually along with daily examples of their constant sacrifices.

Howard was exuberant in his love for Riswanea, and in each letter he found creative ways to express his love: 'Rizwanea, Beloved of my heart and soul', 'Rizwanea, Beloved of all worlds!', 'My blessed, beloved Riswanea', 'my darling, My Darling, MY DARLING!'. Once in a while he is especially exuberant: 'Blessed of all worlds! That's what you are – you blessed, beautiful, charming, lovely mate of my heart! How's that for an opening sentence of a letter from an old married man to his dear little Rizwanea?' And he ends each letter sweetly in various ways as, 'your Howie', 'Eternally thine Howie', 'I love thee My Own. Eternally thine H'.

Often Howard speaks of missing her with words such as these: 'I can begin to count days now before I see & clasp my Riswanea to my heart. Life isn't much fun when we are separated, is it darling? I love you, heart of my heart, & your sweet love & sincere advocation of the Blessed Beauty, and your steadfastness as a warrior in the Path of God – is very blessed & sweet to your Howie. All my heart is thine – your adoring mate of all worlds & ages.'

Frequently his letters to Rizwanea describe their shared lofty spiritual aspirations stimulated by their constant study of the Writings. At the end of one letter dated 15 March 1932, full of practical observations and reporting about their work in sales which they both were engaged in to support their traveling teaching, he closes with this:

> I hope you will get here soon, anyhow, my blessed one, for I want you with me a lot. In fact SOMETHING FIERCE.
>
> Just one word more about our plans for our life together after this experience is rolled up 'as the carpets of yore were folded'. TOGETHER let us try with all our souls to build in our spiritual world a firmer foundation than ever for that eternal union of which Abdul Baha speaks so wonderfully. Let us talk about it a lot. Let us work <u>together</u> and pray <u>together</u> about it and not be satisfied with anything less than perfect spiritual union on the highest plane possible in this world.
>
> I ran across a beautiful and marvelous quotation from the Master's Words in an old note book of mine the other day: 'Immortality is the government of the human soul by the Divine Will.'
>
> The connotations of these words are tremendous to me. We can strive to attain to this Immortality while still in this world. It must be possible or else the Master would not have urged the believers to strive for that supreme Goal.

Many other treasures came to light with each day spent in the Archives over the course of several years – including among other things, unpublished manuscripts, correspondence between other well-known Bahá'ís, pictures, tender letters between him and his family members. As I wondered how to bring this all to light for the many who would wish to know, it became clear to me that I could not be the writer of this biography. Howard Colby Ives's *Portals to Freedom* is loved by so many people who have been touched by its very personal and heartfelt word pictures of 'Abdu'l-Bahá that it seemed clear that another more experienced writer should be the drafter of the book.

FOREWORD

Just before the 100th anniversary year of 'Abdu'l-Bahá's eight-month visit to America in 1912, I had discovered a marvellous book, *'Abdu'l-Bahá in Their Midst* by Earl Redman, and was so taken by it that I read it through four times during that year. In doing so I became quite a fan of the author and nurtured the hope that I might someday meet him. By chance we were introduced via email and I invited him to come to visit when next he and his wife might be passing nearby on their travels around the world sharing the stories in the book. To my delight he agreed, and we arranged a number of story-telling gatherings in the Portland area for them.

I must admit that not only was I an adoring fan, but there was an ulterior motive. It seemed to me that Earl's approach to telling these stories of 'Abdu'l-Bahá and those who met him had all the elements that would be needed for a biography of Howard Colby Ives – deep knowledge of the Faith paired with a warm heart and rich writing experience. Earl's stories always seemed to create the space to let the reader's heart be touched. A biography of Howard Colby Ives would certainly need someone to approach it with great heart. So during their visit I shared the story of the thirteen boxes of Mabel and Howard Colby Ives's papers, described what they contained and asked if he might be willing to take a look with an eye to writing the biography. He left with a flash drive full of all the scans from those thirteen boxes. And so it is that this book has come to life as the result of that collaboration.

Earl has been the main writer, with me serving only as light editor, sometimes adding more information or highlighting some aspect of the story. Everyone who will read this book owes a debt of gratitude to him for bringing to life the story of these two devoted servants of God. Thankfully now many readers will experience the unfoldment of how two souls strove to live lives dedicated to 'Abdu'l-Bahá's ringing words, 'This is the day for VERY GREAT THINGS!'

Erica Toussaint, summer 2022

Acknowledgements

Erica Toussaint's massive accumulation of information about her great-grandfather Howard Colby Ives is what enabled this book to be written, but several other people also made contributions. Doris Dejwakh, who had previously looked into writing the Howard Colby Ives biography, shared her initial data organization and ideas, and answered my early questions. Lewis Walker at the US National Bahá'í Archives, as he has for all my previous books, found and sent me a number of interesting items. Erica Leith shared a copy of an autobiography of Edris Rice-Wray from the George Ronald files that helped to fill out some details. Steven Kolins very kindly shared the results of his extensive research of online databases for information about Howard, Mabel and their families. Violetta Zein helped to greatly improve the Introduction, and finally, Larry Staudt, as he did in some of my other books, edited an early draft of this one. I would also like to thank Andy Qualls for his help in proofreading the book.

And, as she has done from the beginning, my wife Sharon O'Toole was my invaluable proofreader.

I also have to gratefully acknowledge the editing skills of May Hofman, who guided six of my previous seven books to publication with George Ronald. And she had a significant hand in that seventh book as well. Her suggestions and comments always led to a better book. On those rare occasions when I really didn't want to delete a story she indicated wasn't appropriate or maybe was historically dubious, on re-reading the bit under discussion, it was always obvious she was right – even if I didn't like it! This is the last of my books that she will edit – her retirement will be deeply felt. Many thanks, May, for all your help and guidance.

Earl Redman, 2023

1
Introduction

In November 2015, my wife, Sharon O'Toole, and I were headed for an 11-week story-telling trip across the Pacific to Hawaii, Fiji, Samoa, New Zealand, Australia and Tasmania. While the trip was still in the planning stage, Erica Toussaint, who had enjoyed my first book, *'Abdu'l-Bahá in Their Midst*, contacted me and mentioned that she would love to set up some story-tellings in the Portland, Oregon, area if we were to ever pass through that city. From Ireland, Portland is right on the way to Hawaii, so we made arrangements to spend a few days with Erica and do our story-telling. While staying with Erica and Marvin, her wonderfully charismatic husband whose sparkling black face was set off by an amazingly white, bushy beard, Erica asked me about writing a biography of her great-grandfather, Howard Colby Ives, author of the famously intimate *Portals to Freedom*. She had been trying to get the book written for years and thought my writing style could bring the heart of the story of her dedicated ancestor to light.

A biography was a daunting challenge since I had never written one before, but Erica's enthusiasm and the stories she shared piqued my interest enough to make me say that I would like to look at what she had collected and see what might be possible. My small travel computer didn't have storage for the huge number of files she had scanned, so early the next morning, while everyone else was asleep, I went for a three-mile walk, debating whether I was the one who should be writing Howard's biography. When I came across a store with USB drives of sufficient space on sale at a discount, I bought one. That purchase was my decision to at least examine the possibilities. It wasn't until later, after we'd left Erica and Marvin's, that I began to look over the letters and discovered what she'd given me. It very quickly became clear that there was an amazing story there.

In a Tablet to Howard Ives revealed four years after their initial meeting in April 1912, 'Abdu'l-Bahá told Howard of his station:

> O thou speaker in the Temple of the Kingdom!
>
> ... It is recorded in the Gospel that John the Baptist was crying in the wilderness: 'Prepare ye the way of the Lord, make His Paths straight, for the Kingdom of God is at hand.'
>
> He was crying in the wilderness, but thou art crying in populous cities. Although the ministers have brilliant crowns on their heads, yet it is my hope that thou mayest crown thy head with the diadem of the Kingdom – such a diadem whose brilliant jewels may illumine the dark passages of future centuries and cycles.
>
> God says in His great Book, Qur'án, 'He especializes with His Mercy whomsoever He willeth.' That is, God distinguisheth with His favor and bestowal a number of souls, and marks them with His own seal of approval. A similar statement is revealed in the Gospel: 'Many are called but few are chosen.' Now, praise be to God that thou art one of those 'few'.[1]

That was what ultimately caught my attention and made me want to write this book.

Those familiar with *Portals to Freedom* know that Howard Colby Ives wrote very emotionally, intimately and spiritually and he put his heart into that book. His letters are even more intimate. And it also quickly became apparent that this was not going to be a book about just Howard Colby Ives; it had to be a book about Howard and his wife, Mabel Rice-Wray Ives. Her letters are just as emotional, though more pragmatic than his. Together, they formed a powerful teaching team that gave up house and home for 20 years and travel-taught their way across the United States and Canada in the desire to be of service to the Faith of Bahá'u'lláh.

Howard's life was one of dedication, sacrifice and an immense desire to 'attain' the good pleasure of God and so be worthy of being one of the 'few'. His relationship with 'Abdu'l-Bahá from the early days of his study of the Faith had cemented his heart and fealty to the Head of the Faith and this would characterize the rest of his life of service as well.

When I began to look at Mabel, it quickly became obvious that she was a teaching powerhouse in her own right. Helen Inderlied has written about spending some weeks with Howard and Mabel in Scranton, New York:

> Knowing Mabel more intimately made me think of Wordsworth's poem – 'She was a phantom of delight when first she dawned upon my sight . . . I saw her upon nearer view, etc . . .' The 'nearer view' was 'all to the good', better and better as I realized more the depths and facets of her nature. She had her prayers and devotions in the morning and joined Mr. Ives and me about ten o'clock. Mr. Ives confided to me that she was striving for spiritual poise at all times. He added, 'How sweet she is when she comes out from her devotions so dear and poised.' She certainly had attained, for no matter what happened, she was always patient and helpful and wonderful, even tho she was so exhausted she had to leave us and go South for a complete rest. She said to me 'I must go or I shan't be able to hold out. I haven't had a vacation in 15 years.' I did not see how we could spare her. She was the life of the new class she had just started. But Mr. Ives said, 'we must not put a stone in her way'. That showed his great love for her and his noble station.
>
> We Bahá'ís all knew that Mabel Ives was one of the best speakers in the Cause. She was clear, original, magnetic, and inspiring. She could produce a vivid picture of what she wanted to portray, and her spiritual lucidity seemed to allow her to etch her message on the hearts of her listeners,

who did not then forget. I sometimes noticed the expression of her face as she lectured – often of ethereal sweetness. Once when she was dressing carefully in every detail before leaving for the lecture, she said, 'I take pains this way with my appearance for the sake of the Cause.' She lived for the Cause of God and she died serving her most precious Faith!²

So, this book became one about a Bahá'í couple to whom the Faith and its exigencies were the most important things in their lives. Howard became a writer – *Portals to Freedom* was just a beginning – and he was a mesmerizing speaker and teacher of the Faith who had his head in the spiritual clouds. He was similar to Thomas Breakwell in that his spiritual side dominated his actions. He was also a deep student/scholar of the Faith, studying the teachings assiduously, creating compilations to aid his study and guiding new believers in learning how to approach studying the Ocean of God's utterance.

Mabel was more in the mold of Martha Root and became the model of a travel teacher, proclaiming the Faith wherever the National Teaching Committee sent her and being very practical in her approach. During the last half-dozen years of their lives, she was the public face of this powerful teaching duo. She brought souls close to the Faith and Howard was the closer: he confirmed the seekers and deepened the new believers. Both were absolutely obedient to the National Spiritual Assembly. They became a Bahá'í tag-team, each playing the part they were best suited for, and together opening up great swathes of America and Canada to the teachings and the Faith of Bahá'u'lláh.

Doris McKay has described them well:

> By living very frugally, the Ives managed. One wondered how they could have done it. Recklessly they burned themselves out and only through stressed concentration, were they able to balance their Bahá'í activities with keeping alive. They were truly heroes, but they did not pretend to be saints. They kept their enthusiasm all through a life

made up of crises. There would be good food and good times. Always the Ives were human. Always the Ives were fun. Certainly this is a high station: to appreciate the good things that God has given us and, yet, to give them up gladly – to be detached.

Mabel, in her remodelled handed-down clothes was dainty and feminine; Howard in his shiny grey suit was distinguished. Together, they were an aristocracy of spirit.[3]

Howard was a man of grand vision and aspiration, while Mabel was much more practical. Howard wrote several long letters to the National Spiritual Assembly of the United States and Canada with suggestions about accomplishing various big tasks. He also had his books which, in addition to the famous *Portals to Freedom*, included a year-long deepening course for Bahá'ís and a book designed to illustrate the Bahá'í principles and beliefs for those who weren't Bahá'ís – done without mention of the Bahá'í Faith or Bahá'u'lláh. Howard was also a speaker whose talks tended to be expansive overviews of the Faith and how it was to develop. Mabel focused more on the practicalities of conducting teaching projects and how to reach and bring in the masses. In this, she built upon the work of Orcella Rexford and Ruth Moffett and became more powerful through the years. Her abilities peaked during the Seven Year Plan that began at Riḍván 1937.

Most of this book is based on letters sent by Howard and/or Mabel or those received by them. There are over 900 of them, full of the details of their hopes and their struggles: the places they went and the people they met. The correspondence between Howard and Mabel is very intimate and illumines the idea that they were a single soul in two bodies, true soul mates. It is also easy to see when they were apart for any length of time, because they would write almost daily letters to each other. But when they were together, the only correspondence was that which they carried on with friends, family, national committees and the National Spiritual Assembly and, of course, with Shoghi Effendi, Guardian of the Cause of God, and this correspondence lacks many of the very personal stories in their letters to each other. There are large gaps in this epistolary conversation – many of their letters are apparently lost or unavailable. Sometimes, there are long periods where there are many letters from one but none from the other, so often this story becomes rather lopsided and about just one or the other.

Between them both, they received 17 letters from 'Abdu'l-Bahá, also known as the Master, and 28 letters from Shoghi Effendi. Howard's letters to the Master and the Guardian are commonly full of angst, asking for guidance and begging that he may be detached from the material world. Mabel's letters are more directed at how she could be more of service and to teach the Faith. These letters, too, give a fascinating glimpse into the spiritual minds of Howard and Mabel. Between them, they taught the Faith in at least 74 communities in 26 states and three provinces.

But with what we have, a truly amazing story of two completely dedicated and sacrificial servants of the Faith emerges. It has been an amazing adventure to be privileged to write.

2
Howard Colby Ives, the Early Years

The man who would become famous across the Bahá'í world for his writing and spiritual teaching skills was born in Brooklyn, New York, on 11 October 1867 to Gertrude and Julius Ives, the third of five children. Howard's older brothers were Charles and William, four and three years his senior; Theodore and Florence four years and nine years, respectively, his junior. Those first years were spent in Geneva, New York. A year after Howard's father died in 1879, the family moved to Niagara, New York, then returned to Brooklyn in 1884.[1] Howard's maternal grandfather, William Childs, was an active part of the anti-slavery movement and his home was a northern terminal for the 'underground railway', over which escaped slaves travelled from the South to the North.[2] His attitudes on race may have influenced Howard's future work with Black people in the South.

Howard begins to write

In 1886, when Howard was 19, he suffered from a lung problem and his doctor, worried that a cough he had developed would turn into 'consumption', recommended a dry climate and high altitude. Howard went to Wyoming, where he lived for two years on a ranch tending sheep. O. Z. Whitehead has written of this period: 'As he sat by himself in the hills and looked at the stars, he sometimes wrote poetry. Always a passionate "seeker of Truth", he tried to dispel his doubts concerning the existence of God.'[3] Thus began his writing career and his spiritual search. His earliest extant poem is dated 1 March 1886:

Friendship

Knowest thou one whose heart beats send
An answering throb to thine own breast
Whose presence all thy tears arrest
And mingled woe with gladness blend?
Then rest thou soul; tho' fortune tend
To rob all else. Thy heart knows best.
    Thou hast a Friend.

Knowest thou one whose love will mend
The broken string of thy heart's lyre,
And though against thy fond desire
Will not to thy wrong wishes bend?
But from thyself thyself forfend.
Reject thou not that holy fire.
    Thou hast a friend.

Knowest thou one who will attend
Thy guide and saviour e'er to be,
Will more than die, will live for thee,
And for thy joy his own will rend?
Hold fast his hand until life's end.
And then in deathless glory see
    A better Friend.[4]

Another poem, called *We're All Built the Same Way*, looked at what makes us happy:

If dollars grew on bushes
And wine came down like rain;
If dewdrops were real diamonds,
As poets fancies feign;
If all the fame I've longed for
Just clamored to be mine,
And all the thoughts I chose to think
The public called divine;

If beefsteaks dangled from the trees,
And pudding smoking hot
Grew in the fields like cabbages
In every shady spot;
If everything one wished to eat
Came quick at my desire,
And jovial friends to eat it with
I need but to require;

If days were filled with pleasure,
And pain came never nigh;
If notes I gave would ne'er mature
And creditors all fly;
If every night brought drowsiness
And every morn delight;
If all my friends were friends in truth
And all my foes polite;

If houses, lands and horses,
Were just exactly what I want
And not the least bit more;
If everything that I could wish
Came quick as one could wink
I know there's something I'd forget;
Happy? Well I don't think.[5]

Howard returned to New York physically well, but still spiritually challenged. In his book *Portals to Freedom*, he wrote:

> For many years I had found myself unable to accept the conventional connotations of such words as God, Faith, Heaven, Hell, Prayer, Christ, Eternal Life, and others of so-called religious significance. In very early manhood I had come to grips with the goblins of superstition masquerading as churchly creeds and had cast them out, but no satisfying, spirit-lifting convictions had come to take their places. Perhaps for ten years my thought of life was frankly and positively agnostic.[6]

Then, in about 1887, according to his daughter Muriel:

> One evening walking home from his job as errand boy on Wall Street he came up the slight rise on to Brooklyn Bridge. It was sunset and Father walked slowly, shelling the peanuts that always filled his pockets and reading Browning. Suddenly he was overwhelmed. Knowledge and certainty exploded within him. He shouted his discovery. 'There is a God' . . . – right there on Brooklyn Bridge. When he told me this story he burst out laughing – and Father had a wonderful laugh, rich, deep and filled with joy. 'There was an old apple woman going by', he said, 'and she looked scared to death. She thought I was crazy. But I knew I was sane for the first time in my life.[7]

His discovery of God through this Paul-on-the-road-to-Damascus moment was life-changing but it didn't begin to bear fruit for another 14 years.

On 12 November 1890, Howard married Elizabeth Church Hoyt in Kings, New York, and the two began a family. She was four years his elder and was a member of the Daughters of the American Revolution with roots going back to the Mayflower. Her family included President Adams and John Hancock.[8] Their first child was Waldo Rolfe, born on 10 October 1891, but he died just six months later of pneumonia. Hoyt was born on 9 October 1892. He went on to become a doctor, but died under mysterious circumstances in 1917 near Terre Haute, Indiana, an apparent suicide.[9] Another son, Whitney Thayer, was born in 1893.

Soon after Whitney's birth, Howard began attending Williams College in Williamstown, Massachusetts. In order to help with expenses, Elizabeth took boarders into the house. Then, the day before Christmas in 1896, while three-year-old Whitney was in bed with diphtheria, the house caught fire. Someone rescued the toddler from the blaze, but he died a week later. Their last child, Muriel Landon, was born on 31 March 1897. She plays a significant role in the latter part of this story.[10]

Years later, Mabel described these years and Howard's first marriage:

> He would rather have waited, as he wasn't established. Then they began having children. Also he had to take care of her parents, difficult people, very. And of his own mother, for quite a while as well as his young sister. He had the greatest difficulty in keeping his head above water . . . But he was superbly loyal and faithful . . . Years after their little sons had died in infancy, they adopted a boy of fourteen, whose father had committed a crime and had been put in Jail. The boy proved a comfort to his wife and she lavished all her affections on him. Howard put him thru Princeton when he could ill afford it . . . he was continually being forced into debt, and could never get ahead. Finally the boy in his last year at an osteopathic college, after having married, suddenly committed suicide.[11]

Howard's writing career began in earnest in 1895, when he had two poems published. One, *The Wreck of the 'Elbe'*, was published poem in *Frank Leslie's Popular Monthly*

The Wreck of the 'Elbe'
(Lost, with 374 Lives, January 30th, 1895)

Dark, dark was the night
    Underneath heaven's lower,
  For the stars hid their light
    From that terrible hour
When calamity wedded destruction, with the lives
of God's children for dower.

    And the waves laughed aloud
      In their horrible glee,
    And cried to each cloud
      Of disaster to be;

And forth from the sheath of his wrath drew the
sword of his anger – the sea.

> While Time held his breath
> > Prophetic, afraid
> Of the shadow of death
> > That pale destiny made.

Eternity came in a moment – the whole game of
life had been played.

> For out of the night
> > Came horror aleap,
> All mounted in might
> > On the chance of the deep,

And smote; and it was but a step into death from
the dreaming of sleep.

> A moment ago
> > And the sea bore its freight
> Of life all aglow
> > And of hope all elate.

Now 'tis death that she wraps in her bosom; she
has taken gray death for her mate.

> Night mourns to the sea
> > And the land to the sky,
> While the waves lose their glee
> > And remorsefully sigh;

And void into void sendeth weeping and deep unto
deep sobs reply.[12]

Howard followed that poem three months later with a story about an old coat that had reached the end of its usable life. It is almost as if the 28-year-old Howard was describing his future self of 1941:

A Shabby Coat

... 'Tis nothing but an ordinary coat: no eye could dwell on it as a thing of beauty; its days of usefulness are ever passed, but nevertheless such memories crowd the thoughts of it that it is holy.

The smell of mountain lakes is in its thread bare nap; its elbow still bears stains from grass that six years ago died under the Adirondack snows; its sleeve will hold the print of fingers dear then but dearer since. The blue of summer skies is locked in it for me, the gray of kindly eyes looks out from it to mine; long walks and talks are treasured in its woof and far past days are woven with its threads.

It has heavy creases, like those around the mouth of a happy face, running from shoulder to waist as if an habitual smile dwelt ever in its folds. Its half-worn buttons have each its peculiar characteristics, gained as we all gain them, in the wear and tear of life. The top button, new in its innocuous desuetude, peeps falteringly around the lapel as if apologizing for its brazenly good condition. The next button, like the foremost man at the pass of Thermopylae, has borne the full brunt of battle and is dying like a hero, still smiling: its once cloth bound sides have a strangely metallic glint now and it hangs half torn from its roots, reproach in its droop but no complaint in its eyes, usefully filled with thread not uselessly filled with tears.

Its lining has long since lost its ability to continue a definite line of action and yawns disjointed just near enough to the pockets to capture the unwary papers and change should you become so reduced as to wear it to business: while its tattered remnants fringe the coattails in most undignified profusion. Its front bears the scars from many a hard fought battle over office desk and lunch counter; its binding is frayed through mere contact with time; its cuffs are shiny in the baldness of age and its elbows are disgracefully baggy at the knees. And yet its very shabbiness endears it. As Desdemona loved her hero for the dangers he had passed so we reverence it for the days that it has seen. The mind ever reverts to the past and such inanimate things are its mouthpieces to the soul.

Thou art not ludicrous, eh shabby coat! And we lay thee away reverently midst rue and lavender. What thou seemest to the eye is lost in what thou truly art to the mind. Who ever remembers that Napoleon was short of stature? That Caesar was thin and subject to fainting spells? That Aristotle was fat, that Socrates was bald, Cicero cowardly and Bacon pusillanimous? The heritage that the minds of these men left to the world immeasurably transcends the fleeting attributes of the body. So thou dwellest in the mind sacredly embalmed in the memories of the past.

No old clothes man shall make his sack thy tomb; no poor relation shall desecrate thy holiness on the back of his half-grown boy. The spirit of kindly remembered days is in thy napless texture; thy gaping pockets are filled with hours far gone; thy very wrinkles, like those we have seen grow on the brow of a friend, do but speak of happy time spent together.

Life has duties for us all, – what kinder epitaph than this? 'He spent himself in the fulfillment of his duty: the comfort of others was his object and he died still pursuing it.' Such, shabby coat of mine, I inscribe upon thy tomb.

Howard C. Ives – March 14th 1895

Howard left college before Muriel was born and returned to his previous job as an insurance salesman. For three years, the family of three travelled together to every place Howard went to sell his insurance. In 1901, they finally settled down in 'a small yellow brick house' in Philadelphia. While there, Howard and Elizabeth had another son, Douglas. Unfortunately, he lived only a few hours.[13]

Howard becomes a minister

In 1901, Howard made a big decision. One day while perusing the library of a village rector, he came across a book of sermons by William Ellery Channing. Howard wrote that 'His sermon on the occasion of the ordination of Jared Sparks in Baltimore in 1844[14] opened a new horizon. Perhaps one could be free and yet have a guide freely chosen.'[15] Channing addressed four points in his sermon: 1) that reason was necessary for the interpretation of scripture; 2) the unity of God and that Christ was fully human with both a human and a divine nature; 3) the perfection of God; and that the mission of Christ was not to atone for human sin; and 4) that Christian virtue was founded on the moral nature of humans defined by the love of God.[16] The themes in the sermon resonated with Howard's spiritual beliefs and helped him connect with concepts he was later to find in abundance in the Bahá'í teachings.

As told by Muriel: 'One evening . . . while I sat on Mother's lap having my very straight hair turned into ringlets by Mother's twisting it up on rags, Father came to stand in the doorway with a book in his hand. He said, "Beth, I've found it. I've found what I want to do. I'm going to become a Unitarian minister." The book was a volume of William Ellery Channing's sermons and Father was radiant with his discovery.'.[17]

Howard began putting this decision into effect the next year, 1902, when he began attending the Unitarian Theological School in Meadville, Pennsylvania. For the next three years, he studied and Elizabeth became the wage earner. She became a professional photographer, specializing in student portraits. In addition, every Saturday she held sales of things like Oriental rugs and fabric and baked goods, as well as candle shades she herself had painted in watercolour. Howard greatly appreciated his wife, telling her one day, 'It's no credit to you that you're completely unselfish – you're just born that way and there's nothing you could possibly do about it.'[18]

In 1905, at the age of 38, Howard graduated and spent his first year as a minister in Brewster, Massachusetts, on Cape Cod.

15

His next parish was in New London, Connecticut. This small congregation did not have a church when he arrived and met in various club rooms. In 1907, the Ives adopted the orphaned boy of 14. Though they treated him like a son and ensured that he had a good education, the boy 'became an increasing cause of anxiety to Howard and Mabel until the pathetic end of his short life'. As mentioned earlier, after being sent to Princeton University for his education and getting married, the young man committed suicide. Of all their five children and one adopted son, only Muriel lived a full life.[19]

In 1910, Howard was involved with The Apostolic Institute, a school in Konia, Turkey. That year, he was on the Board of Directors. He continued his interest for a number of years. In April 1914, he was the financial secretary of the Institute and had begun a five-year project to raise money for the school.[20]

After increasing the size of the New London congregation, he was able to move to another parish leaving his old one with a small church. Howard's daughter, Muriel, later wrote:

> We lived in New London for five years, during which time father built a very nice, though modest, brick church for the people; then he was called to Summit, New Jersey . . . In Summit, as he had in New London, he built a church . . . modelled after one of the early Christopher Wren's . . . It was from Summit that he started additional work with his Brotherhood Church in Jersey City and also organized his Golden Rule Fraternity – a cooperative idea, as I remember . . . one of his many attempts to help humanity in some organized way. The fact that he made it while he was so active building the Summit Church besides starting the Brotherhood is characteristic of the restlessness that always drove him. One job was never enough. Two might do. Three was better. And four was what he'd like.[21]

In Summit, New Jersey, things went well until 1911. Howard supervised the building of the new church and began the group that called itself the Brotherhood Church. The group's ideal was to be 'a group of brothers of the spirit aiming to express their highest ideals in service to struggling humanity'.[22] The group met in the Masonic Hall in Jersey City and Howard was its 'voluntary guide'.[23] Elizabeth was also active in the Unitarian Church. In September 1910, she conducted the opening session of the 78th Connecticut Universalist Convention.

Howard's world begins to turn upside down

By the autumn of 1911, Howard was 'desperately unhappy' with the life of a minister. As he wrote in *Portals to Freedom*:

> To preach once a week; duly to make my parish round of calls on elderly spinsters and the sick to whom my visits were simply what I was paid to give; to build churches to hold a handful of people; never to forget the collection, for which lapse of memory my treasurer was always scolding me, and to fill in odd hours with reading of the latest modern philosophy in order to pass it on to my unsuspecting congregation with appropriate annotations . . . Was it my own fault that I had missed the point and was I a fool in that I could not adjust myself to that definition of success which found its goal in a wealthy congregation, the whispered, 'That was a mighty fine sermon,' the annually increasing salary?
>
> Well, anyway, suffice it to say I was desperately unhappy. I had tried the orthodox scheme; I had tried to sail the uncharted sea of – 'I don't know'; I had tried the 'Liberal Faith' and I found myself approaching spiritual bankruptcy.[24]

3
Howard Meets the Master and Is Transformed

In October 1911, Howard saw a copy of *Everybody's Magazine* in a bookstall. The magazine contained an article about 'Abdu'l-Bahá and His planned trip to visit America. The very emotive story by Ethel Stefana Stevens began with a description of the martyrdom of a young Bahá'í in Tabriz, then told the story of the history, development and persecution of the Bahá'í Faith. Most of the article is a 'first-hand, intimate study' of 'Abdu'l-Bahá, based on her meeting with Him. Ethel introduced 'Abdu'l-Bahá by writing: 'Regard him well, my friends, for in him you behold one of the most significant figures in the religious world to-day; one who is perhaps doing more for the uplifting of the Oriental than any other force; one who has actually suffered for his faith; one whom nearly two millions of people hold in greatest reverence as the Light in the Lantern, the Knowledge within the Gate.' Ethel was very taken with the great number of people she met in the Master's home; people who came from very different backgrounds, but had found unity in His presence:

> This lean-faced convert at our right is a Fire-Worshipper from the shores of the Caspian; beyond him, he of the yellow skin and silken coat is a Sart from Samarkand; over there is a hungry-looking Parsee from the Punjab, and, in the corner, a keen-faced Japanese. And for each of them the Baha has ready sympathy and sound, comprehensible advice. And therein lies his power. He possesses to a positively miraculous degree the faculty of interesting himself in every human soul that asks his spiritual or material aid, and it is this very power which has made him so

passionately beloved by his disciples. But above all, he possesses that subtler quality of spirituality which is felt rather than understood by those with whom he comes in contact. Gentle, genial, and courteous always, he receives, instructs, advises, and assists with unfailing tact and understanding the cosmopolitan stream of pilgrims which flows so steadily and so increasingly toward this little Syrian coast town.[1]

Ethel concludes her very personal story with an exhortation:

I have shown you now, as best I am able, what manner of man is this Abbas Effendi who is variously held to be impostor, priest, and prophet. Whether he deserves the title of prophet I do not know; no one knows; that, the future alone can tell. That he is a good man and sincere, there can be no doubt. That the faith which he holds and the creed which he preaches might be followed with benefit by us all, there is no gainsaying. Be you Confucian, Buddhist, Zoroastrian, Christian, Moslem, or Jew, to follow the lantern which Abbas lights can bring you to no harm; to abide by his Rule of Love can be no heresy. He preaches a clean and wholesome creed, and though you may question the divine origin of his mission, there is no denying that he is a sincere, courageous man, a figure whose increasing influence is already world-wide in its significance.[2]

Howard's reaction to what he contradictorily called the 'somewhat commonplace story' was that he would 'never forget the thrill' it gave him. He wrote that he 'read and re-read that glorious and tragic story and filed it in my voluminous twenty-five volume scrap-book. There may have been a vague purpose in my mind of making that story the background of a sermon . . . To such human uses do we often put the skyey glimpses God vouchsafes us.'[3] The story touched something deep within Howard's heart that he didn't even know was there.

Around the same time, the Brotherhood Church sprang out of Howard's sense of spiritual unrest and frustration. It was not a church in the normal sense, but a 'band of brothers' whose highest ideal was to be of service to humanity. Howard wrote about how easy it could be to underestimate that great things can be the results of 'even slight efforts undertaken in the sincere spirit of service'. He credited this unofficial church with allowing him to discover the 'Sun of Reality' as soon as he did [4]

The Brotherhood Church was non-denominational and was as free as Howard could imagine. In his daughter's words: 'It had no limitations, no horizons, no dogma, no ritual, no anything. It was just a church, a brotherhood.' One day, a man came into the church while Howard was doing paperwork and asked:

> 'Are you Mr Ives?' He said that he was. The man said, 'I live around the corner and I've been passing your church every day on my way to and from school' [where he was a teacher]. He said, 'The word brotherhood intrigues me. What do you mean by brotherhood?' Father said, 'Well, I mean brotherhood. Brotherhood is brotherhood. Why does it trouble you?' The man said, 'Are there any limitations to it, any limitations as to race or creed or color or national origin?' Father said, 'Of course not. Brotherhood is brotherhood.' Then the man said, 'Just like a Baháʼí.' This was the first time Father had heard the word.
>
> So they began to talk and this was Clarence Moore.[5]

Some time later, Clarence, who by then was on the Board of Trustees of the Brotherhood Church, approached Howard for help. Howard deeply loved and respected Clarence because he was one of the 'humblest and sweetest' men he knew. Though his health and financial positions were both poor, Clarence had 'the key of universal love which unlocks every heart'. When Howard asked how he could help, Clarence said:

> [Y]ou know I have been to some extent interested in a world-wide movement which seems to have great spiritual and social significance. Friends of mine have found in it

much of value and inspiration which so far have seemed too high and deep for me to fathom and explore. It occurred to me that your knowledge and experience in such matters might assist me to a more just appreciation. So, this afternoon I attended one of the meetings of this group in New York and made some rather full notes with the idea of submitting them to you for your criticism and opinion.[6]

Howard had no idea that the meeting Clarence had attended and the article in *Everybody's Magazine* sprang from the same source – the Bahá'í Faith. He also had no idea that Clarence had been a Bahá'í since about 1905 and had even gone on pilgrimage that same year.[7] Furthermore, he didn't want to get involved in 'Oriental cults, Eastern philosophies, and the queer, supposedly idealistic movements of which there are so many', but respecting his friend, he took the notes and read them on the train home that night. The notes were 'interesting, I thought, heart-stirring a little, but that was about all.'[8]

A few days later, Howard was quite surprised when he received an invitation to a 'Bahá'í Meeting' in New York. He quickly connected the invitation with Clarence, which 'disturbed' him. He wrote that he 'had no desire to be drawn into any movement or interest which might distract my attention from my legitimate work'. He was just about to throw the invitation into the rubbish when he thought of Clarence's 'selfless service, his friendship and love' and knew that he could not simply reject it. His initial thoughts were that going to the meeting would mean 'an evening wasted, and a mid-night return to my home which, in my then state of health, was a not inconsiderable hardship'. All of these were material concerns from a man who devoted himself to a spiritual life. Much later, after many years of being a Bahá'í, Howard realized that 'Heaven is not given away, God cannot be had for the asking unless with that asking goes all that one has.'[9]

Howard's world began to turn onto a new axis. He attended the meeting and remembered only that there were no hymns, that the prayers were beautiful, but how disappointed he was because they were read from a book. Something, however, attracted his heart and he asked the speaker, a woman from London, England, to recommend a speaker for his Brotherhood Church group. She introduced him to Mountfort Mills, who came and spoke to the group a couple of weeks later. When he came, Mountfort's talk was on the subject of 'The Divine Springtime' and a lady sitting in front of Howard was enthralled, but concluded 'If we could only be *sure* it were all true'.[10]

His world began to turn ever faster, seeking to find its new pole star. He wrote that the next three months were the 'most remarkable' of his life.' 'The Divine Voice', he wrote, 'calling from on high seemed constantly in my ears.' He began to attend weekly Bahá'í meetings in New York and though much of what he heard he did not understand and sometimes what the speakers said repelled him, 'my heart was in a turmoil and yet incredibly attracted'. He was given *The Seven Valleys* at the first meeting and read it completely on the train home. He wrote that 'it stirred me beyond measure. Not one word in ten did I understand but doors seemed to be opening before me . . . Certain passages struck my heart like paeans from angelic choirs'[11] This was Howard: his heart was constantly soaring in the spiritual world while his mind struggled in the material.

Howard began buying and reading all the books on the Bahá'í Faith that he could find. The congregation soon noticed a new vigour and direction to his sermons – sermons he no longer prepared through study, research and writing, but through prayer and meditation. Prayer took on a wholly new meaning. He wrote that he had 'always prayed after a fashion, but since religion had become a "profession," public prayer – pulpit prayer – had to a great extent displaced personal devotions. I began to vaguely understand what communion might mean.'[12]

Even with all this new information and the resulting amazing spiritual insights, still Howard was not happy. He finally decided that since 'Abdu'l-Bahá was soon to arrive on America's shores, the only way to 'calm' his 'restless soul' would be to meet this mysterious visitor. In February 1912, while walking with Mountfort, Howard listened to the inspiring stories

Mountfort shared of others who had met the Master, 'Abdu'l-Bahá. 'Impulsively', Howard told Mountfort that

> 'When 'Abdu'l-Bahá arrives I would like very much to have a talk with Him alone, without even an interpreter.'
> He smiled sympathetically but remarked:
> 'I fear you couldn't get very far without an interpreter, for 'Abdu'l-Bahá speaks little English and you, I imagine, less Persian.'
> I would not be dissuaded. 'If He at all approaches in spiritual discernment what I hear and read of Him,' I said, 'we would get closer together, and I might have a better chance of understanding, even if no words were spoken. I am very tired of words,' I concluded rather lamely.[13]

Neither of the two men spoke of this very unusual desire again. Six weeks later, on 11 April, 'Abdu'l-Bahá arrived in New York and Howard went to the first meeting at the home of Bahá'ís Edward and Carrie Kinney. The house was packed with people, all eager to meet the man designated by the founder of the Bahá'í Faith, Bahá'u'lláh, as head of the Faith and the Centre of His Covenant. Howard wanted at least a glimpse of this spiritual Figure. He wrote:

> A glimpse was all I succeeded in getting. The press of eager friends and curious ones was so great that it was difficult even to get inside the doors. I have only the memory of an impressive silence most unusual at such functions. In all that crowded mass of folk, so wedged together that tea drinking was almost an impossibility . . . there was little or no speech. A whispered word; a remark implying awe or love, was all. I strove to get where I could at least see Him. All but impossible. At last I managed to press forward where I could peep over a shoulder and so got my first glimpse of 'Abdu'l-Bahá . . . He was just in the moment of accepting a cup of tea from the hostess. Such gentleness, such love emanated from Him as I had never seen.[14]

Howard admitted that he was wholly ignorant of the station of 'Abdu'l-Bahá, and he was mystified at the reactions of others in the room. 'What', he asked himself, 'was it that these people around me had which gave to their eyes such illumination, to their hearts such gladness. What connotation did the word "wonderful" have to them that so often it was upon their lips?'[15] The answers to those questions eluded him on that day.

Howard's world leaps to its new pole

12 April 1912. The story of what happened that day has been told many times and widely read. But it was such a unique moment and had such a dramatic effect on the unhappy pastor, that its telling must again be repeated:

> ... the very next morning, early, I was at the Hotel Ansonia . . . before nine o'clock in the morning I was there . . . Already the large reception room was well filled. Evidently others also were conscious of a similar urge . . . I did not want to talk to anyone . . . I withdrew to the window overlooking Broadway and turned my back upon them all. Below me stretched the great city but I saw it not. What was it all about? Why was I here? What did I expect . . .? I had no appointment. Plainly all these other folk had come expecting to see and talk with Him. Why should I expect any attention . . .?
>
> So I was somewhat withdrawn from the others when my attention was attracted by a rustling throughout the room. A door was opening far across from me and a group was emerging and 'Abdu'l-Bahá appeared saying farewell . . . His fez was slightly tilted and as I gazed, His hand, with a gesture evidently characteristic, raised and, touching, restored it to its proper place. His eyes met mine as my fascinated glance was on Him. He smiled and, with a gesture which no word but 'lordly' can describe, He beckoned me. Startled gives no hint of my sensations. Something incredible had happened. Why to me, a stranger unknown, unheard of, should He

raise that friendly hand? I glanced around. Surely it was to someone else that gesture was addressed, those eyes were smiling! But there was no one near and again I looked and again He beckoned and such understanding love enveloped me that even at that distance and with a heart still cold a thrill ran through me as if a breeze from a divine morning had touched my brow!

Slowly I obeyed that imperative command and, as I approached the door where still He stood, He motioned others away and stretched His hand to me as if He had always known me. And, as our right hands met, with His left He indicated that all should leave the room, and He drew me in and closed the door. I remember how surprised the interpreter looked when he too was included in this general dismissal. But I had little thought then for anything but this incredible happening. I was absolutely alone with 'Abdu'l-Bahá. The halting desire expressed weeks ago was fulfilled the very moment that our eyes first met.

Still holding my hand 'Abdu'l-Bahá walked across the room towards where, in the window, two chairs were waiting. Even then the majesty of His tread impressed me and I felt like a child led by His father, a more than earthly father, to a comforting conference. His hand still held mine and frequently His grasp tightened and held more closely. And then, for the first time, He spoke, and in my own tongue: Softly came the assurance that I was His very dear son.

What there was in these simple words that carried such conviction to my heart I cannot say. Or was it the tone of voice and the atmosphere pervading the room, filled with spiritual vibrations beyond anything I had ever known, that melted my heart almost to tears? I only know that a sense of *verity* invaded me. Here at last *was* my Father . . . My throat swelled. My eyes filled. I could not have spoken had life depended on a word. I followed those masterly feet like a little child.

Then we sat in the two chairs by the window . . . At last He looked right into me. It was the first time since our eyes had met with His first beckoning gesture that this had happened. And now nothing intervened between us and He looked at me. *He looked at me!* It seemed as though never before had anyone really seen *me*. I felt a sense of gladness that I at last was at home, and that one who knew me utterly, my Father, in truth, was alone with me.

As He looked such play of thought found reflection in His face . . . it was as if His very being opened to receive me. With that the heart within me melted and the tears flowed. I did not weep, in any ordinary sense . . . It was as if a long-pent stream was at last undammed . . .

He put His two thumbs to my eyes while He wiped the tears from my face, admonishing me not to cry, that one must always be happy. And He laughed. Such a ringing, boyish laugh . . .

I could not speak. We both sat perfectly silent for what seemed a long while, and gradually a great peace came to me. Then 'Abdu'l-Bahá placed His hand upon my breast saying that it was the heart that speaks. Again silence . . . No further word was spoken, and all the time I was with Him not one single sound came from me. But no word was necessary . . .

Suddenly He leaped from His chair with another laugh as though consumed with a heavenly joy. Turning, He took me under the elbows and lifted me to my feet and swept me into His arms. Such a hug! No mere embrace! My very ribs cracked. He kissed me on both cheeks, laid His arm across my shoulders and led me to the door.

That is all. But life has never been quite the same since.[16]

This was the beginning. Over the next eight months, Howard spent as much time as he could with 'Abdu'l-Bahá. On 19 April, Howard wrote his first letter to 'Abdu'l-Bahá:

Dear Master and Friend

I must try to express my gratitude, which is too weak a word, for the inspiration and help your words and presence have brought to me. I feel as though I have come very near to God and that I may, if I pray and love, keep in close communion with him always. I do thank God most deeply for this blessing, and you as His messenger who brought it to me. I pray that I may receive a full and fuller measure of the Holy Spirit. You will understand all that my halting words cannot express.[17]

He concluded the letter with an invitation for the Master to address his Brotherhood Church, which 'Abdu'l-Bahá did several weeks later.

At that early stage, Howard had but little understanding of the station that the Master occupied and meeting Him actually increased his inner turmoil. He wrote, 'The world and I in turmoil and here was peace . . . It seemed to me that He stood at the heart of a whirlwind in a place of supreme quiet . . . I looked at this stillness, this quietude, this immeasurable calm in 'Abdu'l-Bahá and it filled me with a restless longing akin to despair. Is it any wonder I was unhappy?'[18] For the rest of his life, Howard sought that quiet in his soul. He clung to the passage in *The Seven Valleys*: 'If he strive for a hundred thousand years and yet fail to behold the beauty of the Friend, he should not falter. For those who seek the Kaaba of "for Us" rejoice in the tidings: "In Our ways shall We assuredly guide them."'[19]

As long as 'Abdu'l-Bahá was in New York, Howard could not stay away from Him. One day the Master quoted the words of Christ and interpreted His words quite differently from what Howard had heard before. Howard abruptly asked, 'How is it possible to be so sure? No one can say with certainty what Jesus meant after all these centuries of misinterpretation and strife.' 'Abdu'l-Bahá calmly indicated that it was indeed possible. But Howard's turmoil was exposed as he said, 'That I cannot believe.' He noted the interpreter's 'glance of outraged dignity', as though he was asking, 'Who are you to contradict or even to question 'Abdu'l-Bahá!' Howard wrote that 'His calm, beautiful eyes searched my soul with such love and understanding that all my momentary heat evaporated. He smiled as winningly as a lover smiles upon his beloved' as He quietly suggested that 'I should try my way and He would try His.' His family remembers that throughout the years when he would tell this story, his face would turn beet red at the thought that he had the temerity to try to argue with 'Abdu'l-Bahá. For Howard, those soft words 'unlocked my hard-bolted, crusted and rusted heart'.[20]

Though he had yet to accept Bahá'u'lláh as a Manifestation of God, His words were having their effect. When a man in his congregation came to say that his wife had fallen very ill, Howard instinctively opened his Bahá'í prayer book to the healing prayer, which they repeated nine times together. Howard later wrote that he did not understand what those words actually meant, but he did know that the wife began to recover from that day.[21]

Howard's mind and heart were battling for supremacy during those extraordinary days. Then one day, he suddenly asked 'Abdu'l-Bahá, 'Why should I believe in Bahá'u'lláh?' 'Abdu'l-Bahá 'looked long and searchingly as it seemed into my very soul. The silence deepened. He did not answer.' During this long-extended silence, many things poured through Howard's mind. Finally, the Master stated that when he, as a pastor, preached, prayed or taught his congregation, his heart had to be filled with love for God. And he must be truly sincere. He said: 'One can never be sincere enough until his heart is entirely severed from attachment to the things of this world. One should not preach love and have a loveless heart, nor preach purity and harbor impure thoughts. Nor preach peace and be at inward strife.' When Howard later understood that 'Abdu'l-Bahá had answered his question, those words became his goals for the rest of his life.[22]

Howard had been a smoker most of his life and, though he had tried various times, he had been unable to break the habit. Thinking that the Master could help, he took the question to Him. To Howard's surprise, 'Abdu'l-Bahá gave no 'dissertation on the evils' of smoking, but said that He did not think it would hurt him. He noted that 'men in the Orient smoked all the time, that their hair and beards and clothing became saturated, and often very offensive'. But since Howard didn't smoke so much, it shouldn't trouble him. This He said with a twinkle in His eye. Two days later, Howard had absolutely no desire for tobacco and didn't smoke again for seven years.²³

'This is a day for very great things'

One day, Howard sought out 'Abdu'l-Bahá to ask about a passage concerning renunciation in a book he was reading – 'Prevent me not from turning to the Horizon of renunciation.' When he found the Master, He was just leaving one house to walk to another. There were a dozen others following, but 'Abdu'l-Bahá and Howard walked together a few steps ahead. 'Abdu'l-Bahá spoke about horizons and how though the Suns of the Manifestations each rose from a different point along the horizon, they were the same sun. He even stopped a couple times and drew an imaginary horizon on the sideway with a stick. Since Howard wanted to hear about renunciation, not horizons, he felt deeply disappointed.²⁴

When they reached their destination, 'Abdu'l-Bahá stopped with his foot on the first step and turned to His confused companion. '*This is a day for very great things*,' He said. He repeated the phrase '*so* impressively, *so* earnestly', saying that Howard must never forget it. Howard still could not understand what those words had to do with renunciation. 'Abdu'l-Bahá rose up another step and repeated the phrase for a third time, 'but this time in what seemed like a voice like thunder, with literally flashing eyes and emphatically raised hand: that I should remember His words that This is a Day for *very great things* – VERY GREAT THINGS. These last three words rang out like a trumpet call.' Poor Howard was overwhelmed, thinking and questioning, who was he to do great things? He didn't even know what 'things *were* great in this world awry with misbegotten emphases'.²⁵

'Abdu'l-Bahá then marched up the stairs to His room, with an unthinking Howard being pulled along in His wake. Suddenly, Howard found himself alone with the Master in His own room:

The late afternoon sunlight lay palely across the floor, but I saw nothing. I was conscious only of Him and that I was alone with Him. The room was very still . . . The silence deepened as He regarded me with that loving, all-embracing, all-understanding look which always melted my heart. A deep content and happiness flooded my being. A little flame seemed lit within my breast. And then 'Abdu'l-Bahá spoke: He simply asked me if I were interested in renunciation.

Nothing could have been more unexpected. I had entirely forgotten the question which had so engrossed my thoughts an hour since . . . I had no words to answer His question. Was I interested? I could not say I was and I would not say that I was not. I stood before Him silent . . . Then His arm was around me and He led me to the door . . . During all the long years of renunciation that followed, the memory of that walk with Him; my disappointment that He had not understood; His ringing challenge; This is a Day *for very great things* . . . Indeed I *was* interested and my interest has never flagged from that day to this. But I never dreamed that renunciation could be so glorious.[26]

Howard was anxious for 'Abdu'l-Bahá to speak at his Brotherhood Church, but the Master did not operate by calendars, only as the Spirit moved him. Five weeks after Howard first sat alone with 'Abdu'l-Bahá at the Ansonia Hotel, the Master spoke at Howard's Brotherhood Church on 19 May. Howard introduced Him and told the congregation something of His life and sufferings. Then 'Abdu'l-Bahá arose and spoke:

'Because this is called the Church of Brotherhood I wish to speak upon the Brotherhood of Mankind.' As that beautifully resonant voice rang through the room, accenting with an emphasis I had never before heard the word Brotherhood, shame crept into my heart. Surely this Man recognized connotations to that word which I, who had named the church, had never known . . . To Him all races, colors, creeds were as one. To Him prejudice for or against a soul because of outward wealth or poverty, sin or virtue, was unknown.[27]

Howard had been given a copy of Bahá'u'lláh's *Seven Valleys* by one of the Master's translators and he treasured it. This was the same little book he had been given at his first Bahá'í meeting by Mountfort Mills near the end of 1911. Of the thin volume, Howard wrote:

> I have before referred to the deep impression which this little book made upon me from my very first reading. Since then I had gone through it many times, and phrases, sentences, whole paragraphs had become familiar to me: outwardly familiar, that is, but the deeper meanings, the elusive, spiritual, mystic beauty of the Words and the thoughts they aroused, stirred an inner depth heretofore untroubled. My heart, too, had become 'fascinated by the zephyr of assurance wafted upon the garden of my innate heart from the Sheba of the Merciful' . . .
>
> But, alas, not to me had been given the faintest indication of the meaning of the divine words describing the further experience of the traveler on the road 'from self to God'.[28]

Howard took his copy of the *Seven Valleys* when he went to see 'Abdu'l-Bahá and asked if He would write something in it, 'adding something of my hope to understand more and more of its hidden meanings'. 'Abdu'l-Bahá 'smiled rather more gravely than was His wont and looked deeply into my eyes for a long moment before He signified His assent'. The next day, the Master returned Howard's book without a word. Eagerly opening it, Howard found 'several lines written in the beautiful copperplate Persian characters and signed by Him'. Since it was written in Persian, Howard quickly asked one of His secretaries to put the English translation on the facing page. It read: 'O my Lord! Confirm this revered personage, that he may attain the

Essential Purpose; travel in these Seven Valleys; enter the silent chamber of realities and significances, and enter the Kingdom of Mysteries. Verily, Thou art the Confirmer, the Helper, the Kind.'[29] The inscribed copy of the Seven Valleys has been lost, but Howard included the translation in *Portals to Freedom*.

A wedding

On 7 July 1912, Howard was in New York for the wedding of Harlan Ober and Grace Robarts, his close friends and confidants and who were to figure prominently in his future. Theirs was a marriage instigated by 'Abdu'l-Bahá when he suggested to Lua Getsinger that Grace should marry Harlan, a man she barely knew. With Lua as the intermediary, Harlan immediately accepted the Master's request and travelled to New York to propose to Grace.[30]

'Abdu'l-Bahá performed the Bahá'í marriage, but requested that Howard assist Him by performing the legal ceremony in his capacity as a minister. Though he was there to participate in the wedding, Howard's description of the event focused entirely on 'Abdu'l-Bahá:

> Dominating the scene was the white-robed figure of the Master. From the age of seven He has been addressed and spoken of by this title. Bahá'u'lláh Himself indicated his wish that so He should be addressed.
>
> His right to the title did not rest upon any assumption by Himself of authority or precedence. His whole bearing was ever that of humility and gentle deference. Yet in every home He entered He was the host, in every gathering the center; in every discussion the arbiter; to every problem the answer . . .
>
> I sat very near Him, and, naturally, my every faculty, eye, ear, mind and heart were centered upon that radiant Personality. Nor was I alone in this. There was but One worthy of attention when He was present; but One wholly satisfying.

After the simple wedding ceremony and the bride and groom had resumed their seats, 'Abdu'l-Bahá rose. His cream-colored 'abá fell in graceful folds to His feet. Upon His head he wore a tarboosh, or fez, of the same color, beneath which His long white hair fell almost to His shoulders. Most impressive of all His impressive aspects were His eyes. Blue they were but so changing with His mood! Now gentle and appealing, now commanding, now flashing with hidden fires, now holding a deep, tranquil lambent repose as though gazing upon scenes of glory far removed.

His brow above those wide-set eyes was like an ivory dome. His neatly clipped beard, snowy white, touched His breast, but around His mouth no straggling hairs obscured the mobile lips . . .

He swept the room with a glance at once enfolding and abstracted. He raised His hands, palm upwards, level with His waist. His eyes closed and He chanted a prayer for the souls united by Him and by me . . .

This prayer of 'Abdu'l-Bahá, chanted in tones to me unequalled in all experience, mellifluous (honey-like), is the nearest descriptive word, but how inadequate, is the keenest of all my memories of that evening.[31]

New Hampshire and the end of Howard's Christian ministry

As eager as Howard was to be in the Master's presence, occasionally it was just not possible. On 10 July, he had to turn down an invitation from 'Abdu'l-Bahá for lunch: 'I find it will be impossible for me to take lunch with you tomorrow, Thursday, as you so kindly invited me to do. I shall hope to do so at some early date.'[32]

In August, 'Abdu'l-Bahá was staying in the cool mountain town of Dublin, New Hampshire and Howard happened to be in Peterborough, a few miles away. He wrote to the Master for permission to visit Him:

My dear Master –

I shall be in Dublin Saturday of this week, Aug 10th, and want very much to see you. If you are to be there, and it will be agreeable to you to have me do so, I will plan to stay over Sunday in Dublin.

I have much to tell you, and need your advice and strength very much.

Please have word sent to me in the enclosed envelope what you wish me to do. It should be mailed at once on receipt of this so that I may be sure to receive it.

With the utmost love and reverence.

Your Son, Howard C. Ives[33]

Howard's request was successful and he was again in the presence of 'Abdu'l-Bahá. He attended a luncheon given by Agnes Parsons for a group of prominent and wealthy people and was surprised at how easily the Master mingled with them without embarrassment and simply outshone them. Mrs Parsons greatly wanted Him to tell them about Bahá'u'lláh, going so far as to ask Him to do so and suggesting various subjects throughout the meal, hoping to lead 'Abdu'l-Bahá to give a spiritual talk to these very materially-minded people. But during the meal the only conversation was mundane. When Agnes tried to open a spiritual topic, the Master instead asked if He could tell them a story. He broke the ice with one hilarious tale after another and then others contributed their own stories until the room rocked with laughter. Howard was immensely impressed at the reverence those rich people gave to the Master as the luncheon ended.[34]

Demonstrating His complete impartiality, 'Abdu'l-Bahá left the rich White group and met with all the servants, who were mostly Black, who had gathered in Mrs Parson's boathouse. There He announced the upcoming marriage of Louis Gregory, Black man, and Louise Mathew, a White woman – the first Bahá'í interracial marriage, which the Master Himself had arranged.[35] This was not lost on Howard.

Shortly after leaving Dublin, Howard wrote to 'Abdu'l-Bahá to thank Him for His courtesy and kindness. On 26

August 1912, Howard received the first of seven Tablets from the Master:

> O thou my revered friend!
>
> Your letter imparted the utmost rejoicing, for its contents evidenced attraction to the Kingdom of God and enkindlement with the Fire of the Love of God!
>
> A hundred thousand ministers have come and gone: they left behind no trace nor fruit, nor were their lives productive.
>
> To be fruitless in the world of humanity is the manifest loss. A wise person will not attach his heart to ephemeral things: nay, rather, will he continually seek immortal life and strive to attain eternal happiness.
>
> Now, praise be to God that thou hast turned thy face towards the Kingdom, and art aspiring to receive Divine Bestowals from the Realm of Might.
>
> I have become hopeful, and prayed that thou mayst attain to another Bounty; seek another life; ask for another World; draw nearer unto God; become informed of the mysteries of the Kingdom; attain to Life Eternal and become encircled with the Glory Everlasting.[36]

'Abdu'l-Bahá's Tablets, which Howard read and reread endlessly, were a constant source of inspiration to him.

By the autumn of 1912, the Brotherhood Church was in serious financial difficulties and was forced to close. Howard wrote to 'Abdu'l-Bahá, telling Him of the troubles, but also of his ever-increasing desire to teach the Faith of Bahá'u'lláh. In response, he received his second Tablet from the Master in which He wrote:

> O thou spiritual friend!
>
> Thy letter was received. I was made very sad on account of the event of the closing of the Church of Brotherhood. But when I was in those parts I alluded to you that you should not put your confidence upon these souls. They say

many things but they do not fulfil them. You stated that 'my first assistant is a philosopher.' It is true that philosophy in this age consists in the fact that man be out of touch with God; be out of touch with the Kingdom of God, be out of touch with spiritual susceptibilities, be out of touch with the Holy Spirit, and be out of touch with the ideal verities; to wit: he may be an agnostic and a captive of the tangibilities. While in reality her highness the cow enjoys this attribute and quality. The cow naturally is a denier of God, a denier of the Kingdom, a denier of spiritualties, and a denier of the heavenly verities. She has attained to these virtues without labor. Therefore she is the Professor emeritus. Our philosophers of this age after 20 years of study and reflection in the universities attain to the station of the cow. They know only the senses as the verities; therefore her highness the cow is the Great philosopher; for she has been a philosopher from the commencement of her life and not after the hard mental labor of twenty years.

I have mentioned the fact to you that these promises are unstable. You should not put your trust upon a soul who is without God.

In brief: be thou not unhappy. This event has happened so that thou mayest become freed from all other occupations, day and night thou mayest call the people to the Kingdom, spread the teachings of Baha-o-llah, inaugurate the era of the New Life, promulgate the reality and be sanctified and purified from all else save God. It is my hope that thou mayest become as such. Crown thy head with this diadem of the Kingdom whose brilliant jewels have such luminosity which shall shine upon centuries and cycles.[37]

Howard wrote that this Tablet left 'two distinct and oddly contrasting impressions. The first one, of course,'

> was its wit. It was my first personal encounter with 'Abdu'l-Bahá's wisely humorous attitude toward the accidents of life . . . when I met Him for the first time after the long

Summer's separation almost His first words were to ask if her highness the Cow were not a noble philosopher? And the smile and hearty laughter accompanying the words seemed to sum up the fundamental absurdity involved in most of 'the gloomy dust arising from men of limitation enveloping the world'.[38]

The second point that Howard noticed was 'the command of severance' and promoting the Teachings of Bahá'u'lláh.[39] This Tablet provided the impetus nine years later when Howard and Mabel set out to do what 'Abdu'l-Bahá suggested in the last paragraph.

Responding to the Master's letter, Howard wrote:

My dear Master
I must write and tell you how cheered and uplifted I was by the inspiration of your presence and words yesterday. I have been much depressed lately: the spirit of courage and faith seemed to have deserted me, and things have looked very dark, but all looks brighter now and, God willing, when the clouds gather again I will remember your faith and rise above them. Pray for me, dear Master, I do need your prayers and help sorely. I know so well that nothing will satisfy the soul but God Himself, but the claims of the world, the obligations of society, the necessities of existence, overwhelm me and I lose the vision of calmer times and descend to the darkness of despair. At times the remembrance of you and your words is like a glimpse of daylight. What shall I do when you leave us?[40]

By the end of 'Abdu'l-Bahá's journey across America, Howard had finally accepted the station of Bahá'u'lláh. On 23 November, he attended the Master's final public talk at the Great Northern Hotel in Montclair, New Jersey. It was to be a final gathering for all of the Bahá'ís to celebrate the Day of the Covenant. Unfortunately, the hotel's manager refused to allow the Black Bahá'ís to enter. In recompense, the White Bahá'ís held a special feast the next day where they hosted and served their Black brethren.⁴¹

It was still a significant event for Howard. He noted that no one was there to 'advance any personal or political ambition; not in the interest of any social or financial group'. They were all there, as 'Abdu'l-Bahá said, to promote 'the solidarity and brotherhood of the human race, the spiritual welfare of mankind, unity of religious teaching with the principles of science and reason . . . love and fraternity among all mankind.'⁴² Howard was fully a Bahá'í, now. He wrote:

> I am not a believer because of any preconceived explanation of this fundamental Truth based upon the ideas of those around me, as, for instance, the Christian is such because he was brought up under its teachings, or the Muhammedan is such because he was born where those principles are prevalent, and so with all other followers of the various theologies of the world. I am first of all, humanly speaking, a rational being. I have a mind which requires intellectual satisfactions. I have found in the teachings of Bahá'U'lláh and 'Abdu'l-Bahá much more satisfactory explanations of the meaning, the origin and the destiny of life, than I have elsewhere found . . .
>
> But, and this it seems to me, is conclusive as to the reason for its acceptance. The teachings of Bahá'U'lláh comprise a veritable Universe of wisdom. It is no more possible to define Its limits than for even an Einstein to define the limits of the material universe.⁴³

Howard wrote that 'During the last three days before 'Abdu'l-Bahá left this country I haunted His presence.' One of the Master's 'most fascinating and provocative characteristics,' he said, 'was His ready laughter when alluding to subjects usually approached with extreme gravity.' Howard illustrated this with a description of his final interview with 'Abdu'l-Bahá at the beginning of December:

I was saying good-bye and my heart was sad. Haltingly, I expressed this sorrow that He was leaving the country and that, in all probability, I should never see Him again. We were standing. It was actually the last good-bye. 'Abdu'l-Bahá laid His arm across my shoulders and walked me to the door, saying that I should be with Him in all the worlds of God. And then He laughed – a hearty, ringing laugh – and I: my eyes blinded with tears. – 'Why does He laugh?' I thought. Nevertheless, these words, and even more, the tone in which they were uttered, and His joyous laughter, have been an illuminating light upon my path through all these years.[44]

On 'Abdu'l-Bahá's last day in America, 5 December 1912, the dock where the *S.S. Cedric* was berthed was packed with those whose hearts He had touched. Of course, Howard was there. As he walked up the gangplank on the ship, he found himself 'in the midst of that indeterminate, indescribable rushing about; the bustling confusion of a departing liner.'[45] But this wasn't just any liner. This one was to carry 'Abdu'l-Bahá away. About 100 people, including Howard, crowded into the ship's salon.

> We slowly passed in front of Him. To each He gave a handful of the flowers massed near Him . . . When my own turn came I again forgot all but His nearness and the overwhelming fact that never again in this world would I see Him, or hear that beloved voice. I impulsively dropped to a knee, raised His hand with mine and placed it upon my head . . .
>
> The friends gathered on the wharf looked up at the figure of their Master as the ship slowly moved into the river. 'Abdu'l-Bahá stood at the rail, His white hair and beard moved by the breeze, His erect, majestic figure outlined clearly. In His hand I noticed the rosary which was His constant companion. His lips were moving. I could easily read those lips. 'Alláh'u'Abhá! Alláh'u'Abhá!'[46]

4
Finding His Way

Observation of 'Abdu'l-Bahá's life reflecting perfectly the teachings of Bahá'u'lláh had exercised its influence deeply on Howard's life and this manifested itself in his ministerial work, which reflected the transformation. Because of his new spiritual knowledge, he was 'able, in a deeply transforming manner, to assist souls struggling in the grasp of temptation, sorrow, perplexity of mind and confused with all the intricate problems of life and death'. He had gained what he called 'spiritual intuition' and it was 'an entirely new and very humbling experience'.[1] On 14 February 1913, Howard wrote a long letter to 'Abdu'l-Bahá, pouring out his heart and sharing the developments in his life. He mentions how the advice continued to aid his spiritual growth and guide his actions:

> . . . I have just re-read your two beloved letters to me. I read them often and they always cheer and uplift and enlighten my soul. In this reading I am particularly impressed with one of the closing paragraphs in your last epistle. It is this, in the light of the coming change in my activities it is significant, I hope.
>
> 'In brief be thou not unhappy. This event, (the closing of the work of the Brotherhood Church) has happened so that thou mayest become free from all other occupations, that day and night thou mayest call the people to the Kingdom, spread the teachings of Baha'U'llah, inaugurate the era of the new life, promulgate the reality and be sanctified and purified from all else save God. It is my hope that thou mayest become as such.'
>
> These words of yours, my dear Master, at this time in my life come as words of high encouragement of which I am

unworthy, but I pray that I may become so. I have broken another chain which binds me to the dry and dead philosophies and theologies. I have resigned my church in Summit, to take effect in the Fall of this year, and shall devote all my time to the work for the college in Konia, Asia Minor, of which I told you when you were here. It will be my work to raise money for its extension and support. This college is for the education and relief of the Armenian children who suffered so terribly under the persecutions of the Turk. I am very happy in the thought of this work, and if I ever become worthy to do thy work, teach thy truth, live thy life and help to establish thy kingdom that will be my crowning joy.[2]

Howard emphasized in a later letter to Ella Cooper, however, that

> it is <u>not</u> to be said that I gave up my church in order to talk the Bahá'í Revelation freely. That possibility entered into the decision as a factor, but there is [Albert] Vail doing wonderful work in the pastorate, and Abdul Baha has told me, and him too, that it is often advisable to stay in the ministry, and that during this transition period it [is] allowable to support ones family in the customary way as a minister.[3]

With the Brotherhood Church closed, Howard was free to devote himself fully to teaching the Faith. In the same letter to 'Abdu'l-Bahá dated 14 February 1913, Howard also told Him of the passing of Clarence Moore, his Brotherhood Church companion and the one who had first led him to the Bahá'í Faith. Clarence's wife, Marie, drew great strength from having learned of the Faith directly from the Master. Howard wrote:

> I cannot write all that is in my heart. My tears are blinding me now, but not tears of sorrow, rather of joy and deep emotion which your loving heart will share. Mrs. Moore is more wonderful in her faith and joy than I could tell,

but not more wonderful than you will understand, for your loving heart knows us better than we know ourselves . . .

Oh my Master. I love you but would love thee more. I am hungry, feed me with the bread of life, and am thirsty, give me to drink of thy favor. Tell me what to do and I will do it. I am determined to find God and to serve Him with all my soul. I rely on thee to lead me to Him. Truly I feel that without thee I can do nothing . . .

It is hard to try to say in cold words what is in our hearts. No words could ever express it and we rely on your love and insight to understand, and we know that we do not trust in vain.[4]

In June, Howard again wrote to the Master, pouring out his heart with a longing to follow the right path:

I have many, many things to tell you. Of my great love for you, of my entire acceptance of Bahá'u'lláh as my Lord and God, and of 'Abdu'l-Bahá as the Center of the Covenant. I am overwhelmed with the wonder and beauty of it all. I have become a new creature, I am unworthy of this great blessing – the confirmations of God descend upon me uninterruptedly. I wish I could lay all my heart bare before Thee. I do try to do so in prayer constantly. I seem to always be praying and happiness and peace attend me every moment.

O my Master! May my life be a sacrifice to Thee and to Thy beloved ones! May I sacrifice my spirit and all my possessions for the life of the world. May I become severed from self, the world and all else save God and drop my head on the dust in the path of the Friend . . .

I long to be worthy to aid in the building of the New Kingdom in the hearts and souls of men. I pray constantly for this confirmation. I study nothing but the writings of Bahá'u'lláh and 'Abdu'l-Bahá, I read nothing else and all my heart is set upon doing Thy will and living Thy life. Pray for me my dear Master.

I know how busy you are, with the burden of the world

upon you, but I beg for just a few words from your own hand assuring me of your blessing and warning me against what your wisdom seem to be mistakes. I will follow your commands unquestioningly.[5]

Howard's daughter Muriel becomes attracted to the Faith

Although Howard begged for assistance, he had already set his feet on the path of service and was travelling and giving talks about the Faith in the many cities he visited in his capacity as a salesman. His sixteen-year-old daughter, Muriel, kept contact with him through letters while he was away from home. During a month-long absence in September and October, Muriel suddenly became interested in the Bahá'í Faith. According to Harlan Ober, Muriel initially followed her mother's path of opposing what her father had done. It 'nauseated her to think of it and she felt as if she never wanted to hear [Howard] mention another word about it'.[6] But Harlan and Grace slowly educated her, and on 22 September, she wrote to her father saying that she and Harlan Ober had had a long talk – 'my desire to know things at last got the better of my silly notions so I asked him questions and he told me all about the Message. Isn't it wonderful! I'm so glad that I'm inside and can understand, instead of outside wondering.'[7]

Three days later, she wrote a letter addressed to 'Dearest Daddy-Pop' saying that Harlan had given her a copy of *The Seven Valleys*. She asked her father to send a copy of the *Hidden Words* to her. 'Then', she wrote, 'I can have them both bound and remember both the people who first told me about the Message.'[8] Howard suggested she write to 'Abdu'l-Bahá, but she demurred, writing that 'I don't feel as if I could write to Abdul Baha quite yet – it's come so suddenly that I haven't quite found my bearings yet.' She noted that her Uncle William, her mother's brother, had asked about the Faith. When she told him what she had learned, he brushed it off as 'probably another fool religion', then commented that 'he'd lived so far without hearing of Baha'u'llah and he guessed he could get along without it.' She added that he didn't know her true interest and that she hadn't yet told her mother.[9]

On 27 October 1913, after he had returned home from his travels, Howard wrote to 'Abdu'l-Bahá, his primary news being his daughter's acceptance of the Faith, but also expressing his love and devotion:

> My dear Lord and Master –
>
> I want to write just to tell you of my love for you; of my passionate desire to subject my will to Thine and to spend my life in Thy service and the service of Thy beloved. The past months have been filled with very great joys and with severe tests. I thank God for both – It is my hope that I may be found worthy to suffer greatly in the Cause of God. I have written to Thee twice before and I know that you have answered in the spirit though not by letter. I feel very near to Thee, my dear Lord, and am very happy in the service of Bahá'u'lláh and the Center of His Covenant.
>
> Pray for me my dear Master that I fail not in steadfastness.
>
> My dear little daughter, Muriel, whom you anointed in Mrs. Kinney's house, has lately accepted the Message through Grace and Harlan Ober, and this has made me very happy . . .
>
> Oh, my Master! It is the one desire of my heart to please Thee – to please God, – so that I may learn how to serve Him and the world, that His Kingdom may come on Earth. I earnestly supplicate at Thy threshold for Severance, and perfect evanescence.[10]

Muriel's mention of her Uncle William's view of the Bahá'í Faith foreshadowed a familial conflict. Howard's wife, Elizabeth, was very unhappy with Howard's decision to become a Bahá'í and give up his ministry and its consequent security. Muriel's interest in the Faith also greatly disturbed her. To support the family, Howard took up a job selling the Alexander Hamilton Business

Course, a job that took him away from home for long periods of time. These changes, the increased financial insecurity and her daughter's interest in the Faith, resulted in Elizabeth having a series of nervous breakdowns. She ended up leaving and taking Muriel with her to get her away from her father's influence. In 1918, she obtained a legal separation.[11]

Howard's life was greatly changed by his new Faith. In his diary for 31 December 1913, he wrote:

> This is the most wonderful year of my life. What it all means, what the future has in store, I of course cannot know. But I do know that the experiences of the past year must indicate some great work or suffering that I have to do or pass through. I cannot imagine anyone having much more wonderful spiritual experience. The growth of the soul has been so sudden and so great. Lessons in severance have been learned which last year at this time would have never been dreamed of as possible. – And the more I have given up, the more I have gained. It would almost seem at times as though God were audibly calling me to sacrifice <u>all</u> in His path. I have tried.[12]

After writing that deeply intimate thought, he returned to the material world of being a salesman. He wrote that he took the early train to Philadelphia, had breakfast in the Broad Street Station, then called on clients to collect his due, $20 from one company. He then took a train to Vineland, New Jersey, and got $50 in pledges and cash. On the train, he met Dr C. 3. Kuen 'and gave him the Message'. From Vineland, he took the sleeper train at 10 p.m. for Pittsburgh. On the train, he had 'the most wonderful time of prayer and illuminating thought for two hours'. The New Year came in while he slept in his berth on the train. His meditations in the morning led him to write about his growing sense of confirmations and his strong desire to serve with all his soul. That diary note heralded the spirit and course of the rest of his life:

For just about one year I have accepted wholly, unreservedly, <u>absolutely</u>, Baha'u'llah as my Lord and my God, and Abdul Baha as the Center of the Covenant of God. – And it has been the happiest, most fruitful, most helpful and most righteous year of my life. Surely these are the confirmations of God. With each day my faith has grown firmer. Each day God reveals Himself more and more clearly to me. And now on the threshold of a New Year I feel as though nothing at all mattered. Whether I have home or family, or friends or love or health or comforts or even life itself. I lay it all at Thy feet, O my most Holy Lord. – And I ask for more and more consecration . . . I want to be Thy man <u>wholly</u>.[13]

Replying to those sentiments, in February 1914 'Abdu'l-Bahá wrote in a Tablet to Roy Wilhelm, that 'I am fully informed with the services of his honor Mr Ives in different parts of America and in the meetings of the believers. I supplicate God to make this glorious personage a torch of the Love of God in those regions and innumerable souls may be guided through him.'[14]

Howard received another Tablet from 'Abdu'l-Bahá, written on 28 January 1914. It must have calmed his heart:

O thou my heavenly son:

Thy letter was received. It was a rose-garden from which the sweet fragrances of the love of God were inhaled. It indicated that you have held a meeting with the utmost joy and fragrance.

Your aim is the diffusion of the light of guidance; the resurrection of the dead hearts, the promotion of the oneness of the world of humanity and the elucidation of Truth. Unquestionably you will become confirmed therein and assisted by the invisible powers.

I have prayed on Thy behalf that thou mayest become the minister of the Temple of the Kingdom and the herald of the Lord of Hosts; that thou mayest build a monastery in heaven and lay the foundation of a convent in the Universe of the

Portrait of Howard, 1912, later given to Grace and Harlan Ober

'Abdu'l-Bahá with Howard Colby Ives, 1912

Howard Colby Ives, about 1912

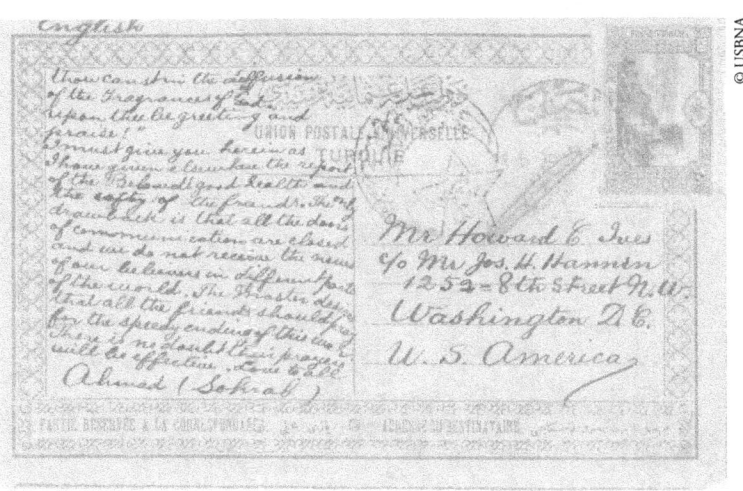

Two months after 'Abdu'l-Bahá wrote the last of the first group of the Tablets of the Divine Plan in 1916, He sent this Tablet to Howard on an open, unsealed postcard, just as He had with the first Tablets of the Divine Plan. Because of the disruption of the World War, mail was being heavily censored by the Ottomans, so the messages were sent on open postcards to allay any suspicions. The quotation from this Tablet on page 2 of this book is in the version later published in Portals to Freedom

A young Mabel Simon, sometime in the 1890s

Mabel in Detroit sometime between 1914 and 1917

Placeless; in all thy affairs that thou mayest become inspired by the Breaths of the Holy Spirit, and that thou mayest become so illumined that the eyes of all the ministers be dazzled by thy brilliancy, and may long to attain to thy station.

Thou art always in my memory. I shall never forget the days of our meeting.

Endeavor as much as thou canst that thou mayst master the Principles of Baha'U'llah, promulgate them all over that continent, create love and unity between the believers, guiding the people, awakening the heedless ones and resurrecting the dead.[15]

This was the first of three Tablets Howard was to receive from the Master in 1914. His instinctive response to the Writings, along with the guidance he received from 'Abdu'l-Bahá, was to reflect deeply on the meaning of each phrase:

Aside from the apparent fact that this letter was a call, a summons, a Trumpet-peal from a higher realm to *advance* – to 'come along *up*,' the meaning, the inner significance, of some of the phrases used eluded me completely at the time and still remain only dimly apprehended.

'Assisted by the Invisible Powers' – 'Minister of the Temple of the Kingdom – 'A monastery in heaven' – and a 'convent in the Universe of the Placeless' – what could such strange phrases mean?

As the years have passed and more and more thoroughly I have become impregnated with the Divine Utterances of Bahá'u'lláh and 'Abdu'l-Bahá a meaning has emerged, elusive yet definite; vague yet alluring beyond words in its appeal to the spirit. What if the orchestra is veiled behind its screen of divine roses, is the music less entrancing, or the certainty that there *is* an orchestra there less convincing because of that?[16]

In March, Howard wrote back to 'Abdu'l-Bahá, responding to His January Tablet:

Thy wonderful Tablet was received, and also the Name stones [ring stones] sent by you through my dear brother Ahmad. Truly I am overwhelmed with Thy Love and Bounty. Were I to write endlessly I could never express my adoring love, my soul-bursting thanksgivings. If I could only be worthy of Thy prayers and expectations concerning this Thy unworthy servant! . . .

I opened Thy blessed Tablet on my knees, and I read it through blinding tears. And now, as I write to Thee, my heart is afire with longing for Thee, and my eyes are overflowing. Truly I am intoxicated with the wine of the Love of God. When I realize that Thou art praying for me, and that the prayers of 'Abdu'l-Bahá are always answered, I am again and again over-whelmed . . .

May I proffer one supreme request? It is that I may come to Thee and be with Thee in that Holy Land. It seems as though that is the one desire of my soul . . . I want to sacrifice myself wholly at the Blessed Threshold, but I am so weak and sinful, so lost in selfishness and littleness that unless I imbibe Thy Spirit I can never attain. I feel that if I could be with Thee – O wonderful privilege! – and learn of Thee I might somehow be fitted . . .

I have been going through many and severe tests and I thank God for them. I pray for more pain and sorrow and suffering in order that these flames may purify me from all of Self. I truly 'long for suffering as a rebel craves forgiveness and a sinner longs for mercy.' I pray, O my Lord, that I may be so blessed as to be ordained to the station of sacrifice. May I give up all in Thy way and pour out my soul freely . . .[17]

'Abdu'l-Bahá's rapid response on 31 March was very uplifting, although it did not answer Howard's request for pilgrimage:

O thou my respected son:

The letter that thou hast written with the utmost love became the cause of perfect happiness. Truly, I say, thou art striving with heart and soul, to obtain the good pleasure of God. It is assured that this blessed intention will have great effect. The good intention is like an ignited candle whose rays are cast to all parts. Now, praise be to God, that thou hast manifested the utmost effort so that thou mayest light a candle of guidance in that region; plant a tree of the utmost freshness and delicacy in the garden of the world of humanity; call the people to the divine Kingdom; become the means of the progress of intellects and souls; gather the lost sheep under the protection of the Real Shepherd; cause the awakening of the sleepy ones; bestow health upon those who are spiritually sick; enlarge the sphere of human minds; refine the moral fibre of the people and direct the wandering birds to the rose-garden of Reality . . .[18]

The following Tablet received early in August 'just about the time of the outbreak of the World War', also highly praised Howard's desire to serve and purify himself, but again did not mention the requested pilgrimage:

O thou respected personage:
Thy letter was received. Its perusal imparted to me great hopefulness, for from its contents it became manifest that through the effects of thy entrance into the Divine Kingdom thou art progressing day by day.
When this progress shall become perpetual and continual, then thou shalt find the Most Great Center in the Universe of God, and shalt clearly behold the Confirmations of the Holy Spirit. Thou shalt be baptized in the Fountain of Life and shalt be freed from all the laws of the world of nature.
Thou shalt become illumined, merciful, heavenly – a radiant candle in the world of humanity.
Endeavor as much as possible to liberate thyself wholly from human susceptibilities – so that the powers of the Kingdom may gain control over thy heart and thy spirit – to such a degree that although thou art living on the face of the earth, yet thou mayest truly be in heaven; that although

outwardly thou art composed of material elements, yet spiritually thou mayest become composed of heavenly elements.

This is the everlasting glory of man! This is the eternal sublimity in the world of existence! This is the never-ending Life! This is the Spirit incarnated in the heart of humanity!'[19]

If Howard was disappointed at not being invited on pilgrimage, none of his collected correspondence whispered of it.

Howard was a speaker at the Green Acre Conference in July 1914. On Tuesday the 7th, he spoke about 'Universal Education – Knowledge vs Wisdom'. Two days later, he spoke on the topic of 'Universal Religion – The Unity of the Spirit'. On the 12th, Howard's subject was 'The Bahá'í Revelation as a Solvent of the World's Problems'.[20]

In August, Howard again wrote to 'Abdu'l-Bahá. He began with the song from his heart: 'My heart longs for Thee. I serve day and night at Thy Holy Threshold. – I am faint with yearning for the fullest confirmation of His Holiness Bahá'u'lláh – May my life be a sacrifice to His beloved ones! Truly I am ever intoxicated with the love of God and my heart dilated always with joy in Him.' Howard then repeats his continual plea for his life to be one of service:

> I am so happy in this assurance that day and night my heart is singing. – Bless me with the great joy of service in the Holy Kingdom. My one request is that my life may be used to advance Thy Cause. I ask for the gift of the Holy Spirit, not for my own joy and peace but that I may bring that joy and peace to the poor, sad, suffering, sinful, <u>warring</u> world. O let me be lifted up, my God and my Beloved, that I may do a little toward drawing all men unto Thee!'[21]

Most of the letter is very newsy. He tells of a new believer, Francis Wattson, from New London, Connecticut, who was mortally ill, but who 'received the message like a little child and in these few months he has attained a wonderful station in the new Kingdom'. This newsiness continued with a note about the people he had met at Green Acre that year:

> Green Acre this year has been a storehouse from which the treasures of the Kingdom have been poured. I am enclosing several programs. – Harry Randall, whose house in Medford, Mass. You blessed when in Boston, was there often, and always filled with the light of the love of God. His brother, Albert W. Randall, accepted the message at Green Acre this summer and his radiant face attracts many others to the Kingdom of El Abha. – Greater and greater unity is being manifested amongst the believers. Juliet Thompson is a wonderful servant. She thinks of nothing day and night but telling of Thy love to this world. She is accepting great tests with joy and gratitude in the path of God. Mrs. Clarence Moore is also growing into a beautiful and fruitful tree in the Rizwan of God. Harlan and Grace Ober have given up their work in New Bedford to establish a school under divine auspices in Dublin with the aid of Mr. and Mrs. Parsons. They have undoubtedly written Thee about it. Great is their love for humanity, and selfless zeal in service.[22]

By the spring of 1915, Howard's reputation as a Bahá'í speaker led Ella Cooper to ask him to speak at the First International Bahá'í Congress at Riḍván in San Francisco. In his response on 4 April, he first apologized for typing his letter, saying: 'Please pardon the use of the machine, I am obliged to use it on account of difficulty in my arm which make the pen a burden.' He noted that he had been travelling for a month, but had managed to sketch out an abstract of his proposed talk, though he warned that 'I won't guarantee to say anything like it when the day arrives, for it is my hope that God will do the talking and not I.' Ella had also obviously asked him for some information about himself, which he provided 'under protest'.[23]

Looking to the future, it is interesting to note that Howard mentions that Mabel Rice-Wray, of Detroit, had been elected as a delegate to the National Convention, but was unable to go. She had asked Howard to be her proxy delegate. Both Howard's and Mabel's marriages were in disarray at this point, primarily because of their dedication to the Bahá'í Faith and their spouses' opposition to their activities.

Howard spoke on 'The Underlying Unity of all Faiths' (see Appendix 1) on 21 April. It was all about the oneness of God, the oneness of religion and the oneness of humanity. He concluded with:

> It is not enough merely to speak the word of God, to preach the truth, to exhort men to be good and pure and holy and just. 'Guidance hath ever been by words,' declares Baha'u'llah, 'but in this day it is by deeds.' He tells us plainly that unless the teacher is disinterested, thinking only of the kingdom of God, careless of himself, considering the interest of others in preference to his own, willing to sacrifice all that he has in the service of his fellow man, his teaching will be of no avail, even though he speak the word of God. . .
>
> It is easily demonstrable that strife and true religion . . . are contradictory terms. Hence it follows that strife is prima facie evidence of atheism, irreligion, idolatry and polytheism. It makes no difference what profession men make if their actions give the lie to all their pious words. The day has come when by deeds alone men are to be judged . . .
>
> There is only one possible basis for world unity and peace, and that is a recognition of the essential oneness of all mankind.
>
> One God implies one humanity. One Father signifies one human family. One divine commander-in-chief means a unified army certain of victory . . . Can such an army be conquered![24]

Howard's talks were carefully crafted and, as in his life, followed Bahá'u'lláh's Writings as closely as possible. From his earliest encounter with the Writings, he thought about them deeply, applied them directly, and sought to use the very words as the guiding light of how to live his own life and how to influence other lives. He was never much interested in his own opinion, favouring instead as direct and clear an application of the meaning of the words of Bahá'u'lláh and 'Abdu'l-Bahá as was possible.

The following year, on 22 June 1916, Howard received the astonishing Tablet from 'Abdu'l-Bahá that was included in the introduction to this book. It is such an amazing and prescient Tablet that it is again placed here. The Tablet began with a note from Ahmad Sohrab that read: 'The reports of your services, your travels and lectures are most stimulating to the friends in the Holy Land and conducive to the happiness of the heart of 'Abdu'l-Bahá.'

> O thou speaker in the Temple of the Kingdom!
> Praise be to God that most of the time thou art traveling, going from city to city raising the melody of the Kingdom in meetings and churches, and announcing the glad tidings of Heaven.
> It is recorded in the Gospel that John the Baptist was crying in the wilderness: 'Prepare ye the way of the Lord, make His Paths straight, for the Kingdom of God is at hand.'
> He was crying in the wilderness, but thou art crying in populous cities. Although the ministers have brilliant crowns on their heads, yet it is my hope that thou mayest crown thy head with the diadem of the Kingdom – such a diadem whose brilliant jewels may illumine the dark passages of future centuries and cycles.
> God says in His great Book, Qur'án, 'He especializes with His Mercy whomsoever He willeth.' That is, God distinguisheth with His favor and bestowal a number of souls, and marks them with His own seal of approval. A similar statement is revealed in the Gospel: 'Many are called but few are chosen.' Now, praise be to God that thou art one of those 'few'.
> Appreciate thou the value of this bounty, and occupy thy time as much as thou canst in the diffusion of the fragrances of God.[25]

Because of the world war then disrupting the mails, Howard did not receive the Tablet until November. Mail was being heavily censored by the Ottomans at that time, so 'Abdu'l-Bahá sent His Tablet to Howard on an open, unsealed postcard, like the first five of 'Abdu'l-Bahá's *Tablets of the Divine Plan*. This was done to allay any suspicions the Ottomans might have had. When Roy Wilhelm informed him that the Tablet had arrived, Howard quickly wrote to Joseph Hannen, who handled his mail, with directions to send it to Allentown, Pennsylvania.[26] With Howard's constant travelling for work and the Faith, he was a hard man to track down. When he reached Allentown on 19 November, the Tablet was waiting for him. His response to Joseph was 'How blessed it is to receive these wonderful Words! Truly they are the Words of Life.'[27]

Joseph asked if Howard could travel to Washington DC, and Howard gladly accepted, writing that 'I pray that we will all be tested and strengthened for the great Days to come when all the world will be anxious to hear the Gospel of the New Kingdom.'[28] Joseph's response to Howard's desire to be tested has not been preserved.

In the middle of January 1917, Howard went to Washington. Joseph had asked whether Howard wanted to be introduced as 'Reverend' and he said yes, if it would attract a single heart to the Cause.[29] Howard offered three topics on which he could speak – 'The Signs of Peace in the Great War'; 'The Spiritual Forces at Work in the World'; or 'The Spiritual Foundations of Humanity'. He told Joseph to pick any of them and he would 'express what God wishes me to say.'[30]

Howard was back in Washington DC in April, again at the request of Joseph. This time, his topic title was to be either 'The Kingdom of God on Earth' or 'The Spiritual Superstructure in the World of Humanity'. Howard noted that in reality, they were the same thing.[31] Just one day after agreeing to the Washington talk, Howard had to add a stop in Baltimore because Joseph said it was important.

Understanding war and God

In April 1918, Muriel, Howard's 21-year-old daughter, married Theodore (Ted) Obrig in Summit, New Jersey, with Howard officiating.[32] Muriel's mother was not there. The honeymoon was short because soon afterwards Ted was in the middle of the war in France. On 31 July, Howard received a letter from Ted describing the horrors that surged around him. Ted wrote about how the unabated slaughter was driving men from God:

> The more that I see of this terrible war the less do I believe that a wise and good God ever had anything to do with it, even as an object lesson to the people of this sad earth – at least the half that I am in is too sad and pained for words. You at home read of what is going on over here but you never know of the absolute horror that is poisoning the minds of the men engaged in this terrible slaughter of all that is beautiful and good. I find that instead of turning them to any kind of a God it is filling their hearts with hatred, with a disbelief in the God they have long thought good and absolute. And strange to say I do not blame them at all. If you could <u>see</u> this hell that is the only way you could understand just what I mean.
>
> I can not believe any longer that this war is for the good and I want to tell you why. For the last three years the men most needed in the world, the big, strong men, the men who would have led the world, if this war had not been, have been killed off. The weaklings have been left. The law of the biologists has been reversed. The hearts of the women and children have been filled with terrible sorrow and a hate that will only die with them. The treasures which the ages have given us have been destroyed without cause. The industries of nations have been turned to the production of the instruments of death – you have this in the States now. The God the people once worshiped is now mocked. The God for the Germans is the fatherland. Is this not a queer perversion of an instructive faith? And Oh, Daddy Howard

I half believe in what seemed absolute not so long ago. I refuse to believe in a God who could have anything to do with this damn war and still what am I to think of a God who has nothing to do with it. That last thought makes the "hopeless God" a vain delusion. What am I getting at? Will this war do away the popular human God? If it does, away goes heaven and hell and an impersonal power alone takes its place. The mass will then have nothing for they can not grasp such a conception. Is this pragmatic? I certainly do not believe so. The lower class must have something more human, something which they can grasp, something like their human fellows. I fear when they lose this God they lose everything including themselves. Oh, I must stop this for the more I think the more complications enter the matter. What do you think of this letter? How I wish you were here to talk to and how glad I am that you are far away from this sorrow . . .

I will wait anxiously for your letter in answer to this wild muddle of thought. Perhaps you can find the end of the string and untie the snarl it has gotten into.[33]

Howard was appalled by what he read. His response ran to three-and-a-half pages as he strove to explain that God had not been powerless to stop the war and that belief in Him was the only salvation for those engaged in it. He got right to the point:

My dear, dear boy,

Your letter of July 31st has just come. I wept over it because it reflected so fully the faithless condition of the world. I hardly know how to answer it but I will try, and I pray for wisdom and a divine eloquence. I do not need to pray that every word may express a deep, deep love for you, dear Ted, and a sympathy and understanding beyond all words. For this is deep in my heart. I could not fail to get that over to you. God is daily proving to me that He has answered my prayer that only love for humanity may be in my heart.

How dreadful all that Hell 'OVER THERE' must be I can imagine. I think I can imagine it very vividly, tho not as vividly as if I saw it: but I do think I can imagine it more vividly than you see it. Do you get what I mean? I see things here in this country which wring my heart but which other men and women seem to pay no attention to, and in some cases actually laugh at. The Eye which God hath opened in the Great Day of Revelation sees significances in everything which speak of His Love and Power. The illumined vision sees God in everything. This is what Jesus meant when He said that the pure in heart see God. The truly pure ones, those whose hearts and consciousnesses are simple, not confused with intellectual subtleties, not obsessed with selfish desires, not wandering in the darkness of theological vagaries, – such see with clear vision, as when the light is suddenly turned on in a dark room.

Of course God did not have anything to do with this war, if by that you mean that He wilfully allowed it, positively foresaw it without being able to prevent it, and planned it without a peradventure. Does the mother plan the spanking when she tells the child she will spank if he does certain things?

But let us not deal with such superficialities. You cannot disbelieve in God, – in a Creator, and Infinite, Wise and Powerful ONE, call Him by what name you will. Your own letter proves you cannot for such disbelief leads to a greater and more terrible dilemma than the belief. Your very agony over this seeming injustice and lack of love on the part of God, the Omnipotent, the Kind, is the greatest possible proof that there is such a God, for if not where did your sense of justice come from which is so outraged. Unless you created yourself, and each man is responsible for his own ideals and faiths, then the Creator, the Self-subsistent and Eternal God is responsible for your very rebellion against what seems to you intolerable injustice.

Ah, dear Teddy, this is just as it should be. Until the heart awakens to such a love for, and trust in, God, that it is able to see Him in all things, and to trust Him at all times, and walk thru the Valley of the Shadow of Death without a fear or doubt, it is better that it should revolt. This very revolt is the Voice of God.

Now let me see if I can say something positive that will help you to see more clearly what it may all mean. My prayers go with every word.

There is no possible explanation except we see this as the Day of God. Think of the time of Christ. Do you imagine that the Romans and Greeks felt any less strongly than you that their gods were falling and all faith impossible, when they saw their empires crumbling, their arts being destroyed, their fellows massacred by the 'Barbarians', and all the world . . . falling into ruins about them?

We say now that their gods were false. No more false than the imagined God of the theologians. Jesus, the Christ, the Anointed One of God, the Humble, Meek and Loving One . . . told us what and Who God Is, and how we should worship and serve Him. Love your enemies, bless them that curse you, give and serve and help all men . . . Have we done this? No. Was it possible to have done it? Undoubtedly, else no one could ever have believed on Christ, or found happiness and peace in trying to follow these teachings.

But Christ foresaw that the time had not yet come for men to learn their lessons perfectly, and He foretold the coming of One who should complete what He began . . . He also foretold exactly these conditions, now obtaining on earth . . .

But you will say, why could it not have been done without such terrible suffering. My dear! my dear! – there are some things even God cannot do. He cannot make men wise except thru their own experience. If he created them unable to sin they would be like animals without a sense of right and wrong . . . The whole object of Creation is to make men into Sons of God, and this needs ages of schooling, and a long succession of Teachers sent from God . . .

Men kill and stone these Divine Ones, and then build

wonderful temples (tombs) for them and worship them. Then straightway they forget, or partially forget, their teachings and revert almost, but never quite, to their former state of selfishness and lust. Then God sends another Messenger of the Kingdom, and with Him comes such a Power of the Holy Spirit that the world takes on a new and Divine Life . . . This very fact arouses all the forces of selfishness and evil against these heavenly armies, and behold, the tremendous WAR is on. It could not be avoided except as man was incapable of wrong doing, which is unthinkable, or being capable of wrong never committed it, which is also unthinkable, for then he would be God and the creation unnecessary. The only other alternative is that being capable of wrong doing, and committing it, he could also be happy and escape any suffering as a consequence of wrong-doing. This is also unthinkable if we assume a good and loving God. For what would we think a good earthly parent who cared more for a child's physical happiness and comfort than for his spiritual, intellectual and moral welfare?

. . . Some of these men you speak of who are now cursing God and losing what they call their 'faith', had it not been for this war would be leading self-satisfied lives, using the name of God lightly . . . Very few of them ever touched Reality, or saw God clearly enough even to deny Him, until brought face to face with His outraged Laws . . .

My dear Ted, I say to you . . . that this war, with all its suffering, all its bodily death, is infinitely preferable to that spiritual death to which Christ referred when he said 'let the dead bury their own dead, come thou and follow Me'. For these men whom you see dying all around you are not really 'dead'. Their bodies are returning to dust, where they would return in a short time anyhow, but their spirits are immortal and the wonderful lessons they are learning every hour of their own weakness and need of God are preparing them for that greater and deeper and richer Life as their humdrum existence never could. . . .

. . . It is not necessary to pass from this body in order

to enter the immortal life. It is only necessary to believe in God, that is to believe in His Manifestation . . . You will say that many do. I say to you that so few do as to be practically negligible. For Belief is only evidenced by deeds. This war has for centuries been seething in the social, political and theological life of this world. It has only come to the surface, like a fearful boil, in the last three years.

I see the same WAR going on is this country. Here we call it Race-Hatred, with its lynchings; Or capital and labor war with its ruinous blood-money methods; Or white slavery with its unspeakable horrors; . . . Or church hypocrisy, with its blindness as to what worship and prayer consist in . . . There is not a department of life, from the way the mistress treats the servant in the kitchen to the way the ministerial sycophant smirks before the wealthy pew-holder, that does not bear witness to man's forgetfulness and denial of God . . .

Oh Ted! . . . I thank God that you are there seeing all this terribleness with your own eyes. You might never have awakened to the Reality of God in any other way. I would rather have you deny Him with curses than be indifferent to Him . . . It is indifference when men say with their lips what their hearts and lives deny, when their lives do not reflect the life of Christ. That only is true belief.

Abraham, Moses, Zoroaster, Buddha, Mohammed, Christ – all came to tell us, and show us what God IS, and they said we must be like HIM. That is we must be spiritual sons of this Heavenly Father. Now Baha'O'llah has come to fulfil the teachings and lives of all His predecessors. He and they are ONE . . .

I pray for you daily with deep love and faith in your safe return to us all. May God illumine your heart with the Light of knowledge of Himself, that you may not be withheld by false voices from beholding the signs of His coming, nor from turning to the Horizon of Renunciation. Such renunciation of self and this mortal vanishing world is the Resurrection spoken of by all the Prophets of God. In this renunciation lies the Path to Immortal Life. I pray that you may attain to this blessed Path while walking upon this earth, and that you may take a sip of the Cup from the Oceans of Eternity, even while drinking from this mortal and turbid cup.[34]

Ted returned home in the spring of 1918 and he and Muriel moved to Washington DC. Howard wrote to Joseph Hannen saying:

> My daughter has only attended one or two Bahá'í meetings and was not favorably impressed, although she loves 'Abdu'l-Bahá. He anointed her when He was here. I am not sure they will even come when I am there; I will not urge them at all. Their hearts are all in His Hands, and he guides whomsoever He will into His way. My Muriel is the sweetest, dearest daughter a father ever had, and of a deep, spiritual nature. The time for her perfect understanding will surely come. Until then prayer and love will suffice for teaching.[35]

Ted and Muriel's marriage lasted until at least 1925 and two children were born, Betsy and Barbara.

Travel teaching and Conventions

Howard was constantly in demand to talk to the Bahá'ís and interested people. In February 1918, he was again asked to go to Washington DC and speak to the friends. Howard offered to speak in Baltimore, as well. Then due to some confusion, Juliet Thompson scheduled him to speak in Baltimore at 3 p.m. on Sunday, while Joseph Hannen scheduled him for the evening of the same day in Washington.[36] One of them had to be rescheduled. Howard gave his talk in Washington and Joseph quickly requested still another visit.[37] This was set up for 26 May with the topic being 'The True Freedom'.

In October 1918, communication was re-established with the Holy land and Howard joyously poured out his heart to 'Abdu'l-Bahá:

O my Master! As this servant writes his heart is on fire and his eyes overflow with tears. All that is in his heart to write to Thee Thou knowest. All the love he would express is as an open book to Thy Heart of Love! This servant supplicates only that his 'advancement in the Kingdom of God may be perpetual and continual,' as Thou didst advise him in a wonderful Tablet which has been a Guiding Star for three years. He seeks only perfect sacrifice in the Way of God; absolute submission at the Holy Threshold; complete effacement of self and humiliation and evanescence in the presence of the servants of God.

And this servant supplicates also that from this emptiness of self may grow perfect servitude in the Kingdom of El ABHA. May he be made worthy to serve the Cause of the Oneness of the world of humanity; may he be enabled to advance the love of Truth and Freedom of Spirit in this poor world of darkness and slavery; may he be strengthened to spread the Gospel of the New Kingdom and to bring joy to the hearts of men thru the knowledge of the Coming of God and the attainment to the Meeting of God.

O my Lord. Truly this servant is aware of the greatness of this supplication. Yet Thou didst tell him when Thou wert in this country, that he was not to seek small things. 'Ask for great things' was Thy command, and ever since he has sought only the greatest things his mind and heart could compass. And yet he is unsatisfied. Nothing but the very highest will ever satisfy his heart. Nothing but the perfection of the world of humanity, nothing but the Virtues of God will satisfy him, nothing but citizenship in the Kingdom of God and membership in the Supreme Concourse. He supplicates at the Holy Threshold for perfect humility and nothingness in order that progress in this High Path may be possible . . .[38]

With all his travelling around for both work and the Faith, some people were having a tough time knowing where to send his mail. Many of his letters included new mailing addresses.

His constantly shifting whereabouts created difficulties for Roy Wilhelm, and he commonly didn't know where to send Howard's mail. Somehow, Roy chose an incorrect one and used it for an extended time. In exasperation at Roy's mail forwarding, Howard cried, 'I can't imagine why Roy persists in sending my mail to Jersey City. My address has never been there.'[39]

In April 1919, Howard attended the Bahá'í Convention in New York City and presented a talk on 'The Coming of the Promised One' (see Appendix 2). He began by contemplating the dawn and how the dark earth is gradually flooded with light. By extending the metaphor to the spiritual dawns that occur once every millennium or so, he described how each Manifestation of God renews that spiritual light, initially seen only by those seekers with pure hearts, but slowly spreading across the world of humanity and driving away the darkness. Those who first see the light have the obligation of helping others to see it:

> Did you ever stand upon a high point and see the sun rise? I have stood among the foothills of the Rocky Mountains and watched the dawn break over the hills, the morning star gradually dimming in its glory, the faint first rosy light creeping up the horizon, and then gradually, above the mountains, the first rim of the radiant glory of the orb; then lifting, and lifting, and flooding the earth with its glory . . .
>
> The Sun of Reality rises only once every thousand years or so, the stars in the heaven precede his dawning, the hearts of men become weary through the night as they watch the stars in the sky and long for the coming of that which the stars promise . . .
>
> My friends, praise be to God, the promised One hath come again. We have waited long throughout the centuries; our hearts have grown into stone, our hearts have become frozen, our hearts have fallen low in woe and weeping. Praise be to God, He hath come again! He hath come again! The Sun of Reality hath risen . . .
>
> Ah, my friends, make the picture, for his human temple

is the Sun of Reality, and within that human temple, which is nothing but a cloud, the Sun is shining to those whose eyes can see it . . .

When the sun rises in the springtime, when the sun gradually crosses the line, what do we see? Do we see all at once the earth burst into beauty and perfection? Do we see all at once the fruits of the harvest appear? Oh, no, we see a blade of grass here and there, a little green leaf, then the rest; we see a tree just beginning to show its buds but these are the new earth . . .

Those who believe in Bahá'u'lláh, those who have turned their hearts to the Center of His Covenant, those who love the Blessed Perfection, were created by the Sun of Reality in the human temple for sacrifice, and by sacrifice shall they glory over the world as He did and establish the Kingdom of the promised One in the hearts and souls . . .[40]

He also read the closing prayer for the Feast of Paradise with 'great spiritual attraction and earnestness'.[41]

During the next Convention in 1920, Howard participated in the marriage of Juanita Storch, of California, and Ahmad Sohrab, one of 'Abdu'l-Bahá's former secretaries, by reading the marriage vow for them to repeat.[42]

In September 1919, Carl Scheffler had asked Howard to speak in Chicago on 3 October. Carl was thinking of showing the moving picture of 'Abdu'l-Bahá at the meeting and asked Howard's opinion. Howard agreed with showing it, but with a caveat – 'I am sometimes inclined to the opinion that the less emphasis is put on the personality, when giving the Message the better.'[43] Two days later, after receiving a reply from Carl in which the date was changed to a week later, Howard replied that the new date was much better for him. He asked for several more copies of the programme to be sent to him and that he thought Mrs Rice-Wray 'would like to see them too – but I will see that she gets one'.[44]

In 1920, Mabel Rice-Wray would suddenly become very prominent in Howard's life.

5

Mabel Rice-Wray, the Early Years

Mabel Simon was born on 21 September 1878 in Montclair, New Jersey.[1] Her parents were Caroline McGrew Simon and Albert G. Simon; her father's parents were German and her mother's were from Virginia with English antecedents. Mabel had a brother, Albert Jr, who was five years older. She also may have also had a younger sister who was born after 1880 and who must have either died or married and moved away before 1900. The only reference to her is a photo of a young Mabel on the back of which is written 'With much love from your sister, Mabel'.[2]

Mabel's daughter and son, Edris and Colston Rice-Wray, recalled: 'From the time she [Mabel] was a young girl, she had an intense desire to find the truth. She felt that surely there was some other answer than traditional Christianity, in which she had been brought up. She investigated every avenue which gave the least promise of being able to fulfill her intense desire to know.'[3]

When Mabel was 16 she lived in Baltimore, and to go shopping had to take a certain streetcar that descended a long hill from the residential part of the city to the shopping area. The journey down the long hill 'passed through an area that was treeless and drab, was lined with small shops and poor houses'. She had made this same trip many times before 1894. There are two descriptions of Mabel's first encounter of the Bahá'í Faith, one from her step-daughter Muriel, and one from one of Mabel's friends, Mariam Haney. Muriel wrote that Mabel

> began to be aware of a strange impulse to get off the trolley car when it was half way down the long hill. This was, of

course, ridiculous. Why would she want to get off the car? There were no cross-streets; she knew no one in the neighborhood, why would she get off and what would she do if she did get off? So – trip after trip she reasoned with herself, talking herself out of it and feeling really very foolish. The feeling persisted – she should stop the car half way down the hill and get off.

Finally, after this had been going on for many weeks, she lost patience. All right – she would stop the car and get off! So, the next time she had occasion to go shopping she did just that. And, as she stood on the curb [of Charles Street] watching the trolley car slide down the rest of the hill out of sight, she felt very silly. So now what was she supposed to do? She turned from the curb and found herself facing a small shop that sold newspapers and magazines and stationery with, maybe, penny candy. Mabel, not knowing what else to do, went over to the shop and walked in. Behind the counter, there was an older woman with a gentle face and beautiful eyes. She asked Mabel if she might help her. Mabel said, helplessly, 'I don't know. I don't know what I want. I don't know what I came for' – and then she found herself telling the woman all about the curious experience she'd had for so long as she came down the hill on a trolley car. When Mabel had finished the woman smiled. 'I can tell you what you came for,' she said. 'Come into my sitting room with me, and I'll tell you the whole wonderful story.'[4]

Mariam Haney wrote that the woman Mabel encountered was Pearl Battee Doty, a woman in her late thirties who was the first Bahá'í teacher in Baltimore. Pearl introduced Mabel to the Bahá'í Faith and invited her to her home, giving her a firm foundation through a series of private lessons.[5]

Whatever the actual details, Muriel always ended the story by mentioning that the woman in the shop was a Bahá'í who ardently desired to teach the Cause. She worked long hours in the shop, and feeling constrained by being confined for so many hours, she had prayed for seeking souls to be led to her.

Mabel was the first person who responded to the mysterious force of divine assistance.[6]

Mabel married Theron Rice-Wray, the son of Ellah and James Rice-Wray, on 16 April 1903. Theron had gone to Baltimore from St Louis in November 1901 on business and had been given a letter of introduction to Mabel. They were attracted to each other and Mabel introduced him to the Bahá'í Faith.[7] Theron was the same age as Mabel and was born in Versailles, Missouri. The young couple were married in Alexandria, Virginia, lived briefly in Washington DC, and then settled in Newark, New Jersey. The marriage was sanctioned by a Tablet from 'Abdu'l-Bahá on 11 March 1903:

> O you two who are advancing toward the Kingdom of God!
>
> Hearts were elated (with joy) on account of your conjunction (marriage) in a blessed and happy day, in this glorious Age. This conjunction is undoubtedly blessed and happy to the people of Faith, inasmuch as both of you are overshadowed under the Tree of Life, have entered the Ark of Deliverance and are attracted to the Fragrances of the Garden of the Kingdom, through the Confirmation of the Lord of Signs. How blessed is this conjunction! How noble is this companionship and union!
>
> Be ye as a pair of Nightingales making a nest in the loftiest branches of the Tree of Life in the Paradise of the Merciful One, and warbling in the most wonderful praises during evens and morns in glorifying their Independent Lord.
>
> Verily I beg of God to ordain for both of you every good, to quicken you with a pure life, to enable you to do righteous deeds and to cause blessings to descend upon your friends and kinsmen.
>
> How excellent is this conjunction (marriage) united through Faith, and which has coincided with (the time when you were) attracted to the Beauty of the Clement One![8]

Following their marriage, a second Tablet arrived:

> To Mr and Mrs Rice Wray (Upon them be Baha'Ollah)
> O you two myrtles in the Garden of the Love of God!
> Happy is your condition! for ye have made your house a nest and dwelling for the birds of the Grove of Truth; that is for the beloved of God and the maid-servants of the Merciful! The meeting of the worldly people of other religions is the cause of dis-union, but the assemblage of the people of the Merciful One is conducive to Union and Love amongst the spiritual ones. In whatever dwelling the assemblage of the friends is organized, the Light of Guidance will shine therein, the Cloud of Gift will rain and the Breeze of Providence will waft by. Happy is your condition, for ye have become the cause of love and harmony among the friends![9]

In 1905, Theron's sister, Ella, learned of the Faith from Mabel when she visited them and quickly accepted the Message. Ella took it back to St Louis and shared it with her mother, Ellah, who also accepted it, thus beginning the St Louis Bahá'í community. Ellah wrote:

> When the Bahá'í Message reached me, I had the belief – based on Ancient Teachings – that: The assertion of a truth becomes a truth according to the Reality of the Truth and the strength and persistence of the asserter. I was using – Jesus is the Christ the Son of the Living God – having again united with the Christian Church after many years away from conventional religion, though never away from God, so I asked: 'What is the Word?' and was given 'Allaho Abha.' Briefly – I learned that Word and used it and it brought me into the New Revelation and daily increases both my strength and my glory in God and all His Manifestations.[10]

'Alláh-u-Abhá' was considered by the early Bahá'ís to be a very sacred word and not to be given out or used freely. It was kept secret until a seeker accepted the Faith, at which point, they were given the holy 'Word'.

Both Ella and Ellah became strong, life-long Bahá'ís and energetic teachers of the Faith. Theron, too, became actively involved in Bahá'í activities and held 'Abdu'l-Bahá in great esteem, but had difficulty with the Faith apart from the Master, whose Will and Testament he was unable to accept.[11] Mabel and Theron had three children in the following years: Edris Roushan was born on 21 January 1904, Landon Carter in 1905, and Rouhi Colston on 17 October 1906. 'Roushan' and 'Rouhi' were names bestowed by 'Abdu'l-Bahá. Landon lived just a short time. Helen Inderlied shared the story as told to her by Mabel:

> She related how she had the great sorrow of losing by illness a beloved baby [Landon]. She said, 'Imagine my grief intensified by my great weariness of nights and days of nursing ending in defeat and sorrow.' A woman came to call. She asked this poor mother, what the Bahá'í Faith was. Mrs. Ives [Rice-Wray] thought 'Must I tell her now – can I not be quiet now with my grief?' But she was not content to do that. She proceeded to explain the Faith she served to this inquiring soul.[12]

Mariam Haney wrote about the effect of the child's death: 'Mabel and Theron were so pathetic, so tragic at that particular moment. They knew no one but the Bahais; they had only been in Newark a short time. The way they held on to me was sad – they needed all the comfort I could give them. We had our little spiritual service for the baby, and then the three of us laid it to rest in the cemetery.'[13]

During the first years of marriage, they had the bounty of deepening their knowledge of the Faith with many strong Bahá'ís: Paul and Mariam Haney, Ellen Beecher, Ali Kuli Khan, Harlan Ober and Hooper Harris. Mariam remembered Mabel's 'beauty and radiance but particularly her spiritual capacity, so unusual in such a new believer and especially in one so young. "She was one of those rare young souls who was always longing to go forward on the path, always reaching out for more and more of the teachings . . . There were signs ever present which indicated her earnestness and longing, born of the recognition of the Manifestation of today which was like a pressure upon her soul, pushing her ever on and on to the mission she was to fulfil, to the destiny all her own.'"[14]

In 1906, Mabel received her first Tablet from 'Abdu'l-Bahá in response to a letter she had written to Him (but which is not now available to the authors). He wrote:

> O thou maid-servant of God!
> ... I hope you will become confirmed by the Good-pleasure of God. Do ye think at all times to practice the Advices and Exhortations of God. If we characterize ourselves in a befitting manner with the Fragrances of Divine Holiness and live according to the instructions of the Blessed Perfection, undoubtedly we will hear with the ear of the mind, the melody of the Holy Spirit, and the Harmony of the Kingdom.
> The supplication which you have asked for the children is forwarded along with this Tablet. Each child may memorize as much as he can from this supplication.[15]

New Orleans, Louisiana

The Rice-Wrays lived in New Orleans from about 1907 until 1909, staying in the Casa Grande Apartment Hotel. According to Edris, they had a 'black "nanny" who did our house work, cooked, and cared for us children'.[16]

A move to Los Angeles

In 1909 or 1910, the family moved to Tropico in the Los Angeles area, where Mabel became a good friend of Kathryn Frankland, one of the distinguished early American believers. With Kathryn's help, Mabel began to serve the Faith quite diligently. She held firesides and study classes in her home, and became active in women's organizations.

Mariam Haney wrote that Mabel

was hungry . . . for the companionship of Baha'is. She used to come over to our home in Los Angeles as many times as she possibly could, and with her understanding heart and mind helped me so very much with my son Paul [appointed a Hand of the Cause in 1954] who was then a baby. No one but the Lord knows how much I appreciated her service. She always helped us, too, with the Feasts at our home and with meetings . . .[17]

On 18 October 1912, 'Abdu'l-Bahá arrived in Los Angeles. Mabel's reaction was related by her daughter, Edris:

When Mother heard the electrifying news that 'Abdu'l-Bahá was in Los Angeles, we were in the midst of moving to a new house. She had a terrible time finding our clothes as part of our things were already in the new house. My grandmother threw up her hands in despair and exclaimed, 'Mabel, you are out of your mind! How can you drop everything and go to Los Angeles?' The movers were also surprised and said, 'Lady, where are we going to put the furniture in the new house?' My mother replied, 'Just put them anywhere. I have to go to Los Angeles!'

So off we went to Los Angeles to the hotel where 'Abdu'l-Bahá was staying. He was out so we sat in the lobby waiting. Soon, 'Abdu'l-Bahá entered, followed by two Persians and a few of the L.A. Bahá'ís. We joined the group of L.A. Bahá'ís and when we got in the elevator, we found that 'Abdu'l-Bahá was with us. My mother said that He stood behind me, put His hands on my shoulders and closed his eyes. She thought that he was praying for me. When we all got to His room, he sat in a big arm chair and reached out for my brother and me, and put one of us on each knee. He motioned to one of the Persians to give Him a box of cookies which were on the Bureau and gave each of us a handful. We sat there happily munching the cookies while He gave a short talk to the Bahá'ís present. I felt happy and content. It was like sitting on the lap of a kind grandfather. Afterwards as we left the room, my mother leaned down and whispered to me, 'Edris, what did you do with the cookies?' I replied, 'Why I ate them!' I don't know what she wanted to do with them, save them for posterity?[18]

Edris wrote that 'to us he was as a kind grandfather, but to our mother it was a moment of rededication, a moment of increased awakening. She became inflamed with the deepest longing to serve this Cause.'[19]

Mabel received another Tablet from 'Abdu'l-Bahá in the summer of 1913. She had apparently asked about the 19-Day Feast, which 'Abdu'l-Bahá called a 'spiritual meeting':

> O thou daughter of the Kingdom!
>
> Thy letter was received and its contents imparted the utmost of happiness, because it was an indication of thy firmness and steadfastness in the Covenant. Today whosoever is firm in the Covenant he will become ignited like unto a candle in the Assemblage of the World and the Confirmations of the Kingdom of Abha shall encircle him from all directions. Thank thou God that both thyself and thy respected husband are confirmed in the firmness of the Testament and from every standpoint you are serving the Kingdom of God. His Holiness Baha-o-llah has manifested infinite favors toward you and I hope that under all circumstances he may make you triumphant.
>
> Thou hast written concerning the spiritual meeting. The spiritual meeting must be in the utmost of ecstasy and tumult. The supplication must be perused, the Tablets and verses be read, eloquent speeches be delivered, divine proofs be explained, the audience be encouraged and incited to enter the Kingdom of God, the news received from different parts be read and at the end they may collectively (ensemble) read (or chant or sing) a supplication.[20]

Detroit

In 1913, Theron changed his business and moved to Detroit, leaving Mabel and the children in Tropico. A year later, Mabel was at her wits end trying to handle two quite rowdy children by herself. She wrote to Theron saying, 'I can't handle these children alone anymore'. Realizing that his children needed a father, he brought the rest of the family to Detroit in 1914. Edris remembered that the train trip was awful, 'two nights and 3 days sitting up on the train'.[21]

Mabel's teaching activities in Detroit enabled the formation of a group and she learned about renunciation: 'I turned to God, saying that I wanted nothing but His Will – that I asked no personal happiness, nothing but one thing – to be permitted to serve His Cause. Whatever was his Will was mine'.[22] Wishing to follow God's will instead of her own became her guiding standard.

Mabel's health problems started early. In late 1916, in a letter to Joseph Hannen, Mabel noted that she was in the hospital convalescing from an operation. In spite of that, her teaching efforts were already well underway. In the letter, she states that she had promised Sandusky, Cleveland and Akron, all in Ohio, that she would visit. There was also an invitation from Washington DC. She was still recovering from the operation at the end of January 1917.[23] In Detroit, Mabel was able to introduce the Faith to Henry Ford, the founder of the Ford Automobile Company.[24]

As the years passed, the differences between Mabel and Theron became great. Edris wrote that 'the chief reason that she married him was to get away from her parents'.[25] She also noted that 'My mother and my father lived in different worlds. He was dynamic, forceful, and brilliant, but very worldly when compared to her. He had high ideals and a great admiration for 'Abdu'l-Bahá and often said that the standards of his life were based on the words of 'Abdu'l-Baha, but he never became an active Baha'i and later could not accept the Will and Testament'.[26] In 1918, Theron was no longer capable of being in her spiritual shadow and left the family, filing for divorce soon thereafter. The divorce was finalized in 1920.

With Theron's departure, it was a very unhappy Mabel who went out and found work as a saleswoman, but she hardly slowed down her teaching activities. Beginning in 1917, she was deeply involved with the National Conventions. That year, she was on the Credentials Committee, a delegate from Detroit and actively involved in the various consultations.[27]

The next year, she was again a delegate for Detroit and involved in the consultation. At one point, during consultation on a few so-called Tablets from the Master that were being circulated as authentic, Mabel was able to point out that one was someone's dream that had been written down and was being passed off as an authentic Tablet from the Master.[28] The years 1917 and 1918 were a time of Covenant-breaking activity in Chicago. Mason Remey was appointed to chair a committee to look into the activities of a group headed by Luella Kirchner, who had rejected the elected Chicago House of Spirituality and formed their own Local Spiritual Assembly.[29] In a letter to Joseph Hannen in February 1918, Mabel wrote:

> I do hope, dear Brother of mine that unity in protecting the Cause is again holding the servants of the Cause together – and a stronger unity, as usually follows these periodic 'violation' experiences. If Abdul Baha had not foreseen these very occurrences would He have warned us that tests would become so violent in America that strong trees would be uprooted by them? This Chicago affair was certainly one of the tests of which He speaks and comes through the subtlety of the Nakazeen [from Náqidín – pronounced nakazeen – meaning Covenant breakers] poison. Only by absolute unity and obedience to the glorious center can we pass thru this fire of tests.[30]

In January of 1919, Mabel received another Tablet from 'Abdu'l-Bahá. It contained another powerful exhortation with an interesting note to her father at the end. Albert G. Simon had a dramatic change in character later in life: as he grew older he changed his business and then his politics. And at the age of 95, he finally accepted the station of Bahá'u'lláh:[31]

> O thou dear maid-servant of God:
> Thy letter dated Oct. 23. 1918 was received. Thou hadst written that the kingdom of God is being spread abroad and the friends and believers of God are in perfect steadfastness. The diffusion of fragrances is the magnet of confirmation of the Lord of Lords. I have therefore become hopeful that the assistance and confirmation of the Kingdom of Abha shall encompass that city and within a short period of time the signs of assistance shall become manifest. Strive therefore, heart and soul, that ye may instruct ignorant souls, vivify the dead and enkindle the dispirited. For the bounties of the kingdom of Abha are the life of souls, they bestow sight and perception. Wherefore teach ye through morality and deeds for this is more effective than teaching by words. The moral characteristics of the kingdom constitute the magnetic power which draws souls to the Divine kingdom. Strive therefore to bring about amelioration and rightness of morals, for the morals of every soul are totally transformed as he enters into the Divine kingdom. If he has been ignorant he will gain knowledge; self-conceited, he will become self-sacrificing; proud and haughty he will become humble and submissive; ambitious after worldly riches he will strive for donations; bad and harsh in character he turns out meek and mild. These are the signs of entrance in the kingdom of God. I pray God that all the friends may be assisted thereunto and may admonish and advise one another.
> Strive thou, therefore, that the moral characteristics of the kingdom may be disseminated among the friends. Convey on my behalf to all the friends and the maid-servants of God longing greeting. Convey on my behalf the kindness of the kingdom to the respectable Mrs........ and embrace and clasp affectionately in thy arms her young daughter.

> I pray and beseech the Exalted Lord that He may bless that child and may cause praise-worthy results to be manifested among men from her existence.
>
> I pray God that Rowshan and Ruhi may become resplendent and life-giving. Show kindness and affection to them on my behalf.
>
> Convey my message to thy respected father and say unto him: Entrance into the kingdom bestows a new power; it turns an old man young and makes strong the feeble. I trust that Divine Bounties will cause thee to attain this station.[32]

At the 1919 National Convention, Mabel was a delegate from Detroit, the chairman of the third session, on the Committee on Permanent Organization, appointed to the 19-member Teaching Committee and a member of the Nominating and Credentials Committees.[33]

In 1920, both Mabel and Howard wrote to 'Abdu'l-Bahá requesting pilgrimage. She received her answer from Him in March saying that although He wished to see her, He would prefer that she stay and serve on the homefront:

> O thou, the maid servant of God:
>
> Thy letter arrived. Its content was spiritual and conducive of the dictates of conscience. Thou hast asked for permission to come to me. Thy presence (here) is also my wish. But at present if thou couldst remain there thou wouldst be confirmed in service. This service is better and more delightful. Nevertheless thou art free to choose.[34]

With 'Abdu'l-Bahá suggesting that she remain and teach the Faith instead of going on pilgrimage, Mabel chose to stay and teach, beginning two decades of constant travel teaching across half of America and Canada.

On 30 January 1920, Howard applied for a passport, stating that he hoped to depart in March. On a supporting note, he wrote:

On January first I received a cablegram from Abdul Baha Abbas, of Haifa Palestine, reading as follows – and Dated Dec 30th 1919 from Haifa.

Wilhelmite Howard Ives New York Permitted to come. Abbas
   I wish to go to see him on important matters relating to religion and am planning to sail sometime in March, possibly earlier.[35]

'Wilhelmite' was Roy Wilhelm's business telegraph address.

The passport office was obviously a bit worried by Howard's reasoning. A note attached to his application read: 'U-H has no record of Mr. Ives. However, the application appears to me to be somewhat peculiar and I do not quite understand the religious motive. I believe it would be well to find out if the Department of Justice or MID [Military Information Division] has any record of Ives before granting the application. It may be perfectly alright but it won't hurt to be on the safe side'.[36]

In response, another note was appended to Howard's file: 'There have a no of applis [applications] gone thro – like this – I saw one of the letters explaining a certain few would be permitted to have an audience with Abdul Baha – There is a religious sect call "Baha'is" and I know some very prominent people belonging to it.' In the end, Howard was not able to make the pilgrimage he had dreamed of ever since 'Abdu'l-Bahá's departure from America.

Mabel was busy at the 1920 National Convention in April. She co-chaired the first session of the Congress with Dr Frederick D'Evelyn and was a member of a Teaching Committee of 19 who represented the five regions written to by 'Abdu'l-Bahá in the *Tablets of the Divine Plan*. She was also on the Nominating and Auditing Committees. The Nominating Committee was unusual. It was to be a committee of nine.

> . . . appointed to present a list from which to elect a teaching committee . . . This nominating committee . . . would

not be bound in any way as to the number of the teaching committee it shall recommend to the Convention, and also that the nominating committee should include some recommendation as to the best means by which the Convention may handle the other matters mentioned in the book entitled, The Divine Plan, which are matters associated but not necessarily identical with the work of the teaching committee . . .[37]

Howard and Mabel were both on this committee and both were single at this point.

6
Howard and Mabel Get Married

Mabel meets Howard

At the National Convention in 1919, Howard and Mabel began to get acquainted. She wrote:

> Grace [Ober], Harlan [Ober], Howard and I had breakfast together, at the McAlpine Hotel . . . He was a very old and dear friend of theirs, and I knew him as I knew other Bahai teachers. At this breakfast, I was telling the Obers about my wonderful job with the National Industrial Speakers Bureau, and how our speakers were bringing understanding between the management and men in industry. Howard took fire at that and said he wanted to go in for it too. He had a fine position with the Alexander Hamilton Institute, and was making as much as $10,000 a year out of selling their course. I think he had been with them three years. From a business standpoint he shouldn't have left . . . but his naturally idealistic nature got the best of him, and also, no doubt, he was guided by a higher wisdom then any of us at that time imagined, as had he not taken that step, we would not have been thrown together, and our marriage . . . would not have taken place . . .
>
> Well after the historic breakfast at the McAlpine, I long-distanced my headquarters in Cleveland and they were delighted to have Howard come out to see them. They sent him to Chicago, where he encountered some difficulties in selling their Bureau, so they sent him to Detroit to work out of my office which I had established! How strangely Fate (or God) works . . .[1]

Howard and Mabel were strongly attracted to each other and Mabel was torn. They spoke a lot about their spiritual attraction and the love of God, but she knew the Bahá'í laws on marriage and fought that attraction, writing in the same letter that she had felt: 'I don't want to fall in love with him, I couldn't.' Finally, she wrote him a letter saying that they should end their relationship. He never received it and the more they saw of each other the greater that attraction became.

The resolution to their problem came from their respective spouses. Both marriages had broken down and neither of the couples had lived together for years. Then both Mabel's husband T.C. and Howard's wife Elizabeth began demanding divorces. Mabel later wrote in the same letter quoted above about what she did:

> Finally I turned to Baha'u'llah and from the very depths of my being, I made a complete renunciation of everything, saying (and meaning it) that I was willing to stay as I was married to T.C. in a way, with all the misery that meant, to the end of the chapter, if that was His will. That I wanted nothing but His will. That I asked nothing, no personal happiness, nothing but one thing, that He would permit me to serve His Cause . . .
>
> Almost immediately after that T.C. became determined that he should have his freedom, and put such pressure on that there was nothing else I could do.

Mabel was divorced from Theron, but Howard was still legally married to Elizabeth. She, too, wanted a divorce, but because of his understanding of the Bahá'í teachings on the sacredness of marriage, he could not bring himself to agree. Howard wrote to the Master asking for advice and His response was to be patient. Although Howard was patient, Elizabeth still demanded a divorce. Then on 15 June 1920, Howard received a cable from 'Abdu'l-Bahá that read: 'TELL HOWARD IVES REFER HIS CASE HOUSE OF SPIRITUALITY NEW YORK ABBAS'.[2]

With the support of May Maxwell, this they did. Mabel

later wrote: 'At last the fateful night came . . . On first entering we were asked if we would accept and conform to their decision whatever it might be. We agreed.' 'I was asked to remain in another room as the matter did not concern me. . . . I sat alone and prayed, . . . Our fate was being decided in the next room.'³

A few days later, they were notified by the Assembly that after thorough investigation of the laws of Bahá'u'lláh about marriage and divorce, Howard was justified in getting a divorce. Mabel wrote to Doris McKay that May had told them that 'she felt that we, by our act of complete obedience, had established the Administrative Order in America'. It seems that it was the first case in which so personal a matter was trusted to the Local Spiritual Assembly.⁴

This act of complete willingness to obey the Bahá'í administration, even in the face of what could have been a huge disappointment, was a hallmark of both Howard and Mabel's devotion to the Cause and absolute obedience to the Covenant. This obedience became a hallmark of their lives.

On 29 October 1920, Mabel and Howard were married in New York City. He was 53 and she was 43. Mabel described the wonderful event:

> Then in [October] 1920, we were married, Grace and Harlan coming down to the City Clerk's office at the City Hall with us for our civil wedding (which Mountfort, who was our spiritual father and advisor) insisted was necessary, tho we would much have preferred just our Bahai wedding. That evening we had the loveliest Bahai wedding at my apartment, which then became our apartment. The dear Kinneys were there (that is Saffa was), and chanted divinely. Bert Randall, Mountfort and others of the believers most near to us, Grace had managed to get a wedding cake. I remember we all stood up in a circle holding hands, as we repeated the beautiful words.⁵

In a card they sent to friends and signed as Howard and Mabel Rice-Wray Ives, the new couple wrote that they had a 'heavenly occasion'. Jináb-i-Fádil [Mazindarání] sent a letter that was read at the ceremony. He also sent a 'name-stone' blessed by 'Abdu'l-Bahá.[6]

On 19 December, the newlyweds sent their first letter to 'Abdu'l-Bahá, saying:

> Our Beloved Lord:
> These servants, whom Thou hast united for Thy service in the Kingdom, turn their hearts towards that Holy Spot with great love and admiration.
> On Oct. 29th, 1920, in the presence of nine of the friends we were united by the Bahai ceremony, as ordained by His Holiness Baha'O'llah, following a civil ceremony in the afternoon. We enclose a copy of the paper signed by witnesses. Thy saintly ambassador, His Holiness Jenabi Fazel, who has gone thru this country transforming hearts by the Power of Thy Love, wrote a letter which was read at our wedding, bringing Thine own confirming Love and Blessing.
> Since our union how marvelous has been Thy Bounties to us in opening the doors to the inner world! We have been so conscious of Thy Presence, and of the reuniting of the two halves of this one soul, and of its return, after the long Journey, to the Home of the Beloved. We supplicate for Thy Divine Confirmations upon this union that it may be a bounty to the Cause of God and an instrument to Thy Hand.
> Praise be to God this home is being used, thru Thy Bounty, as a center for the diffusing of the Divine Fragrances. New and eager souls are gathering here. We beg that the Holy Spirit may aid these souls.
> A group for the cementing of a divine unity meets weekly for loving prayer and meditation consisting of Juliet Thompson, Mr. and Mrs. Kinney, Mr. and Mrs. Ober and these servants. May these prayers be the means of great service in the Kingdom of Love.
> We are hoping to make the Pilgrimage to Thy Blessed

Marriage 'Certificate' for the marriage of Howard Ives and Mabel Rice-Wray, Oct. 29, 1920

```
9999999
9     9
9     9
9999999
      9
      9
      9
      9
```

YA BAHA EL ABHA

We, the friends of God, and of the Family of the Kingdom, In the PRESENCE of HIS HOLINESS ABDUL BAHA, the CENTER of the COVENANT, having gathered for the purpose of witnessing the firm covenant in marriage between Howard Ives and Mabel Rice-Wray, hereto subscribe our names as partakers in that lofty and holy ceremony:-

"The City of the COVENANT" Signed:
(New York City) Mountfort Mills
October twenty-ninth Johanna M Storch
Nineteen Hundred and twenty. Juanita S. Sohrab
 A.W. Randall
 Isabel F. Chamberlain
 Mahrah Molenar
 Edward B. (Saffa) Kinney
 Harlan Ober
 Grace Ober

Howard and Mabel drew up their own marriage certificate, which they sent to 'Abdu'l-Bahá.[8]

Presence in the early Spring, and beg that Thou wilt open all doors.

> Our heads are at Thy Holy Threshold
> Thy humble and loving children[7]

Howard and Mabel began their married life on 83rd Street in New York. Their Bahá'í community included Harlan and Grace Ober, Edward and Carrie Kinney and Juliet Thompson. The newlyweds taught the Faith from their apartment and tried to settle into a normal life. Howard called Mabel Riswanea, so from that point on, she was always Riswanea and he was Howie.[9]

Harlan and Grace Ober

Harlan and Grace Ober were two of Howard and Mabel's closest friends. Of Howard, Harlan wrote: 'He was the most welcome of visitors. He was collecting contributions for an orphanage in Turkey and from time to time he would come our way. He knew where to find the key and often the first we knew he was in the house would be when we would smell the coffee, followed shortly by the vigorous call to breakfast!!'[10] The Ives and the Obers went into business together and for some time lived in the same house in the 1930s, along with Willard and Doris McKay.

Harlan Ober had become a Bahá'í in 1906 and was privileged to be on a very early and gruelling teaching trip to India at the behest of 'Abdu'l-Bahá. On 17 July 1912, Grace and Harlan were married at the suggestion of 'Abdu'l-Bahá. The Bahá'í wedding took place in His presence. Later that same day they were married again by the laws of New York when Howard Colby Ives performed the legal ceremony.[11]

Harlan served on the Bahá'í Temple Unity Executive Board from 1918 to 1920 and on the National Spiritual Assembly of the United States and Canada from 1938 to 1941. Harlan and Grace made many teaching trips in the United States and Canada. Harlan's great friendship with Louis Gregory, who was posthumously appointed a Hand of the Cause of God, took Harlan into the American South and consequently Harlan was in demand as a speaker at Race Unity Conferences.[12]

Grace, who said that she hoped she would 'die with her boots on', passed away during the National Convention in May 1938. Harlan had just been re-elected to the National Spiritual Assembly and called Grace to speak on her recent travel-teaching trip to Louisville, Kentucky. Finishing her talk, as she passed Harlan, she whispered, 'I want to congratulate you now. I may not have time later.' Grace then sat down in her seat and quietly bowed her head – and her soul passed to the Abhá Kingdom.[13]

Some years later, in 1941 Harlan married Elizabeth Kidder and in 1956 they pioneered to South Africa, where they remained until Harlan's passing in 1962.[14]

Beginning to teach in the Black community

Along with the Obers, Howard and Mabel began working in Harlem with the Black community.[15] They were very conscious of the exhortations by 'Abdu'l-Bahá and later by Shoghi Effendi about the absolute equality between the races in the eyes of God. In his encounters with 'Abdu'l-Bahá, Howard had witnessed 'Abdu'l-Bahá's focus on and joy in seeing the friends serving the cause of racial unity. One of the most well-known episodes is his account in *Portals to Freedom* of 'Abdu'l-Bahá and the boys who came to visit him after seeing Him walking in the streets of New York. In that account, Howard described how 'Abdu'l-Bahá singled out the only Black boy in the group and with a radiant smile, referred to him as a 'Black Rose', before passing out handfuls of chocolates. Looking into the nearly empty box:

> He picked from it a long chocolate nougat; it was very black. He looked at it a moment and then around at the group of boys who were watching Him intently and expectantly. Without a word He walked across the room to where the colored boy was sitting, and, still without speaking, but

with a humorously piercing glance that swept the group, laid the chocolate against the black cheek. His face was radiant as He laid His arm around the shoulder of the boy and that radiance seemed to fill the room. No words were necessary to convey His meaning, and there could be no doubt that all the boys caught it.

You see, He seemed to say, that he is not only a black flower, but also a black sweet. You eat black chocolates and find them good: perhaps you would find this black brother of yours good also if you once taste his sweetness.

Again that awed hush fell upon the room. Again the boys all looked with real wonder at the colored boy as if they had never seen him before, which indeed was true. And as for the boy himself, upon whom all eyes were now fixed, he seemed perfectly unconscious of all but 'Abdu'l-Bahá. Upon Him his eyes were fastened with an adoring, blissful look such as I had never seen upon any face. For the moment he was transformed. The reality of his being had been brought to the surface and the angel he really was revealed.[16]

Howard had probably heard or read about 'Abdu'l-Bahá speaking to groups in New York and Washington DC:

> How conducive to peace, confidence and happiness if races and nations were united in fellowship and accord! The Prophets of God were sent into the world upon this mission of unity and agreement: that these long-separated sheep might flock together. When the sheep separate, they are exposed to danger, but in a flock and under protection of the shepherd they are safe from the attack of all ferocious enemies.[17]

> This is a beautiful assembly. I am very happy that white and black are together. This is the cause of my happiness, for you all are the servants of one God and, therefore, brothers, sisters, mothers and fathers. In the sight of God there is no distinction between whites and blacks; all are as one.

Anyone whose heart is pure is dear to God – whether white or black, red or yellow.[18]

Shoghi Effendi reemphasized this concept in a letter to the American believers in April 1927:

> As this problem, in the inevitable course of events, grows in acuteness and complexity, and as the number of the faithful from both races multiplies, it will become increasingly evident that the future growth and prestige of the Cause are bound to be influenced to a very considerable degree by the manner in which the adherents of the Bahá'í Faith carry out, first among themselves and in their relations with their fellow-men, those high standards of inter-racial amity so widely proclaimed and so fearlessly exemplified to the American people by our Master 'Abdu'l-Bahá.[19]

For the rest of their lives, Howard and Mabel did their best to share the Faith with both Black and White and bring about the unity of the races.

7
A New Plan of Action and the Beginnings of a Life of Sacrifice 1920–1925

Mabel again asked 'Abdu'l-Bahá for permission to make a pilgrimage to Haifa and on 13 February 1921 applied for a passport, noting that she planned to leave in March and visit England, Switzerland, Italy, France and Egypt en route to Palestine. Her reason for going was to 'visit friends'.[1] The Master's response, if there was one, is not known.

The Ives worked at both teaching the Faith and earning a living. This lasted less than a year. After a failed business venture, Howard and Mabel made a monumental decision:

> Our plan had been to earn a lot of money rapidly . . . enough to make us independent so that we could give the rest of our life to spreading the Cause. This had proved a chimera, and our dream of travelling and teaching was no nearer. Then one day we realized that we might go on the rest of our life trying to earn enough so that we might <u>some day</u> go out in the teaching field; and never do anything but just simply work and dream of a future, so we decided that because it was utterly impossible and couldn't be done, as we had no money, that we would go out and teach.[2]

So, with the help of God, they determined to do the impossible. On 29 September 1921, Howard and Mabel sent what would be their last letter to 'Abdu'l-Bahá:

> These, Thy worshipping and adoring servants, longing for complete effacement and dispersion before Thy Holy

threshold, send this short supplication unto Thee, entreating Thy acceptance of our humble service and Thy confirmation in the path of heralding Thy Kingdom, upon which we are starting out.

With Thy help these servants are endeavoring to put everything behind them, and renounce everything except servitude: and are intending to spend the remainder of their lives, going from city to city and country to country, according to Thy wish and guidance, in the hope of attracting souls to the Kingdom.

These servants are eager and longing to sacrifice all their conditions for Thy Condition, and to serve uninterruptedly the Threshold of Oneness. And they beg that Thou wilt test them to the point of absolute purification.

There are no earthly means, and certain souls, as Thou knowest, are entirely dependent upon us. Yet, depending upon Thee, we are going forth endeavoring to earn sufficient for all as we go.

Helpless are we without Thine assistance. We beseech Thee to pour forth the Power of the Covenant upon us that these weak mosquitos may be transformed into soaring falcons. Thou knowest our hearts and our entire longing to serve Thee and to be a cause of Unity among the friends of God. We are Thy slaves, Thy thralls: command us, O Abdul Baha . . .

We supplicate Thy Divine approval and confirmation. Without that we are weak and incapable. With that these insects will become soaring eagles, and these timid sheep transformed into raging lions and conquering hosts.

Our hearts are longing to make the Blessed Pilgrimage to the Holy Threshold. O open Thou the way that we may avail ourselves of Thy gracious permission when the time that is in accordance with Thy will arrives.[3]

Not many people have the courage to ask to be tested 'to the point of absolute purification', but over the next 20 years, their wish was fulfilled. They ended their letter with a joint appeal for pilgrimage: 'Our hearts are longing to make the Blessed Pilgrimage to the Holy Threshold. O open Thou the way that we may avail ourselves of Thy gracious permission when the time that is in accordance with Thy will arrives.' Unfortunately, 'Abdu'l-Bahá ascended two months later and they never received a response.

With this declaration, Howard and Mabel decided to give up a life of stability and a fixed address for an itinerant life teaching the Faith. Mabel wrote: 'When Howard and I decided to leave New York City and go out and teach the Cause of God in 1921 or 1922, we either gave or sold everything we had but what would go in two suitcases and two trunks, and after we bought our railroad tickets to Pittsburgh we had $7.00.'[4] So it began. They advertised for jobs as salesmen who wished to travel and received 21 replies. Off they went to Pittsburgh.

Edris described their new lifestyle:

> From then on [they] never stopped. At first, they earned their living making show-cards for store windows. They had a little machine that printed these show-cards in different colors and styles. Later they sold an adult education course which included the books and the arrangement for classes and the group leader. I often think of the difficulties which beset these two precious souls, both of them past middle life; Howard who had been trained to be a minister and who knew nothing about business. Mabel who had been brought up in the South to be a lady and was no better equipped. They were like two babes in the woods when it came to dealing with the world of business. Anyone who has been in selling work knows the extreme difficulties of cold canvassing and this is what they did. They worked hard calling on prospective customers all day and then spent their evenings holding lectures, classes and fireside groups. Their housework and all that goes with it was sandwiched in between. Mother once wrote me from somewhere in New York State that they were such interesting experiences and hoped that God would permit them to learn the lessons

that they were supposed to learn from these experiences. One of these 'interesting' experiences was an incident where one afternoon they found themselves down to their last twenty-five cents and in a new city. If they didn't make a sale that afternoon, they would neither eat nor sleep that night.[5]

Years later, when asked what it was like to be 'homeless' and itinerant, Howard's response was:

> You ask me how we can accustom ourselves to homelessness. Our own vine and fig tree is a natural desire to the children of men; there is nothing reprehensible in this desire. Bahá'u'lláh has provided for this in His Law, dignifying the home and hospitality as a means of serving God. Nevertheless there are a few of us to whom He whispers in the ear 'Make My Home thy Mansion, boundless and holy.' 'Riswanea' [Mabel] and I often have a yearning for a permanent place to bestow ourselves and our few goods. Just as sure as this longing finds a place in our hearts we are moved again . . . 'Abdu'l-Bahá's words 'Homeless and without rest' ring in my ears, when He is describing the attributes of the Apostles of Bahá'u'lláh. Rest assured that God does not take away an earthly home without providing a heavenly one right here on earth if we accept His Will with radiant acquiescence . . . Rejoice, my beloved daughter, in the little home which Baha'u'llah has provided for you. If you are worthy He will move you into other homes and other hearts, and you will then rejoice again: for the bounty of a wider horizon of service has been given you; a greater freedom of spirit has been vouchsafed you and a few more chains of this world have been knocked from your limbs.[6]

Early in the new year of 1922, with the passing of 'Abdu'l-Bahá the previous November, Howard was anxious to have the latest news from Haifa and requested a copy of the Master's *Will and Testament* from the National Spiritual Assembly to share with the worried Bahá'ís. Alfred Lunt responded on behalf of the Assembly: 'I do not believe there is any chance that the will and testament of His Holiness, Abdul Baha, will reach this country for some time yet. I understand that Shoghi returned to Haifa in order to translate this and certain other important documents and Tablets which were revealed just prior to the Ascension.' He went on to share what news he had of what was happening in Haifa:

> The Master's body was placed in the tomb of the Bab on Mt. Carmel and a very large gathering of people from all over the country attended, including the Governor-General of Jerusalem and other officials. The casket was borne up the mountain on the shoulders of the believers. It is said that this was a most impressive spectacle. Nine addresses were made which will be translated later. It appears that He had arranged all matters and unquestionably knew exactly the time of His going, and had said something to the family the week before which they afterwards understood to mean just this.[7]

This was a time of great uncertainty for the Bahá'ís, and Howard recognized the challenges ahead. It wasn't until March that the Bahá'ís in America began to receive copies of the newly-appointed Guardian's first letters and 'Abdu'l-Bahá's *Will and Testament*. Every Local Spiritual Assembly in the country was sent a copy of the Will. Mabel asked the National Assembly for their own copy so that they could deepen on it. The response was that the Assembly would consult on the matter and in a letter, Alfred Lunt noted: 'I hope very much I will be enabled to send you a copy as I know you will treasure it and not allow it to go out of your possession.'[8]

Before leaving New York, the call of the Faith kept them busy. On 1 January 1922, Howard wrote to Dr Frederick D'Evelyn, saying that he had been asked to visit the new Local Spiritual Assembly in Pittsburgh on the 7th while Mabel would be meeting with 'a group of attracted and devoted souls' in either

Syracuse or Buffalo, New York, the same night. These teaching trips were quite uplifting: 'It is very wonderful to have the great experiences of meeting the flaming and attracted hearts in each city. We are constantly in awe at the confirmations of the Center of the Covenant and the supreme fulfillment of His great Promises. Truly it is the Day of God and His confirmations descend unceasingly upon those who do even the smallest service.'[9]

Howard and Mabel wrote their first letter to Shoghi Effendi during the summer of 1923. Their response came from 'Azízu'lláh Bahádur, whom the Guardian had left in charge of correspondence while he was away for the summer. The explanation of the Guardian's absence was interesting: 'Shoghi Effendi has gone to some summer resort owing to our humble request in order to protect his precious health from the heat and malaria which are unbearable here in the summer.' He went on to write that 'The members of the Holy Family have rejoiced much over your good news. They pray for your happiness and success, too. You say that Jináb-i-Fádil has advised you to write to our dear Shoghi Effendi. Jináb-i-Fádil is right in doing so for he knows that your letters bring good and refreshing news and consequently the dear heart of the Heart of the Cause of God, or the beloved Guardian will be delighted thereby.'[10]

Material reality and spiritual challenges

Howard and Mabel set off on their new path. First they went to Pittsburgh for six weeks, where they held 36 Bahá'í meetings in addition to pursuing their sales business.[11] Then they moved their work to Youngstown, Ohio, where, during their ten-day stay there, they held several meetings to teach the Faith, one of which had 50 interested people attend. Then it was on to Buffalo, New York, for 19 days. Upon their arrival, Mabel was tired and took a nap, but Howard went out for a two-hour walk and returned with four speaking engagements. They ended up giving 17 talks in their 19 days. From Buffalo, the couple went to Syracuse and Rochester, New York, followed by Columbus and Birmingham, Ohio.[12] This became the pattern for the rest of their lives, filling their time in each city or town with talks and interviews, continually seeking every opportunity to spread and strengthen the Faith they loved.

The material challenges began very quickly. Their first selling job was a bust and they lost everything they put into it. Then they began selling an illustrated encyclopedia and their sacrificial efforts suddenly bore fruit. One day they stopped in a small farming village and stayed in a tiny hotel. Over the following weekend, the Ives were warmly welcomed by some and angrily rejected by others:

> In Howard's calls the next day he called upon a delightful woman who had lately retired to her farm after years of active life in a large city. To meet a man of Howard's caliber was a blessed experience, and she insisted that he must speak at the church the next day (Sunday), so, as she was evidently the moving spirit in the community, she arranged it, and he gave a challenging talk, which so inspired the people that they asked him to speak again in the evening. That night the whole countryside turned out and the church was full. We divided the evening, and after our talks were over and Howard had invited questions, one man arose, bristling fairly, and let out a tirade directed at the 'this man and his companion', saying that we were leading the people to the devil. And that they shouldn't listen to us. That we were Muhamedans, etc. He went on and on. Howard listened with perfect calm and courtesy, and then finally broke in and said pleasantly that perhaps someone else would like to express themselves, and so the man who proved to be an evangelist, ceased talking, with the parting fling, that as for him, he stood firm in the love of Christ.
>
> Then when Howard closed the meeting, this evangelist and his party, two women and another man, gathered all of the audience he could get around him and laid down the law to them in emphatic language, finally leaving fairly bristling with wrath. In the meantime about half of the

In Van Cortland Park, New York, 1918. Among those present are Hooper Harris, Howard Colby Ives, Hooper Harris, Carrie (Vaffa) Kinney, Mountfort Mills and Ahmad Sohrab

Van Cortland Park, New York, 1918. Left to right: Della Lincoln, unknown, Valeria Kelsey, Robert Kelsey, Howard Colby Ives and Curtis Kelsey

Howard with a group of friends, 1918

audience had gathered around us, and we were backed up against the wall. They however were most friendly, and asking eager questions. Before we left, one of the leading men of the church, who had been conferring, I had noticed, with several other men, came over to me and said; 'We have been talking this matter over, and we have come to the conclusion as to who was really "firm in the love of Christ"'. Which was a lovely tribute to the heavenly and wise attitude which Howard had taken toward this disturber . . .[13]

In a letter written in March from Columbus, Howard told Agnes Parsons, "We are having some beautiful experiences here. Many friends and attracted souls are arising. The experience is not so pronounced as it was in Rochester, where a real, alive Assembly is functioning. Praise be to God!"[14] The Ives immediately realized that one of the greatest problems in Columbus was race unity. Howard proposed a race unity conference to be held after the National Convention, writing to the National Spiritual Assembly:

> The race question here is an absorbing one. There is an opportunity for large service and thru that service to establish the Cause in Columbus for permanent work on a large scale. There are about 40,000 colored people here and the need for active work towards spiritual unity is very great. I have talked with the President of the University and the Chairman of the Race Relation Committee of the Urban League and have aroused interest.
>
> If such a congress could be arranged it would lead to great results, I think.
>
> If Mrs. Parson[s] could come here, or assist with her experience thru correspondence, and Jenabi Fazel come and Harry Randall and some others of the wonderful friends and also some representation leading white and colored people (of course Louis Gregory), our Lord would bless the endeavor thru the gift of the Holy Spirit most surely . . .
>
> I have given the message to the Secy of the League, Mr.

Allen (colored) and to his brother who is a pastor of a Meth. Church here. The latter received it most enthusiastically and will, God willing, become confirmed . . .'[15]

Unfortunately, the National Assembly, though 'sympathetic' with the idea, replied that they 'felt that the Tablets and instructions which Abdul Baha had given in which he mentioned several American cities where it would be well to hold such Congresses should be looked into and if possible such cities taken care of first.'[16]

Howard, though living at that time in Columbus, was also involved with the Bahá'í community in Rochester, New York. Shortly before Riḍván in 1923, Alfred Lunt, the Secretary of the National Spiritual Assembly, asked Howard to help Rochester form their Local Spiritual Assembly. Alfred wrote: 'I suggest you write them to hold their election the first day of Rizwan which will bring them in accordance with an important letter and cable received from Shoghi Effendi within the last few days. All the Assemblies are to be asked to hold new elections on that day.'[17]

Mabel and Howard made a travel teaching trip to Louisville, Kentucky, in the spring of 1924 and she gave two talks that were broadcast over radio station WHAS. The manager was quite excited about the reaction to them:

> At any time you expect to be in cities where there are large radiocasting plants, I am sure that the managers of those stations will be grateful to me for introducing you to them. Your two talks from WHAS made a very distinct impression, if we are to judge from the nine or ten hundred letters we received about it, and let me take this opportunity of cordially inviting you and Mr. Ives to speak for us at any time in the future when you happen to be in Louisville . . . Assuring you of our appreciation and regards and once more congratulating you upon the most fortunate reaction your talks created among radio listeners . . .[18]

The first years of their high-minded aspiration quickly became one of constant struggles in both the material and spiritual worlds. In the material world, their attempts to earn a living as salesmen became a battle between high expectations based on the spiritual nature of their endeavour and the dark abysses of material reality. Things were not going very well in the material world and these tests led to spiritual tests.

As he travelled, Howard was on the lookout for possible business opportunities and also constantly looking for ways to reduce expenses. He wrote to Mabel that 'Monday night while I was praying I had an inspiration which since then I have been putting into practice. I am trying to save $5.00 a week extra by cutting off little things that I can do without by sacrificing.'[19] The next day, in a letter from Eire, Pennsylvania, he wrote, 'Here I am at the old stand, but I am not staying at the Lawrence [Hotel] – but right across the street at the Y.M.C.A. to the tune of $1.25 per night. I fear I won't be able to see Muriel this week after all as business has been so poor I can't afford the trip: for I surely don't want to go down there with no money in my clothes, and that is about the condition I am in.' Trying to drum up some business, Howard noted that 'I have called on and phoned to several old prospects but so far have had no success. This evening I will call in what looks like a good prospect . . . All these experiences are good for your Howie. He needs a lot of pruning down.'[20]

Howard was truly grateful for Mabel's love and support. A lot of time was spent travelling separately and he eagerly watched for her letters. They wrote to one another nearly every day whenever they were teaching in different places, which was often. These intimate letters give us a glimpse of their struggles and triumphs, along with the enduring deep love for Bahá'u'lláh and for each other which permeates each letter. He wrote to her on 7 August 1924 from Fredonia, New York, expressing his amazement and gratitude for her deep spiritual insights and also to his complete devotion to her:

> Mabel – Beloved of all worlds! Thy blessed and wonderful letter came to this servant this morning. I do not need to

tell you what it meant to me. Praise be to God for this tremendous vision of Reality that has opened before thee. This is what for many years my heart has known: this is what has made me seem so 'impractical' and 'visionary.' When Abdul Baha looked into my eyes and heart then, for the first time, I began to be able to balance the real with the imaginings of my untutored soul. Now, praise be to God, thy Clear and practical and inspired envisaging of all the aspects of man's problem in this world and his education through severe tests for the preparation for the 'world of the Placeless' will enable <u>us both</u> to go forward, God willing, on the Supreme Path and reach this Divine Grail soon – ah soon! God grant it may be so!

Nothingness is needed that we may kindle the fire of existence and become acceptable in the Path of Love. Love will not accept a soul alive to material things.[21]

Mabel, too, gained much support from her husband and was just as eager for his letters as he was for hers. In her reply, she wrote:

My real Mate and Beloved of all the Worlds,
I am looking forward with eagerness to renewal of our life together alone and the spiritual flights which I am sure we shall take. This summer has been invaluable to me. Such an expansion of spiritual consciousness! And my Howie has grown so. With only half the chance!
I do so long for one week alone somewhere in the open – just you and I – before the summer passes – perhaps in Sept. Where we can meditate continuously and pray and you study – or prepare. I feel that we are starting out on a second journey in the Cause – of greater service bearing eternal results.[22]

During this time, Howard and Mabel were in a business arrangement with Harlan and Grace Ober. Apparently, the business was having difficulties and this was creating problems between the two couples. A part of one of Howard's letters was about unity and materialistic pursuits:

> All that you say and intimate, regarding the spiritual nature of our unity, (we four), this servant also utters from his heart. Indeed we have proven these last few weeks how pitifully insignificant that so-called unity became when we attempted to prostitute it to 'business' ends. That is not what God has called us together for. Neither our unity, Riswanea dear, nor Harlan and Grace's unity, nor the larger unity of us all has been given to us for this world's uses and ends. Our Lord has brought us together in the realms of the spirit in order that we may function as one soul in 4 bodies and so prove how the Kingdom of God is to be established in the foundation of loving and severed hearts; hearts humbled at the Threshold of Oneness; hearts longing to be consumed in the fire of His Love; hearts absolutely ready at any moment to place themselves beneath the feet of the beloved of God.
>
> This is not to be accomplished thru worldly prosperity. This is not to be done by allowing our minds to revolve around material problems. This is only to be accomplished thru complete self-dedication in the Cause of God and self-sacrificing love for one another.[23]

Howard's head was always in the spiritual worlds and having to live in a material one was a problem that afflicted him his whole life. He had high spiritual aspirations, but struggled with the worldly troubles of earning enough to live on materially.

A few days after the above letter, Howard was in Geneva, New York, from where he wrote to Mabel, outlining a possible course created by Dr Albert Heist they could sell. He wrote that his

> plan for educating the adolescent youth [is] a very wonderful and practical one and would undoubtedly be very easy to sell. I have looked up Dr. Heist's record at the banks

and the Chamber of Com. and his friends and enemies and find nothing against him and much for him. I am going to spend the evening with him and it is now 6:30 p.m. and I have not yet had my dinner . . . He and his wife are much interested in the Message and our talk, I hope, will revolve around Divine and Eternal things – even when we talk education and business. One thing I am resolved on. If any business arrangements are entered upon it will be on the basis of my (or our) control absolutely of all business and financial and educational policies. His part will be to furnish the mass of data and his knowledge and experience of character and vocational training of adolescent youth for which we will be paid on a royalty basis -- $3.00 or $5.00 (for instance) in every course sold. He thinks that $30. per course would be about right. This would include a series of booklets, about 20 of 'em, some group lectures before parents and children and teachers and individualized training by a local 'Counselor'.[24]

Dr Heist became a dedicated Bahá'í, serving on the National Teaching Committee and speaking at race unity conferences.

Mabel and Howard constantly supported and encouraged each other. On 9 September, Mabel wrote to Howard:

Well, darling, I have just been praying and sending you strong thoughts for success. How many wonderful things we are learning these days. How beautiful to know that everything we have belongs to the Beloved. It is His anyway, as Abdul Baha said, since we count it as His, not ours that all the boundless heavens of His wealth is ours to draw upon as we will. That He is guiding us at every step and bringing things to our attention at the moment where we should know them and that He is supplying all our needs, and that we are resting upon Him and knowing that He is caring for all our necessities. How lovely just to rest and trust in Him and go forth to do our work with our best and keenest, and all the time knowing that He is taking care of the results,

A NEW PLAN OF ACTION

and that in His perfect and infinitely wise way. That our faith makes all things possible.[25]

On the same day, an excited Howard wrote to Mabel about a 'most interesting experience!' He had spent an hour with his 'friend', Congressman Reed, about a proposal. The Congressman said that 'he would not hesitate to back me financially if he had the money! and explained at some length why he could not'. He did call up a Dr Rieger and told him that Howard was coming to 'see him with a most interesting proposition'. Howard then spent until 11 pm with Rieger, who 'was also completely sold on the plan and is going with me to lay it all before Maj. Haquelenburg on Sunday'. Howard wrote Mabel that he felt

> very strongly guided to think this matter over through the wonderful friends that our Lord has raised up for this servant here. What the outcome may be I cannot know, of course. But I feel quite confident that enough actual cash will be subscribed here to make a start in Rochester very soon. Perhaps it is a real advantage, and a plan of the 'Master Schemer,' that Maj H. could not see me this week, and Mr. Nelson was not in Jamestown, for that forced me to bring the matter up with others so I will go to those men later with fine moral backing.
>
> Thy Howie is passing thru real furnace fires these days. I pray that he may be absolutely purified by this conflagration and all of self be burned away. It is a very serious financial situation that confronts me. I have made four full presentations this morning – (it is near lunch time.) All were favorable, but none actually closed, tho two of them probably will be. But you know how these 'probablies' turn out. I am so sure of my guidance, however, and see in this situation simply the 'spur' that forces me higher, that my spirit remains calm and my assurance unshaken.
>
> Praise be to God for my Mabel who understands and whose prayers and faith are such a wonderful anchor to the heart.

> 5 P.M. Another very active day. This aft. I just got my dander up and started in making cold calls and pushing the A service. I got one A right away but only $5.00 down and wrote checks for bal. monthly $5.00. But it was a start and I kept at it and dug up two more fine prospects . . .[26]

Mabel responded that

> I too know, dear, that the door must open and that thru faith and intelligent effort <u>will</u> open it [sic]. It seems as tho the Lord is showing us that we must use our power and faith and abilities to make a real go of it financially in order that we may <u>serve</u> in a bigger way. And it's brains not brawn that will do the trick. Of course, you will get your $5 . . . if not from one man from another and remember all the time that the treasures of the Lord are inexhaustible and that we have abundance of means – plenty of means – right <u>now</u>. It is ours. We are really very wealthy. Of course we are. Know it. I think it all day long. Let your reaction to every experience thru the day be that of one with abundance back of him.[27]

On 2 February 1925, Howard wrote to Mabel from the Hotel Martin in Utica, New York, about these high hopes and the spiritual nature of their efforts:

> I decided to go to a hotel for a few days. It sounds much better from a business standpoint and it is much more convenient. I have a good room without bath in the 2nd best hotel for $1.75 per diem . . .
> My train was 1½ hours late getting into Utica. Such a lot of snow I never saw since the great Blizzard of 1888 – which <u>you</u> don't remember – you were too young and besides you didn't live where it was, and they say another storm is on the way.
> . . . I kept on the job until 6:15, when I finished talking with the Nat'l Executive Secy. of the Zonta Society. She is to send me a complete list of the Utica members . . . I also

got a list of Rotarians and a promise of a list of Kiwanians tomorrow . . .

Coming down on the train I read much of the time from the Baha'i Scrip. and got great inspiration and happiness from this communion. The inspiration took a business turn. It came to me clearly that we can get anything we go after if we go after it in the right spirit and by the right method. I'll pass along to you, my sweet mate, what I dug up. In the first place, we must be more methodical and steady in our efforts.

We have been too apt to rush ourselves to death for a week or two or a month or two, then do little or nothing for a while.

2nd: we must keep always in a calm and tranquil state. We must <u>know</u> at all times that our Helper and Refuge is the Omnipotent Lord. If we really are conscious of that we will never be anxious or hurried or flurried. And we will always carry with us an air of conquering success which in itself will <u>bring</u> success.

3rd: we should study our proposition more and be at all times overflowing with faith in and desire to <u>serve</u> people with it . . .[28]

Their letters are full of notes and comments on their finances. In one letter, Howard wrote, 'I am living on very little so far as my eats go, but car fare etc. counts up something fierce. 7 ½ cents car fare and . . . 3 cents for "exchange" rides.'[29] In another letter, he wrote that he had breakfast of 'fruit or cereal, toast and coffee with cream – 35 cents. Luncheon at the Automat or some such place, or fruit and milk and [undecipherable] or something like that, and dinner at the Club – oysters, soup, roast, salad, vegetables, coffee and dessert for $1.00 – I can't do it any cheaper anywhere and this way I live decently.'[30]

In one letter, he counted up their weekly expenses:

I have to figure in at least $25 a week exp. That is small if business is decent. So I simply have got to do good business.

R[iswanea] meets			H[oward] meets	
Maxwell payments and upkeep	16		Bus. Exp.	25
Saving	10		Food and inc for self	12
Food and inc	12		Rent and upkeep	28
Clothing and anything else	<u>12</u>		Bath	<u>25</u>
	50			85

Anything more that is earned goes for debts and savings etc. We each pay our own Hakouk.[31]

Mabel began fasting in the hope that would help their selling efforts. Howard wrote: 'So my blessed one is fasting! Good work! I am sure it will help. . .' Mabel did make a big sale, but her fasting worried Howard: 'I didn't speak of your fasting and your great victory in going out Monday and landing the sale under such difficult circumstances. I'm proud but anxious. Please don't force yourself that way. You might do yourself great harm. It isn't necessary dear and think what a calamity it would be to have you ill.' But having told her of his anxieties, Howard waxes positive, writing: 'Isn't our life a wonderful thing! I go all day in an atmosphere of peace and love and happiness. You are with me constantly. All that I think and do involves your companionship. All the worlds await us dear. But these next few years are years of great responsibility. Untold and unimagined results hang on what we do and sacrifice in these remaining years here. Praise be to God!'[32]

Howard and Mabel were living on a financial knife-edge and small pleasures were not taken for granted. Howard noted in one letter that he had his 'hair cut – bought a new hat, and will wear my new shoes! Grand and wonderful. Just had to get the hat, dear. Am having the other one cleaned and so will have two good hats.'[33]

Difficult as things were financially, both Howard and Mabel were constantly uplifted by the recognition that they had dedicated their lives to the Cause of Bahá'u'lláh. Being broke and in debt only bothered them to a point. While on the train from Albany to Utica, NY, on 5 February, Howard wrote to Mabel that

> I am thoroughly 'sold' on the idea that our Lord expects us to get out of debt quickly and become independent of all save Him just as soon as hard work and sincere faith in Him will get us there. Now your part in this is to do what you can do calmly and easily. You will never accomplish really great things if you work nervously and push yourself beyond the normal. Please don't overdo and don't feel strained.[34]

'Abdu'l-Bahá's exhortation to do 'really great things' was constantly in Howard's mind.

A few days later, he wrote: 'Another day without any business! . . . felt sure this week would be a record breaker with the start I had. Well – you never can tell!' Though disappointed, he still managed to look on the spiritual side of things: 'How wonderful it would be to be really free from all personal attachment and perfectly content with spiritual unity in the real world! We can at least recognize that this is the Real World and long for that content and seek true unison in the heart of our Lord – the Center of the Covenant of God.'[35] The next day he was disappointed again: 'Another day gone without any enrolments! – now what do you know about that?', but undaunted, he continued, writing 'Praise be to God! I'm still going strong and happy as a clam at high tide.'[36]

Howard's driving was also a problem. He loved to memorize prayers, so he would paste his favourites on the dashboard of the car. In one of her talks Muriel described the result: 'Father, even without the distracting prayers on his dashboard, was not a good driver – there were too many interesting things to think about.'[37] She described an example of her father's driving:

> To drive with my Father, as my stepbrother, Colston Rice-Wray, said, was, 'You know, anyone who didn't believe in

God would have to believe in God after driving with Unk [Uncle] because nobody else could protect him.' And this is true. I went to visit Father . . . He met me and it was in the evening – the train got in about 8 o'clock – and I had my daughter Barbara with me. Barbara was then about 2. So Barbara and I climbed into this car with Father. It was not a reliable car to begin with, and we started off. It was dark and it was snowing, a real blizzard, winds, snow blowing everywhere. We were going down a long hill and it had little trolley car tracks and the trolley car tracks were off center, so that on the right, where we were going, there was only room for one car between the trolley car and the curb . . . So we started down this long hill and very casually, Father said that 'You know, I have no brakes.' I sort of caught my breath and when we were about half way down the hill, another car was coming up . . . And here was the trolley car tracks with a [trolley] car on it. There was us with this other car coming up and no brakes . . . So, Father got about 25 feet from the oncoming car and a filling station showed up and Father turned into the filling station and sailed passed the pumps out the other side. I said, 'Father, did you know that filling station was there?' He said, 'Oh no, but something always is.'[38]

8

Spiritual Struggles and Tests

All during these early years, as material tests pummelled them, both individually and together, spiritual ones both added to their burdens but also gave them the strength to forge ahead. They recognized the tests for what they were and took great encouragement from the belief that God was challenging their resolve, giving them the opportunity to reach higher levels of spiritual detachment. Howard's letters are filled with his thoughts on their tests:

> Darling all of these things are just <u>Tests</u>. Nothing is important except 'supplication, communion, prayer and obedience.' That is to say everything we do must be done in this atmosphere of perfect evanescence and submission. That means that we do not overwork, do not over strain, etc.[1]

> Darling, I want you to know one thing, and know it with all your heart, that the present situation is <u>not</u> thru any fault or failing or lack of effort on your part, or because there is anything wrong with you. This is a test in the path of God, and if it had not come in one way it would in another.[2]

> I am depending on you not to get downcast either my beloved one. It is all right. These are necessary experiences to train us and test us and make us worthy of that which He hath ordained unto us. There is only one thing I really desire with all my heart and soul, that I fail not in the task laid upon me – the task of learning the obedience and humility and courage and radiance and faithfulness and steadfastness

– the development of these spiritual organs in the womb of this world which shall make me able and worthy to take up the <u>real life</u> with my eternal mate, my Mabel, in the world of Reality. What has the earning of a few dollars to compare with that tremendous attainment? The dollars are necessary and enough will come to us, but the great achievement is to be found in the world of the spirit. <u>Together</u> we shall strive and attain and someday we shall <u>laugh</u> at these days of confusion and effort and realize how supremely valuable they were.³

It is terribly hard to be separated from you so long. If I should listen to my longings for a <u>moment</u> I would take the first train for Rochester. But there is a great wisdom in all this. We are both gaining victories. We are both serving the Cause. We are both learning trustfulness and self-denial. And success here in Phila. means ultimate freedom from the financial stress and anxiety. So let us put out of our minds our little petty yearnings. Let us once and for all set our minds and hearts determinedly on the goal to be attained and get there solidly, steadily and <u>permanently</u>. Soon this will all be a dream.⁴

Mabel took great comfort from his thoughts and responded with her own. 'My darling,' she wrote, 'I hope that we can and will live on a high plane together, indeed we must, that is our destiny. Our lives are dedicated to the service of God and we must ever be in an attitude of attention, and service, ever be open to the guidance of the Spirit, ever be ready and at all times know that all our affairs are in His Hands'.⁵ And again: 'Perhaps it will make you happy to know that your sufferings of the last few days were accepted as a sacrifice in the Path of God – and that thru them your worthless Mabel has come nearer to Reality, perhaps than ever before.'⁶

Mabel took great solace in the words of Shoghi Effendi and meditation on his writings. One day, she wrote:

This morning in meditation I realized that one of the outstanding things about Shoghi Effendi was that at every instance he obeys the command of God – that is, the laws and commands of Bahá'u'lláh and that in this is the secret to attainment. The same unfolds like a flower and the spiritual life takes care of itself automatically if we concentrated upon obeying this command.

For instance, he will not utter one word of criticism of or against anyone nor will he permit a word to be uttered in his presence. Therefore naturally and automatically, he sees the good found in each person and enlarges upon it and brings out the best in each.

This is why the Commands of the Manifestation are the healing for the individual and social ills . . .

O I want to talk to you much about all of this. But pray about it and it will all come clear to you. I feel that much of uncertainty of where to turn in prayer is gone now, that some way I have found God, the point of control with God in Shoghi Effendi. I know now where to turn in prayer . . . It is like the true point of control in the field of the crystal, on the crystal radio set. The air is full of music. You do not hear it until you get the needle on the exact point of contact on the crystal. Then the music floods the room. So tho the universe is full of the Holy Spirit, you do not control its power. It arose thru the past Manifestations.[7]

There was considerable confusion about the stations of the Báb, Bahá'u'lláh, 'Abdu'l-Bahá and Shoghi Effendi within the Bahá'í community during this time. Mabel displayed this confusion in the same letter: 'It is significant that Abdul Baha said that the Manifestations ended in [Bahá'u'lláh]. That the Báb and [Bahá'u'lláh] were Manifestations, but that he was only the servant of God. Well, Shoghi Effendi says that the Báb, [Bahá'u'lláh] and ['Abdu'l-Bahá] were Manifestations and that he is only the Guardian. What will the next one say.'[8]

Some of Howard's and Mabel's greatest tests came from other Bahá'ís. In one of his daily letters to Mabel, Howard describes the friction and disunity in a community he was visiting. Personalities of believers who were sincere and devoted, but whose styles rubbed each other the wrong way, had interfered with the ability of the community to progress. At the end of the note he laments, 'How can the Cause of God grow when there is no unity? God forgive us all. How merciful and loving and patient He is!'[9] And the following day he wrote to her: '. . . the Cause has been taught here for 25 yrs. And so little unity and love and truth established. What can be the matter with us all!'[10]

Defence against tests

Howard and Mabel recognized the spiritual and material problems as tests given them by God to purify their souls. Prayer and meditation were their primary defences against all the financial and spiritual woes and worries. Both the Ives relied heavily on these spiritual faculties, but in different ways. In his letters to 'Abdu'l-Bahá and Shoghi Effendi, the spiritually-minded Howard wanted to be tested to purification. He wrote to 'Abdu'l-Bahá:

> May my life be a sacrifice to Thee and to Thy beloved ones! May I sacrifice my spirit and all my possessions for the life of the world. May I become severed from self, the world and all else save God and drop my head on the dust in the path of the Friend.[11]

> I have been going through many and severe tests and I thank God for them. I pray for more pain and sorrow and suffering in order that these flames may purify me from all of Self. I truly 'long for suffering as a rebel craves forgiveness and a sinner longs for mercy.' I pray, O my Lord, that I may be so blessed as to be ordained to the station of sacrifice. May I give up all in Thy way and pour out my soul freely.[12]

> These servants are eager and longing to sacrifice all their conditions for Thy Condition, and to serve uninterruptedly

the Threshold of Oneness. And they beg that Thou wilt test them to the point of absolute purification.[13]

And to Shoghi Effendi:

With my head at the Holy Threshold this servant humbly supplicates that his whole being may be a sacrifice to the Kingdom of Abhá upon this earth, and that he may be so blessed as to be acceptable in the army of the Lord of Hosts of which thou art the Leader and Commander.[14]

Mabel, the more practical of the two, begged Shoghi Effendi over the years for guidance on how to become a better teacher of the Faith:

I desire nothing except to spend every remaining hour of my life in your service. I want to make a fresh and complete dedication of my life to the Faith, and I supplicate your prayers that the dross of my being may be removed and only that which may be serviceable to my Lord remain, that the Holy Spirit alone may flame in my heart. Please pray that I may become a <u>mature Bahai</u>, and be able to attract, not a mere handful of souls to the Faith, but thousands, and people of capacity.[15]

Knowing your staggering burden of responsibility, I have refrained from writing you, but I so long to make a closer contact, to work more directly under your guidance that perhaps you will forgive me for doing so now.[16]

We beg your prayers that the quality of our service may be ever nearer to the lofty standard which Bahá'u'lláh has called us to, and of which you are setting the example.[17]

Because of your loving prayers and the assurance which your cable brought, this servant was able to hold on to life, although it would have been so easy to go. But the feeling that you wanted me to stay and that Bahá'u'lláh had more work which He wanted me to do, strengthened me to fight through the crisis of the complications, following the operation; and now recovery is taking place but it seems to be a rather slow process in the face of the needs of the Teaching at this time and the pressure from the National Teaching Committee to get back into the strenuous campaign work during September . . .

It is difficult to know what to do, as you told me to follow the advice of my doctors and yet the need seems so great and one is tempted to feel the request of the N.T.C. should be followed and that, if I trust Bahá'u'lláh and depend upon Him, that he will carry me through and strengthen this servant to do his work.[18]

Their correspondence illustrates their understanding of their tests. In a letter to Mabel in 1925, Howard wrote:

This morning I left Pottersville [New York] where I spent the night (at the foot of Schroon Lake) at 6 AM and a few miles out stopped in a retired nook and before sunrise went through the Dawn Prayer and had a most wonderful time of meditation . . .

I realize now as never before how important it is to have long periods of meditation and prayer if one is really to attain. That is why [Bahá'u'lláh] spent two years in solitude; why Christ had his 40 days in the wilderness and why all truly spiritual souls feel oppressed by the world and a need to flee from it at times and for rather long periods. In this day we can attain much of this by inner contemplation even while in the world: – But we must have the other too . . .[19]

Their problems extended beyond their finances. The lack of spiritual awareness of the people, the disunity of the Bahá'ís, and the struggles of the members of their own families were also causes of heartache and concern. In April 1925, Howard received a letter from his brother, Theo, about the loss of his fruit farm. There had been bad words in the past between them and Howard was very glad to be back in contact, even though, as he wrote to Mabel, he had to ignore

> everything in the past that might be imagined a cause for disagreement. You see the tone he writes in. I would not send it to you if it would make you feel the way it did me, but I just want you to know that I did what I could to make the world a little easier for him and to release him from the chains of hatred. Please pray for him and for Will and Florence, the other two of my family that are laying up for themselves such a harvest of unhappiness in both worlds.[20]

The troubles of his brother brought to Howard's mind the words of Shoghi Effendi:

> Humanity, through suffering and turmoil, is swiftly moving on towards its destiny; if we be loiterers, if we fail to play our part surely others will be called upon to take up our task as ministers to the crying needs of this afflicted world.
>
> Not by the force of numbers, not by the mere exposition of a set of new and noble principles, not by an organized campaign of teaching – no matter how worldwide and elaborate in its character – not even by the staunchness of our faith or the exaltation of our enthusiasm, can we ultimately hope to vindicate in the eyes of a critical and sceptical age the supreme claim of the Abhá Revelation. One thing and only one thing will unfailingly and alone secure the undoubted triumph of this sacred Cause, namely, the extent to which our own inner life and private character mirror forth in their manifold aspects the splendor of those eternal principles proclaimed by Bahá'u'lláh.[21]

Howard's primary personal focus was on the spiritual side of life in a material world. His belief was that by becoming more purified, he would be better able to share the Message of Bahá'u'lláh.

Mabel wanted to be a better Bahá'í and was intent on becoming a better teacher of the Faith in the material world.

The bond between husband and wife

Through all the ups and downs in these early years, Mabel was Howard's rock and he was her spiritual guide. Each supported the other through their almost daily letters. They almost constantly used 'thee', 'thy' and 'thou' instead of the everyday 'you'. His letters to her overflow with deep love and emotion:

> I love you beyond words. Our unity is so perfect that in a sense we are never separated. I feel your presence so clearly when I am praying for you.[22]

> Blessed of all worlds!
> That's what you are – you blessed, beautiful, charming, lovely mate of my heart! How's that for an opening sentence of a letter from an old married man to his dear little Rizwanea?[23]

> What a wealth of divine love and assurance and comfort and power your letter bore to thy mate. Surely there never was such a wonderful wife since time began.[24]

> Your letters are such a joy! You dearest and darlingest of mates! I have some pretty fierce times of longing for my dear one too. We were never made to be very far apart after we had once found each other. I get considerable comfort out of your picture. It is more truly you than any other picture I have seen. It stands on my dresser and it cheers a lot...
> I love thee my own Mabel. Thou art in my heart of hearts every instant and throughout all eternity we are one. The Fire of the Love of God has welded our beings into one.[25]

I wish I could begin to tell you all the comfort and blessing you are to your Howie. To think that this servant has found his Eternal Lord and his eternal mate in one life time! How seldom that happens! Only the Supreme Bounty of God could bestow such a gift. How can anything but constant and radiant happiness, selfless and joyous service and absolute trust and confidence be the atmosphere in which we live.[26]

Mabel completely reciprocated those feelings:

What an infinite joy and inspiration you have been to me and to us all this past weekend. The glory of the Most Glorious One shone thru you and illumined us all. How Blessed thou art. Thou are truly under the protection of the Most High.[27]

O my God, Howie darling, I am simply speechless before your divine energy and faith and courage. It is sublime! Couldn't it be hitched just as well to something which could be done – dearest work under the Guardian's directions! You are a whole power house – a dynamo and with your now spiritual maturity it seems you might render outstanding vastly important services to the Cause and leave eternal traces. I adore you, my darling. I know that Baha'u'llah loves you.[28]

My Precious One –
Was so happy to get your letter today. I just live for the mail . . . Until tomorrow, my darling. I shall meet you in prayer tonight and in the morning.[29]

Where tests commonly are a challenge to a marriage, Howard and Mabel understood why they were being tested and this forged an ever-closer bond between them. It was a bond that grew stronger and more profound over the years.

The whole purpose of sacrificing home and resources was to teach the Faith. Their abilities to do so quickly became apparent.

The McKays and the Collisons – Geneva, New York

In the autumn of 1924, Howard and Mabel's teaching efforts began to flower with three couples. Rex and Mary Collison (who were atheists at that time, but who later became Knights of Bahá'u'lláh during the Ten Year Crusade), Willard and Doris McKay (who became long-time travel teachers and pioneers), and a Christian physician and his wife together began reading a newly published book called *Bahá'u'lláh and the New Era* in Geneva, New York. Doris noted that the book had been 'left by someone named Howard Ives' who had passed through the town. Soon, Willard's mother joined them. The book piqued everyone's interest.[30]

Then in January 1925, the group met Howard and Mabel at the Collisons' home. It was a life-changing evening:

> Over the handshakes we caught the message of Howard Ives' eyes. Most eyes are veiled at first contact, the first meeting. Perhaps some are veiled always. But these eyes spoke. They said, 'My dears, this is a meeting of souls. We cannot hide from one another.' The moment passed and we saw his eyes to be deep set and brown under bushy brows. They were set in a lined face with strong features. He had a mobile, speaker's mouth. The man was spare, a little bent. Close to him stood his wife, Mabel, his physical opposite, not very tall, exceedingly pleasing and pretty with blue eyes and dark curly hair. She looked both merry and wise.[31]

'The aura of the two guests enhanced the atmosphere of the room' and it was an eager group who listened to the teaching duo. Doris later wrote:

> We were to see the skilled operation of an experienced team of husband and wife. Mabel spoke first on the world aspects of the Bahá'í Faith, stressing its call to universality. She listed and explained the Bahá'í principles derived from the Writings of Bahá'u'lláh revealed over a century ago. Among these were

a list of concepts. In those early days they were challenging, even explosive – far reaching in their call, not to a locality, but to the whole world. For example, mankind is one, the religions are one, all racial, national and religious and class prejudice must be abandoned. There must come universal education, a universal language, a world court, a world administrative body. By eliminating the roots of dissention, she said, universal peace would ultimately follow.

'How can we achieve such a state of mind?' somebody asked.

'By still another Bahá'í principle,' she responded. 'The independent investigation of truth.'

There was a thoughtful silence. We had all been seekers, each in our own way. We had remained cool to the insistent dogmas of the church, the weird statistics of psychical research, the egoistic goals of the modern cults into which we had probed. Had we perhaps been perishing for a firm belief in something reasonable, something scientific, and at the same time something warm?

Mabel's strong confident voice laid every treasure before us in dazzling array, and somehow, truth could never again be piecemeal. In our minds a new thought exploded: the concept of oneness – a concept to be loved as a reality, for itself! In that flash of illumination we accepted the integration of our ideas and of our world.

Speaking quietly, Howard, told us of an Entity, veiled in light, whom he called 'the Manifestation of God'. This being had borne the name of Zoroaster, Krishna, Buddha, Moses, Christ, Mohammed, and, in recent times, the names of the Báb and Bahá'u'lláh. Their words were the Messages of the Holy Spirit made vocal, each in its own day. . .

Here, indeed, was a new idea, a Christ returned! 'Like a thief in the night,' said Howard. When he invited questions, our instinctive need was to relate to our previous beliefs the supreme fact that he had revealed. But how could his answer be reconciled to such a group as were gathered before him? The agnostic and atheistic scientists, the churchman, the searchers in the humanistic cults.

Sometimes it seemed as if Howard had left us when, with open palms and head thrown back, he sat in silent prayer. Then he would rise up, his deep eyes flashing, his white mane vibrant on his head, and the answers would come through an electrified atmosphere.

He told us, 'Instead of giving up Christ you will find Him. Yes, God spoke through His prophets. Did He not say to Moses, "I am the Lord, thy God." Yes, this is in fulfilment of prophecy. The prophecy of all the prophets foretold this Day.'

'Science?' asked Rex Collison.

'Science and religion will enhance and prove each other. How can one truth contradict another truth?'

'Reincarnation?' That was my question.

'It is true that we are born again after leaving this world, but not in the sense of reincarnation. In the next world we will continue to advance into higher stations, if we so desire. Births will be necessary to attain to these, just as tonight a new world and a new birth lie before you. Your first birth was from the womb. Even in this world, a "second birth" is available to the awakened soul.'

'Proofs of the prophet?' Here is the challenge to investigate truth. Howard told us. 'The life of the Prophet and His Teachings are the unassailable proofs.'

'How do we know that They were sent by God?'

'Whence came that dynamic power to uplift humanity of the world religions that bear their names?'

His voice stopped as did our questions. We sat silent, amazed by another and personal proof. We had beheld a man communing with an Unseen Power. We had watched him bring inspired, reasonable, and acceptable answers back from another realm.

Such was the power in the room, our eyes, too, were suddenly opened to it. A place of spirit had, somehow, signalled us. The man, Howard Ives, had become a part of his message, had become something more than the flow of words, the voice, the movement of hands in prayer. More than his eyes looking into ours with a compassionate comradeship. Our defenses dispersed. The Message flowed into our separate worlds like a sudden flood. I believed. We all believed. . . .

I had one last question for Howard as he held my hands in a goodbye: 'How does one pray?' Howard and Mabel exchanged the look of conspiring parents.

He said, 'Dare I?'

She nodded, and he slipped into my hands his own worn prayer book to take home.[32]

Doris wondered what she had learned from 'the passionate sincerity of Howard's words.' She was astounded that when asked a question, Howard could withdraw to the spiritual worlds and ask for assistance. Suddenly, she knew that 'there was a world of spirit and that there was an Essence there – a knowing and responsive ENTITY. That Howard had addressed this Being and had been inspired in the answering of our questions. That it followed that we, too, could pray, establishing a kinship with this Power, with Bahá'u'lláh as an intermediary.' The three couples were now on a different plane.[33]

Howard and Mabel continued to return 'with parental concern' to 'instruct and inspire' them. They introduced the new Bahá'ís to Grace and Harlan Ober, who invited them to attend a Feast at their home in Buffalo. Doris wrote that Howard's spiritual teaching was occasionally impacted by the material world:

We took flight like seven young birds following their parent birds to a clime where always the sun shines and roses bloom. Those who rode in the Ives' car had the added advantage of a tour, with Howard as guide, through *The Seven Valleys*. On we flew through the spiritual landscape of the Valleys that symbolize the seven stages of the progress of the soul: the Valleys of Search, of Love, of Knowledge, of Unity, of Contentment, of Wonderment.

'Now,' proclaimed Howard, 'we come to the seventh Valley, the Valley of Annihilation.' Just then a heavy truck tore past with a screech of doomsday – missing us, it seemed, by only half an inch. 'Praise be to God,' said Howard, watching the road a little more carefully the rest of the way.[34]

When Doris wrote what she called her 'me-moirs', *Fires in Many Hearts*, she dedicated the book to Howard Colby Ives – 'A lighter of fires in many hearts: his spiritual sons and daughters, impregnated with the love of God, spread first over the eastern United States and Canada. His spiritual progeny have multiplied through the generations to become an army. I am one of his daughters and, to me, he will be always "Daddy Howard".'[35]

Travelling and teaching

As Howard and Mabel struggled with finances, separation and other frustrations in 1925, they filled in any extra time working for the Faith. Wherever they travelled, the Bahá'ís in the communities they visited organized both private and public talks. While in Philadelphia, Howard spoke to a Black spiritualist group one day and a White spiritualist group the next. Of the Black group, Howard wrote that 'Last night I had a unique experience at the Colored spiritualist church. About 20 colored people, lots of singing and considerable noisy expressing on the part of the minister Mrs. Coleman. A very beautiful atmosphere was developed. But all very sincere and open-minded'.[36] The next night with the white group, he wrote, 'Last night we had quite a wonderful meeting at another spiritualist (white) church. Only a few there but they seemed quite enthralled, and the atmosphere was very pregnant with the Breath of the Holy Spirit.'[37]

In July, Howard was in Springfield, Massachusetts. He wrote to Mabel that 'The meeting last night was very beautiful. Our Lord does confirm His servants even tho they are personally so worthless and weak, doesn't He dear!' Though the meeting had gone well, Howard managed to drive 'off with Mrs.

Greenleaf's suitcase on the running board and had to leave it at Keens for them to send for. Mrs. Parsons told me to do this on the phones. Too bad!'[38] On another occasion, a man walked up to Howard in a men's room, tapped him on the shoulder and asked, 'Isn't this Mr. Ives?' It was a man Howard had wished to share the Faith with for weeks, but whom he had not been able to find. They 'had a fine talk and breakfast together this a.m. He is on his way to Jacksonville Fla. and wants the names of some Bahá'ís there.'[39]

Howard's manner of opening up a new city was sometimes quite circumspect. In Elizabeth, New Jersey, on 4 November, he spoke on eating and health. Under a headline reading 'Diet to Stretch Man's Life to 100', he described how an intelligent approach to diet could extend the average lifespan. The *Elizabeth Journal*, in its story on the talk, closed with a reference to the Bahá'í Faith:

> Mr. Ives, who was formerly minister of the Unitarian Church at Summit, but who for the last twelve years has given much of his time to the spread of Bahaism, is an ardent devotee of the cult, which now includes in its fellowship about 15,000,000 persons.
>
> When Abdul Baha visited the United States several years ago Mr. Ives became interested in his philosophy of life and left his pulpit. Mr. and Mrs. Ives are engaged in a business enterprise, but a large part of their time is devoted, without remuneration, to the winning of men and women to belief in the ideals of Baha.
>
> 'The Bahai religion,' says Mr. Ives, 'does not ask any man to forsake his faith, but rather tries to make him see the good in all creeds. It is not merely a religion, but a movement on the part of the world to bring harmony and peace out of chaos. Through the teachings of Abdul Baha and his father the religions of the world are being unified . . .'[40]

A month later, in mid-December, Mabel gave a talk in Cranford, New Jersey. A newspaper story noted that 'Mrs. Ives has a well-poised and pleasing manner, and wore a very pretty gown' before describing her talk as a more 'practical view of her subject "How to Attain a Radiant Personality" than its title would suggest, which was an agreeable disappointment, since mystical interpretations are of comparatively small value to persons compelled to live on the plane of ordinary daily existence.' The subject, as described in the paper, focused on the ways that this radiance could be achieved:

> Health of mind largely depends on health of body and she gave some excellent advice on diet, sleep and exercise . . . Breathing exercises and internal and external cleanliness were also insisted upon. After this came the topics of recreation or change of occupation . . . The fact that good habits as well as bad ones may be cultivated to become automatic . . . Mrs. Ives then spoke of constructive and cheerful thinking, and the necessity of some central interest in life outside one's self, which will do away with fear, malice, jealousy and similar mental disabilities. Passing on to the spiritual side, she said that love, faith and thankfulness were equally essential to radiance. Perhaps the most valuable of her practical hints, because less often brought to the attention of such audiences was her advice to take a few minutes for slowing down, every day, a short time in which to step aside out of the bustling procession and relax body and mind by being still. To put Mrs. Ives' meaning in popular language, do not become so hopelessly caught up in the whirl of hustle and boost that you are too hurried and dizzy to take your mental and spiritual bearings. Take time to form a definite idea, and then persist in trying to attain it. Everybody is sacrificing on some altar, worthy or unworthy, so stop to choose one that is worth while, and remember that the spirit of love is the greatest of constructive forces.
>
> The speaker was given a standing vote of thanks at the close of her address . . .[41]

9
Race Unity Work
1926–1931

Howard and Mabel's service was inspired by their desire to faithfully carry out every wish of Shoghi Effendi. They wrote to their second letter to the Guardian on 6 January 1926:

Our beloved Guardian:
   We have longed so much to see you and to lay our foreheads at the Holy Threshold, but circumstances have not as yet permitted. It is our hope, assisted by your prayers, God willing, that soon this will be possible . . .
   These servants, after five years of wandering and working have, under the Guidance of 'Abdu'l-Bahá, settled in New York. We are entering upon a new life of teaching and service and we supplicate that your prayers for us may be that we may become daily more severed, more selfless, more devoted to the Cause of God: and that in all our affairs we may be under the Guidance of 'Abdu'l-Bahá, that we may be protected from error, that we may assist in establishing perfect unity amongst the friends of God, and that with wisdom and humility we may be confirmed in helping to bring to pass the 'Very Great Things': which His Holiness 'Abdu'l-Bahá told this servant to expect and pray for.
   Dear and Blessed Shogi Effendi! We dedicate our lives to thee. Thy will is our will; thy commands are our joy; thy slightest wish shall be to us a Divine Law. What greater joy could there be than this! To lay our lives at the Holy Threshold and give up all for the service of Bahá'u'lláh![1]

The letter also contained requested prayers for some of the Bahá'ís in Geneva and Rochester, New York, Detroit, Michigan and Keyport, New Jersey. The reply promised prayers for all those mentioned in the letter and went on to say:

> Shoghi Effendi greatly appreciates your constant services. He hopes that you will always find success in your work, especially now that you are determined to stay in New York. This city is an important center and if the Cause should obtain a firm standing in it, that will reflect on other centers, for it is a place to which people of different nationality, religions and modes of life come. If they receive the message, they will carry it back to their homes and introduce it to their circle.[2]

In his personal note at the end, Shoghi Effendi wrote: 'May the Beloved enable you to motivate and consolidate the all-important and most vital work of teaching and assist you to win to the Cause exalted, devoted, and enlightened souls. I will pray for you that He may aid you to fulfil your heart's desire. Your well-wisher, Shoghi'.[3]

By July 1926, Howard and Mabel were in Ithaca, New York. They gave talks to the Rotarians, the Cosmopolitan Club and the Hill Club. Howard's talk at the Hill Club was titled 'A Plan for World Unity' and repeated the rather amazing statement that there were 15,000,000 Bahá'ís in the world. In it, he defined what a Bahá'í was: 'a follower of the light. He has an open mind and harbors no prejudices. He finds truth in all religions. He is a man with an out-look and not a back-look.'[4] Howard commonly used the number 15 million when referring to the number of Bahá'ís in the world, because that figure was commonly used in newspaper articles during 'Abdu'l-Bahá's visit to America. While in Ithaca, the Ives were visited by Ruhi Afnan, Shoghi Effendi's cousin and one of his secretaries.[5]

Mabel was in Ithaca for the last half of March 1927. A local newspaper headlined her 18 March talk with, 'Woman Power Must Be Organized to Insure Peace'. She began her talk by looking at the world – 'Nations arrayed against nations, races against races, classes against classes, all of which conditions contain the seeds of war'. She then laid out eight points necessary for the creation of world peace, partly coming from the Bahá'í principles and partly inferred:

1) Individually, we can slough off our individual prejudice ... and treat all men and women as brothers and sisters who are created by and worshiping the same God.
2) We as women can assist in the establishment of an international court of arbitration.
3) Gradual reduction of arms and armaments.
4) Teach peace through education, through the rewriting of history text books in which the achievements of peace rather than those of war will be emphasized.
5) Ask bankers not to loan money for war purposes.
6) Work for permanent peace treaties between nations.
7) America is the most powerful nation in wealth of resources today. She is the creditor nation. She should take the initiative in all of these peace movements.
8) All nations shall stand together in readiness to use such police power as they have retained to check nations who by force will offend against other nations.[6]

On 31 March, Mabel was joined by Harlan Ober for a World Peace meeting. The next day, Mabel's talk was a 'Plea for World Peace' and outlined 'Causes of Present Chaos'. She titled her talk 'From World Chaos to World Peace' and began it by asking the question, 'Is this civilization going to continue or not?' Mabel listed what she called the 'five basic delusions as 'national, religious, racial, class, and economic prejudice'. Her solution to the world's problems, as it had in her 18 March talk, came from Bahá'u'lláh, with a few interpreted bits:

> an international court of arbitral justice, a gradual and simultaneous disarmament of all nations, universal education in the principles of peace, freedom of the seas for all, a few battalions of international police to preserve internal

order, refusal of financiers and bankers to grant loans to finance wars, refusal of railroad and steamship companies to transport war munitions, demand of soldiers to know the justice of all wars and an enduring treaty of peace between nations.[7]

During the summer of 1927, Howard and Mabel stayed with Doris and Willard McKay in Geneva, New York. That autumn, they moved on to Ithaca, New York, home of Cornell University. The Ives commonly returned to Geneva on weekends and stayed with the McKays. Forsyth Ward, a Bahá'í in Ithaca, introduced the Ives to the Cornell Cosmopolitan Club, which 'represented the cream of their Indian, African, Oriental and South American cultures. Their faces were a garden of hues.'[8]

Race unity work in New York State

Binghamton

Helen Inderlied lived in Binghamton, New York in 1928 and encountered Mabel in a psychology class:

> The first time I saw Mabel Ives she was delivering a lecture with a chart (based on Abdul Baha's teachings) at a psychology class – Mrs. Harriet McCullom had started the class and successfully conducted it for some weeks. I had just departed for other fields. I thought the substance of the lecture excellent, but what interested me more was an extremely strong attraction I felt for the speaker without any reason I could give. It was a strange experience – like a magnet drawing me to her presence. I pushed up to her and inquired bluntly, 'Are you a lecturer?' She smiled and replied, 'Well a parlor lecturer, perhaps'. I then asked crudely, but driven on by a force larger than I understood, 'Where do you live?' 'Well', she cheerfully said, 'I think I shall live in Binghamton'. 'Binghamton!' I said to myself

– To think she was going to live in Binghamton! I walked dazedly away. It was too good to be true, but it was true. Later to my intense surprise I discovered that my experience described above was not unique to me. More than a dozen other members were similarly affected and it was these attracted souls that became the Charter members of the Binghamton Baha'i Community.

Year 1928. It seems that just previous to this 'historic' lecture, Mr. and Mrs. Ives had arrived in Binghamton and were not yet settled in their apt. when Mrs. Ives put on her hat to go out. Mr. Ives protested on the ground of her weariness but she explained that she had seen in the Press the notice of a Psych meeting that night and she had a' 'hunch' to go, that she felt it would be a favorable opportunity to make contacts (For the Baha'i Movement which they were in the city to promote). She continued to attend these meetings accompanied by Mr. Ives and was made President of the Psych. Class. One evening at her request, Mr. Ives reviewed a book by Evelyn Underhill for the group. In that way we contacted him too and were deeply impressed. After the book review, Mr. Ives asked all who seemed especially attracted to their apt. on Conklin Ave. on a different night than that on which the Psych. class was held. These meetings continued weekly in 1928-1929 until in Aug. 1930 19 of us accepted the Baha'í Faith and an assembly was formed. Mr. and Mrs. Harlan Ober came from Pittsburgh to assist and also Baha'is from Geneva. Evidently the hour had struck in Binghamton for this great step. Mr. and Mrs. Ives, we realized, were great Teachers with a unique message – Through it they could answer questions that had never been clearly answered; they loved humanity in a deeper, broader more vital way than we had ever witnessed; they sacrificed time and strength more completely to teach us and 'counted it but joy'. They displayed infinite patience as they gently and skillfully led us into that higher state of consciousness revealed by Baha'u'llah.

After Mr. and Mrs. Ives left the city, they wrote to us

marvelous letters, returned to inspire us from time to time, and sent us other outstanding Bahá'í Teachers to develop our nascent consciousness. Mrs. Ives was under a Doctor's care while in Binghamton but she took almost no time out. She would on occasion 'rest a moment' when forced to it, but only to rise and forge ahead steam on!⁹

Howard and Mabel spent most of 1928 living in Binghamton, but by September they were considering a change. They were both tired from the constant travelling and separation and when they heard from Rex and Mary Collison about John Bosch's work in Geyserville, California, they decided to look into joining him. In their letter to John, they wrote:

> The idea came to us at an opportune moment for Mrs. Ives and I have been considering for some months buying a small farm where the strenuous life we have been living could be simplified, and where there was opportunity for service to the Cause.
>
> The change is necessitated by the condition of my health. A milder climate is proscribed and some lessening of activities.
>
> Will it be too much trouble for you to write me as soon as possible giving me an idea of what a small farm, or ranch, could be purchased for, with a bungalow on it, enough fruit for our use, etc.? We do not expect to go into the fruit business. Perhaps Turkeys or chickens will interest us. Anyhow we would want from five to ten acres. We would prefer to be near some good sized city where no Bahai Assembly is as yet established, and yet not too far from Geyserville, in the neighborhood of Santa Rosa or Sacramento, for example.¹⁰

This blissful idea never came to fruition and the Ives continued their stressful life. From this point on, however, both Howard's and Mabel's health began to have an impact on their lives. But that simply led to more sacrifices for the Faith.

In late August 1929, several carloads of Bahá'ís went from

Geneva to Binghamton, a city about a hundred miles [160 km] to the south. Howard and Mabel were especially excited. They had been living at Quaker Lake near Binghamton and had invited everyone to a 'houseparty' and to either stay with them or with some of the Binghamton Bahá'ís. Harlan and Grace Ober came down from Buffalo. Doris noted, 'Baskets of food were taken down to the pine trees by the lake and, after reading a selection of 'Abdu'l-Bahá's words on the subject of love, we feasted.'[11]

The next day, about forty people sat down at picnic tables for breakfast in the 'highest spirits and, beyond the hilarity, was the feeling that this was a special moment.' Howard read a prayer 'with the power that was in his voice', then called for talks. Harlan and Grace spoke about the reality of servitude. Others spoke from their hearts. At the end, Howard laid a long sheet of paper and a pen on the table and said, 'All those from Binghamton who wish to become Baha'is, write your names on this paper.' Nineteen people stepped forward to pick up the pen and sign their names.[12]

In December 1929, Howard and Mabel received a letter written on behalf of the Guardian. Shoghi Effendi encouraged them to maintain contact with the groups and assemblies that they were helping to form so that they would become deepened and steadfast. The letter said:

> It is needless also to say how happy Shoghi Effendi becomes of such news. The important thing, however, is to keep in touch with them. You should not let the iron cool until you have moulded it into its proper and final shape. He hopes that you will arrange with the teaching committee and neighbouring groups to visit them every now [and] then and keep them in touch with the Cause and its spirit. We also hope that you have encouraged them to collect the important books and form a library that would be for their common use. They surely need to deepen their knowledge.
>
> One member of this group, whose name I do not know, has already written us. It was my good fortune to acknowledge her letter. It was most interesting for her questions

were the result of great thought and deep study. I hope that her problems would gradually be solved.

Please convey to every member of this group Shoghi Effendi's loving greetings and assure them of his prayers. He hopes that every one of them will become a torch and give light to others. We need helpers if we are to succeed in our endeavour to bring about the reign of peace and brotherhood in the world.

May I also assure you of Shoghi Effendi's prayers. He is always and anxiously awaiting such news from the soldiers of the Cause who in the field of service are constantly winning ground and setting back the forces of darkness. Perhaps it is fortunate that your most permanent home is the Cause. It has helped you to establish many centers and we hope it will guide you to many more. May God's spirit always assist you and keep you.[13]

As he usually did, Shoghi Effendi closed with a personal message: 'With the assurance of my loving prayers for you at the Shrine of Bahá'u'lláh.'

Howard was a prolific letter-writer and on 25 June 1930 he wrote to Doris McKay, beginning the letter as he usually did by saying that it would be a short one. He then proceeded to write about recent events and his health, which was not good. Doris noted that, as usual, 'by the time he finished describing his health, he would be struck by a train of inspiration streaming gold'. From this long letter, his 'gold' was that

> Unity is the great key to spiritual progress. The unity of believers must be of such a character that never, NEVER, must one single thought of anything but love and sympathy and kindness and reverence enter into such a heart. 'Abdu'l-Bahá says that when we see even the slightest traces of love for Bahá'u'lláh in any soul, we must reverence that soul. How great then must be the reverence we have for those souls who are fully confirmed in the Cause of God and have arisen for service . . .

But our great task, as individual believers, is to see that, in the group in which God has called us to serve, never does the slightest breath of anything but love arise. And that constantly, at every moment of our spiritual journey, every selfish desire, every human attachment [must be banished and we must] find our greatest joy in becoming 'as dust beneath the feet of the friends . . .' This is the station of unity in this Day to which the believers of God are called . . .

Upon thee be glory and peace! Upon thee be all the confirmations of holiness and sanctity!
In His Name and love, Daddy Howard [14]

Syracuse, New York

In the early spring of 1929, Howard and Mabel began preparations for an Interracial Amity Conference in Syracuse, where they were living at the time. Unexpectedly, in March they ran into some opposition. Initially, they had been given the use of the auditorium at the Syracuse Central High School for a talk sponsored by the National Inter-Racial Committee of the Bahá'ís of the United States and Canada. Several local people had agreed to serve on a committee to host the talk, but due to an article in the local newspaper, in which the Faith was called a 'Persian cult', a number of them resigned, thinking it was part of the 'Bahá'í movement' and that the reason for the talks had been misrepresented. They also worried that the talks were an underhanded way to convert people to the Bahá'í Faith. Mabel rebutted the accusation, saying that 'The Bahai Movement is not a cult. It is a world-wide, international and inter-religious movement, in which all nationalities, races and religions are represented. It has for seventy-five years been working earnestly and successfully in every country of the world to bring about better international, inter-racial and inter-religious understanding.'[15]

Howard also responded, writing:

> As to the accusation quite openly made that misrepresentation was used, that is, of course, quite untrue. In every case I mentioned the fact that the conference was to be held under the Bahai's auspices, but I also said that the Bahai movement as such would not be featured, nor anything like proselytizing attempted. Such a thing is directly opposed to the Bahai teachings . . . These Inter-Racial Amity Conferences have been held in many of the large cities of the country and always held in exactly the same way that the Syracuse conference is planned . . .[16]

He then went on to list other successful conferences in Washington DC, New York City, and Philadelphia. Continuing, he said:

> At all of these conferences Bahai men and women acted as chairmen, and some of the speakers on the program were usually a Bahai. Quotations from Baha U'llah and Abdul Baha were used on the programs as well as quotations from Jesus Christ and from the other great spiritual leaders of mankind. But in no case was there any attempt to urge the Bahai cause upon the attention of the public. Every endeavor was bent towards unifying and harmonizing the relations between all nations and to fostering the spirit of good will, friendliness and understanding between the different races and peoples of our common country.[17]

As might be expected, the resulting brouhaha ended up giving the Faith much publicity which increased the interest of many people. Howard and Mabel even ended up giving a talk explicitly on the Bahá'í Faith so that the people of Syracuse would understand its principles and teachings. In addition, many locally prominent people arose to defend Howard and Mabel and the aims of the Interracial Conference. Syracuse's Mayor met with Howard and reported that 'Mr. Ives has convinced me that his meeting is for the purpose of inter-racial understanding, and I see no reason for stopping it.'[18] When Howard gave his talk at the Hotel Syracuse, most of the 60-strong audience were impressed and asked many questions. One man, however, had not liked what he heard and, 'making violent remarks, stormed out of the room'.[19]

Geneva, New York – The second Blossom Picnic illustrates race unity

The Blossom Picnic in Geneva was the time when the Bahá'ís from Geneva, Binghamton and Rochester, New York, gathered for two days of spiritual unity. It was a unique gathering in that the Bahá'ís from Rochester were Black and those from the other communities were White. Howard and Mabel were integral parts of the weekend.

This was a special event for James Hubert, a Black man and Secretary of the Urban League, in Rochester. He liked what he had heard about the unity of the races from the Bahá'ís, but said, 'I wish it were true, but it can't be done. I won't believe it 'til I see it done.' When he arrived at the picnic, he saw a 'crowd of boys were playing ball in a field. They were of both races, black and white. Here was something that Mr. Hubert had never seen before'. When he left, he said, 'I had to see it to believe it!' One Black woman remarked to Doris, 'If the Bahá'í movement makes you love us like this, it must be the return of the Christ spirit!'[20]

Many well-known Bahá'ís were there, including Howard and Mabel, Grace and Harlan Ober, Louis Gregory and May Maxwell. A total of 80 people participated over the long weekend. Howard and Mabel conducted a series of lectures and formed a Bahá'í study class. Doris McKay wrote, 'We have had a big picnic for each of four days. Barefoot dancing on the lawn, Oscar Wilde stories by firelight, 'Abdu'l-Baha's Tablets at sunset on the hill with a young moon rising.'[21]

Michigan and Pennsylvania

Louhelen, Michigan

In 1930, Lewis (Lou) and Helen Eggleston bought a farm outside Davison, Michigan, that they hoped to develop into a Bahá'í summer school. Their plan had the backing of both the National Spiritual Assembly and the Guardian and became known as Louhelen, by joining their first names. The first summer school was held from 1 to 9 August 1931, with 35 full-time participants from six states and another 50 people who attended at least one session. Sessions 'were held that year in a wooded area sloping down to a clear stream, either in a lodge on the hillside or in an open-air amphitheater'. Mabel and Howard, along with Grace Ober, were the primary teachers, and Dorothy Baker and Fanny Knobloch also shared their knowledge and understanding of the Faith. Howard's class was about the spiritual teachings, emphasizing the Hidden Words, while Mabel 'drilled' into the participants how to publicly present the Faith. Grace's class was about the social and economic teachings of the Faith.[22]

Washington DC area

Howard was in Chevy Chase, Maryland, on 24 January 1932 to attend an interracial meeting whose aims were simply to 'gather the two races in a friendly, natural way together for the discussion of general themes vital to all.' In addition to meetings, Howard visited a number of individuals. One couple had been in a 'dreadful' car accident and been hospitalized for three months. The husband of another couple had been run down by a car and been incapacitated ever since.[23]

The interracial meeting went well, with a variety of speakers. Howard was only supposed to participate in the resulting discussion; however, moments before the program began, a note was handed to him saying that 'one of the speakers could not attend and I was to take his place and darned if they didn't call on me the first one. And my note seemed to be the chord to which the other speakers tuned in.' A minister from Haiti, Mons. Bellegarde, spoke in French and 'was translated by Stanwood Cobb. He followed me and referred to the talk of Mons. Ives as "thrilling him to his very heart".'[24]

Howard's schedule for Washington DC during the following ten days included a study class and speakers training class on the 25th, and a meeting on the afternoon of the 27th at Stanwood Cobb's home followed by one at Agnes Parsons'. On the 28th there was to be a meeting with a large group of Bahá'ís at Bessie Hopper's home followed the next day by dinner with Dr Irani and a meeting at his home. On the 30th, a meeting was set for the home of Mr and Mrs Davis. On Sunday, 31 January, there was to be a public meeting and there would be a group meeting the next day at the home of Mrs Stewart. On 2 February, Orcella Rexford was to take Stanwood's study class since he would be out of town. Finally, Howard would spend all day on 4 February in Baltimore.[25]

10
Howard Breaks Down

The Great Depression was being felt everywhere, and the storm of the financial and social problems affected everyone. Howard had been really struggling with the material world in 1930 and 1931. Already in 1930, Mabel could readily see his strains and wrote him a letter in which she lovingly, but bluntly, told him why he was having such a difficult time in the world:

> I was praying for my Howie today, while I was taking my walk, praying and meditating as to what could be done so that he might be free to do the work for which he seems to be fitted and to which he seems to be called. And I had what I think was a real illumination . . .
>
> It seems to me that you are what psychologists call a 'sensitive'. That is you are tuned up to a higher vibration than most people and consequently the harsh notes of the world jar upon you terribly. It is like the true artistic temperament: a great artist or musician is keyed up to a high nervous tension, he must be in order to create that which his vision has revealed to him, and while in that creative mood he does not fit into this world at all . . . You are of this type and this explains why you had such a difficult time adjusting yourself to the world of your boyhood, youth and business life . . .
>
> You have, in the natural course of things, not a great many more years to live on this plane of being. I want to help you so to adjust your life that these remaining years may be the most productive of that for which God has placed you here . . .
>
> My thought is this: that we should so arrange our lives that you will be enabled to spend, perhaps, three-fourths

of your time in writing and teaching. This work is to be your <u>real</u> work, it is this around which your whole thought should revolve. Then when you need some money go out for a few days, relying upon Abdul Baha's help and guidance, and earn what you need. It may not be necessary for you to do very much of this kind of work, for our Unity with Harlan and Grace may, under the guidance of Baha'U'llah, provide the means . . .

There are three things that in the past have prevented you from doing your best work in the world, the work for which you were created. First: You have been constantly thwarted in your highest endeavors, by the long years of constant struggle to express yourself on <u>your</u> plane of being while the world around you insisted that you express <u>that</u> plane. You have been trying to put a round peg in a square hole; you have been constantly torn between two worlds . . .

One reason why you have not been able to function in this world is that your mind has never been occupied exclusively with it. You are greatly lacking in the faculty of observation on the plane of materiality, while being keenly observant in the spiritual world.

The combination of these, and many others of course, conflicts in the inner world have brought you during the passing years to the extremely nervous condition through which you have been passing . . .

The <u>Second</u> of these three causes of your condition is this: Your spiritual vibrations being constantly tuned up to a high degree, attenuated, so to speak beyond the vibrations of this world, you are very easily thrown off balance . . . [A] good illustration is that of a speeding automobile. A car going at the rate of sixty miles an hour [100 km per hour] cannot make the slightest deviation from the straight track without disaster, while one going at the rate of twenty miles an hour [32 km per hour] can afford to take chances with slight deviations, and a slack hand at the wheel does not do much harm . . . This is symbolic of the vibrations on the spiritual plane. You are highly tuned and to attempt to drive at sixty miles an hour in traffic accustomed to only twenty miles an hour naturally leads to disaster.

The <u>Third</u> of the three causes is a most important one, and in this no one can do anything for you except to advise and encourage. You have to do most, if not all of it, yourself.

You have been living all your life under the influence of a number of bad habits: bad in the sense of unhealthy, and when the Temple of the Holy Spirit is incorrectly managed, badly kept, improperly functioning, it is only to be expected that the Holy Spirit will not be able to express itself through that channel as completely as it otherwise would.

Some of these bad habits you have conquered. Tobacco and coffee, to which you have been a slave for many years, have now ceased to enchain you . . . There remains, however, another very bad habit to which you have been a slave all your life, i.e. the habit of overeating and improper eating . . . It remains for you, and only you, so to set your will and determination at this problem and task that you shall be a complete Master of the Temple of your body, so that you will eat <u>only</u> to secure the necessary strength and energy to accomplish the supreme task which Abdul Baha has set before you, the spreading of His Cause and Kingdom in the world . . .[1]

While there is no record of Howard's response, we know from their many letters how he welcomed her loving counsel and support.

Howard and Mabel spent the summer and autumn of 1931 near New Castle, Pennsylvania, in a house surrounded by orchards. It was a difficult time and Howard was trying to find ways to support their teaching efforts. Doris McKay wrote, 'The Depression was deepening in the city. Guards were being posted at night in the foodstores. There was even some talk of closing the schools. Willard and I were almost penniless; Harlan's funds were diminishing. The miasma of desperation, constantly combatted by prayer, seemed to drift into our minds like polluted air infiltrating a house through chinks, crevices, and keyholes.'²

By November 1931 Howard and Mabel had moved into the home of Harlan and Grace Ober in Pittsburgh. Doris and Willard McKay were also living in the house. This was called the Tilbury Tenement, in which they lived in close proximity and gathered in 'prayerful conferences together, [with] the divine spirit of mutual consideration and open discussion of everything pertaining to [their] mutual interests'.³

During a visit with Howard the previous summer, Doris McKay wrote that 'With his characteristic enthusiasm, Howard had fallen in love with some beautiful (lucrative, he said) white rabbits.' He planned to buy all he could afford – 60 of them – and, after moving in with the Obers, keep them in an old barn on Tilbury Street. Settled in the multifamily house, Howard bought his rabbits and put them in the old barn. One day, Doris and Mary Ober, Harlan and Grace's daughter, visited the budding business:

> We stood in the doorway, saw Howard there, and went inside. He proudly displayed his neat rabbit crates, stacked in twos and threes.
>
> 'Aren't your rabbits rather small,' said Mary pertly, her high-boned Slavic face animated.
>
> 'I bought the small rabbits because they were cheaper, more of an investment I thought,' replied Howard.
>
> At breakfast a week later Howard announced, 'I am ready to mate the two largest rabbits, to set them up in a home of their own in a nice, new crate, I have named them "Grace and Harlan",' he told us. After that they were a great source of fun – until the morning when Howard joined us with a disturbed face.
>
> 'I found Grace and Harlan's cage full of white fur this morning,' he said. 'They have attacked each other. I am very much afraid that both Grace and Harlan are male rabbits.'
>
> The rabbit tragedy then unfolded. Every morning Howard went to the barn. The bags of food grew smaller in

proportion to the increased appetite of the rabbits. Could he afford to buy more feed? He tried to sell the rabbits, putting a sign on the barn and an ad in the newspaper. The day arrived when Howard came home in mid-afternoon a broken man. He had slain his rabbits, skinned and dressed them, and put the meat into cold storage. A murderer would have had no deeper lines on his brow. Howard's spirit dwindled into gloom.

The forecast of meat for the winter was fulfilled . . . We had rabbit stew, baked rabbit with stuffing, minced rabbit with spices, rabbit 'a la king' with white sauce and pepper rings and cold rabbit salad. I would enhance their attraction by calling them hazenpfeffer or jugged hare . . . Said Mabel, 'Those rabbits should be grateful. They have entered the human kingdom.' Rabbits taste rather like chicken and were a prized addition to our diet.

The rabbits even made a contribution to the Temple dome. When a plea came for sacrifice to the Fund, we invited all the Baha'is for a baked potato and rabbit gravy dinner. The friends were to contribute the cost of a normal dinner at home. We collected fourteen dollars for the Treasurer to send. Henry and Bessy Seker asked us all to their place, the next week, for another economy dinner.[4]

Everyone was having a tough time, but Howard's problems suddenly burst out into the open. A doctor told Howard that his nerves were 'stripped' and Mabel was suffering from stress. Even so, Doris McKay wrote:

> Those wonderful Ives. There is no one like them! It is their temperament to be either in heaven or in hell – nearness to God or separation from Him. The process seems necessary for the release of their special powers. Whatever their emotions in reacting to conditions, there is no variability in their passion to teach, never a cooling of their love for Bahá'u'lláh. It is only that they are sometimes in contact and sometimes disconnected from the Object of their love.

They are always in a state of spiritual excitement and the people they reach are awakened and stirred, as we ourselves were touched and awakened the night we met them.[5]

A month later, Howard's nervous problems had intensified. He ate his meals alone in his room and the whole 'family' hushed because of his condition. Everyone tried to keep out of his way. One evening, Howard was in the McKays' living room alone and Harlan went in to talk with him. Howard erupted. He 'began to shout, repeating over and over, "I want to be alone. I want to be ALONE!" Mabel came running down the stairs crying, "Oh, Howie," in an agonized voice. Then she took him away and held him in her arms the rest of the night. He told me [Doris] later that he would have died had he not in his memory that night, the words of Bahá'u'lláh.'[6]

It was an uncomfortable night for everyone: Howard was on edge, Mabel tried to calm him and Doris prayed. In the morning, Doris was in the kitchen preparing breakfast when Howard came in, dressed to go out. He went up to Doris, took her in his arms and called her his daughter. Howard then made coffee for her and asked her to eat breakfast with him. Mabel joined them and the three celebrated his victory over himself. Howard then went out. Doris wrote:

> Later in the afternoon Howard returned, exhausted. His face was leaden and had terrible lines in it. He sent Mabel to ask if I would put my hands on him and perhaps put him to sleep. Oh, would I! I sat beside him with my hands on his head and neck, and I prayed. My whole personality was dissolved in prayer. The prayer had the effect of moisture on a hard crust, it dissolved the shell that encased him. After a time he caught my hand, kissed it, and held it to his cheek.
>
> I sat with him a long time and sometimes he would speak to God, or to me. I did not tell him what a test he had been to me as well as to the others. Yet I blamed myself for having withdrawn from him, my spiritual father, in those dark days. How shallow we were – how selfish and blind.[7]

On 11 January 1932, Howard called Mabel, the McKays and the Obers together. He told them, 'I have come to a turning point in my life and I intend to waste no more time. Perhaps I will go away from you all and not come back.' Mabel had her head back and her eyes closed. Doris said that her heart was 'thumping'. Howard continued, saying, 'I had a letter from Washington. They want me on a two-week teaching stay. Perhaps I will buy only a one-way ticket, trust the Lord, and go about my business.'[8]

The others thought his plan was irrational. With his age, poor health and tenuous finances, it did not make any sense to them. When they told him this, he 'became violently disillusioned with all of us and broke away to his room, shouting over his shoulder that he wished he had not confided in us.' Everything was extremely difficult at that time and the tensions of the house, the lack of work, of money and of a direction had crushed Howard down and he simply wanted to escape. The others were in a misery and that night they called to the Guardian 'to take our prayers to Bahá'u'lláh, the "Remover of Difficulties" and the Healing prayers.'[9]

The next morning, Howard asked to talk with Grace Ober and she told him the truth: 'how everything in the house had had to build itself around his self absorption; how the boys kept out of his way; how Mary at age seventeen was angry with him because he treated her like a tiresome child; how we deprived ourselves of food to give special luxuries.' It was shock treatment – but it worked. The change was almost immediate, 'a healing from on high. He came back to his loving friends. He won the boys. He apologized to Mary. He let us play the radio at dinner.' A week later, he left for his two-week teaching trip in Washington DC with a new understanding of himself. He told the others that 'never before had he met himself face-to-face in just this way.'[10]

Later in the spring, Doris was able to write that Howard is 'bubbling over with zeal. His personality is flooded with power from on high. After the events of last winter, he is a miracle confirmed.'[11] Howard's suffering had been traumatic for everyone, but the following years became the most productive ones of his life in service to the Cause.

11
Early 1932

A proposal to the National Spiritual Assembly

On 28 January 1932, Howard and Mabel made a proposal to the National Spiritual Assembly to achieve what they thought were goals from the Guardian's letter of 21 March 1930, entitled 'The World Order of Bahá'u'lláh, Further Considerations'.

> The plan, . . . as a corollary to the New Plan of Unified Action, is proposed with the utmost humility, and with perfect willingness to lay it aside if not considered wise by your body after consultation and prayer. Only the present extreme need, as manifested by world conditions, for conforming to the wishes of the Guardian; and the fact that this servant was indirectly responsible for the adoption of the Plan for Unified Action in the first place, having proposed its broad lines at the Green Acre Convention in 1925, gives him courage to hope that the inspiration of the Holy Spirit may be the source of the present suggestion. . .
>
> The letter of Shoghi Effendi dated March 21st, 1930, and published under the title of 'The World Order of Bahá'u'llah, Further Considerations'; reinforced by the rapid succession of shattering world events within the last few months; and still further reinforced by the majestic and authoritative letter just issued under the title 'The Goal of a New World Order,' – all indicate, too clearly for any but the most superficial minds to neglect, a rapid disintegration of world civilization as we have known it. Judging by what has happened during the past two years this means a reduction of all income and means of subsistence to a much lower standard than even now is forced upon us.[1]

The Guardian's letter described the collapse of the old world order and Howard felt a sense of urgency. The National Spiritual Assembly had adopted the Plan of Unified Action and Howard was offering what he thought was a practical way to actually win that urgent goal. The Plan of Unified Action had been developed by the National Spiritual Assembly to spread the Faith across the continent and to raise funds for the completion of the first unit of the Mashriqu'l-Adhkár. ('Dawning place of the remembrance of God', a Bahá'í House of Worship).[2] What the Ives put before the National Spiritual Assembly was a plan to cover the necessary costs of teaching and construction.

This plan summed up all the necessary expenses, which they estimated as $375,000 for the Mashriqu'l-Adhkár and $17,500 for operating expenses for the National Spiritual Assembly. Their plan consisted of five points:

1) That the N.S.A. . . . set the example to the believers by declaring that since the completion of the Temple is of such paramount importance, the usual annual convention will be omitted this year, and suggesting that the believers donate the sum thus saved to the Temple Fund.
2) That the N.S.A. appropriate the amount which has heretofore been appropriated for convention expense to the furthering of the above six months plan.
3) That a duly authorized representative of the N.S.A. visit every Assembly in the United States and Canada to acquaint the believers with all the details of the plan; informing them of the great and immediate need; suggesting ways and means by which the efforts might be directed to the successful completion of their quota, and in a general way act as a loving friend and counselor.
4) That the Sec'y. of the N.S.A. be directed to send to each Assembly a letter outlining the above plan, recommending it to the prayerful consideration of the friends and preparing them for the visit of their representative.
5) The sending to each Assembly a regular report of the

progress of the Fund, preferably at short intervals. Thus keeping alive the interest and enthusiasm of the friends.[3]

To achieve the financial goal, they proposed that 1,586 dedicated Bahá'ís contribute $300 each to meet it. The National Spiritual Assembly, however, did not think that his plan was 'advisable as there were several other plans proposed and they thought it better to stick to the original New Unified Plan.'[4]

Meeting Senator Borah

On 30 January 1932 Howard had an interview with Senator William Borah, a Republican politician who was then the Chairman of the Foreign Relations Committee. Howard called the interview 'very interesting'. His first question to the Senator was, 'We would like to have your opinion on the present world conditions. What hope do you see of a successful termination to the Disarmament Conference to be held in Geneva, opening next week?' The Senator replied that 'What our people want and need and what all the world needs is economic stability; harmonious commercial relations; the revival of trade and commerce. For myself, I am perfectly willing, when I see a program which to me seems to insure economic rehabilitation of the world, I shall be perfectly willing to use the debts as a part of our program.'[5]

The Senator strongly condemned the treaty that had ended the First World War, stating:

> the Treaty of Versailles was not a *Peace Treaty* at all, but was really a document which perpetuated the envy, rivalry and hatred which was the cause of the war in the first place. Not until that Treaty is revised or discarded in favor of some just and equitable international agreement can we hope for a durable Peace in the world.
>
> Another reason for the many smoldering fires in world affairs is the perpetual economic unrest due to the unstable condition created and kept alive by the reparations and war-debt questions. We are, of course, justly entitled to the

payment of the war debts. But we are far more interested, in my judgement, in the economic recovery of the world and escape from this awful depression.⁶

Senator Borah was strongly against the use of force in any case, even when all the nations of the world might arise to subdue any unjust or warring nation. When Howard spoke about Bahá'u'lláh's plan for a world government with an international army and navy, Borah was dismissive:

> I am assuming now that you are talking of a world government, a government which brings under its control and direction all peoples. If it were possible to do a thing of that kind, we would have a wholly different situation from what we have now. But when you speak of an international army and fleet to bring into submission a recalcitrant nation, you are still dealing with different nations, and so long as you have different nations, I do not believe that force can be made effective as a peace measure. The moment you employ force against a sovereign you have war.⁷

Baltimore, Maryland

Howard headed for Baltimore on 4 February and sent Mabel a suggestion for the National Teaching Committee. His idea was that he would 'travel throughout the country teaching and lecturing on the Cause with especial reference to the Temple'. He had been offered slides of the Temple and could aim his lectures at 'popular audiences'. Howard wrote that 'A very great service could be rendered, God willing. And I could interview prominent men all over the country at same time.'⁸ This did not come to pass.

In a short preliminary trip to Baltimore, Howard spoke to a group of 15 at the home of Charles and Mrs Mann. Half of the group were young of the 'enkindled, energetic modern Bahai types, including the four Mann children, whose ages were 18 to 28 [Grace, Amelia, Jessie and Roland]. We had a wonderful meeting, really. Eyes enkindled; hearts aglow; love shining . . .' Howard kept trying to close the meeting, but Grace Mann told him that 'Some people [want] you just to be in the same room with them. I feel as tho I could stay here all night.' When he finally did leave, Mrs Mann gave him a sum of money that he initially thought was to cover his expenses, which he felt comfortable accepting. But when he discovered that she had given him a whopping $16, he tried to return it, saying that he could accept money for expenses only and not as a gift. Mrs Mann said, 'but this *is* for your expenses part and [for expenses] to come in the Cause of God'. She hadn't known that Howard had used his last dollar bill to buy his train ticket to Baltimore.[9]

Howard consulted with the Mann family the next day on how to begin to form a Local Spiritual Assembly and said that he would continue to visit Baltimore and give lectures and study classes. When this idea was presented, Grace exclaimed, 'Opportunity is knocking at our door.' Howard promised to return on 6 February.[10]

The Baltimore Bahá'ís officially invited Howard to come to the city 'for an indefinite period, as long as I could stay, at least two or three months', They would take care of his expenses.[11] So, on 8 February, Howard left Washington for Baltimore. He found a 'lovely room, ground floor' with a private bath and a big desk. It also had a large parlor where he could meet guests and hold meetings.[12]

Things didn't always go smoothly when teaching the Cause. A member of one of Howard's study groups told some of her friends about what she had learned and was accused of 'teaching a new religion, a Persian cult'. She was worried because someone had said that 'she ought to be run out of town if she were teaching a new religion.' Eve (Nicklin?) explained that the Bahá'í Faith was not a new religion or a cult, then gave her some of the principles and a short history of Bahá'u'lláh.[13]

During this time, Howard was, as usual, down to his last pennies. In his daily letter to Mabel, he wrote that 'I am not producing financially these days and I feel that the clothing and food that are absolutely necessary Abdul Baha will provide if I keep my heart and soul constantly at the Holy Threshold.'[14] In another letter, he noted that

> Mrs Thompson is going to darn my socks and put new cuffs on my shirts . . . I am living within a rigid budget which allows me . . . eighty cents a day for food and an outside limit of $2.00 weekly for clothing repair and all incidentals. When you think that the trolley fares are 10¢ and that I have to ride a lot in seeing people, and I ought to make lots of contacts, of course, you will see that I don't have much to spend on getting hats cleaned [which Mabel was planning to do]. Another item of expense that I cannot neglect is keeping the two colored boys doing janitor and elevator service happy with tips.[15]

Mabel, teaching in New Castle, had written to the Guardian in January, in a letter not now available, and received a reply written on his behalf on 18 February.

> Even though he does not often hear from you and Mr. Ives, through indirect channels he hears of your services and the great sacrifices you make in spreading the Faith. Your success should be a constant source of gratification and pleasure, especially in these days when we see around us nothing but physical suffering and economic stress. In his moments of prayer and meditation he will think of you and ask God to guide and assist you.
>
> There are wonderful chances of service before the friends in America, if only they do not let them slip away. Through the great crisis that is now sweeping over the world, men are becoming more and more conscious of the futility of a purely material civilization and gradually turning their attention to God and what is eternal and abiding. Should at this turning of the way the Bahá'ís be ready to spread the Message and diffuse its spirit, large numbers will enter our ranks and find the realization of their spiritual longings in our precepts.
>
> Shoghi Effendi hopes that your efforts at New Castle

will prove successful and a new centre be established. He is especially glad that group is constantly visited by different Bahá'ís and their interest in the study of the teachings kept up.[16]

Shoghi Effendi added his personal note at the bottom of the letter: 'With the assurance of my deepest appreciation of your many and continued services to the Faith, and of my constant prayers for your welfare and spiritual advancement. Your true brother, Shoghi.'

By 20 February, Howard was planning his trip back to visit Mabel, who was having more health problems. She wanted him to take the train, but he said he couldn't afford it and that the bus was less than half the price:

I shall not spend one cent unnecessarily upon myself: and by 'unnecessarily' I mean that I shall for six months do my durndest to live as though I did not have a dollar to my name. As a matter of fact I have not. All the money I have, and all that you have, (since we are spiritually ONE) belongs to God, to Baha'u'llah and His Cause and Kingdom. If I spend any of this I am directly responsible to Him for an accounting. Since I have been away from Pgh. [Pittsburgh] I have not spent a cent on myself except four collars which I sadly needed and which I got at half-price at a sale. No soft drinks, no movies, no magazines, no car-fares where I could possibly walk, no expensive foods, no restaurant fare, in fact nothing at all that has not passed the judgement bar of Abdul Baha's consent. You see I am really forced to this position by the logic of my letter to the N.S.A. Whatever you may do with the money you earn is your own affair, but if I use any of it for my own gratification, no matter how specious may be the rationalism with which the 'Satan of Self' presents the argument, I am surely recreant to the high Trust reposed in me by God and He will surely withdraw His support from me . . .[17]

Howard took the bus to New Castle, Pennsylvania, to collect Mabel and together they went to Pittsburgh on about 25 February for a week. He noted that things were starting well in Pittsburgh and that attendance at his talks was increasing.[18] Howard and Mabel spent ten days in Pittsburgh working for the Faith, then he returned to Baltimore and she to New Castle.

Howard attended a meeting of a group who worked with the Black people in Baltimore. The meeting was held at the Urban League and was attended by a dozen people, including two Black ministers. Howard was warmly welcomed and asked to speak for five minutes. He did so and stopped when the time was up. The host, Mrs Mason, then said he could have another five minutes. Ultimately, Howard spoke for 45 minutes and the two Black ministers urged him to attend a 'colored minister's conference' the next week.[19]

Howard faced some serious opposition when he called on one woman who was interested in the Faith. Her husband was 'violently opposed' to it. He told Howard that he 'did not know anything about it and DID NOT WANT TO KNOW either'. Howard suggested that they would only talk about things that the husband would be interested in and when his wife was free, she and he would talk about things that she was interested in. 'At this he flew up in the air again and said: "Look here, don't you come around here in my absence and try to influence my wife" . . . When I left he put his hand on my shoulder and said: "I like you personally, Mr. Ives, but I would like you a lot more if you were a Christian."' His wife still attended Howard's meetings.[20]

Howard spoke to 150 men at the Kiwanis Luncheon Talk on 10 March. The chairman knew and admired Roy Wilhelm, a very well known Bahá'í, so gave Howard a 'personal and friendly' introduction. The audience consisted of 'hard-boiled businessmen' and Howard was surprised at the level of interest they had. In a letter to Mabel, he wrote that 'It is easy to be courageous when whipped up by an enthusiasm that overrides personal timidity . . . But to maintain a calm, judicial, simple and humble bearing and at the same time say quietly the most startling things, the most penetrating and comprehensive utterances, this is a divine art.' That evening, he spoke to the YMCA Forum. The Chairman told him that he should not try to 'forward any movement' and Howard agreed. He spoke on the 'Challenge of Present Crisis to our Social, Economic and Relig. Institutions.' He talked for 35 minutes, then 'there were a rapid-fire lot of questions which brought out the whole Message'.[21]

In mid-March, Howard wrote to Mabel saying that he really needed her there in Baltimore. He particularly needed what had become her greatest skills, 'how to approach groups and individuals, the contacts you are able to make which I cannot, though I might assist in following them up after you have opened the way; your ability in teaching a certain phase of the Cause so much better than I can . . . All this has demonstrated how important it is for us to stick together.' At that time, Mabel was packing up to move from the 'Tilbury Tenement' where they had been living with Harlan and Grace Ober, but the Obers were moving, so Mabel was getting ready to find another place.[22]

Louis Gregory was in Baltimore for two days in the middle of the month. He talked to a group in Howard's room that was so large that it taxed its capacity. Nineteen were present and Howard called it a 'wonderful session'. One Black Baptist minister was very excited after Louis finished speaking that he 'practically acknowledged his belief in the Message.'[23]

Howard returned to Washington DC for an overnight stay about 20 March. At his evening talk, there was a large crowd. The biggest thing in his letter to Mabel, however, was about her coming to Baltimore. He wrote: 'Do you realize that we shall be together alone and unhampered for the first time since we were in Glenn Falls a year ago last fall? Ever since then we have either been separated, or you ill, or someone else always hanging around. Now we can get acquainted all over again.'[24] Mabel arrived in Baltimore on 26 March and stayed until 7 April.

Howard was back in Washington on 11 April to interview Kansas Senator Arthur Capper: 'He was a delightful man to talk with. I sensed a real spiritual quality in him that I did not meet in either of the other two interviewed. I wrote him just now sending him "Goal of New W[orld] O[rder]" and Horace Holley's "World Economy of Baha'u'llah'. He seemed much pleased when I offered to send him some more information.'[25]

12
Howard's Weekly 'Hakouk' Letters January–March 1932

During this time Howard was, as usual, financially strapped, and in one letter he debated whether to get a haircut or send the money to the Guardian. The 'Hakouk', or as it is now written, Ḥuqúqu'lláh, was a law of Bahá'u'lláh and mostly unknown in the West at this time. Howard had read an early, unauthenticated translation of the Kitáb-i-Aqdas done by an individual Bahá'í and wanted to follow its stipulations, though the translation gave him no real concept of what Ḥuqúqu'lláh actually was. In reality, the law of Ḥuqúqu'lláh, or the Right of God, is a payment described by Bahá'u'lláh as a 'spiritual obligation and bounty'. It is based on a percentage of whatever excess a believer might have after all necessary expenses. He also writes that 'the acceptance of the offerings made dependeth on the spirit of joy, fellowship and contentment that the righteous souls who fulfil this injunction will manifest. If such is the attitude acceptance is permissible, and not otherwise.' Howard understood it to mean that it required an even greater sacrifice than giving to the Bahá'í fund, which he assured the Guardian that he was continuing to do, while he paid 'Hakouk' out of even greater sacrifices from his meagre resources.

Beginning on 29 January 1932, Howard began a series of weekly letters to the Guardian, writing a total of nine letters. In response, he received four letters back from Shoghi Effendi. This represents a unique conversation between a devoted soul and the Head of the Faith. Howard had two reasons for sending his letters: to renew his consecration to the Faith and renunciation of material things, and to contribute small amounts to what he called 'Hakouk'. In his first letter, Howard wrote: 'Now

I feel that I must write, for I am strongly impelled to utter to you the renewed consecration of heart, soul, spirit and body that has taken possession of me within the last few weeks, and which has been infinitely strengthened and reinforced by the wonderful letter from you which has just been issued by the N.S.A' [The Goal of a New World Order].[1]

This theme continues through all of the letters:

> 5 February 1932 – May this servant again request the prayers of the Guardian at the Holy Tombs that the rest of my life on earth may be absolutely and wholly devoted to the Cause of God?

> 12 February 1932 – In humble expectation of the Supreme confirmations of the Holy Spirit . . .

> 19 February 1932 – Humbly but with all the sincerity this servant is capable of . . .

> 26 February 1932 – This slight offering, symbolizing as it does the sincere dedication of my spirit and life to thy service, has been a great comfort and confirmation to this heart.

> 4 March 1932 – With my head at the Holy Threshold this servant humbly supplicates that his whole being may be sacrificed to the Kingdom of Abhá upon this earth, and that he may be so blessed as to be acceptable in the army of the Lord of Hosts of which thou art the Leader and Commander. May my life be a sacrifice to Thy Command!

> 18 March 1932 – Would that my words could convey the feelings with which I write the above. The majestic meaning of 'The Guardian' grows upon this servant day by day. 'The Dawn Breakers' has just come to me this morning and, truly a New Dawn is coming to my spirit. Praise be to God!
> . . .
> My head is at the Holy Threshold and I seek only thy

heavenly Will and good pleasure. I supplicate that I may be confirmed in the utmost state of absolute steadfastness, to such a degree that not for one moment may my efforts falter in the great task to which the guardian has called the servants.[2]

Howard's first 'Hakouk' letter to the Guardian was a news-filled one written on 29 January, outlining their activities for the previous years:

> Beloved Guardian of the Cause of God; Leader and Director of armies of the Lord of Hosts and repository of our Love for God . . .
>
> Some months ago, before we left New Castle, Pa., where my wife and I spent the Summer, we began a letter to thee, attempting to make an exhaustive report of our activities in the Cause since we wrote you from Binghamton, N.Y. some two or three years ago. (I am ashamed to think how long it has been.) But my health has been far from good, and at the time of that writing it was very difficult for me to concentrate on details, so the letter was never finished . . .
>
> This servant is having the high privilege of serving in Washington, D.C. for two weeks, and we have been addressing meetings every day, sometimes twice a day, and having many wonderful interviews with attracted souls. This has been made possible by the loving cooperation of our dear and blessed friends in God, Harlan and Grace Ober. On Oct. 3rd last we moved to Pittsburgh and into the same household where already Willard and Doris McKay, our spiritual children from Geneva, N.Y., had made their home. So that now we three families totaling nine souls, are cooperating in a miniature Bahá'í community.
>
> Owing to this great economy in living expenses my services as bread winner can more easily be dispensed with, and in consultation with the whole group it has been decided that this servant shall be released from all such responsibilities and may devote all of his time to the spreading of

the Cause of God. You may imagine with what joy I have accepted this great trust.

May I supplicate again that your prayers may be raised at the Holy Shrines that means may be provided so that this servant may travel thru-out the country, if it be God's will, bringing to the friends of God renewed consecration in the Field of Sacrifice to the completion of the Temple Fund, and spreading the knowledge of the Great Plan of the World Order of Bahá'u'lláh to all parts of the country... I am entirely submissive to the Will of Bahá'u'lláh and desire only that wherever I may be every breath may be inspired by the Breaths of the Holy Spirit, and that the dedication of every moment remaining to me in this life may not falter for one instant.

Since writing you from Binghamton, N.Y., where there is now a flourishing and active Assembly of about thirty-five confirmed souls and new members being confirmed almost weekly, we have been working principally in Hartford, [Connecticut], and New Castle, Pa. [Pennsylvania]. In the former city there is now a confirmed group ready for the formation of an Assembly. In New Castle there is a wonderful group of deeply attracted souls about ten or twelve of whom are either confirmed or very deeply attracted...

The other soul is Eve Nicklin. She is a Deaconess in the M.E. Deaconess Home, at New Castle, Pa. She is a very wonderful soul, as is demonstrated by the fact that her position in an extremely orthodox institution has been no barrier to her spiritual sight. She says: 'At last I have found the Goal of my heart's desire.' She has given her whole heart to Bahá'u'lláh and both she and Miss Drury have joined the Pittsburgh Assembly as non-resident members. New Castle is not very far distant from [Pittsburgh].[3]

Eve Nicklin later became a long-time pioneer in South America. The Guardian's reply, as written by Ruhi Afnan, was that

Shoghi Effendi wishes me to acknowledge the receipt of

your letter dated January 29th 1932. He was very glad to hear that circumstances are favouring your travelling for the benefit of the Cause. You should be very thankful to those who have made it possible for you to enjoy this great privilege and blessing. For what blessing is greater than meeting the friends and spreading the message throughout the world. Many long for it but only few find the way before them clear and easy.

In his moments of prayer, Shoghi Effendi will think of you and ask God to guide you and assist you in carrying through your plans of service. How deeply pleased he becomes when he hears that a new competent soul has dedicated his life to the spread of the teachings. We need such men, we long to see them arise and respond to the call.

In his own hand, Shoghi Effendi wrote:

My dear and precious co-worker:
I am greatly pleased and heartened to learn of your splendid record of service and of your unwavering determination to persevere and extend the scope of your notable activities. I will assuredly remember you in my prayers at the holy Shrine and wish to assure you of my heartfelt appreciation of the spirit of self-sacrifice that animates you in your work. Persevere and rest assured that the hosts of the Supreme Concourse will reinforce and assist you to achieve your heart's desire. Your true brother, Shoghi[4]

In his second weekly letter of 5 February, Howard wrote to the Guardian about his activities and an interview of he had had with Senator Borah, Chairman of the Foreign Relations Committee:

My fourteen days of service in this city closes tonight. We have held twenty-one meetings here and in Baltimore, and had twelve more or less important personal interviews relating to the Cause: one of those was with Senator Borah, U.S.

Senator from Idaho. This interview is to appear in the Feb'y number of the Bahá'í Magazine.

The Baltimore believers have requested that this servant spend a few weeks in that city, endeavoring to strengthen and enlarge the work being done so faithfully, and under such discouraging circumstances, by the self-sacrificing and illumined believers there. We are supplicating that only the Will of the Master may be done.[5]

The Guardian's reply, in a letter written on his behalf, was that

Shoghi Effendi was very glad to hear of your interview with Senator Borah. How wonderful it would be if these people who are guiding the affairs of the nations and shaping the future of the world could be imbued with the spirit of the Cause. Even though they do not fully accept the teachings, they could put the principles of the Faith into practice and hasten the inauguration of the era of peace into the world. The friends should pick such ones among them who promise to be receptive and introduce them to the spirit and teachings of the movement. Shoghi Effendi will be waiting eagerly to read your article, reporting your interview, which you say will appear in the Bahá'í Magazine.

In his moments of prayer at the Blessed Shrines, Shoghi Effendi will think of you and ask God to guide and assist you in carrying through your programme of service. May God bless your work and make you a perfect channel for the diffusion of His spirit.[6]

Howard's interview with Senator Borah has been described in Chapter 11. His next letter to Shoghi Effendi was sent on 12 February from Baltimore. Howard wrote:

You will be interested to know that I was requested to leave my first rooming place because of my Bahá'í faith. The landlady was good enough to say that she liked me personally but she would consider herself a traitor to the religion of

Christ if she harbored me beneath her roof. We had a most interesting conversation with the dear soul, who was at least sincere and courageous, for she sadly needed the rental I was paying her. I think she will long remember our conversation.

I have secured a much more desirable place and last night the friends held their first meeting here.[7]

Howard's stay at his new place was also short-lived. On the 10th, his new landlady came and 'very positively informed me that she was greatly opposed to the Bahai work – anti-Christ, etc. She is a fundamentalist thru and thru. Well, it was a remarkable interview. She said lots of nice things about me personally, but feared I would be eternally lost unless I repented. She did most of the talking while I did the smiling.'[8]

On 19 February, Howard sent his next weekly letter to Shoghi Effendi. It was newsy:

We held our first meeting of the weekly study class last Tuesday evening. The Young People's Group is in process of formation. Its first meeting will be held, God Willing, about March 4th. Contacts have been made in the past week with many important centers of influence. Among them are, 'The Urban League,' colored and white folk working together for better conditions. A large group of young people holding weekly meetings Sunday mornings to discuss 'The Sore Spots of Civilization.' This is under the auspices of one of the largest churches here. I have submitted a list of the subjects I speak on and shall attend their meeting Sunday. Also have been asked to speak before a small group meeting weekly at the office of one of the prominent physicians here, who is a very liberal and philanthropic soul, Dr Donald Hooker. Also have visited Morgan College, a colored educational institution. Had luncheon with the Dean of the College there today. He is to have me out there to address the whole student body, over 500, early in March, or the first open date possible.[9]

The Guardian's reply to Howard, written by his secretary, praised his efforts and gave him guidance about teaching, though it did not mention his accommodation problems:

> Shoghi Effendi wishes me to acknowledge the receipt of your letters dated respectively February 12th and 19th 1932, and to express his deep appreciation for the wonderful services you are rendering to the spread of the spirit and teachings of the Faith. In his moments of prayer at the Shrines he will remember you and ask God to guide and assist you in this noble work you have so earnestly undertaken. He trusts that through the Master's loving guidance and your persistent and sacrificial endeavours many souls will be attracted to the Cause and find in its divine precepts the hopes and ideals they have always sought and longed for. Your past achievements along such lines of service have been remarkable and Shoghi Effendi hopes that in the future they may be even more arresting and wonderful.
>
> It is surely always better for a teacher to stay in a town for two or three months and continue his work until a definite group is brought together and made to embrace the Faith. To just deliver few lectures and make few contacts would not be, so experience has taught us, of any appreciable value.

The Guardian's personal note at the end of the letter read: 'May the Beloved guide your unsparing efforts, and sustain you in extending the scope of your invaluable and exemplary activities in the service of this sacred Cause. Your true brother, Shoghi.'[10]

In his 19 February letter, Howard noted that he had asked the Guardian for a prayer for Baltimore, adding that he had compiled a prayer for the believers to use. For a former Christian minister, composing prayers was a normal activity. Shoghi Effendi, however, responded:

> Concerning that prayer you have compiled for the friends in Baltimore: Shoghi Effendi does not consider such a

method advisable, for supposing every city were to follow such an example, how confusing the prayers would then become. Every prayer that Bahá'u'lláh revealed outwardly was in honour of a certain person but in reality was meant for all the world, for every single soul both living and to be born. All the prayers of the Báb, Bahá'u'lláh and 'Abdu'l-Bahá therefore apply to and could be read by the friends in Baltimore. Why therefore compile a new one? Would the name of Baltimore mentioned there make such a difference when all provinciality is to be demolished?[11]

When Howard wrote to the Guardian on 26 February, he mentioned his daily study of the Guardian's newly received letter to the American Bahá'í community, "The Goal of a New World Order":

It has been forcibly impressed upon this servant in the last few weeks of service in Washington and Baltimore that the emphasis in our public teaching work should be laid with increasing force upon 'The New World Order.' It seems very apparent that this civilization is preparing its own funeral pyre, and that the duty of the Bahá'ís is to prepare the foundations of the New Order as expeditiously and as firmly as possible. I am studying daily your great State Paper of the New Order and upon it base all my utterances.[12]

He also described his work in Baltimore, focusing on the Black population and the racial prejudice in the city:

The situation in Baltimore as regards Race Prejudice and the whole status of the colored people is very critical. In some respects the prejudice there is worse than in any other city in the country. The largest and best department stores absolutely refuse to wait upon colored people, and publicly state that they are not wanted within their doors. On every hand they are publicly insulted and ill-treated. On the other hand I have met in that city some of the noblest, best educated and cultured people of this race, or any other race whom I have ever met. Especially would I mention the family of Dr. and Mrs. Joe. Mason, who with their four lovely daughters I had the privilege of spending last Sunday evening with [sic]. We talked of the Cause for over two hours: then they kept me to supper. It was a most beautiful and worthwhile contact. And this is only one of several great experiences with these dear people. Last Saturday I attended a Luncheon of the 'Cooperative Women's League', a colored organization. There were over 300 present, most of them colored folk. I spent four hours with them. A more charming, cultured, friendly and attractive group it has never been my fortune to be with. Please pray for these dear people in Baltimore, and that this servant may be confirmed to bring the solace to their souls that only the Cause of God can bring.[13]

Looking over their rather chaotic life, Howard and Mabel had decided that it would be better if only one of them worked full time for the Faith. Through consultation, they decided it would be Howard. On 4 March 1932, In his sixth weekly letter to the Guardian on 4 March, Howard wrote:

Ever since my wife and I determined that one of us should give all our time to the service of the Cause, and it was thought best that I should be that one for the present, our material affairs have been ever so much better . . .

In his letter, Howard said that he had spent ten days in Pittsburgh with Mabel, who had been there for four months. He said that she 'has been able to do in the last month as much as we both accomplished together in the previous three months'. Howard himself was beginning a ten-week period of 'intense and concentrated work in the Cause' in Baltimore. The friends, he wrote, were 'supporting the work with great zeal and love', and that they were 'depending greatly upon thy prayers at the Holy Tombs in our behalf'.[14]

I hope you do not object to my speaking of these things. It is only because I want you to know that your prayers and the promises of our Master have been answered and fulfilled . . .

Especially I am earnestly desirous of making the influence of the Cause felt amongst the colored population of the city. I am endeavoring to make many influential contacts with representative members of that race. Some have already planned to attend our Bahá'í meetings. This, I believe, has never happened in this city, although in Washington, which is only a few miles away, there are many confirmed Bahá'ís among the Negros.[15]

Howard's weekly letter on 11 March informed the Guardian of this work with the Black community:

So much has happened in the work for the Cause here since I wrote that letter that it seems incredible that it is such a brief passage of time.

Sunday next, Mar. 13th, we hold our first public meeting and the interest is growing every day. Especially is this true in my work among the colored people. Very fine contacts with these friends are being made. I have been invited to attend and speak before the weekly conference of colored ministers next Monday. The clergy of that race are not nearly so prejudiced as their white brothers of the cloth.

I spoke before the Public Forum at the white Y.M.C.A. last Thursday and had a most friendly and appreciative reception. Also spoke at the colored Forum last Sunday with like result. These lead to many more and wider openings.

I am overwhelmed with thankfulness. Surely thy prayers at the Holy Shrines are drawing the heavenly confirmations. Your assurances that they will continue to descend are most encouraging.[16]

Howard's eighth weekly letter to the Guardian on 18 March told of his gratitude for his prayers and support and of Louis

Gregory's visit. Louis was in Baltimore for two days in the middle of the month and talked to a group in Howard's room.[17] Howard wrote:

> You will be glad to hear that our dear brother Lewis [sic] Gregory has been with us here in Baltimore. He spoke to quite a large group in my apartment last Wednesday [evening], and there were present six of the finest, most influential and spiritual colored people in the city. One of them was a young minister, still without a charge. He had only heard of the Message a few days before when this servant spoke before a colored ministers Baptist conference for about five minutes. But in those few minutes I read the wonderful "Exhortation" of 'Abdu'l-Bahá, and these Divine Words evidently attracted his soul. At this meeting when Lewis spoke this young man practically accepted the Cause, and his words had all the fire and fervor of a true believer. All present were deeply moved, and the impression on the other newly attracted souls was very deep.
>
> If it were not lest I weary you I could relate many other most inspiring events happening daily in this city. Suffice it to say that thy prayers at the Holy Shrine are being answered and the confirmations of His Holiness Bahá'u'lláh are descending upon the devoted group who for so many years have been steadfastly upholding the Cause of God under great discouragements in this city. We thank God for this great bounty.[18]

In his ninth 'Hakouk' letter to the Guardian, Howard described his interview another high-ranking politician, Secretary of the Interior Roy Wilbur:

> It has been a most confirming experience for this servant and it is his hope that it has not been unacceptable at the Holy Threshold. It has always seemed that such slight services as we have been able to render could not be interesting to you, except in the knowledge that we are striving

to spread the Divine Message to the best of our ability. To write you often seemed like an additional tax upon your already overburdened time and strength. It has been a joy to write and a greater joy to receive the heavenly letters from that Holy Spot.

Last Monday I had the opportunity of talking for a half hour with the Hon. Roy Lyman Wilbur, the Secretary of the Interior in President Hoover's Cabinet. This interview was arranged for me by Allen McDaniel and an account of it will appear in the April number of the Bahá'í Magazine . . .

I found Mr. Wilbur most receptive. He had heard of the Bahá'í Movement but had no realization of its scope and world-wide purpose. I gave him Horace Holley's late publication 'The Bahá'í Movement' and a copy of your last letter, 'The Goal of a New World Order.' He promised to read them, especially the latter, which I told him I considered the first World Paper of the New Era. Mr. Wilbur is a very broad-minded, fine spirited gentleman and I am praying most earnestly that his mind may be more and more receptive to the great illumination.[19]

In his response, the Guardian's secretary acknowledged Howard's 'Hakouk' contributions: 'He knows how much sacrifice such contributions entail and he is sure it is fully appreciated in the sight of God. It is not the amount donated but the spirit with which it is donated that counts in the sight of God.' He then wrote about the world situation and Howard's interview with Mr Wilbur, encouraging him to take advantage of every such opportunity, while guiding him about how to avoid getting entangled in politics:

The report of your services brought great pleasure to Shoghi Effendi. He sincerely hopes that the spirit of Bahá'u'lláh will guide you and enable you to confirm many souls in the Faith. Present world problems and general suffering have undoubtedly awakened many souls to the significance of the spiritual life and forced them to consider the things of the world in their proper value and not with exaggerated importance. They are seeking therefore for some movement that will answer their need and satisfy their craving. Such being the case, it is time for the friends to arise and, remembering the provisions of the last Will and Testament of the Master, teach the Cause throughout the world. Thank God the number of those participating in teaching activities is daily increasing and achieving great success.

Shoghi Effendi fully approves your meeting of important men who are in power and have the reins of government in their hands. In fact he would urge you to avail yourself of every such opportunity that presents itself. But you should be very careful not to discuss matters that are political and that are points of contention between the different parties. That would drag the Cause into political affairs, a thing which was strictly forbidden by the Master. Your concern in meeting such people should be to familiarize them with the teachings of the Cause and imbue them with the spirit of the movement. Should such men embrace the movement they would lead with themselves thousands of others into the Cause.

In his general letter Shoghi Effendi has not glorified war. Far from it, he absolutely condemns it. When he says "upon the consummation of this colossal, this unspeakably glorious enterprise" he means the unification of the world and the attainment of the goal created by Bahá'u'lláh for our warring and divided humanity. Shoghi Effendi hopes you will make this point very clear. We should consider the war as the inevitable evil rather than a good.

In his moments of prayer at the Shrines Shoghi Effendi will think of you and ask God to guide and assist you in this wonderful service you are rendering to His Cause. He trusts that every single soul you meet and to whom you deliver the message would gradually embrace the Faith, and then become your spiritual child. Please extend Shoghi Effendi's greetings to Mrs. Ives. He hopes that she also will render many distinguished services to our beloved Faith.

In the Guardian's personal note at the bottom of the letter, he wrote:

> Dear and valued co-worker,
> I was so pleased to learn of your interviews with men of eminence and authority whose knowledge of the Cause is not only fragmentary but superficial and defective. It is our supreme obligation to endeavour to bring the knowledge of this Revelation to the highest authorities and the leading personalities among our countrymen, but to refrain from associating ourselves or identifying our Faith with their political pursuits, their conflicting ambitions and party programmes. May the Almighty guide and sustain your high endeavours, and enable you to win for His Cause the most capable, the most virtuous and the most enlightened leaders of public opinion in that land.
> Your true brother, Shoghi[20]

13

Travel Teaching and a Boarding House 1932–1935

Challenges in Ohio: Why didn't we know this before?

The National Teaching Committee asked Mabel to work in southern Ohio and she arrived in Columbus on 10 April 1932. This was a relatively new community that, unlike most Bahá'í communities at that time, was 'a cross section of society'. It had some serious problems that Mabel tried to help resolve. The Faith had originally been brought to Columbus by a certain woman who had 'unlimited generosity and a truly loving spirit', but who also suffered from 'emotional outbursts and tactless criticisms' due to mental challenges. Combined with the oldest believer in the community, who knew 'the Cause quite well, and is a sincere Bahá'í, but who felt she was the teacher and insisted on monopolizing the meetings', those meetings were fraught with problems. The Bahá'ís spent more time discussing subjects such as numerology and astrology than on teaching the Faith or strengthening the Administrative Order.[1]

Mabel's solution was to meet individually with a number of the Bahá'ís and train them about the Bahá'í Administrative Order, consultation and assembly meetings. Up to that time, the Local Spiritual Assembly had not met 'except for five or ten minutes at the end of a general meeting'. When the group began meeting together again, they planned study meetings, had rotating chairmen, and stressed the importance of coming to meetings prepared. Mabel ensured that everyone present had a chance to contribute to the consultation. The group was amazed at how great a difference real consultation made to the affairs of the community. Over and over, they would say, 'Oh why didn't we know all this before? We could have saved so many mistakes!' At the end of her time in Columbus, Mabel wrote, 'The thing which struck me most forcibly was the real, and almost pathetic, eagerness with which each one reached out to be set straight, and the longing which each seemed to have to help build up an harmonious and smoothly functioning Assembly.'[2]

Mabel's intense activity landed her in hospital on 2 May and she apparently had a minor operation of some sort the very next day. Howard was surprised at how quickly it all happened. There is no indication in their letters of what the problem was.[3]

While Mabel was in Columbus, Howard was still in Baltimore. On 4 May, he met with the Junior Citizens of the World, a group of children. He wrote:

> There were over 25 children there, which was a large proportion of the membership to get together on a school day, for that meant an hour and a half or so taken out of their play time. And it was such a charming lot of young people. My heart just went to them all, and I think they must have felt it. I talked to them about the 'Five Deadly Sins' (prejudices) and illustrated it with several A.B. ['Abdu'l-Bahá] stories and they were really deeply interested and responsive. Hazel [Langrall] just now spoke of my talk and the children's reaction so enthusiastically. She said that her oldest daughter referred to the talks as 'swell', and she said that they all had such an interesting conversation at the dinner table tonight about it all. Hazel is really one of the most sincere and illumined Baha'is I know.[4]

Manchester, New Hampshire

Howard and Mabel planned to spend the summer in Manchester, New Hampshire. Howard finally left Baltimore on 15 May and travelled up to Pittsburgh, where he packed the car 'to the roof' with everything Mabel wanted him to take. The next evening, he had a meeting with 30 Bahá'ís.[5] On the 17th, he drove to Mansfield, Pennsylvania, and Binghamton, New York, then to Geneva, New York the next day.[6]

Howard's goal once he reached Manchester was to find a place to live. He contacted a real estate agent who took him to Pine Island Park to look at what Howard thought would be a good temporary place. He wrote to Mabel that he didn't think it was what they would want when she joined him, though the location was beautiful:

> It is very small, kitchen, one bed-room and a good sized (fair) sleeping porch. No living room, no bath, no running water, must go some little distance to a spring . . . But the situation is lovely. On a small lake, only four miles [6 km] from Manchester, trolley line to the spot, for Pine Island Park is an amusement park, skating rink, roller coaster 'n everythin'.
>
> But the cottage is not at all near all that, I can't hear a sound except sometimes a distant thunder of the roller coaster.
>
> As I sit here now, with my typewriter resting on your stool and me on the steps of the back porch in the sun, I look directly upon a little river about fifty feet distant, which runs out of the small lake before mentioned. The lake itself [now called Pine Island Pond] is also visible to my left about 300 feet distant. The cottage is one of quite a number of similar ones, all placed pretty close together, which is another reason why it will not exactly suit us. The neighbors are not of a class, either to be attractive as friends or Baha'i prospects, tho most kindly and friendly. But OH the sun and the sky and the lake and the fresh air are glorious . . .
>
> The discomforts have been ludicrous. I have not minded at all, for the advantages more than made up. Electricity not connected so I went to bed by the light of two candles. Stove pipe disconnected and the electric stove (two plate hot plate) also unusable of course. No sheets or pillow cases but plenty of blankets . . .

> I had for breakfast the juice of three oranges with the yolks of two eggs dropped into it. This is highly recommended by Dr. Kendrick...
>
> Later a neighbor offered me a cup of coffee and some toast which was very acceptable. For my dinner I had a large can of mixed vegetables which the same neighbor kindly heated for me on her stove, some canned grapefruit and some swedish bread, you know the crisp stuff. For supper tonight I shall eat a large part of a head of lettuce which I brought with me last night, another 'pep-cocktail' and more grapefruit.[7]

Mabel left Ohio for Indiana on 23 May and Howard hoped that she would reach Manchester by 1 June. In his letter of 28 May, he wrote: 'Do you realize it has been over 4 months we have been separated with the exception of the 10 days in Balt.'[8] The Ives remained in Manchester for the summer.

Many people were transformed by Howard and Mabel. One of these was John S. McHenry II, who first learned of the Faith from Zia Baghdadi when he bought Zia's house in Wilmette. He was then connected with Howard and Mabel. He often 'expressed his gratitude for having been blessed with such marvelous souls who taught him and [his wife] Elizabeth the Faith'. Howard was his first teacher, instructing him downstairs in the house, while Mabel taught the Faith to a group upstairs.[9]

Howard's boarding house experiment

In June 1933, Howard wrote to the Guardian and described his plan to set up a boarding house in Brocklyn and to try to help men find jobs. The Depression had made many people either homeless or in desperate poverty. He describes what they were trying to do:

> For some time the poverty and suffering of the millions in the great cities has burdened my heart. The Master has laid such stress on serving the poor and the comforts I have

always had begun to be bitter in my mouth. About the first of last March certain events occurred which put the decision fairly up to me whether I had the courage and faith to make the effort and the sacrifice necessary. My decision to make the attempt was unavoidable without great cowardice and faithlessness.

About the 20th of March a thirty-six room house was secured for a very low rental. About this time I spent a night in one of the cheap lodging houses, 'flop houses' they are called. And I experienced myself for one night what so many thousands of men here in N.Y. are undergoing all the time.

. . . I am doing this entirely on my own responsibility. There is no mention of the Baháʼí Cause in connection with it, though, of course, that is the ultimate goal. I am now beginning to talk to the men of 'The New World Order' and building up in their consciousness a spirit of fraternity and cooperation. I will also enclose some clippings from the Brooklyn papers which have several times mentioned my work with approval. The chief executive of the 'Emergency Work and Relief Committee' which has spent upwards of $23,000,000 in the last three years on the relief of the unemployed in N.Y. said to me that this work of mine is on the most constructive lines of any with which he is acquainted.

I have also become interested in quite a large plan to settle a group of destitute families on five acre plots in Southern New Jersey. The land has been secured and we hope to have our first settlers there before fall. We take destitute families, give them a small house, and chicken house, 500 chickens, necessary tools etc. Then we market their product for them and in a year and a half they will own their plot; or at least a half equity in it, paying off the balance in small instalments. It is the same idea on which my work here is being run but on a larger scale and adapted to rural conditions. There is a fair possibility that this may develop into a real Baháʼí Community as my associates seem inclined to receive my ideals sympathetically. Here again my whole being is engrossed with the thought of the Kingdom. I have prayed most earnestly at every step of the way. One reason, perhaps, why I have delayed writing to you was because I did not want to tell you of what I intended to do but wanted to wait until I could report something actually done.[10]

The Guardian's response was very supportive:

> Your long and inspiring message of June 8th, 1933 brought much joy and comfort to our Guardian's heart and he has requested me to convey to you his kindest regards and to assure you of his whole-hearted appreciation of the noble work in which you are so devotedly engaged. The services you are so freely and so generously rendering the poor he highly values as they give you a good opportunity to put into actual practice the social and the humanitarian teachings of the Cause. It is hoped that you will persevere in your endeavours and will gradually widen their scope so as to draw the attention of the public and to enable it to realize the effectiveness and the practicability of the Bahá'í teachings. Yours is a living faith since it expresses itself into fruitful and constructive action, in selfless service to the cause of the poor.
>
> Shoghi Effendi is firmly convinced that the work you have undertaken to achieve constitutes an important medium of teaching the Cause in an indirect and practical way. You can achieve a good deal by following this method of teaching.
>
> Shoghi Effendi will offer his prayers on your behalf and will implore for you God's assistance and blessings . . .[11]

In March, when Howard wrote to Mabel about the boarding house, it was obvious that they were both struggling and suffering the effects of trying to make it work. He wrote:

> My heart is torn when I recall our conversation this evening

because I realize that I should have been far more gentle and considerate. You are really going through a very trying and difficult experience and while I realize that from my standpoint it would seem that you exaggerate some details of the situation without at all understanding others, yet that fact does not make your mental and physical sufferings any less and I should have appreciated this instantly instead of two hours later. I can only ask you to forgive again as your loving, faithful heart has always done.[12]

In spite of the difficulties, Howard soon had several men lined up for his boarding house and was hoping they would sign on the 'dotted line' and stay there. It was the getting them to sign part that was frustrating. But Howard was ever optimistic: 'Even if this plan as a whole proves impractical and if even, the whole thing fails up, which God forbid, even so these two men have felt the touch of the Lord God and inhaled the fragrance of the Immortal Rose Garden.' Howard explained to Mabel how his plan was to work:

> We can see our way reasonably clear to get our 30 men into the house. The only question is how <u>quickly</u>. If I can raise the needed $300 I can do it within two or three weeks. I feel also reasonably sure that as these men come in I can find work for them (with what they can find for themselves . . .) so that they can pay in either service or cash the necessary 1.15 per day to provide their lodging and 3 meals. The returns from these 30 at this rate will be $360 per month from the 40¢ for lodging and about 20¢ a day surplus in their food apiece. Which makes another $180 a month – a total of $540 monthly. This seems incredible but you can figure it up. The rent is $150. Gas, heat, elect. Lt. [lights] and phone average $25 a month and of course there will be other expenses . . .[13]

Mabel told Howard how things were going at the boarding house while he travelled:

Mabel and Howard out for a pleasure cruise, about 1919

Mabel and Howard on the tennis court, about 1920

Mabel and Howard with Dr Albert Heist in about 1924, possibly in Geneva, NY

Bahá'ís of Rochester and Geneva, NY on the McKay farm in Geneva on 19 May 1928. Howard is in the back row at the left; Dr Albert Heist is holding the menorah in the front row, third from right

Willard McKay, Howard and Mabel picking flowers on Emerald Hill in Willard's garden, 1928

The Race Amity Conference in Harlem, New York City, 8 November 1930. Louis Gregory is the tall moustachioed man in the first standing row. Howard is to his left. Also in the photo are Harlan (second right of Louis) and Grace Ober (seated in front of Louis), Reginald and Mary Collison, Doris Holley, Kenneth Christian, Mary Hanford Ford (front row left), Ali Kuli Khan (front row), Mela Bechtold and Harvey Burley, a noted singer and composer

> All the men were working Saturday. One steady job secured at $10 per mo. 9 hours a day. A large job in a foundry using 3 men for 2 weeks at $3.00 per day a piece is starting tomorrow. Several of these big things in the offing. More furniture coming in . . . Probably a radio and much also to tell but which will keep till your return – a probable (practically arrived) donation of a hundred lbs of coffee, sugar . . . meat from another mail; soap from a manufacturer and Mr. F. thinks he can get good suits of clothes for the men.[14]

Howard's idea was that if this worked, Mabel would be able to spend the summer at Green Acre for a thorough rest. In mid-May, Mabel was in Brooklyn and wrote that she was

> enjoying the lovely rock garden and pool – and feel much better already. I slipped over to N.Y.C. this a.m. and made a sale (for Yonkers Chapter). N.Y.C. and Newark are off. How would you like to have me help you sell the Farm Plan for a few weeks? I could be one of your sales force . . . I had a lovely afternoon and evening with Evelyn yesterday – we sat on the roof and went deep into the spiritual realities. She and Muriel are probably coming over tomorrow for a service. If you draw a check better draw on the Brooklyn Bank. I have only $9.00 in the Yonkers Bank.[15]

Howard's boarding house had 17 men living in it by early June and he expected that to increase to 25 within a week. In his letter to the Guardian, he wrote, 'The work of the men supports the house. It is cooperatively managed. Every morning we have a "consultation" period, in which I speak of the principles of the Cause and next Sunday I shall probably begin with some simple teaching, gradually building up a confirming influence in their hearts. Please pray that great results may come.'[16]

By the middle of June, however, the boarding house project was struggling and Howard was faced with the possibility of having to close it. He wrote to Mabel that 'Unless I can get $100 with the bank pretty damn quick the food for the men, and my credit with the gar[bage]. phone and elect. people will be shot . . . I live from day to day. I am hoping to get the needed $100, but if I don't and we can't keep going – well that will only mean that I can concentrate on the Farm Com[munity] Plan . . . with you this summer.' Later on that same day, Howard wrote, 'I feel it in my bones it is pretty nearly over but I am still fighting. Too bad for the work is coming in and things are better organized than ever . . . We are in His Hands and they are Powerful, Loving and Merciful Hands.'[17]

Mabel's answer was philosophical:

> I agree with you darling it has been worth all its cost in what you have gained out of it all. Whether that particular house and group continues is not of great importance. You have helped and served them all and someday they may understand what was in your heart. And my dear you Love it – the real thing. This experience will give you entrees to men whom you should meet in the future. It has all been a wonderful experience. If Baha'u'llah wishes you to keep going, you will certainly be able to do so as you are doing everything humanly and divinely possible.[18]

The end of the project came quickly. On the evening of 17 June 1933, Howard wrote that the three men he depended on most at the boarding house 'have lit out . . . taking practically all the money the men paid in'. This left Howard deep in debt.[19] Edris became one of their prime means of support from this time, sacrificing much so that Howard and Mabel could continue their teaching work.

After initially writing to Shoghi Effendi about the boarding house project, Howard did not write to him for two years, waiting until 2 December 1935. When he did, he opened with its failure:

> It is not because I have not wished to write that so long a time has elapsed since last a letter went to you and I received your comforting and encouraging reply. My heart

is always filled with thoughts of you and prayers that I may be worthy of your guidance.

The venture in Brooklyn, of which I wrote you, resulted disastrously. The men robbed me of everything I had, and the strain broke down my health. I am now incapacitated from activity in business and, owing to the heavenly love of my wife's daughter, who is as near and dear as if my blood were in her veins, Dr. Edris Rice-Wray Carson, am devoting all my time and strength to spreading the Revelation of Baha'u'llah through the spoken and written word.[20]

The Guardian's response, through his secretary, was:

The Guardian is in receipt of your very kind and encouraging letter of the second instant, and is, indeed, pleased to hear from you after such a long silence. It gives him great pleasure to realize that in spite of the severe material difficulties with which you have been confronted during all that time, and notwithstanding your physical ill-health you have been working so hard for the Cause, particularly in the field of teaching.

Shoghi Effendi's personal note at the end of the letter was very encouraging and uplifting:

Dearly beloved co-worker: I grieve to learn of your illness, as I regard you and your services as constituting a most precious asset to our beloved Faith. Your literary accomplishments, your remarkable ability in presenting the Cause to the general public, your understanding, devotion, zeal and experience eminently qualify you to take a leading and decisive part in the nation-wide campaign of teaching inaugurated by the American believers. I will pray for you from the depths of my heart. Rest assured and persevere. Affectionately Shoghi[21]

Howard was still trying to pull the boarding house business

out of the fire in July, making an arrangement with one of the residents to run it. In the interim, life in the house was close to the bone: 'We are living more simply than I ever have. Mostly shredded wheat and milk and fruit. You see we can't cook anything. We make our breakfast coffee on the fourth floor. Once in a while we blow ourselves to eggs. Even so it is nip and tuck to get even this much ... I really don't mind, and it is giving me the experience of true poverty which is valuable in its spiritual significance.'[22]

Being separated so much was unavoidable given Howard's and Mabel's chosen lifestyle, and it was a constant theme in their letters. Howard wrote to Mabel, 'When we are separated like this in body always I feel very close to <u>you</u>. And I do love you with all my being. Someday, when this pitiful world has passed like the dream it is, <u>only</u> Reality will be visible: all the mists that hide us from each other will have dissipated before that glorious Sun and the "Eclipse of the World" will be over.'[23]

Muriel rediscovers the Faith

When Howard became a Bahá'í, his wife, Elizabeth Hoyt Ives, couldn't reconcile herself to his change of religion and left him, taking their daughter Muriel with her. Muriel, as was mentioned earlier, met 'Abdu'l-Bahá when she was 16. She had followed her father into the Faith in 1913, but with her removal from her father and the Bahá'ís she had known, her declaration could not be supported by strengthening or confirming her in the Faith and, with the breakup of her parents' marriage and her mother's antagonism towards the Faith, Muriel continued to seek the truth for years. She described what happened to her family later, saying that she remembered only two things:

> First, that 'Abdu'l-Bahá had insisted that she kneel. She commented, 'the Bahá'ís never believe me about this; so many times people tried to kneel in respect to His greatness and he had always lifted them to a stand, insisting that they not to do so. But me, he told to kneel. I remember

seeing the hem of His Abba against the floor.' The other thing she remembered is that Abdu'l-Bahá told her that she would 'grow like a tree'. This statement, as far as she was concerned, just confirmed that 'Abdu'l-Bahá was simply a strange old man.

Many years later, when she was in her 70s, Bahá'í travelers would often stop to visit with her. One such visitor was a young man, a student whose had majored in forestry. He spent the night as a guest of Muriel and her then husband, Leland. The next morning, during breakfast, the young man asked her about when she met 'Abdu'l-Bahá. She recounted her two recollections. He then asked her how long after that meeting she had declared herself a Bahá'í. She told me that she always felt embarrassed to answer this question, because it was so long. It took her 20 years. When she shared this fact with the young man, he became quite animated, saying, 'That is the average maturing rate for a tree!' Finally, so many years after Abdu'l-Bahá had told her that she would 'grow like a tree', it finally made sense.[24]

Muriel rekindled her interest in the Bahá'í Faith as a married woman of 28, but she still had to keep her growing interest in the Bahá'í Faith a secret from her mother. In the spring of 1925, Howard had written to Mabel:

> It would have been lovely for our dear daughters to meet, but it would not be feasible yet. Muriel would have to hide the fact from her mother and I could not suggest that. But they will be great friends someday. In the meanwhile I am content to see her gradually get more and more of the Bahai spirit.[25]

Muriel and I had even more confidential and helpful talks and she let drop several allusions which indicated her deep interest in the Bahai Cause and how she was constantly standing up for it. The most interesting thing was that she arranged with a very dear friend of hers, a young married woman, to come in to talk with me because 'she needed spiritual help and advice' – was suffering much and Daddy could help her, and she (the friend) had been reading Some Ans. Ques. which Muriel had loaned her, and was interested, etc.[26]

Suddenly in 1933, Muriel changed into a 'flaming believer'. She was now 37 and had two daughters of her own.[27] Her youngest, eight-year-old Barbara, Howard's granddaughter, wrote her first letter to Shoghi Effendi in June, and Howard included it in his own letter. Barbara's letter said: 'Dear Shoghi Effendi, I am sending a prayer I made up yesterday. I also made a string of prayer beads. They only have 46 beads for that was all I had. Mother and I go around two times. I hope I can meet you sometime. Lots of love, Barbara Ives.' In her eight-year old handwriting, she created a folded card on the cover of which she printed: 'My Prayer For Shoghi Effendi from Barbara Ives'. Inside the card, she included a prayer, arranged like a poem:

> O My God, I thank Thee for a lovely day,
> I thank Thee for my food and home,
> I thank Thee for the clothing that I wear
> Please heal the sick and make them well
> Verily Thou art the powerful[28]

Howard wrote to the Guardian about Muriel and Barbara:

> I must tell you of the great joy that has come to me because of the confirmation of my daughter Muriel. When the Master was here twenty-one years ago she was sixteen years old. She knelt before him and he blessed and anointed her, saying amongst other wonderful things that she would become confirmed and would 'grow like a tree'. For all these years she has been germinating. Never antagonistic, in fact for the last five years she has called herself a Baha'i. But about three months ago she suddenly leapt into a flaming believer. She is dedicated and severed and serving to a

most remarkable degree. Several souls have become confirmed fully by only one or two talks with her. My heart is so filled with thankfulness and joy. She is now my daughter throughout all the worlds of God. She is very happily married and has a most remarkable little daughter, Barbara, (eight years old) who is also of a deeply spiritual nature. She has been using the Master's little prayer for several years. She speaks of keeping the mirror of her heart pure so that it may reflect the characteristics of God.[29]

When the Guardian's reply came, it said: 'Please convey his loving greetings to your beloved wife, to your daughter and to little Barbara whose prayers have greatly impressed him and for the realization of which he will surely pray.' Shoghi Effendi also added his own note at the end:

> The news concerning your daughter and the light which she radiates as a result of her faith in the Cause brought much joy to my heart. I will supplicate on behalf of those whom she has interested in the Faith, and for all those whom you are interesting and attracting to the teachings. What you have already achieved is indeed worthy of the highest praise and my fervent and loving prayers will continue to be offered for so devoted, so distinguished a servant of Bahá'u'lláh. Your true brother, Shoghi[30]

Maine

Mabel spent July and part of August 1933 in Portland, Maine, and Green Acre. She returned to New York sometime in August and apparently the Ives were together there until December. After that, Mabel was constantly on the move, both for her sales business and for the Faith. She was in Lewiston, Maine on 4 December staying at the Y.W.C.A.[31] Two days later, after receiving a letter from Howard (which we do not have), which apparently described his struggles and self-doubt, she wrote back with spiritual encouragement:

You are wonderful my beloved one – don't get any other ideas in your head. I know how wonderful you are. Your patience and self-control and sweetness have been simply marvelous thru this whole situation. Your Riswanea knows! Also Abdul Baha knows! Your growth is remarkable – you are not so aware yet but I see it constantly. And remember Baha Ullah is 'opening the doors, preparing for us the means, rendering the Path safe and paving the way' to our real and outstanding and concentrated service to the world, aided by Baha Ullah. He is providing the means – all that we need – so that we can give all the rest of our lives in His service. Know this darling. Go forth each day knowing that doors are opening on all sides – that plenty of means are coming from every direction – that His Plan for our service to the Kingdom can never be defeated – that our ordained destiny is along the lines of 'very great things' – that we know that He is guiding us. That all that we need is already here – that our work is already provided – that the doors are now open. We know this – we thank the Blessed Beauty for it.[32]

Howard's reply on receiving the letter was joyous: 'Honestly, I think you are the Queen of the world. What unbounded resources of love and tenderness and spiritual energy . . . You know my heart and there is nothing too high to say about my Riswanea. I love you more and more as years pass and I see you growing into all that you were ordained to be by the Creator . . . What fun we shall have together when we have dropped this veil and weight of the body.'[33]

In Lewiston, Mabel gave six talks and made a quick trip to Portland, Maine, to give a talk at the Eastland Hotel.[34] She was back in Portland on 15 December trying to do business and wrote that there were 'A few nibbles, but not a real bite. Came home about 6 and rested and did a wonderful lot of praying for my Howie and us both. You see we really desire only to teach His Cause and herald the World Order of our Beloved.'[35] A few days later she went to Augusta, again searching for business during the day and meeting with those interested in the Faith in the evenings.[36]

Near the end of the year, Howard and Mabel were together in Portsmouth, Maine, for a few days, then travelled together to Albany, New York, where they remained for a few weeks doing both business and teaching the Faith.[37]

In January 1934, Howard and Mabel were in Albany, New York. Mabel spoke at three meetings and Howard at two. Leaving Albany on 16 January, they spent a few days in Binghamton where Mabel addressed five meetings and gave two radio broadcasts. They continued on to Cleveland, Ohio, and South Bend, Indiana, in both of which Mabel made presentations. In February, Mabel was in Cincinnati, Ohio.[38]

14
Howard Discovers His Writing Skills

In March 1934, Mabel and Howard were in Knoxville, Tennessee, where they remained until September. Things were really bad financially, but Mabel described what happened next:

> Well, when we were down in Knoxville we had just about hit bottom financially; we just didn't seem to be able to sell at all. The situation was growing rather desperate and Howard's business which was different from mine at the time was a complete flop. So we decided that since he was getting nowhere plugging at his business; he had much better forget it and turn his attention and time to some direct service to the Cause, so why not do the thing that the Guardian seemed to want him to do, as he had mentioned it several times in his letters to H[oward], and which Mariam was continually begging him to do, namely interview outstanding men. So as the T.V.A. [Tennessee Valley Authority] was then at its height, and Mr. Arthur Morgan, the President of it, was in Knoxville, which was the headquarters of the T.V.A., H. sallied forth to interview him. This interview resulted not only in an article, but while there, Mr Morgan offered H. a job in the publicity dept. of the Co. to write articles about the T.V.A. for magazines which were dunning him for articles on the subject and which he did not have time to write himself. So he was assigned an office, all the facilities of the large business plant at his disposal from which he could get information, the Company photographer at his disposal etc. He came home with this story at the end of one of the most discouraging days in my business history, and it seemed so wonderful as he unfolded it that I simply wept and wept for joy and relief.

How truly God never deserted us. We had reached just about our last dollar, and the new salary (a SALARY! such a thing had never come to us – always commission before) and also, I think, the first week's salary in advance. So Howard for the first time in his life, begin to live the life he had always dreamed about, a quiet office, all his own, where he could write undisturbed by outer interruptions, and by inner pressure that he ought to be out earning his bread and butter; with reference books and all other facilities right at his hand. With time and a sense of leisure in which to think, and doing the thing he loved best to do, and had longed all his life for. He had made many previous attempts to write, but daily pressure was too great and he had not quite got into the swing of it. This lasted just one blessed month, but it was enough to shape his whole career and give him a new lease on life . . .

At the end of the month, Mr. M decided that H. could write to better effect as an outsider than as an employee of the Co., so he turned over the requests for articles about the T.V.A. to H. and H. was to write them and then get the checks direct from the magazines. That was alright. The month had brought us $200.00 . . . so altho disappointed, and H. missed his office, we secured a lovely place in the country (it was summer) . . . Howard had his own room and quiet. He received $25 or $35 for his articles and all was well, and the big thing was that he was finding that he could write acceptably.[1]

The Tennessee Valley Authority was building three dams on the Tennessee River, as well as a town called Norris to house the workers. Howard's job was to write articles about the huge project. He wrote three articles, the first two of which were published in the *Christian Science Monitor*. The first article was published on 4 May 1934 and opened by stating, 'Things are happening in the Tennessee River Valley which will affect our national life for generations. And it is not only what is happening objectively, it is the animating spirit that is making them happen which strikes the new note in our national life.' Howard highlighted the outstanding unity of all those involved in the project and put this forward as 'a new social order now being prepared for the inspection of the American people'. He predicted that 'the reactionaries, more in love with their own well-being than with human welfare, will most of them find their appropriate resting place in costly mausoleums and a new generation will have taken their places trained in body, mind and soul for service to the social life of which they are a part'.[2]

In June, Howard's second article, titled 'Training for Living: How the Norris Educational Plan Aims to Fit Men and Women for a New Social Order', was published. He wrote that the Norris school emphasized human life over conventional education.[3] A third companion article was published in July in *The World Outlook* magazine in July. Titled 'Putting Humanity First', the article, which was about the people living in the Authority's town of Norris, stated that 'this Norris spirit which puts humanity first has a great chance of establishing a new type of civilization in this country' and concluded that the people involved with it 'are working and planning to bring about a new social and economic order in which poverty and ignorance and enforced idleness will be things of the past'.[4] Howard obviously liked the Bahá'í-like ideals of those working on the project.

Howard and Mabel were still in Knoxville in July, but their financial problems had returned. Both she and Howard had been suffering health issues. On 1 July, Howard suddenly 'staggered and then fell unconscious on the floor by his bed'. Mabel wrote, 'I reached him as he fell, he was still vomiting and in great pain. We got him on the bed, and called a doctor. He [the doctor] thought the pain in his heart was angina, tho later he was not quite sure whether it might be a broken rib as he had struck the side of the bed in his fall. Anyway, he lay there in agony . . . I turned to Bahá'u'lláh and asked for help.'[5] Howard had had a heart attack.

At that point, Mabel was at her wits end because she herself had an infected leg. The doctor promised to send medicine for Howard, which they couldn't pay for and which thankfully never came. But three checks for Howard's writing came unexpectedly in the mail.

Mabel wrote to her daughter Edris on 28 July, 'We are both up and around now. I let the nurse go last Saturday. I kept her here just one week. My leg seems to be OK and Unk [Uncle Howard] walks a little every day and gets around the house and out on the porch. We lay blankets on the lawn in the evening and lie there till the house cools off. Has been 101 [38°C] here . . .' She went on to write that Howard 'has been trying to write the last two days, but doesn't seem to be able to get much of anywhere with it. He got very dizzy today just sitting at the typewriter. But he is getting back his strength.' Howard had been ill for a month. She closed her letter saying that 'As to our finances, we are down again to zero, except a little we have put aside for the Bahai Fund. We are under the protection of Bahaullah.'[6] Howard and Mabel were always operating on a financial shoestring. During the 1930s, Mabel's daughter Edris commonly sacrificially deputized their teaching trips.[7]

Howard's daughter Muriel later wrote about their circumstances around this time:

> At this time they – she and my father were living in a particularly difficult situation. It was a furnished room and the landlady was constantly complaining of everything they did. They used too many lights, they took too many showers using up too much water, and the clacking of Father's typewriter was driving her crazy. So, one morning, Rizwanea told Father how she felt: She had come to the end; she could endure no more; she was unable to go one step farther. They had a long period of consultation, and at the end, Father told her that, of course, he would do as she wished, but would she, in turn, do one thing for him? Would she wait just one more day before making a truly final decision – and would she spend this day in prayer? She agreed. So after Father had left her to go out and attend to his business details, she kept her promise. She began to pray. And as she prayed, it came to her just what, in its

depth and beauty, submission, detachment, and servitude really meant. And it came to her that submission – true and complete submission to the Will of God – was the first basic step. So she began to pray for submission – she prayed and prayed, and finally, submission came to her – but with it came the realization that submission was not enough.

Well, then, what was enough? What should she pray for now? And she remembered that Baha'u'llah had written that we must be grateful for the circumstances to which we were submitting. Grateful? Grateful for this horrid little room? Grateful for the beastly, complaining landlady?

Well, all right – if Bahá'u'lláh said so she, Rizwanea, would be grateful. But it wasn't easy. She was pacing the room, thinking, praying, fighting and now she went to the window to stare out into the street. 'Teach me to be grateful! Teach me to be submissive! I will be grateful! I will be submissive!' She clenched her small fists. She fought and she suffered. And, finally, the first warm touch and then the warmer flow of submissive gratitude surged over her. But, the next moment, she realized that even this was not enough. Not enough? When she'd fought so hard and she was so tired. What then was left? What should she pray for next?

And it came to her that now she must pray for love; love for her nerve-wracking circumstances; love for her harsh landlady; love for the whole situation that had led to the crisis – the blessed crisis that had forced her to learn this lesson. So, now, Rizwanea prayed that she might love that she might be filled with love that she might be able to pour out this love.

And her prayers were answered. When Father returned to her, it was to meet a radiant woman – a woman filled with the glory of complete submission to the Will of God – a woman rich with the glory of gratitude for tests – a woman overflowing with the clear crystal waters of the love of God.

And, for many years more, she poured out these waters for the glory of the Cause she loved so well.[8]

A tour through the Midwest

At the beginning of January 1935 Howard was in Urbana, Illinois. He had arrived there 'without a penny – gave my last 8¢ to the porter with apologies'. His whole trip, which he described as 'a most enjoyable and fruitful experience', cost a total of $9. On the 12th, he was at a large gathering with a buffet supper. Howard told stories about his experiences with 'Abdu'l-Bahá and answered questions until 9:30 p.m. The next day, an 18-year-old student came to talk with him. Howard noted that he 'thinks he will enter the ministry and so is faced with a serious problem'. That night, he spoke to a non-Bahá'í group on 'The Relation of the Baha'i Movement to Christianity'.[9] Howard rejoined Mabel in Chicago on 14 January.

Moving on to Winnetka, Illinois, north of Wilmette, between them they gave about 30 talks at the Chicago Bahá'í Rooms and at the Mashriqu'l-Adhkár. They also gave 23 talks in Milwaukee, Racine and Kenosha, Wisconsin, 12 to various fireside groups, 4 in Urbana, Illinois, held weekly study classes in Winnetka and spoke to several women's clubs in Chicago.[10]

By the end of July, they were apart again, Mabel travelling to Detroit and Howard staying in Winnetka. When Mabel left, she apparently told their landlord something that made the landlord think that they were moving away. Howard was surprised when the landlord brought possible new renters to view the apartment. He assured her that they were staying for the winter.[11]

Howard's health continued to plague his efforts. In late September, he noted that 'I am entirely incapacitated, so far as heavy or long-continued and exhausting work is concerned. My heart difficulty has become accentuated so that any work except writing is taboo. Our darling daughter, Edris, put her foot down hard early last Spring and absolutely forbade me any attempt to work, and delegated Riswanea (Mabel) to spend all her time teaching the Cause and looking after me.'[12]

He was able to write again, however, and in October, he produced a poem to Mabel. He told her, 'I had been reading one of my fool stories up to about 9:30 and then decided to go to bed. Just as I laid down the book, and without any particular thought of you in my mind . . . the words came into my mind: "What is this strange thing beating in my heart? It can't be love".' He said that he immediately got up, grabbed a pen and within an hour had written it. 'I wonder where such things come from,' he asked.[13]

To Riswanea

What is this strange thing beating in my heart?
It can't be love, for love belongs to youth
And I am nearing three-score-years-and-ten.
Yet when she is not near the world's a place
That has small meaning: and when she returns
Each slight thing takes significance again.

What is this strange thing beating in my heart?
It can't be love for love's a thing of fire
That burns to ashes in a few brief years.
But, somehow, this strange thing within my heart
Has fire which like a jewel burns that leaves
No ash, and years have no effect at all.

What is this strange thing beating in my heart?
It rings like mailed and marching hosts upon
A mighty bridge which spans all time and space.
It has a cadence like a trumpet call;
And there's a fragrance, too, as though its beat
Touched roses lightly, crushing not a one.

What is this strange thing beating in my heart?
It can't be love for love is bound by death.
But this strange thing that beats – and beats – and beats
Has wings – perhaps it is those wings I hear –
Has wings that soar and do not vainly beat,
And when they speak of 'Severing Death' – I smile.[14]

Mabel responded to this love letter from her beloved:

> My Poet!
> I'm just thrilled and deeply touched over your lovely poem. How adorable of you to write it. I know just what you mean, darling, but it took my poet Howie to put it into that lovely form. I felt that same way, as I left you and for hours while driving down. It is something that belongs to a deeper world than we can understand now – but I get glimpses every once in a while. If what that real bond is in the eternal world, it is inexpressible but infinitely satisfying. This world seems so terribly limited.[15]

Their financial difficulties were the subject of Howard's next letter: 'The dollar you sent was a god-send . . . as I had already dipped into my reserve fund to the extent of $3.00 . . . [Edris] doesn't realize, the dear girl, that although I have had my dinner with them each night, yet my breakfasts and lunches do cost a little, especially as I have to have oranges and eggs pretty often . . .'[16]

Howard's approach to the study of the Writings, and Nancy Phillips

Howard was by nature a deep student of the Faith. He continually sought to understand the meaning of Bahá'u'lláh's words more deeply, and early on developed a discipline for his own study. He had a practice of creating note-cards and notebooks filled with compilations of the Writings by subject, cross-indexes of topic, annotated books and personal journals. His purpose was to understand how Bahá'u'lláh defined His own words. Disinterested in his own (or any other's) opinions about their meaning, his quest was to find Bahá'u'lláh's meanings in the Writings themselves. He instilled this same discipline in the many souls he taught, giving them to tools to study the teachings deeply themselves. Many of his spiritual offspring received a monthly lesson with quotations from the Writings on important themes. Howard passed the approach used for his own study down to many of the souls he taught, including his own descendants. An anecdote shared by Erica Toussaint, his great-granddaughter, gives an example of the continuing generational influence of his approach:

> During the second day of the 2008 International Convention, I spotted Hooper Dunbar, who was retiring from his service as a member of the Universal House of Justice at that time, standing alone preparing to walk through the large display of photographs from around the world. For many years I had noticed that Mr. Dunbar's approach to the study of the Teachings was very similar to the approach that our family used, and had wondered why that was. So I joined him and as we walked through the beautiful exhibit, I finally had the opportunity to ask him about it. He chuckled and said that there was an easy answer. When he became a Bahá'í, Nancy Phillips was the person who first deepened with him. Early on she sat him down with a few of the letters she had received from Howard Colby Ives, who had been her Bahá'í teacher. She instructed him to copy – and follow – the contents, which contained specific guidance about prayer, meditation, and how to study of the Writings. Mr. Dunbar explained that those instructions guided his approach from the very beginning for his own study. They were reflected in the many youth deepenings that he famously held for decades. As he finished telling me the story, he concluded that we had both been trained by 'Daddy Howard'.
>
> When I returned home I contacted Nancy, who was living in Ontario, Oregon. She was delighted to receive Hooper's greetings, confirmed that she still had the letters, and invited me to come visit. We had a delightful visit, and instead of allowing me to copy the many letters she had saved from her spiritual father, she handed them to me to assist in the research for the biography that would be written about Howard and Mabel. She passed away within a few months.[17]

Nancy Phillips was a young woman in her latter 20s when she met Howard in Winnetka. She was introduced to Howard and Mabel and began going to their house in Chicago every evening after work to learn more about the Faith. Nancy noted that Howard and Mabel had very different teaching methods: Howard taught using the words of Bahá'u'lláh, which touched the heart, and Mabel taught using charts, which educated the logical mind. Howard's way was the one that drew Nancy deeply into the Faith.[18]

In 1936, after she had married, Nancy moved from Chicago to Jerome, Arizona, and she and Howard began a running correspondence in which he kept deepening her and helping her to find her way. Nancy was eager to raise up a Bahá'í community, but her teaching efforts weren't going as well as she had expected. She was wondering if she should go elsewhere. Howard's advice was that

> it really makes little or no difference what part of the little globe our feet rest upon, nor what experiences our bodies and minds go through in their contacts with material things. All these are much the same everywhere. But everywhere are Souls. And these immortal beings are searching, just as you are, for Reality, for Peace, for a satisfactory answer to their perpetual questionings.
>
> You have at least got on the trail of a satisfactory answer. God has put it to you . . . You just must do one of two things. Follow that Trail even if it leads through fire and flood, or else stand looking at it with wishful thinking. You will do the former . . . for once having got a glimpse of the Promised Land – Land of Peace, Servitude and ecstasy – such a Soul as thou art cannot rest until you rest in Him.[19]

An example of how Howard counselled her is this:

> Do not feel hurried about this. Make friends amongst the people who to you seem to have capacity and pray constantly for guidance. You will surely receive it. I have just

been re-reading Baha'O'llah's wonderful book – 'The Tablet to the Son of the Wolf,' . . . Let me quote a passage or two on this matter of teaching method.

'O people of Baha! Consort with all people with joy and fragrance. If you possess a word or principle, of which another is deprived, reveal and communicate it in the language of love and affections . . . The language of love is the touchstone of hearts and sustenance of spirits; it is like unto the significance behind words, and a horizon for the dawn of the sun of wisdom and knowledge.'

'Ask God for attentive hearing, piercing sight, a rejoicing breast, a generous heart. Perhaps men will turn towards the Friend, and find the Desired One.'

Are these words not lovely? And so piercingly true and wise as a method of attracting hearts and souls. I am constantly being more and more impressed with the entirely new attitude which Baha'U'llah enjoins upon men in their approach to life – its problems and its contacts. It is as if He would warn us against reliance upon a purely intellectual approach. Instead of advising us to use our heads alone, He urges resort to the heart first and afterwards the use of wisdom and discretion. For instance: in the same Tablet above referred to He has much to say about courtesy. I will quote two passages.

'Indeed We have chosen courtesy, and have made it an order to the elect. It is a garment which becomes all, both great and small. Happy the one who adorns his body with it, and woe unto him who deprives himself of this supreme grace.'

'I declare by God that the sword of virtue and civility is keener than blades of steel!'

Think how wars and all strife, both in the home and on the

battlefield could be so simply avoided by obedience to these Divine Commands.

The way to every heart is not by argument, nor even by persuasion. It is by the Royal Path of love, servitude, happiness – and by the clothing of oneself in the garments of the attributes and qualities of the Manifestation of God.[20]

To the reader who might think that these quotations seem only partially familiar, they are from an early translation made by an unknown person or persons. When the Guardian finished his own translations, he sent them to George Townshend, an Irishman who later became a Hand of the Cause, and who served the Guardian by beautifying the English translations of Bahá'u'lláh's Writings. Shoghi Effendi sent almost all of his translations and writings to George for this editorial work. After the Guardian and George Townshend translated and beautified the first passage above, it became this:

> Consort with all men, O people of Bahá, in a spirit of friendliness and fellowship. If ye be aware of a certain truth, if ye possess a jewel, of which others are deprived, share it with them in a language of utmost kindliness and goodwill . . . A kindly tongue is the lodestone of the hearts of men. It is the bread of the spirit, it clotheth the words with meaning, it is the fountain of the light of wisdom and understanding.[21]

In addition to advice as above, Howard regularly sent Nancy, a series of lessons he had prepared. In a letter of 10 September 1936 Howard provided this counsel:

> During the first five years or so of my own Bahá'í experience I was travelling much throughout the country, or my business kept me often for many months away from any possible association with the friends.
> But those months and years were most profitable from a spiritual standpoint. I spent all the time available from necessary work in study and prayer. I copied endlessly from

the Creative Word. I made book after book of compilations on various subjects. I indexed every book I studied with cross references showing where in other writings explanatory phrases were used, throwing light on otherwise obscure passages.

It is possible that such separation as you are to have for a while may be productive of Very Great Things in your spiritual development and in your preparation for great usefulness in the Cause in the future.

All such events are tests of our sincerity, our severance, our self-sacrifice, our capacity for greater and greater service. In other words, it is a definite call to Spiritual Heroism. St. Francis, St. Theresa and many other great souls withdrew voluntarily for many years from all human companionship. You remember Jesus' forty days in the wilderness. Bahá'u'lláh withdrew from the world for two years during His Baghdad exile...

In a word . . . this is what I would say to you. Dedicate your life wholly to God – to Bahá'u'lláh – to servitude in His Path, to self-sacrifice in His Way. Regard each day as time given you to fit yourself for a great service in the future. You will find that this self-dedication and constant prayer will enable you to be of such assistance to _____ that nothing else could compare with it. You will find souls being drawn to you and opportunities for spiritual and material service multiplying on every hand. You will find yourself being asked to tell where you achieved such power and love. In a word if you place yourself unreservedly in the Hands of Bahá'u'lláh, of the Supreme Concourse, of the Holy Spirit, you will find yourself guided and guarded and supported on every hand.

In 'Abdu'l-Bahá's second Tablet to me I find a passage so appropriate to our thought that I will quote it. These words are for you just as much as for me. God calls all souls to these high attainments. The chosen ones (those who rise when called and choose themselves to march at His Command) take such High Words as these and appropriate them to themselves and MAKE their lives a mirror of their beauty. In closing His Tablet 'Abdu'l-Bahá uses these words:

'In brief: be thou not unhappy. This event (substitute your present isolation for the event He refers to) has happened so that thou mayest call the people to the Kingdom; spread the Teachings of Bahá'u'lláh; inaugurate the era of the New Life; promulgate the Reality and be sanctified and purified from all save God. It is my hope that thou mayest become as such. Crown thy head with this diadem of the Kingdom which has such illumining power that they shall shine upon centuries and cycles.'

Never regret being alone with God. This is a great Bounty from His Hand. Try to get the habit of long communion. Ask Him for advice and counsel just as you would if you could have a personal and face to face talk with 'Abdu'l-Bahá. Listen for His answers just as eagerly and with even more concentration for He is really there even though you cannot see Him. Visualize Christ if that comes easier or more naturally to you. Only make it real and practical.

Keep some kind of a record of your spiritual experiences which you may use in the future to help others from and by. This will also make those experiences more vivid and real to yourself right now.[22]

On 3 March 1937, Howard again advised his spiritual daughter:

This solitude and silence may be most productive of spiritual growth if wisely used. I cannot emphasize this too strongly. Bahá'u'lláh has placed you just where you are for a definite purpose. Remember, my dear, that you are still a youth – about 26 years old I think you told me once. Just think of this: I was 46 (20 years older) when I first heard of this Divine Message, and that was just 25 years ago right now. Think what those years have meant to me and to the hundreds of souls Riswanea and I have contacted during that time. And then envisage what your future life may be – and SHALL be, God willing.

A DAY FOR VERY GREAT THINGS

You have, at the normal expectancy of life, some 40 to 50 years ahead of you on this little planet, and untold ages of work and true life ahead of you in 'all the worlds of God'. There is not a question in my mind, and I pray that there may be no question in yours, that Bahá'u'lláh has given you, from His Generous Hand, these few months or years of solitude for the express purpose of your preparation for the years and ages ahead of you. Do you recall the 40 days in the wilderness of Jesus? And the two years of solitude of Bahá'u'lláh when he spent while in Baghdad? . . .

Every soul must have some such preparation before he or she can be prepared for their true LIFE. Praise be to God that you have been selected for this great bounty!

Now may I make a few practical suggestions for the use of this invaluable time of quiet and solitude?

(1st) Set aside a particular time each day for prayer, meditation and study. I would suggest not less than two hours. You will find that as you get more and more deeply absorbed in this divine task you will gradually extend the time so that it will be difficult for you to tear yourself away from this abstraction from the mundane, the 'contingent' world. For, truly there is no happiness to be compared with this absorption in the things of the spirit, for 'the spirit alone is real: all else is as shadow'. Read again . . . the Tablet of Ahmad . . . Here is a perfect picture of the unimportance, the absolute worthlessness of the visible world compared with the invisible.

(2nd) Start indexing every book you read. Examine each Word, each line, each paragraph with anxiously attentive eyes and soul lest you miss something of these heavenly significances which may throw light on your own immediate needs and opportunities. For 25 years I have done this, and annotated the margins of each book freely. In the back of each book I read I use the blank pages for such indexing. Placing all, or similar passages under their appropriate headings. And also be careful to note those passages which throw light upon each other. For instance: . . . you will find the words – 'but some of the people understand and remember and some remember but do not understand.' This passage puzzled me for some time until I happened up on the passage in the Tablet to the Christians . . . the passage referred to you will find . . . as follows – 'whereof some know and bear witness, but the majority bear witness and do not know.' Evidently the translation of the first passage is most faulty; in fact Shoghi Effendi says that it is VERY badly translated as are many of the English versions of the Holy Utterances. The first passage should read like this: 'But some of the people understand (what they are saying) when they utter remembrances of Me and some utter these remembrances and do not understand (their inner significances).'

The second passage makes this very clear for He says: 'some know and bear witness (utter remembrances) but the majority bear witness and do not know.' (what they bear witness to, but are simply uttering empty words).

You will find many such parallel passages the careful study of which will bring great light and illumination to your spirit. But you must discover them for yourself, only so will the full fruitage be bestowed.

(3rd) Begin making compilations. If you have no typewriter make them in long hand. For many years I have done this and the results have been most worthwhile. Take such a subject as 'Prayer': or Immortality or Eternal Life; or Life of this world – Oh there are scores and hundreds of vital subjects. Such a compilation will be of inestimable value to you right now, for the making of it will force your attention closely upon each passage you copy. And in the future years it will be of still greater value in your teaching work.

(4th and Final) Find – dig up – correspondents, or even one soul, to whom you can write and pass on the results of your study and meditation. I would suggest your sister . . . except that I am not sure that she would welcome such, and there is no use in 'offering the cup unless a soul is thirsty'. But surely amongst your many friends you will know of at least one who will welcome letters written wisely and tactfully according to the capacity and thirst evidenced.

I am sure that you will pardon these suggestions. They come from a heart FILLED with love for you, with absolute certainty of your great capacity and with a sure faith that your future years will be filled with work for Bahá'u'lláh and the feeding of hungry souls.[23]

These excerpts not only give a clear picture of Howard's rigorous approach to personal study, but offer through his own description a glimpse into his own spiritual aspirations, his approach to prayer and meditation, all the while focused on the practical application of what he was learning in service to the many souls he encountered as he sought to live up to the demands of living in the day for 'Very Great Things' announced to him by 'Abdu'l-Bahá in 1912.

View of a future Covenant-breaker

A letter from Howard to Mabel had a fascinating insight into the nature of Rúhí Afnán (also spelled Rouhi), Shoghi Effendi's cousin and secretary:

I have thought several times of what you said regarding Rouhi Afnan's remarks on prayer, and his spending so little time at it. I had not realized all what such a remark connoted and rather hastily, I fear, may have given you the impression that I agreed with him. On the contrary I do not agree, tho I sometimes feel that many of the friends think of prayer in a somewhat limited and emotional way. But as for Rouhi the reason for his attitude was shown by Edris' telling me this morning that Rouhi confessed to her (they had quite a long talk about it) that the inner spiritual life was a closed book to him. She said it was unaccountable to her and it certainly is to me, living where he does and with such a heritage. How incomprehensible! But it now explains many of the things he says.[24]

These comments are especially interesting, coming as they did at the end of 1935. In 1941, Rúhí Afnán completely cooperated with his sister's marriage to a Covenant-breaker. The Guardian tried to redeem him, but in 1953, after Rúhí Afnán began to correspond with Ahmad Sohrab and other Covenant-breakers and attack the Faith, Shoghi Effendi was forced to declare him to be a Covenant-breaker, as well.[25] It was an ignominious end to someone who had been in such close association with the Guardian and had been held in high esteem by pilgrims and Bahá'ís around the world.

Cincinnati, Dayton and Lima, Ohio

Mabel left Wilmette on 27 October 1935 with several Bahá'ís from Cincinnati, to begin a teaching campaign in that city. They were joined two weeks later by Dorothy and Frank Baker. Dorothy was a powerful and effective teacher of the Faith who later became a Hand of the Cause. In Cincinnati, Mabel gave four public meetings between 30 October and 8 November. She also gave two fireside talks, two study classes and a number of personal interviews. In Dayton, Ohio, she gave one public talk and then another 15 talks, study classes, firesides and other meetings in Lima, Ohio. The public meetings in Cincinnati and Dayton had up to 23 people, while in Lima, about 50 participants attended.[26] Mabel also helped a number of young people to form a group and got some much needed rest, writing that the 'last two days have been warm and flooded with sunshine and I have a southern porch off my room, where I lay for hours in the mornings'.[27] She wrote of the 'Truly wonderful spirit there and the magnificent activity of that group. There are meetings of some kind almost every day, and the spirit of love and unity among them is truly inspiring. The clergy of Lima have again and again denounced the Cause from the pulpits, and three of the Believers have been excommunicated from their churches, when they joined the Bahá'ís.'[28]

Howard was busy as well. He addressed six different meetings, and at one gave the first public reading of his 'epic poem' *The Song Celestial* (this poem will be described Chapter 16).²⁹ By the end of the year, Howard was beginning to feel 'oppressed' by how much had to be done. Mabel strongly suggested that he go to Dayton or Lima for at least a week. Dorothy Baker would drive him there and set him up with a room and a desk to work where he could be undisturbed. She also suggested that he would be able to try out a Bahá'í deepening course he was developing for an advanced study group. Mabel wrote that at the last Sunday night at the Bakers she had spoken to about 50 people about the Ma<u>sh</u>riqu'l-A<u>dh</u>kár in Wilmette, using the model lit up from inside. The next night, she had met with a group of youth. Mabel told Howard that his being oppressed was 'all the more reason why you should have a change. I strongly suggest that you accept Dorothy's invitation.'³⁰

Madison, Wisconsin

Mabel was busy in the upper Midwest beginning in December 1935. She spent five days in Madison, Wisconsin, and held five meetings. She noted that 'Madison has real possibilities' and that the wife of the head of the Astronomy Department at the University of Wisconsin and several students were Bahá'ís. She also gave talks in Milwaukee, Kenosha and Racine, Wisconsin; and in Winnetka, Urbana and Wilmette, Illinois. In Winnetka, Mabel and Howard were staying with Mabel's daughter, Edris Rice-Wray. Dorothy Baker came at the request of the Winnetka Local Spiritual Assembly and also gave a talk, entitled 'The Bible Understood,' in Edris's home to a group of over 20 younger people. Howard then went to Urbana, Illinois, for three days and gave four talks, also meeting with many individuals.³¹

In early 1936, Howard was in Winnetka and, as was so often the case, down to his last few pennies. He wrote to Mabel:

> I am having great game keeping things going on little or no money. This morning I had just 45¢ in the world. So I walked down town for I wanted to see the Tribune literary

editor about a book review [for *Portals to Freedom*]. She was out to lunch . . . I remembered that Bill Hayes asked me particularly to let him see the book . . . so I dropped in there. I had only one copy to leave with the Tribune so I showed him that . . . Bill wanted it and my autograph in it and paid me $2.05.[32]

Mabel was also in Winnetka where she was contacted by a field agent for the Federal Works Project of the WPA (a programme that employed millions of the unemployed for public works projects during the Depression. The programme included employing people in artistic fields to work on literary projects). The agent was researching the Bahá'í Faith in Illinois and asked Mabel to help. Mabel contacted the National Assembly and discovered that another agent had already been given a story and photograph of the House of Worship.[33]

15
Howard Writes *Portals to Freedom*

Beginning in 1935, Howard and Mabel began to follow different paths of service. Mabel had blossomed into an incredible travel teacher, carrying out large-scale proclamation projects in many areas, while Howard, with his health declining, spent the last six years of his life primarily concentrating on writing.

Howard began to seriously write starting in Knoxville in 1934 while he was working for the Tennessee Valley Authority. He was 67 years old, but 'suddenly he found the knack of writing vivid prose'. As described by Doris McKay in her 'In Memoriam' article for *The Bahá'í World*:

> In the late spring and early summer he sat four hours each day at his typewriter in the unaccustomed heat of Tennessee . . . He had found a gift which might have resulted in a relief from economic stress only to lose the use of it almost at once. His health, always precarious, was now undeniably gone, also his eyesight and hearing began rapidly to go, and he now, already facing an end that might come at any moment, began to struggle for time. Time to put down in his new found style the memoirs we have referred to as 'Portals to Freedom.' Forbidden to use his eyes, he learned the touch system on the typewriter and completed the book . . . in 1937. Then followed his book-length poem, the 'Song Celestial.' He wrote two later works which have not as yet been published. From Winnetka he wrote: 'I am content to wait. It may be that Bahá'u'lláh has still some work for me to do. As you say, the doctors are often mistaken. I remember an old doctor friend of my mother's, who, when I was eighteen years old, said I would not live beyond twenty-five. Yet here I still am.'[1]

On 2 December 1935, Howard wrote to Shoghi Effendi and included manuscripts for several things he was working on: *Portals to Freedom*, *The Ocean of His Utterance* and *Song Celestial*.

> A book of about 75,000 words is practically completed, 'Portals to Freedom', of which the first two or three chapters appeared in the now defunct 'Bahá'í Magazine', which attempts to set forth the wonderful awakening that came from my contacts with the Master in 1912. God willing, this will be ready for publication before Spring.
>
> I am now engaged in the preparation of an advanced study course which I have called, 'The Ocean of His Utterances', designed for confirmed souls who wish to penetrate further into the illimitable Universe of the Spirit unfolded by His Holiness Baha'u'llah . . .
>
> Also I completed during the past summer and fall a long poem, a copy of which is going to you with this letter. It is to ask your advice, approval and prayers regarding my future work which is the principal objective of this letter . . .
>
> My whole desire now is to use what time and strength remains in the service of the Cause, mainly in writing.[2]

Portals to Freedom

Howard's private interview with 'Abdu'l-Bahá in April 1912 was an emotional experience demonstrating the spiritual power of 'Abdu'l-Bahá. When Howard and Mabel were living with Mabel's daughter, Edris, Edris managed to persuade Howard to write the story of that event as well as his other experiences with the Master.[3] In addition to Edris, Mariam Haney said that she 'literally pestered him into a state where he felt almost forced to produce that great work to get rid of me!' She 'begged and begged him to do so that we might run it as a serial in the magazine'.[4] These led to the writing of what became *Portals to Freedom*. The Bahá'í Magazine had also been begging Howard to write about his experiences with 'Abdu'l-Bahá, so he began to write.[5]

Howard first told Shoghi Effendi about the book in his letter of 2 December 1935, quoted above. By February 1936, he had completed the manuscript and sent a copy to the Guardian. He had to apologize for the messiness of the draft, writing that 'I found it utterly impossible to do all the typing myself and the kind friend who made the four copies necessary was not as accurate as might be, so many corrections had to be made'. Howard also sent a draft to the Bahá'í Reviewing Committee of the National Spiritual Assembly, 'as I want their suggestions and advice before publishing, although the N.S.A. will not be asked to assume responsibility for publishing'. In his eagerness to see the book in print, he also sent it to a publisher, who indicated that he would have to sell at least 500 copies at $2.50 each and have 100 pre-orders before he would agree to do the printing.[6]

The process of writing the book energized Howard. He wrote to Shoghi Effendi on 12 February 1936:

> The happiness experienced in writing the story of my spiritual autobiography under the tutelage and inspiration of the Master is beyond words. I seemed to be living again through those wonderful days, and His Voice and Presence seemed with me as though He were present. The scenes described were, and are, as vivid as at the time experienced. It is my most earnest prayer that this record of those great days may be of lasting service to the Cause to which my life has long been dedicated.[7]

At the end of his letter, Howard asked if he could dedicate the book to the Guardian of the Bahá'í Faith. The reply 8 March 1936 on Shoghi Effendi's behalf said:

> The Guardian has been also very happy to receive the manuscript of your book 'Portals to Freedom' and is looking forward to the pleasure of reading it very soon. He trusts that the publication of this work will effectively assist the friends in their teaching activities, and will give them a renewed stimulus in their labours in that field. He can

well realize the great amount of time and effort you have devoted to the preparation of this autobiography and it is his hope that the results achieved will be such as to fully reward your painstaking labours.

The Guardian also wishes me to assure you of his approval of your suggestion to have the 'Portals' dedicated to him. He would leave the matter of wording the dedication entirely to you.

With his renewed greetings and good wishes, and with the assurance of his supplications at the Holy Shrines for your protection and guidance.[8]

Howard then sent the Guardian his proposed dedication, which read:

> To Shoghi Effendi
> The Grandson of 'Abdu'l-Bahá
> By Him Appointed
> Guardian of the Bahá'í Faith, head of the Coming
> International House of Justice, and Director of the
> Destinies of the New World Order
> This book is lovingly dedicated.[9]

Shoghi Effendi requested that Howard make a change, asking that he omit the words 'director of the Destinies of the New World Order' and 'Coming' in relation to the House of Justice.[10] The final dedication read: 'To Shoghi Effendi, The Grandson of 'Abdu'l-Bahá, By Him Appointed Guardian of the Bahá'í Faith and Head of the International House of Justice, This book is lovingly dedicated'. Editions published after the Guardian's passing removed the line about being the Head of the International House of Justice.

The Guardian's personal appended note on the 8 March letter said that 'I am delighted with your literary accomplishments. Your writings are an asset to the Cause and enrich its literature. I am arranging for some of your poems to be included in the forthcoming issue of "The Bahá'í World'. May the Beloved bless richly your efforts in this sphere of activity, inspire and sustain you, and enable you to render still greater services.'

In his next letter to the Guardian, Howard asked if Shoghi Effendi would write a foreword to *Portals*. To support his request, he added,

> As you must know the book was written primarily in the hope that souls may be attracted to the Divine Light which has brought to me such happiness and peace. I have bared my very soul as I never have thought it possible to do with only this hope and purpose.
>
> It is probable, nay certain, that if it meets with your approval sufficiently to warrant your expressing yourself in such a foreword many souls might read it with more attention and interest than would otherwise be the case.[11]

The Guardian responded to Howard's request in a letter written on his behalf:

> He is exceedingly sorry not to be able to comply with your wish, in view of the fact that as a matter of principle he has never accepted writing any foreword to any book, due to his manifold and increasingly heavy occupations. This is a general rule to which he has never allowed, and can never allow any exception whatsoever, for the simple reason that to establish preferences in such matters would be unjustified and hence would displease many people.[12]

By 30 June 1936, Howard had received suggestions for changes from the Reviewing Committee and the National Spiritual Assembly. He wrote to Nancy Phillips saying, 'I have been very busy for some days going all over my book "Portals" again, making some changes which the Reviewing Committee and the NSA recommended. This will delay the publication at least two months.'[13]

In late August, Stanwood Cobb wrote to Howard with news of *Portal*'s impending publication:

> I fervently hope that your plans for the publication of Portals to Freedom can be successfully carried out. My connection with the material of this book when it was being published in the Bahá'í Magazine has caused me to realize deeply its value, not only now to Bahá'ís and to non Bahá'ís as a teaching medium, but also to posterity as a vivid and spiritually understanding recording of 'Abdu'l-Bahá as He was in daily life during his tour in this country.
>
> These precious memories and impressions of Him which you so inspiringly record must live for posterity. It is an inestimable treasure, which the Bahá'ís of today can enjoy and find inspiration in, and be the means of passing on to future generations.
>
> I hope the Bahá'ís of this country will make such an eager response to your pre-publication as to make possible its immediate publication. I am especially delighted that E. P. Dutton are to undertake its publication for their imprint in the review publicity and the sales it will bring will be a real advantage to the Cause.[14]

But delays seemed to dog Howard's every attempt to have the book printed. The National Assembly, following the guidance of the Guardian to be rigorous about verifying statements attributed to 'Abdu'l-Bahá, asked him to remove the quotation marks around the words of 'Abdu'l-Bahá, advising that actual quotes must be distinguished from Howard's remembrances of the words of the Master. In a letter to the Guardian, Howard wrote:

> I have entirely re-written those parts of the book in which the Words of 'Abdu'l-Bahá appear so that the quotations shall be read in indirect form. This necessitated considerable work and I feared at one time it would weaken the force of the scenes considerably, but it seems not to have done so to any great degree, and I am more than happy to conform to the wishes of the NSA and to yours in this matter.
>
> The publication of the book has been delayed owing to

lack of funds. May I supplicate your prayers on this behalf? I would not venture to mention this to you except that the reviewing committee and the members of the NSA as well as many others who have seen the first chapters of the book as published in the Bahá'í Magazine two years ago, seem to think that 'Portals' will be of some assistance in the teaching campaign now being so vigorously pushed.

May I tell you how the matter stands? Last Spring I sent out the first notices of the book to most of the Assemblies of the world. The Orient as well as the Occident being covered. The response to this brought in about $250. Only one Oriental group was heard from. Beirut ordered three copies, which brought happiness.

Then the Bahá'í Publishing Committee took the matter up and sent out a letter to all the Assemblies in the U.S. and Canada, also a notice was published in the Bahá'í News in August. The response to this brought the subscription up to over $400. I am now trying to persuade E.P. Dutton and Co., the publishers to begin work when I can pay them $500. I think there is fairly good hope of this. If so the book should appear by February. The full cost of publication 1200 copies is $1100. Four or five half tone portraits of 'Abdu'l-Bahá will be included. The price is to be $2.25, but the pre-publication price is $1.85. I am giving these details so that you may be informed of my problem. Again I request your prayers that if it is the Will of Bahá'u'lláh this book may be of service to His Faith.[15]

The road to publication of *Portals to Freedom* had been long and difficult, but by November 1936, things were finally coming together. Shoghi Effendi's secretary wrote that

> he is indeed gratified to learn of the success of the steps which you have, in collaboration with the Bahá'í Publishing Committee, taken for its publication. He hopes that the response of the friends, both in the East and the West, will be such as to enable you to start immediately with the

printing. He is confident that when published this book will be of valuable assistance to the extension of the teaching work. You should therefore persevere in your efforts, and strive by every means in your power, to enlist the support of the believers for the publication of this volume which, he thinks, will be fully utilized as a teaching medium throughout the states and beyond its confines.[16]

The Guardian also ordered 50 copies of the book and sent a draft for $100 in payment. In his hand-written note at the bottom of the letter, Shoghi Effendi added, 'I deeply value your constant services and your literary accomplishments and strongly urge you to persevere and to never feel disheartened, however formidable the obstacles that confront you. I will continue to pray for the extension of your services which I regard as an asset to the Cause of God. Your true and grateful brother, Shoghi.'[17]

Pre-publication book orders, in addition to the Guardian's, were coming in. Howard gratefully acknowledged Shoghi Effendi's order and described how things were going:

> I have been busily engaged in writing the N.S.A., enclosing a copy of your letter, and writing the Publishing Committee giving instructions to them to forward immediately to E.P. Dutton and Company a check for $500. as the first payment on the printing of the book. Your draft alone made this possible.
>
> Strangely enough on the same mail with your letter came one from Dutton making a later proposition, in reply to one from me asking for better terms, offering to print the book for an initial payment of $500 and, on payment of $300 more to bind and deliver to me five-hundred copies, and on payment of the final $300 to deliver the balance of 700 copies.
>
> They will announce the book in their spring catalogue and are reserving 300 copies for their salesmen to handle. Stanwood Cobb is particularly delighted with this provision as it will put the Cause before the public in a way

which we could not do. Those 300 copies are not deducted from my 1,200. The full edition will be 1,500.

We have now about $85.00 towards the second payment of $300. and when it becomes known, as I hope it may be through the News Letter, that printing is actually begun through your generosity, the friends will rally nobly to the support, I feel confident.[18]

Financing the publication was very difficult for Howard since he had almost no money of his own to cover the costs. Mabel's daughter, Edris, tried to help by soliciting donations from Bahá'ís. One letter went to Siegfried Schopflocher. He in turn asked the National Spiritual Assembly about the matter and they responded that

> the National Assembly has not sanctioned any such method of financing Howard Ives' book by personal appeals.
>
> Under the Guardian's clear instructions, given many years ago, all appeals for Bahá'í contributions are to be general in character, and issued only by Bahá'í administrative bodies.
>
> The National Assembly has tried to cooperate with Howard by publishing a notice of his book in Bahá'í News, and the Publishing Committee is sending out a general letter to local Assemblies announcing the reduced price given on advance orders. Aside from this, no further action has been authorized and approved . . .[19]

In January 1937, the National Assembly authorized an advance of $100 to help cover the costs. The Assembly set out how things were going to work:

> We realize that after copies have been supplied to meet all advance orders, you will still have a supply of books which it will be necessary for you to sell, and it can be assumed that the Bahá'ís are your natural market for those copies.
>
> In order to avoid all confusion among the friends about Bahá'í literature, that is, about the manner in which it is

sold to believers, the N.S.A. adopted the ruling that authors who publish approved books through a non-Bahá'í firm are to bring such books to the attention of the friends in ways approved by the Publishing Committee, and the Publishing Committee is to undertake the distribution of notices, etc. and do the actual selling. Otherwise, Assemblies and individuals could receive announcements of Bahá'í literature from many sources, and confusion and inefficiency would result.[20]

Howard's book was forcing the National Spiritual Assembly to examine the question of books written by Bahá'ís that were other than the 'Creative Word' and how they were to be sold. This was new territory and the National Assembly had to develop a whole new policy to deal with the personal recollections of individual Bahá'ís.

There were many problems, some small and others larger, for which the National Assembly had to bring Howard into its developing view of how his books should be handled. The Bahá'í Publishing Committee, and Clara Wood as its chair, tried to balance both the National Assembly's requirements and Howard's financial needs. Unfortunately, there didn't seem to be much consultation between the Committee and Howard. The Committee laid out how it planned to handle Howard's books. They would buy the books for $1.25 each and would sell them, charging him a small 'charge for handling'. Also, the National Assembly had unexpectedly deposited the $100 in Howard's account to help pay the publisher. Howard laid out his dilemma in a letter to the Committee:

> The cost to me, in addition to the charges you will make for your assistance in selling the first 400 copies, is $1115.00 which I am obligated to pay Dutton [the publisher] before the final 600 copies are delivered to me . . .
> Now if I sell them to you for $1.25 apiece that will leave me about 25¢ profit per copy. That means that on the 200 copies still remaining out of the 600 copies delivered as

soon as the second payment of $300 is made, I stand to receive a grand total of some $50. And out of this I am expected to pay Dutton his final $300 plus the NSA $100 plus your charges for work done.

You will see now why I am tempted to use the word 'absurdity' in describing all this . . .

If I should accede to your demands, and deliver the whole edition into your hands at $1.25 apiece I should stand to receive a total profit for all my work of about $186.00.

So that brings me to the final point. I cannot accept the $100 from the NSA under these conditions. I have waited many months for the friends to subscribe about $400. I think I can be patient enough to wait another few weeks for them to subscribe a final $60.[21]

Howard concluded that he would pay Dutton and then send the final 600 copies of his book to the Publishing Committee at a 1/3 discount ($1.50) off the regular sales price of $2.25. If that wasn't workable for them, he would have to find some other way of selling the books.

Howard then proposed that the National Assembly buy 50 copies of the book at a 20% discount from the list price. He also laid out his plan, which was to sell out the current edition in order to be able to reprint it by Christmas, though he worried that 'this may seem to you and possibly the other members of the N.S.A. as an over-ambitious program'. To back up his proposal, Howard included some of the comments made about the book: Stanwood Cobb had called it 'a transcendent enterprise'; Shoghi Effendi had written that 'He is confident that when published this book will be of valuable assistance to the teaching work.' Howard then asked if he could send one copy on consignment to each Local Spiritual Assembly who had not yet ordered any. He concluded this lengthy letter praising their support (both emotional and financial), writing: 'As you probably know, or can guess, it is due almost entirely to Edris that I was given the leisure and strength to write the book. In answer to all my remonstrances she said that she thus became a partner in my work; that she could not write the book but by giving me the opportunity to write it she could think of herself as really being of service to the Cause Of God.'[22]

The result of Howard's letter was that the National Assembly used the $100 it had 'loaned' him to buy copies of the book at the advanced purchase price of $1.85 each.[23]

Money was not the only problem for *Portals to Freedom*. A Florida Bahá'í was very concerned that the National Assembly was involved with the book at all and complained about Howard's 'high powered salesmanship methods'. The man insisted that any money the National Assembly had, should go toward the publication of the 'Creative Word' and not 'eulogies of the Master and personal experiences'. He complained that 'the NSA spiritual control should not be destroyed by anyone seeking personal remuneration and leadership. I need not perhaps remind you of the Curse. "May he perish who seeks of God aught except Himself".'[24]

At long last, on 24 March 1937, Howard joyfully wrote to the Guardian, 'Portals to Freedom comes off the Dutton Press today.' He noted that the Guardian's fifty copies would be on their way to Haifa in the next couple of days. Of the initial print run of 1,200 available to Howard, 950 had been purchased at the pre-publication price of $1.85. Howard was trying to handle the book sales himself and expected the first printed edition to sell out within months. He wrote:

> . . . it seems probable that by June or July another edition will be needed. I am planning to issue 2,000 in paper covers, so that the price may be within the reach of all, and also another 1,000 or maybe 2,000 in cloth like the one you will see.
>
> Praise be to God! It does seem as though many souls may be attracted to the Cause in this way. I can say from the depths of my heart that this was the sole purpose in my mind and spirit from the moment when the book was first conceived or the first word put on paper.[25]

But then the National Assembly had two problems with the jacket of the book – it had a photograph of the Master and had

Howard's name in large letters over the Master's in small letters. One member felt that using a photograph of 'Abdu'l-Bahá was 'improper'. Someone who saw the book at the National Convention wrote to the National Assembly that the effect was that the photograph was 'an advertisement of the book'. The end result was that the National Assembly asked Howard not to use a photograph of the Master on the cover.[26] Mabel wrote about the name size problem:

> Howard was horrified by the way the jacket was made up by the artist of the Dutton Co. He had sent on a sketch of approximately what he wanted, in which the name of Abdul Baha was in large print, at the top of the cover, and his in small print at the bottom. The artist reversed this, to our intense disappointment and regret. But it was too late to do anything about it. We even considered having it done over, but that was too expensive. The N.S.A. blamed Howard for this, and thought that it was his wish and his desire to put himself forward, and instructed him to scrap the jackets, and had the Pub. Com remove them. Anyone who really knew Howard would know that his whole desire was to place his Master above himself in every way.[27]

This jacket problem delayed shipment of the books to Shoghi Effendi. Howard explained in a letter that 'Unfortunately, the printer made a serious mistake in printing the jacket, and the whole 1200 had to be reprinted.'[28]

On 26 May 1937, Shoghi Effendi's secretary wrote that the fifty copies of *Portals to Freedom* had arrived and

> some of them have, at his direction, have already been placed in the library of Bahá'u'lláh's Mansion at Bahjí. Copies here also been sent to various Bahá'í libraries in the Holy Land. The Hebrew University Library in Jerusalem, which is the largest of its kind in both the Near and the Middle East and which contains nearly 300,000 volumes, among them some important Bahá'í publications, has been presented with a

copy, the receipt of which has been acknowledged with much gratitude by the librarian.

The Guardian hopes that in America too the book is being widely distributed, and that you have made arrangements to have one copy placed in various important libraries throughout the country.

He trusts that the perusal of its most impressive and faithful account of the reminiscences of your meeting with 'Abdu'l-Bahá will serve as a means for the attraction and confirmation of many souls who are eager to respond to new spiritual realities.[29]

Pilgrims visiting the Mansion of Bahjí can see copies of the book on bookshelves today.

Shoghi Effendi's personal note of encouragement read: 'May the spirit of Bahá'u'lláh sustain you in your incessant and unforgettable services, and graciously assist you to achieve still greater triumphs in the days to come. Your true and grateful brother, Shoghi'.

For Howard, it had been a very difficult year with all of the many letters that went back and forth between the National Assembly and him. He had been immensely concerned about how to pay his financial obligations and the National Assembly had to develop a workable set of guidelines for Bahá'í authors.

But the struggles were not yet over. On 22 March 1938, Howard received word that the Publishing Committee had purchased the final 210 copies of *Portals to Freedom* from the publisher. These were the copies the publisher had planned to sell itself and were over and above the number Howard had ordered and paid for. Howard also learned that the Committee was also given all the plates of illustrations and other materials. He asked if this meant that ownership of the book had passed to the Publications Committee. In his letter to Horace Holley, he wrote, 'All the material used in the printing and binding of Portals belongs to me as I paid for it.' Howard expected royalties to be paid him on all the 210 copies sold.[30]

The National Assembly's response, written by its secretary

Horace Holley, indicated that the copies were from those extra 300 copies above Howard's printing and were therefore owned by Dutton so no royalties would be paid.[31] This exasperating situation, in which both sides were becoming a bit upset, continued. Howard responded to Horace's letter, 'I hardly know what to say . . . but as it looks from here the Pub. Committee has taken advantage of a situation to make money from my book.'[32] Horace responded by laying out the facts of the matter, concluding that 'the Dutton Co. had every right to sell their remaining books to the Publishing Committee, and the Publishing Committee had every right to purchase them'.[33] Howard apparently accepted Horace's explanation, because nothing more was said. This was all particularly difficult for Howard because the National Teaching Committee had told them that financial support for their travel teaching activities would be eliminated at the end of April and he was very worried about where the money would come from to teach the Cause.

On 29 August 1938, the National Spiritual Assembly wrote to the Ives saying that 'it was voted to refer to the Publishing Committee the information about the inexpensive edition of *Portals to Freedom* and authorize the committee to issue the book through the Scranton [Pennsylvania] printer if satisfied with the quality of their work, and arrange a royalty basis with Howard. This of course is entirely dependent upon Howard's consent.'[34] In November 1938, Howard wrote to the Guardian and told him that the National Spiritual Assembly had appropriated $350 to defray the cost of a paperback edition of *Portals to Freedom*. Howard said that he would receive a royalty of 25%.[35]

By February 1940, Howard felt that the whole process was out of his hands. The first edition had completely sold out and the National Assembly had voted the money to print the second, but nothing seemed to be happening.[36] On 13 March, Harlan Ober wrote to explain why:

> The action taken by the N.S.A. does not in any way interfere with your right to publish it, independently if you wish to do so, now that the Pub. Com. is not able to do it.

> This failure is due primarily to the needs of the Temple in the immediate future; and certain other expenses that may run high, as teaching and certain legal matters.
>
> Because the sales of Portals have not been very large during the past year and the demand not very great, it was decided to postpone any action now since the demand for funds elsewhere was and is so great . . . Action taken by the N.S.A is for now – this minute, and not for any future.[37]

The National Spiritual Assembly had to focus on different priorities from Howard's. Howard apparently reconciled himself at this point because there is no further information about *Portals to Freedom* after this time from him. The book was finally reprinted in 1943 by both the Hobson Press in America and George Ronald in the United Kingdom. *Portals to Freedom* was one of the first books ever published by George Ronald.

16
The Song Celestial

On 1 July 1935, after having completed a draft of *Portals to Freedom*, Howard began another large writing project – an 'epic' poem. He said that it seemed to want to be written, with as many as 2,000 words being written in a single morning. It was completed by 1 August. In December 1935 he wrote to Shoghi Effendi, 'It seemed to pour through me as a bounty from Bahá'u'lláh – I do not regard it as my own work at all.'¹ Mabel wrote, 'Sitting out under the trees, he would write pages and pages in a morning. How often he would call out, in a delighted voice, "Come and see what has come to me!" And he would read aloud, the beautiful verses of his poem . . . He wrote it all in three months.'² Howard hoped that the poem would attract 'certain types of intellectuals'.³ It was called *The Song Celestial* and was written as a conversation between Man and God.

In the April 1936 issue of *World Order Magazine*, a selection from the poem was published under the title 'The Divinity of Labor'.⁴ In July, a second selection was published with the title 'The New World Order' ⁵ A year later, in July 1937, a third selection was published in the same magazine as 'The Creational Book.'⁶

Howard sent a copy of *The Song Celestial* to the National Assembly's Reviewing Committee in April 1938. He noted that he was 'endeavoring to arrange for its publication and if success crowns the effort would like to have the little book bear the ensign of the Publishing Committee'.⁷ This was requested at the same time that he was struggling with the Committee over *Portals to Freedom*. The National Assembly responded that they didn't feel that a poem needed to be reviewed, because the reviewing process was to check the accuracy of 'material written about the Cause and founded on the Teachings and it is really not possible to apply this function to a poem, the value of which rests on it aesthetic quality'.[8] Howard then proposed that the Publications Committee begin to publish more types of works.[9] The National Assembly consulted about the possibility, but decided it could not do so.

In June 1935, Howard sent the Guardian a copy of a 'circular letter' he had sent to a few who were interested in his poem, noting that he had not approached the Local Spiritual Assemblies at that point. The letter stated:

> The poem is arranged under three divisions entitled 'HOURS'. These Hours are times of meditation during which 'Man' asks God certain questions regarding Life, Death, Resurrection, Heaven, Hell, Immortality, Labor, Poverty, and other questions constantly arising in the mind of the sincere seeker. Especially does 'Man' beg for a Guide Who will lead him 'through Life's thorny desert'.
>
> God answers 'Man's' questions in the Words and spirit of the Revelation of the Bahá'í Faith, although these Names are not mentioned.
>
> The purpose in the mind of the author of this poem has been to attract to the Cause of Bahá'u'lláh those souls who might avoid the teachings through ignorance of the mighty purpose of the coming of the Manifestation of God, but who might be interested in a presentation of the essence of these teachings if presented in an attractively artistic form.[10]

On 30 June, a letter from the Guardian's secretary noted that Howard's letter had

> considerably refreshed and rejoiced the heart of our Guardian. He fervently hopes that this latest production from your able pen will bring wide response from the believers and that they will all co-operate in giving it the publicity it truly deserves, and thus help it realize the purpose for which it has been written, namely to introduce the Faith through the presentation of the Teachings in an attractively artistic form.[11]

The first printing of *The Song Celestial* was done in October 1938.[12] In the preface to the 12,000-word epic poem, Howard wrote:

> Song Celestial is, in a very real sense, a spiritual history. The author, filled with questions of that vital nature which probe the very foundations of man's being, the satisfactory answers to which the serenity of soul, and which, unanswered or falsely answered, mean a life thwarted of all that really matters, asked of God, manifest again in this Day of His Revealment, all the questions he has put into the mouth of 'Man' – all these and thousands of others – and was fully and completely answered. Truly he can say from his deepest heart that –
>
> Upon his mind there fell a shower
> From Fount Celestial, and his heart found ease
> Which only God can give.
>
> This poem, then, is not a mere effort of the unaided mind to probe those infinite reaches of Cosmic wisdom. The world has for uncounted ages been filled with such vain endeavors. To add one more is the last thing author wished. Rather, he has attempted the all but impossible task to pass on to other searching minds and hearts a few gems from the infinite mine of the revealed Word of God in this Day.[13]

The 62-page poem opens with Man trying to find God:

> *Man Speaks:*
>
> Why dost Thou hide Thyself from me, O God?
> Where'er throughout the ages man hath trod
> His mind and soul hath sought Thee. All in vain!
> He can but hope and trust: but I would know.

I search through far-flung depths of stellar space;
I grope adown the labyrinths of mind;
I peer into each microscopic place
And find all else: but Thee I cannot find.

God Speaks:

It is not I who hide, 'tis thou art blind.
Thine insight is so dimmed thou canst not see
That My Creation's Book revealeth Me;
That every atom is an open door
Inviting thee to enter and explore!

What dost thou hope to see
When thou goest seeking Me?
A Face? A Voice? A word writ on the sky?
If I should speak who are thou to reply?
If I should write some guiding Word to men
Could they interpret My Supremest Pen?

By the end of the poem, Man has found God:

Man Speaks:

O Glorious Lord! My heart is living song;
At last I glimpse the light for which I long.
My heart bursts with the hope of meeting Thee!
Now all my questions, asked and unasked, flee
Before Thy Mighty Word.
        O, may I be
Enrolled with these, Thy chosen ones? May I
Be privileged to die, unknown, for Thee;
Or, self-forgetting, be allowed to live
And all my dedicated powers give
That my own fellow-men no more may lie
In graves of their own digging?

So may Thy
Long-promised Kingdom now be built on earth;
That so in midst of plenty may be dearth
No more, and from all sorrowed, weeping eyes
Shall tears be wiped away, and anguished cries
Replaced by joyous song!
        My eager being flies
To seek my longed-for promised Guide;
Nor is the night so dark nor world so wide
But I shall find Him and His Word obey.

O, Voice of God! Assure success, I pray!
Confer illumination on my day!

God Speaks:

When Man calls unto Me with heart sincere
As thine, Lo! I become the very ear
With which he heareth My assured reply.

Unto thy eager knock
My Love all doors unlock.

Man Speaks:

Now to myself at last – at last – I die!
And, risen to true Life, armed with Love's sword,
I march beneath Thy banner, nor care when,
Nor where, nor how I meet my shining Lord
Enthroned in Man, for I shall know Him then!

God Speaks:

My glory rests upon thee. On thy head
My confirmations fall.
        Before thy tread
All obstacles shall fade and I will lead

Thee to thy heart's desire.
        I grant release
To thee from bondage; from all fear surcease.

To every soul who followeth Guidance – Peace.[14]

The printed poem was available by late October. One of its earliest recipients was Henry Crane, a Methodist minister, who was enraptured:

> 'The Song Celestial' this exquisite poem from your heart and hand and head, has just come to hand. Immediately I sat down and read it through without a pause. I am utterly enraptured, and likewise overflowing with gratitude. You have sung your message into my heart, and I shall hold it there always – proud of the harmony it perpetually distils. I congratulate you most enthusiastically upon this superb achievement, and may God bless your message a thousand ways as it touches innumerable persons throughout this wide world.[15]

In July 1939, he received a letter from the secretary of the National Spiritual Assembly referring to the 30 June 1938 response of the Guardian hoping that the poem would 'introduce the Faith through the presentation of the Teachings in an attractively artistic form'. The Assembly felt that this was not met in the poem as published in the *Bahá'í News*:

> This purpose does not appear to be realized at present in view of the fact that the book does not in any way attribute the source of the fundamental ideas to Bahá'u'lláh. The National Assembly therefore voted to request you to submit the text of a printed slip which can be inserted in the book rectifying this omission. When the text is approved it is in any later edition to be substituted in place of the present prelude. The prelude unfortunately conveys the thought that the book was entirely personal inspiration, and would not possibly indicate

to the non-Bahá'í reader the fact that Bahá'ís turn to the Manifestation for the source of their spiritual knowledge.[16]

Howard responded to the National Assembly that

> of course whatever is in accordance with the wishes of the Guardian and the N.S.A. will find full cooperation on my part. But it seems to me that such a radical change in the whole spirit and purpose of the poem should have the Guardian's approbation before made, as its present form was that to which he gave his approval.
>
> The words you quote from one of his letters, for instance, were almost word for word taken from my letter announcing the forthcoming publication, which stated clearly that its purpose was to attract non-believers and for this reason no mention of the Cause was made, nor any reference to its protagonists.
>
> I am enclosing for the information of the NSA some extracts from the many letters I have received which will give to them some idea of the effects produced.
>
> ... Again, let me repeat, whatever is best for the Faith's promulgation in the opinion of those who direct its forces, will always be my first consideration.[17]

Howard immediately wrote to the Guardian, including a copy of the National Assembly's letter and the Prelude, asking for his advice. The Guardian quickly replied through his secretary:

> Now, as regards your poem 'The Song Celestial' and the N.S.A.'s recommendation that the Prelude be discarded and specification be made that the fundamental ideas contained in the Song are directly based on Bahá'u'lláh's Writings, the Guardian indeed approves of the recommendation, but would advise that any alterations that would be necessary to make this point clear should be introduced in all future editions of the book, and the present edition be left in the present form. He considers it even unnecessary to have a

printed slip inserted in the volume rectifying this omission, and is writing the N.S.A. advising them to this effect.[18]

The Guardian usually supported such decisions of National Spiritual Assemblies because, as Bahá'u'lláh wrote, they should be obeyed. But when needed, he also gave them more nuanced guidance to help them find better answers. Shoghi Effendi added a personal note to the letter above that read: 'Dear and valued co-worker: This is to assure you in person of my keen sense of gratitude for the very notable services you are rendering our beloved Faith, and which will no doubt greatly assist its furtherance and establishment. I will specially pray that you may be given the strength and guidance to extend the range of your distinguished services in the years to come, and thus ennoble the record of your past achievements.'[19]

In the end, Howard did not rewrite the Prelude, but did add the following at the end of it in accordance with the National Assembly's request: 'It is his earnest hope and prayer that the reader may thus be tempted to search for himself into the vast universe of spiritual Truth revealed in the writings of the Glory of God; the intellectual and spiritual treasures which being the infinite wealth to be found in the writings of Bahá'u'lláh and 'Abdu'l-Bahá'.[20] Since the book was not reprinted during Howard's lifetime, the addition was never used.

In November 1938 Howard was able to write to Shoghi Effendi and say that pre-publication subscriptions for *The Song Celestial* had reached 300, thus defraying the costs of publication, though he needed to sell 650 to break even. Howard was worried about achieving that goal because of publication difficulties.[21] By the end of the year, sales had reached 400.[22]

In November Rúḥíyyih Khánum gave Howard much-needed encouragement in a hand-written note in which she wrote, 'I very much like the style of your verse.' She added, 'I often read of all you and Mabel are doing for our beloved Faith and it cheers me – as it does our dear Guardian.'[23]

Mabel began to actively search for a good publishing company for a second printing with the modified Preface in late

July 1939, contacting Albert Windust about companies in the Chicago area. He recommended Kingsport Press, which claimed to be the 'largest complete book manufacturing plant in the country today' and capable of producing 100,000 books a day.[24] Unfortunately, the book was not reprinted until the early 1960s, when it was reissued by Howard's granddaughter Barbara and her husband Erich Reich through his Erich P. Reich Enterprises. By that time, none of the information from 1938 was known, so that edition does not contain either of the Preludes.

A sequel to *The Song Celestial*

Howard had no sooner completed his epic poem in 1935 than he began a very ambitious sequel called *The Song Celestial, The Antiphony*, that was to be a conversation between Man and the Báb, Bahá'u'lláh, 'Abdu'l-Bahá and others.

As he usually did, Howard wrote to Shoghi Effendi for advice:

> Now what I particularly wish to ask your advice and opinion about is this: In the poem just completed [the original Song], the Names of the Great Revelators are not mentioned, nor is the Cause referred to. Man is instructed by the Holy Spirit as he communes in his inmost heart, and these instructions are taken entirely from the Creative Word.
>
> Ever since it was completed there has been growing in my heart a longing to write a sequel in which Man finds his Guide and is told the whole Message from Its inception in 1844 to the Guardianship and the New World Order.
>
> Won't you please tell me if such a work would be acceptable, and, perhaps a suggestion as to the wisest form in which it should be constructed? The hesitation in my mind arise from two causes: first a feeling of intense inability in the face of such a vast undertaking – and second: a subtle fear lest the form in which the story would have to take shape might not meet with your approval.

My thought at present, (subject to alteration and adjustment or your desire) is to couch it also in the form of a dialogue or dramatic personification. Perhaps a conversation between Man (the seeking soul) and 'Abdu'l-Bahá, in which the Master answers all Man's questions and the complete history of the Cause is developed. This might follow to a degree the model of Dante's journey through Purgatory under the guidance of Virgil. This would give an opportunity for the 'Guide' to bring the seeker into contact with the great Souls of the time of His Holiness the Báb, the exile and imprisonment of His Holiness Bahá'u'lláh, and of the Master's period of teaching and heavenly example.[25]

On 31 December 1935, Shoghi Effendi's secretary replied:

He has received and read with deepest interest the manuscripts you had enclosed with your letter, one entitled 'The Ocean of His Utterance', and the other consisting of a long poem in which you have made an attempt to present the Cause indirectly.

As to the last one, he approves of your suggestion to write a sequel to it, and to refer more directly to the Cause. He would, however, advise you to couch the whole subject in such a form as to make it interesting and appealing to the non-Bahá'í reader. The direct presentation of the Teachings is surely highly important and even indispensable nowadays. But it should be done with utmost care and tact, and in a manner that would appeal to the non-believers . . .

The Guardian is entreating Baha'u'llah to help you in accomplishing this important piece of work, and thus enable you to contribute your full share towards the promulgation of His Message.

May He also give you strength to continue your labors in the teaching field.[26]

Shoghi Effendi's personal note was full of praise: 'Your literary accomplishments, your remarkable ability in presenting the Cause to the general public, your understanding, devotion, zeal and experience eminently qualify you to take a leading and decisive part in the nation-wide campaigns of teaching inaugurated by the American believers. I will pray for you from the depths of my heart. Rest assured and persevere. Affectionately, Shoghi.' The teaching campaign was the first Seven Year Plan.

By February 1936, Howard had written an introduction and chapters on the Síyáh-<u>Ch</u>ál and the martyrdom of Sulayman <u>Kh</u>án. As in the original *Song Celestial*, the new poem begins with Man begging for a spiritual Guide:

> How shall I find my Path in this dark night?
> I turn my face, O God, unto Thy Light.
> Illuminate my spirit that my feet
> May be directed by Thy Love! I greet
> The longed-for Day; I dedicate my life
> To Thee and to my fellow-men.
>
>   Thy Fire
> Is burning in me, O my Lord, and through
> My members doth Its glowing radiance run.
> 'Tis in Thy strength that I gain strength to do
> That which without Thee vainly I aspire.
> O, tell me, has my last great task begun?
> Is there, beyond this night Thy Splendent Sun?
>
> I seek the Heights! No more am I content
> With baser ways till now ignobly trod.
> Upon a Goal divine I am intent:
> Naught shall suffice but Thee – Thyself, O God!
>
> And yet, alas! Alas! Thou art so far!
> Thy spirit breathed within my inmost soul,
> And I, anon, dared dream Thy Guiding Star
> Would light the way to my so longed-for goal.

> But now again the shadows gather near,
> Thy Voice no longer whispers in mine ear;
> I am alone – a wanderer in the dark,
> My very spirit seemeth cold and stark,
> The wilderness so vast, the desert wide!
> And through the heavy murk there's not a gleam!
> A Guide, my God! O, send to me a Guide![27]

From this point, the poem becomes a dialogue between Man and 'Abdu'l-Bahá, with the Báb and Bahá'u'lláh chanting now and then.

Since Shoghi Effendi had encouraged this sequel, on 12 February 1936 Howard wrote to ask: 'Is the dramatic form in which it is couched acceptable? I have taken some liberties, poetic license, in that I have coupled incidents as occurring at one time whereas they actually happened at different times...'[28] In a letter written on behalf of the Guardian, his secretary wrote, 'He thinks that the Song is beautifully written, and sees no objection that it be couched in a dramatic form',[29] but in a subsequent letter noted that it would be disrespectful to have any of the three Central Figures as characters. The reply written on behalf of the Guardian noted:

> As to your question concerning the advisability of dramatizing Bahá'í historic episodes: the Guardian would certainly approve, and even encourage that the friends should engage in such literary pursuits which, no doubt, can be of immense teaching value. What he wishes the believers to avoid is to dramatize the personages of the Báb, Bahá'u'lláh and 'Abdu'l-Bahá, that is to say to treat them as dramatic figures, as characters appearing on the stage. This, as already pointed out, he feels would be quite disrespectful. The mere fact that they appear on the scene constitutes an act of discourtesy which can in no way be reconciled with their highly exalted station. Their message, or actual words, should be preferably reported and conveyed by their disciples appearing on the stage.[30]

Still unsure, Howard asked again about what part the Central Figures could play in his poem. He also misunderstood the use of the word 'stage', thinking that it meant the stage in a play. His letter back to Shoghi Effendi read, 'Of course there has never been the slightest thought of ever having these Personages appear on the stage. Such a thought is horrifying! The poems are meant only to be read. If, at any time in the future an attempt is made to adapt the poems to pageantry work such changes would be made as to have the Words spoken by their disciples.'[31] The Guardian's comments about not including the Central Figures and the enormity of the sequel project brought this effort to an end. Howard had used all the Central Figures to carry the dialogue, and the work of redoing it all may have appeared overwhelming.

The Síyáh-Chál

While working on the sequel to *The Song Celestial*, Howard asked about a number of historical events that he wished to include or allude to in the new narrative. He had apparently asked about the Síyáh-Chál in Tehran, where Bahá'u'lláh had been imprisoned. On 15 May 1936, Howard received a note from the Guardian's secretary enclosing a first-person narrative about the prison: 'The Guardian has instructed me to send you the enclosed material on the Síyáh-Chál of Tihrán where Bahá'u'lláh was imprisoned, in the hope that it may be of some use to you in writing your poems'.[32] The narrative was the personal experiences written by Dr Yúnis Khán Afrúkhtih when he visited his father, who was imprisoned with Bahá'u'lláh. Howard responded, 'Your good letter with its most valuable and inspiring enclosure made us all very happy . . . I think such an inspiring and heart rending account should be widely spread . . .'[33] It is included in its entirety here.

Síyáh-Chál and Qarih-Kahar

It is fitting that Bahá'ís should bear in their memory the names of two loathsome agencies which like those monsters of primeval times have now vanished from the earth. Let us give them a place in the museums of Bahá'í thought, that their names may endure throughout the ages to come. In my childhood I saw those two baneful powers; one I saw from a distance, the other I touched.

The Black Pit (Síyáh-Chál) was the underground dungeon used during the reign of Náṣiri'd-Dín Sháh; here such murderers, robbers, and highwaymen and rebels as were condemned to die and were thought deserving of torture and the rack, would be consigned for a time to await their death in this dank, foul-smelling and lightless place. In the narrow, winding vault where daylight never penetrated and no candle ever shone, the captives, guilty and innocent, lived out their hours in the hope that some glimmer of pity would stir the heart of Náṣiri'd-Dín Sháh and he would let them go free into the light again, or else that their agony would end and death come to summon them.

As to the Night-Black Horse (Qarih-Kahar) this was the name given to the chain used in the Black Pit, which because of its great thickness and weight was not referred to as a chain; and this was thought suited to the wasted necks of the dungeon inmates. The chain was about thirty-five feet long and set with from five to seven heavy iron collars, each with its separate lock; into this chain seven men would be locked in a row. Each prisoner held a stick with two prongs, on which the heavy collar rested, the prisoner leaning his own weight against its base; except when, sitting on the damp bricks of the dungeon he would prop his stick against the floor. Needless to say, the prisoner could neither sit nor walk under such a weight, for no athlete however powerful could carry the links of Qarih-Kahar; he could only sit tailor-wise on the ground, clasp the stick in his two hands and lean his chin between the prongs, while his eyes looked upward toward the darkness of the roof.

Such in brief was the Síyáh-Chál. And Bahá'ís should remember it for this reason, that the holy Abhá Beauty passed some time in this dungeon, and that years later a number of believers were blessed and privileged with kissing that threshold and carrying that heavy burden. But how did I come to know of such a place, I who was neither worthy to enter that dungeon nor strong enough to bear that weight? Fifty-three lunar years ago, when still a child, I had the blessing of visiting my father Mashhadí-Ḥusayn who was among the captives of that time; and when I saw the terrifying scene and the pitiful physical condition of the prisoners, I was so much moved that in fifty-three years I have never forgotten it and I never shall. Most astonishing of all was the fact that I found those ailing, debilitated beings happy and cheerful, and that, too, will stay in my mind forever. The reason for their joy was first, that they had been committed to the dungeon because of their love for Bahá'u'lláh, and second that His August Majesty Náṣiri'd-Dín Sháh had today in a moment of pity commanded that the prisoners, who for thirty days had been breathing the foul air of the pit, should be taken out into the bitter cold, to stay two hours in the light. Thirdly they were happy because through my coming they learned that their families were safe and well, and content with the will of God. For the jailers had given them to understand that the people of Ṭihrán had risen against the Bahá'ís and annihilated them and their children in a general massacre, and that it was in order to check the uprising that the Government had transferred them from their former prison to the Black Pit; now my presence showed that all the prisoners' families were safe and well.

On my arrival I found myself in a courtyard about a hundred yards square and saw a group of infirm and sickly men seated on the ground in the sun. My father had become so pale and emaciated that although he called to me I did not recognize him. I first looked at the late Mullá 'Alí-Akbar-i-Shahmírzádí, known as Ḥájí Ákhúnd, who still retained something of his former stoutness, and who was locked into the same chain as my father, and then I recognized my father. I sat a few minutes on his trembling knees, while malevolent guards surrounded us and stared fiercely down at us. I spoke a few words to the prisoners, gave them the good news of their family's safety, and at the same time I watched, and moved with my hand, the great links of the Qarih-Kahar, which were covered with rust from the underground damp, and I saw before me the mouth of the Black Pit. My father said that a month before they had been transferred from the general prison to the Pit, and that today for the first time by permission of the Sháh they were being allowed two hours in the sun. Such was my meeting with the prisoners in the courtyard of the Síyáh-Chál. Fortunately their imprisonment in the dungeon did not last more than six or seven weeks, and then they were returned to their former prison in the same neighborhood. Here in raised alcoves giving onto a long, underground corridor they would sit by day chained in groups of seven; by night they sat on the ground. Their feet were fastened into wooden stocks (kund-i-Khalílí) but they were not deprived of daylight and were furnished with lamps at night. Whereas during these seven months they had been teaching the Cause in secret to the thieves who were their fellow-prisoners, they could now speak openly with them, and at night when the jailers were asleep the believers would loudly chant such prayers and tablets as they knew by heart, and would spend happy, spiritual hours in this way. When I visited them once or twice a week they would describe their happy nights to me, and now that the violence, blows and brutality had ceased and pity had moved the hearts of the prison officials, and that they had become accustomed to prison life, they no longer desired their freedom.

At last circumstances induced the Sháh to release these believers one after another. After they were freed they often talked of the happy nights they had spent in prison, whereupon their hearers would call to mind this verse:

'How I envy the captives their happy feasts by night
When the sweets of their board are the links of their chain.'[34]

17
Howard's Other Literary Work

The Ocean of His Utterances

Howard's experience in creating a series of lessons that became a basic deepening tool for the Bahá'ís may have inspired him to create an advanced study course for the Faith that he called *The Ocean of His Utterances*. In his letter of December 1935 to Shoghi Effendi, he wrote:

> I am now engaged in the preparation of an advanced study course which I have called, 'The Ocean of His Utterances', designed for confirmed souls who wish to penetrate further into the illimitable Universe of the Spirit unfolded by His Holiness Bahá'u'lláh. This was undertaken at the request of some members of the National Teaching Committee to supplement the course of 36 lessons which have been available for several years. We have begun a class here in Winnetka which is using these lessons as they are completed, so that the advantage of actual experience may assist in their preparation . . . The matter is before the Temple Program Committee at present but no final decision has been made.[1]

The Guardian's secretary responded on 19 April 1936: 'He is very pleased to learn that your work on the study course "The Ocean of His Utterances" is progressing fairly well. He is entreating Bahá'u'lláh to give you health and strength to carry on this important and most useful piece of work to successful completion.' In his own hand, Shoghi Effendi added: 'With the renewed assurance of my lively gratitude and appreciation of the services you are rendering and of the literary accomplishments that distinguish your work in the service of our beloved Faith. Your true brother, Shoghi'[2]

Two years later Howard was re-writing his study course 'in the form of a book'. It had twelve chapters: six involved with 'the deepening of the individual spiritual life, and six with the expression of that life in society – The World Order'. Each chapter was to be a month-long study accompanied with excerpts from the Bahá'í Writings and daily readings. It was, therefore, a year-long study programme of the Bahá'í Faith 'laid out for students who wish to go deeply into the teachings'.[3] The chapter headings were:

The Mysteries of God
The Heaven of Significances
The Two Natures of Man
The True Station of Man
Immortality and Eternality
Real Life and Death. The Resurrection, Day of Judgement.
Heaven and Hell
The Gift of the Holy Spirit
The Kingdom of God on Earth
The Meeting with God
Prayer and Meditation
The Science of the Love of God
The Word of God

Howard told the Guardian, 'It is rather a formidable task for one of my age and precarious health to undertake, but I constantly bear in mind your constant encouragement to let nothing dismay or discourage me. I rely entirely upon the Assistance of the Supreme Concourse, and your precious prayers.'[4]

In the Introduction, Howard explained the purpose of the study course:

> The object of this course of reading and study of the holy utterance of the Divine Revelation of this day of God, is a very practical and inspiring one. It is simply this, that we

may thereby be induced to take the first few steps towards the unveiling of the sublime potentialities lying dormant in the true self.

'An effort is needed that we may annihilate the animal condition that the meaning of the human may become manifest.' – Seven Valleys.

... This course of reading and study is designed for those who are intellectually convinced of the truth involved in the revelation of Bahá'u'lláh, who have accepted him as the Manifestation of God the Father foretold by Christ; who wish to probe further into the hidden mysteries of God as revealed in utterances, books, tablets of Bahá'u'lláh and 'Abdu'l-Bahá, and are willing to pay the price of sacrifice of the lower self in order that the true self, the divine self, 'The Self of God', may manifest.

The Revelation of Bahá'u'lláh is a divine mine whence endless wealth of spiritual realm is to be dug. Endless are these tremendous promises to those who fulfil conditions necessary for their attainment. IS NOT THE GOAL WORTHY THE STRIVING?

Can there be anything more important than this wisdom, this solution of all problems of life, so overwhelming in this crisis of human destiny? When the portals of true knowledge are opened to us should anything deter us from entering? Is any price too great to pay for this understanding which makes the path of life clear before us and enables us 'to pass from sorrow to happiness, to return from sadness to joy, and changes depression and dejection to gladness and cheerfulness?'

May the assistance of the invisible attend every sincere heart. The goal set before us is nothing less than the eternal life of the spirit; the life of ideal happiness and peace; the life of freedom and love; citizenship and service in God's Kingdom on earth and preparation for boundless, ancient and eternal life.[5]

Howard also defined how the study groups should conduct themselves. Participants in modern study circles will recognize his suggestions:

> 1. To avoid wandering off the path of the study course, comments will be welcomed on the readings, but will be avoided when directed to the comments.
> 2. A short pause for reflection will be observed after each reading from scriptures or prayers.
> 3. Each participant will read in turn unless for any reason (s)he wishes not to do so. The study outline commentary will be read by one individual to assist in identifying them, and to avoid confusion between comments and quotations.
> 4. We suggest that each participant review the material and concepts covered between classes, and that a short period at the start of each session be devoted to sharing any insights and observations made between sessions . . .[6]

Expanding horizons

In December 1937, with *The Song Celestial* seemingly done and *Portals to Freedom* published, Howard turned his ever-questing mind to another endeavour, one he ended up calling *Expanding Horizons*. In a letter to Shoghi Effendi, he wrote, 'I shall try to show what real Life is as contrasted with this ephemeral existence which, to such a large majority of mankind, constitutes all the life they know . . . I may not refer much to the Bahá'í Faith, but aim to reach the popular mind and appeal to the spirit of heroic sacrifice rather than to the purely animal selfishness of men.' He went on to note that he had already written about 25,000 words and was very interested in any suggestions the Guardian might offer.[7]

In June 1939, Howard told Shoghi Effendi that a full draft had been completed and the first part evaluated by the Reviewing Committee. He was still considering the title of the book and had a list of possibilities, including *Pearls From the Ocean's Depths, Cosmic Consciousness, The Light of the Universe, The*

Divine Zodiac, The Cosmic Calendar and *Humanity's Expanding Horizon*. He preferred *Expanding Horizons*, but noted that 'This is subject to your approval. I should deeply appreciate it if you would yourself suggest the title for me to use.'[8]

In a significant addition, Howard had put a series of questions at the end of the first chapter, but was uncertain about their utility. 'I am not decided', he wrote to the Guardian, 'whether to use such questions or not. Hence have only added them to one chapter. Would you consider such questions helpful and necessary?'[9]

Shoghi Effendi's response, through his secretary, was that

> The manuscript of the first part of your new book has also duly reached him, but he regrets very much indeed that owing to pressure of work he was unable to read it over carefully. He has, however, reread certain passages, and his general feeling is that the work, both in the form and scope, is quite satisfactory, and he wishes me to assure you of his approval to this effect. He thinks it would be preferable to omit including any questions at the close of chapters, and as regards the title of the book he feels that of the various names you have suggested 'Expanding Horizons' would be the most suitable and the best.[10]

Shoghi Effendi closed the letter with a personal note, writing that 'I will specially pray that you may be given the strength and guidance to extend the range of your distinguished services in the years to come, and thus ennoble the record of your past achievements. Your true and grateful brother, Shoghi'[11]

Howard set his theme at the beginning of the book, quoting 'Abdu'l-Bahá speaking in New York:

> Day and night you must strive that you may attain to the significances of the heavenly Kingdom, perceive the signs of Divinity, acquire certainty of knowledge and realize that this world has a Creator, a Vivifier, a Provider, an Architect – knowing this through proofs and evidences and

not through susceptibilities, nay, rather, through decisive arguments and real vision – that is to say, visualizing it as clearly as the outer eye beholds the sun. In this way may you behold the presence of God and attain to the knowledge of the holy, divine Manifestations.[12]

To a large extent, *Expanding Horizons* was a reworking of *The Ocean of His Utterances*, something obvious when the tables of contents of the two works are compared. Howard rewrote it with the aim of attracting those who were not Bahá'ís. His table of contents details the concepts in the book:

Introduction	–	The Light of the Universe. The Importance of the Study of the Word of God.
Chapter 1	–	The Sun of Reality and Its Mirrors. The Manifestation of God's Names and Attributes.
Chapter 2	–	The Heaven of Significance. The World of Reality. The Mysteries of God.
Chapter 3	–	Man, Human and Divine. Beast-like or God-like. The necessity for a Divine Exemplar.
Chapter 4	–	Immortality. True Life and Death. Resurrection. Heaven and Hell. Eternal Life.
Chapter 5	–	The Word of God. Its Study. Its Importance. Its Effect. Its Power.
Chapter 6	–	Celestial Manhood. Race Maturity. Citizenship in the Kingdom of God. The True Believer.
Chapter 7	–	The Kingdom of God on Earth. God Himself Its Ruler.
Chapter 8	–	The Education of the Citizens of the Kingdom.
Chapter 9	–	The New Science of Economics.
Chapter 10	–	The Social Relations of the Citizens of the Kingdom.
Chapter 11	–	International Relationship Between Citizens of the Kingdom.
Chapter 12	–	The Administration of the Divine Kingdom.

Again, those who have studied the Ruhi series of courses will recognize many of these concepts. Howard begins this book describing man's position in this material world and then his position in relation to the spiritual world. The material world, he indicated, we can see and navigate, but the spiritual world we cannot see on our own. Many people try to find their way through the spiritual worlds, and Howard quickly brings in the concept of the Manifestation of God:

> To the People of the Country of Thought – We do not live in America, or England, or Turkey, or China, or on a certain street in any certain city. We live in a World of our own creation, and in a city built by our own controlled or uncontrolled thoughts. Of course our bodies have a certain postoffice address, but that may be said to be only a matter of convenience. We are, very literally, 'people of the Country of Thought' as Bahá'u'lláh so trenchantly puts it. We do create the world we live in. It is the kind of thinking we do which determines the atmosphere, and the altitude of that Country, and the well-being of its people.
>
> The world we live in is not only created by ourselves, it is also limited only by ourselves. We may make that World as small or as large as we wish. Its boundaries are only circumscribed by the lines we draw. Like the material world, the 'contingent world' as Bahá'u'lláh calls it, that world of our creation, is traversed by many thoroughfares and all of us may travel if we will. There are provincialists of this Country of Thought as well as of the countries of geographical status. And there are also adventurous souls who dare the unknown realms of the mind and heart, as well as invaders of polar regions and Columbuses of unknown seas.
>
> There are needed Captains to lead these adventurous souls. Knowers are needed to instruct the ignorant; Pilots to navigate us through the uncharted seas. Souls vastly more experienced and courageous are needed for this task than any Marco Polo or Richard Byrd. To dare the uncharted seas of the world of sense is child's play compared to the venture

into the Realms of the mind and heart under the direction of the Divine Navigator, the Holy Mariner, He Who alone is able to guide us to His 'abiding rest beneath the shadow of the Tree of Knowledge,' The Divine Cartographers of that Universe of Celestial knowledge and understanding are to the atlas-makers of this little world as the 'Creator of all the Worlds of God' is to the ant on its ant-hill.

The recognition of the fact that we are living in the Day upon which has dawned the Sun of Reality is of little worth to the traveller unless he provides himself with the map of this New Country of Thought, and diligently studies it and faithfully follows it. A certain alertness of mind, a practical attention to details, a careful scanning of near and far horizons are essential to safe journeyings. Of what value the knowledge that the Divine Pilot has appeared if His Chart is ignored? Of what possible advantage to the traveller is the Celestial Road-Map if way-side taverns are lingered in too long?[13]

Howard's conclusion at the end of the book makes it clear that there is no end to the wisdom of his Captains:

As one reviews the attempt to sound the depths of a depthless Ocean; to probe a vast expanse with limited vision; to wing flight across a boundless universe of Revelation, ever expanding as wings strengthen – how futile all endeavors seem!

And futile, indeed they are if the goal set is the complete conquering of that illimitable expanse. But that is not the goal. When the Wrights launched their first flying machine into the air at Kittyhawk, N.C. did they set as their objective an Atlantic flight, or the circumnavigation of the globe? It was sufficient for them to prove the possibility of conquest of gravitational limitation, to emulate the eagle. When Columbus set out in his cockle-shell to map a new route to India was he disappointed when land was sighted after daring the perils of an unknown sea? Even though he later found that land was other than his ignorant fancy had pictured, yet it was LAND which was, though he never knew it, to be greater than any India.

So the mariner traversing the Sea of the Revelation of Bahá'u'lláh; the diver in the limitless ocean of His Word; the dauntless defier of the animalistic law of gravitation – the law which commands man not to attempt to escape the bondage of the material world – needs not to envisage in this aspiration more than the CERTITUDE of the possibility of escape from that bondage. What undreamed realms open before him if he finds he is able to look down upon that 'contingent world' which only yesterday, when afoot, presented such formidable obstacles. To get a glimpse of that spiritual panorama, and inhale the Breeze from that East of Power, is that not victory enough?

Just as our forefathers were forced to abandon all that they had amassed through generations of toil and seek new lands of freedom, so we, in this Great Day when undreamed of Freedom awaits us in Lands of spiritual emancipation is opening before us [sic], find forces beyond resistance impelling us to dare unknown Lands of the Spirit.

When in far-distant ages our ancestors were forced to abandon homes and lands, the heritage of countless generations, before the advancing glaciers which made life impossible, how far beyond their powers to envisage the fertile lands awaiting them, the far more beautiful homes destined for their children's children! And, which is far more significant, how could they dream of the new possibilities of mind and heart opened to them because of the seeds of character developed by that very renunciation and courage. They were Forced to that renunciation, but how gladly would they have embraced it had they known! This severing of anchoring bonds; this conquering of terrors created, perforce, in the depths of their beings those powers which have, as the generations have developed them, made our civilizations possible . . .

So with those souls in this Day who, abandoning all

else save Him, have advanced perforce into the untrodden realms of free spirits, find themselves faced with unknown dangers and unforeseen responsibilities. But the very facing of them, the unreserved acceptance of that spiritual station; the joyful treading of those untrodden paths revealed by the Divine Guide, develop such new powers, such new capacities of eye, ear, heart and mind, that all we have abandoned are seen as childish toys . . .

We too are embarked upon a new sea; we too are forced by the on-sweeping glaciers of a destructive materialism into new and untrodden Lands of the Spirit; we too are encountering such new demands upon resourcefulness, courage, patience and steadfastness that all past experiences and precedents are powerless to aid.

But we have a Guide, a Helper, a Protector, a Counsellor. We not only have an infinite Universe of Spirit to explore but we have a Sun of Reality to illuminate it. The complete and unfaltering certitude of both of these truths is the hallmark of the true believer and transforms him, 'weak and vanishing mortal that he is', into a veritable mirror of that sun.

Does it not follow, then, that to disregard the slightest suggestion of that Infallible Guide; to neglect a single Command of His; to cast one backward glance upon those abandoned lands of imprisonment; to 'place any knowledge above His Knowledge' or any riches above His Wealth; or any happiness above His Peace, is to prove ourselves still entombed with our spiritual ancestors, still slaves cringing under the lash of materialism.[14]

Howard developed the concept of studying the Word of God through 351 manuscript pages, finishing his full draft on 31 July 1939. He was anxious to get the book published and hoped to get it to the printer by September or October. Everything, however, was dependent on the verdict of the Reviewing Committee. He poured out his worries to Shoghi Effendi:

The whole work is subject to your approval and to its being passed upon favorably by the Reviewing Committee. If it is so approved there still remains the important question of its publication. I cannot ask the Publishing Committee to undertake it as I know their funds are extremely limited. There remains only, so far as I know now, the method I used in publishing Portals and the "Song", viz. securing pre-publication subscriptions at a slightly reduced price. May I ask that you express to me your ideas and suggestions on this detail?

... As my health and strength are very uncertain I have to economize both and that makes planning definite times difficult. I feel assured that only your prayers and the assistance of Bahá'u'lláh have enabled me to do what so far has been done. I do beseech you for your most earnest supplications that all Bahá'u'lláh's desires for my service to Him may be accomplished. More than that I do not wish.[15]

In his reply, the Guardian's secretary wrote:

... the Guardian wishes me to urge you to strictly avoid over-taxing your energies, and to have always in view the necessity of safeguarding and preserving your health in the best condition possible, even at the cost of some delay or even curtailment in your activities for the Faith. Rest assured he will continue to pray for your strength, guidance and confirmation, and for the fulfilment of your fondest hopes in service to the Cause.[16]

In August, Howard wrote to Horace Holley, secretary of the National Spiritual Assembly, in advance of the Assembly's next meeting, about his hopes to get the book published. Everything depended on the Reviewing Committee completing its evaluation before anything else could be done. Albert Windust had recommended Kingsport Press in Kingsport, Tennessee, as a potential printer and Howard had arranged for them to send the National Assembly a cost breakdown before the next

Assembly meeting. Howard saw the publication schedule slipping by and told Horace that one of the reasons he was

> anxious to get the book out before the holidays, or as soon as possible, is that I feel the importance of relieving the Nat'l. Teaching Com. as soon as possible of responsibility for Mabel's expenses, which, of course, in my present state of health, includes most of my own.
>
> Judging from experience with Portals and the Song Celestial, income from the three books should within a year or less provide funds to nearly, if not entirely, pay our living expenses.
>
> This, I think, will make clear to the N.S.A. that my interest in an early decision is not prompted by anything in the nature of impatience. If it is the opinion that the decision should be postponed and publication of the book put off until Spring or later, I am perfectly agreeable.
>
> The question upon which I would appreciate decision is: Providing the Reviewing Committee recommends the publishing of Horizons under the auspices of the Baha'i Publishing Committee, would the same methods of securing pre-publication subscriptions be approved in this case? I am enclosing copies of the letter sent out by the Committee and of the mimeographed notice sent out with their approval, so that you may I to what I refer . . .
>
> The book can be published to sell at list $2.50, 520 pp. Cloth same size as Portals, but slightly smaller type. The pre-publication price would be $2.00 plus postage.[17]

The Reviewing Committee completed its evaluation in December, but the result was not what Howard had hoped for: 'My new book – Expanding Horizons – was finished, at least I thought it was, last August, but our reviewing committee suggested so many changes and corrections (wise and necessary ones) that I have had long weeks of work on it, and this, in my low state of health, has been [a] very slow and tedious job.'[18]

By February 1940, Howard had finished all the changes

suggested by the reviewing committee, but felt stymied. He told Shoghi Effendi that 'the matter of its publication, if at all, is entirely in their [the National Spiritual Assembly's] hands. It does not seem probable, at this writing, that it will be done within the near future, as the second edition of Portals to Freedom has not made any progress, in spite of the fact that the money was voted many months ago by the N.S.A., and also that the first edition is entirely exhausted and there is considerable demand amongst the friends and the newly attracted souls for the book.'[19]

In May, Shoghi Effendi responded to Howard's February letter about what Howard should write about next. On behalf of the Guardian, his secretary wrote that he

> feels that for the present you should better concentrate on teaching the Cause, particularly in the pioneering field, especially as the publication of your new book 'Expanding Horizons' has not yet been undertaken, and no definite action been adopted by the N.S.A. in this matter. He still hopes, nevertheless, that some arrangement will soon be made whereby the book may be printed, and that its circulation will serve to awaken widespread and genuine interest in the Teachings.[20]

The Guardian finished the letter with his handwritten note: 'May the Beloved guide every step you take and aid you to continue rendering the Cause services that will enrich its annals, and extend the range of its beneficent activities. Your true and grateful brother, Shoghi'

Howard passed away a year later and *Expanding Horizons* was never published.

Poetry and other writing

Howard was prolific in his writing, with many poems and proposed books in addition to the books he actually wrote. He talked about books called 'Life and How to Live it', and 'Great

Journeys in the Universe of Baha'U'llah', but unfortunately, we have found no manuscripts or other information about them.

Beyond his literary creations described earlier in this chapter, he wrote poetry, the talks he gave, and even the beginning of a novel. His poems almost all dealt with spiritual themes and finding truth. The following was entered in the 'Most Interesting Poem' contest:

The Question and the Answer

The Question

Man's age-long future? What do such words mean?
I see death stalking all the world. He takes
The high and low. The tree of life he shakes
Remorselessly and man drops from the scene.

He pays no heed to pleading nor complaint;
His cold hand strikes the sinner and the saint.
The heart of mankind bleeds and, bleeding, breaks.
Man is – is not. He lives and then – hath been.

The Lords of Life assure me of a bliss
Beyond the sky, and I would fain believe:
But learned men scoff sneeringly at this
And snatch from me the faith I would conceive.

'What is the sky,' they say, "tis empty space
Stretching away illimitably far'.
They point to Arcturus, that distant star
And tell of Light Years, while I hide my face
In dread to dream that I could find a Place
A home, in that vast gulf. I vainly pray.
My hopes allure me while my fears betray.

The Answer

O son of man! Death have I made for thee
As tidings glad: at its approach why flee!
That darkness have I for thee kindly made
A beckoning glory, not a threatening shade.
Why dost thou hide thee from this splendid light
And close thine eyes insisting it is night?

Look thou with keenly penetrating eye:
Canst thou in all My universe descry
A trace of death? 'Tis change thou seest here,
A change which leadeth but to life again.
Death is a superstition born of fear.

Think how the unborn babe should fear the pain
Of parturition. If he could foresee
That venture vast would he not be aghast?
Would he not say that life can nowise be
Outside my mother's womb? "Tis her life-blood
That nurtures me: it is her heart that beats
In mine; my life', he'd say, 'is in her breath,
Tear me from her! Ah, that, indeed, were death!'

Yet, could he think, were he not wholly blind,
Within his very being he would find
A proof most plain of wider life to be:
For, in his organs, forming in the womb,
Is evidence that soon he will be free
To use them. Thus, my son, 'tis so with thee:
For, in the matrix of this world thy part
It is to build thy future life; thy heart
Of love to nurse; thine insight keen attend;
Thine ear instruct; thy limbs to service bend.'

Thy world, compared to Mine, is more a tomb
Than life: thou shouldst prepare thee to ascend.

For, in this transient tavern now engaged
Thy hunger for true life is not assuaged.

While 'The Question and the Answer' was about death, Howard also wrote a poem he called 'Life':

Life

A beginning: a cry in the darkness
    A hush on a mother's breast;
A stretching of hands to the dawning,
    A trying of wings from the nest.

A dreaming of battles and glory;
    A glimpse of the summits sublime;
A face turning steadfastly upward;
    A girding of limbs for the climb.

A losing of missions at mid-day;
    A glare on the hot dusty way;
A burden so heavy it crushes;
    A soul that awakens to pray.

A step growing slower and weaker;
    A heart growing firm and assured;
And eye that, though dim, sees but clearer
    Because of the darkness endured.

A stilling of limbs in the silence;
    A sleep that no calling can rouse;
A folding and softly composing
    Of the beautiful, tenantless house.

A Father's hand reaching through darkness;
    The light of a new day and sun;
A joyful arousing and winging,
    For O, life has *begun*.[21]

A DAY FOR VERY GREAT THINGS

The following is a poem written in 1894 and given to Muriel on her birthday in 1940. It has been shared widely by the various generations of the Ives family. Muriel had typed it up, and often would read it at gatherings, Barbara shared it at times with youth and others, and Erica Toussaint and her siblings have shared it as a dramatic reading over the years at times:

Tirzah
A Legend of the East

Tirzah, the mendicant, who one time sate
In the cool shadow by the city gate
Asking for alms, has come to die – is dead,
And her dark soul, unblessed of good, has fled
To the great doom prepared. There, ages long,
Tortured by vain regret, lashed by the thong
Remorse, which Memory wielded ceaselessly,
At last was touched by Sorrow, and her cry,
Laden with hope, with penitence and love,
Reached Azrael, God's messenger, above
Her pit of torment passing. Circling wide
He turned and listened. Seeing, Tirzah cried:

'Oh, Help of God, carry my prayer to Him
Without Whom long I lived, my soulsight dim
with Earth's unnumbered wrongs. But now I see,
Earth having passed, beseech Him pity me.'

The Angel heard, and, sad, resumed his wing,
Taking to God this plea of suffering.

He soon returning this brief message brought:
'God says: One act of selfless kindness wrought,
Careless of praise or any hope of gain,
Shall be the test of succor from thy pain.'
Long pondered Tirzah, searching through the past
For one poor deed, one beam of sunlight cast

Across her shadowed years on earth. At last:

'One act, so slight, of such small worth
God will not count it as of any price
When weighed against my many years of vice,
Is all I can remember. Once there crept
Into my hut when all the city slept
A poor, a half-starved wretch beseeching food.
All that hot day had I in the market stood
Begging with outstretched palm, and had received
Nothing but two small carrots. One relieved
My fast at even and but one remained.

'Oh, Messenger of God! My pity gained
The victory o'er self. I hungry sate
All the next day beside the city gate.
But that was nothing. Had I only known!
To live midst suffering four-score years and own
But one small deed of all I might have done
To base eternal happiness upon.'

Gently the Angel said: 'Tis God alone
Can judge the value of a kindness done.'
And, saying, rose again on eager wing,
Taking to God this plea of suffering.

When he returned he bore with gentle hand,
And tenderness which none might understand,
A carrot. Shading it with jealous wing
As 't were a holy and a sacred thing.

'God says: "One selfless thought, one kindly deed
Hath power to aid thee in thy need."
Have faith. Doubt not. If thou but lovest well
That Love shall triumph o'er the clutch of Hell.'

Speaking, he bent, reaching the humble weed

To Tirzah, and, behold! She's all but freed.
The carrot and the wings of Azrael
Are lifting her from out the depths of Hell.

Lifting, but not yet freed, for, 'round her feet
She feels the arms of some poor soul entreat

For Heaven too. Casting a glance below
She sees that wretched soul whose moment's woe
She eased by that small gift so long ago.
'Ah, friend!' She said, 'God's aid belongs to thee.
Except for you there were no hope for me.'

With that they faster rose, yet still a weight
Dragged heavily toward their baleful state.
Glancing again – Behold! A living chain
Of damned souls seeking surcease from pain.
More numerous than mind or eye could seize;
Feet clasped by hands, arms interlocked with knees;
On every side the doomfilled pit was riven,
All Hell in motion, reaching out for Heaven.
Horrored by this appalling sight she cried:
'Oh, Angel Azrael, bid them abide!
Will not the carrot break! Those wings of thine!
Did these do good? Was not the carrot <u>mine</u>?'

Alas, with that the carrot broke. The chain,
Tirzah and all, into the pit again,
With many a cry returned. The while above
The Angel moaned: 'Did not I bid thee <u>love</u>?'

Then hid his face, and Heavenward winged his way,
And there was sorrow 'round God's Throne that day.[22]

One of Howard's more interesting efforts was an untitled novel about the discovery of a future, more spiritual world during wartime. Howard was quite optimistic about its appeal:

I am inclosing the outline and first chapter of a book which, I believe has more appeal right now than war stories, because it is a story of the world after the war, which subject has assumed a greater challenge. It has the same type of appeal which made of Lost Horizons a best seller and of Looking Backward a book which has survived thru three generations. I hope that you will consider it carefully, because this book is going to sell. It is going to be read. And I very much want you to be the publisher as your unique genius for getting a book before the largest number of people in the shortest possible time. That is what I particularly want for my book.[23]

The book begins with a pilot being shot down over France in what is obviously the Second World War, because Nazi Germany is mentioned. The pilot is mysteriously transported into the future and awakes in an utopian era, where everyone is at peace, and unity and prosperity are universal. When he meets the inhabitants of this age, he learns that the war in which he fought was the last great war. It had so exhausted the countries involved that all the peoples of the world finally rose up and forced their governments to sign a peace treaty and participate in a universal conference where all their problems were resolved. Through the four chapters that exist, Howard creates what Bahá'ís would recognize as the future Golden Age of the Bahá'í Faith. It is not known whether he ever finished the book – it was never published.

18
Opening the Seven Year Plan
1936–1937

Shoghi Effendi began to implement 'Abdu'l-Bahá's *Tablets of the Divine Plan* in 1936 and gave the National Spiritual Assembly of the United States and Canada a Seven Year Teaching Plan on 1 May. It was the Guardian's first international teaching plan and it gave the North American Bahá'ís the responsibility of opening all of North and South America to the Faith. From the time he had become the Guardian in 1922, Shoghi Effendi had slowly built up the Bahá'í Administrative Order and this was the beginning of a 16-year training period during which he gave every National Spiritual Assembly in the world teaching plans to help them learn to systematically spread the Faith. In 1953, he gave the Bahá'ís of the world the Ten Year Crusade which was designed to elect the final piece of the Bahá'í Administrative Order – the Universal House of Justice.

In his message to the 1936 National Convention, the Guardian wrote:

> Appeal to assembled delegates ponder historic appeal voiced by 'Abdu'l-Bahá in Tablets of the Divine Plan. Urge earnest deliberation with incoming National Assembly to insure its complete fulfilment. First Century of Bahá'í era drawing to a close. Humanity entering outer fringes most perilous stage its existence. Opportunities of present hour unimaginably precious. Would to God every State within American Republic and every Republic in American continent might ere termination of this glorious century embrace the light of the Faith of Bahá'u'lláh and establish structural basis of His World Order.[1]

The Guardian amplified this message on 30 May:

> I fervently hope and pray that the year into which we have just entered may be signalized by fresh conquests and unprecedented triumphs in the teaching field within the United States and beyond its confines. A systematic, carefully conceived, and well-established plan should be devised, rigorously pursued and continuously extended. Initiated by the National representatives of the American believers, the vanguard and standard-bearers of the radiant army of Bahá'u'lláh, this plan should receive the wholehearted, the sustained and ever-increasing support, both moral and financial, of the entire body of His followers in that continent. Its supreme immediate objective should be the permanent establishment of at least one center in every state of the American Republic and in every Republic of the American continent not yet enlisted under the banner of His Faith. Its ramifications should gradually be extended to the European continent, and its scope should be made to include those countries, such as the Baltic States, Poland, Greece, Spain and Portugal, where no avowed believer has established any definite residence. The field is immense, the task gigantic, the privilege immeasurably precious. Time is short, and the obligation sacred, paramount and urgent. The American community must muster all its force, concentrate its resources, summon to its aid all the faith, the determination and energies of which it is capable, and set out, single-minded and undaunted, to attain still greater heights in its mighty exertions for the Cause of Bahá'u'lláh . . .
>
> The American believers, if they wish to carry out, in the spirit and the letter, the parting wishes of their beloved Master, must intensify their teaching work a thousandfold . . . The Tablets of the Divine Plan invest your Assembly with unique and grave responsibilities, and confer upon it privileges which your sister Assemblies might well envy and admire. The present opportunity is unutterably precious.[2]

This was exactly the call that Howard and Mabel had been waiting for and it opened a new chapter in their services to the Faith. Before the Plan, most of their teaching efforts had been concentrated in the American Northeast and nearby upper Midwest: New York, Maryland, Maine, New Hampshire, Illinois, Ohio and Wisconsin. With the Seven Year Plan, their field of service became Canada, North Dakota, Nebraska, Ohio, and the American South – Tennessee, Arkansas, Mississippi, Alabama, Georgia, Louisiana. Mabel went to New Mexico and Oklahoma after Howard's passing.

The Seven Year Plan would see Howard and Mabel rise to the peak of their service to the Faith: Howard with his books and Mabel with her travel teaching and proclamation.

During the summer of 1936, Howard and Mabel began the new Plan in the older, familiar country of Utica and Albany, New York, and Kittery, Maine. On their way back to Winnetka at the beginning of September, they stopped in Schenectady and Utica to speak to different groups.[3]

Mabel in Omaha, Lincoln and Council Bluffs, Nebraska

Mabel began the new phase in their teaching work during the autumn of 1936. In September, Sylvia Mattheson began a teaching project in Omaha and Lincoln, Nebraska and Mabel joined her on 26 October.[4] She wrote that Sylvia, Prof. Forsyth Ward (who later, with his wife Janet, would be the caretakers of the Shrine of Bahá'u'lláh in Israel) and four members of Sylvia's class met her at the station.[5] Mabel found a room, but needed a few items, so asked Howard to send her a number of things; 'long chart in our closet (and put a stick in it so it won't break), and I could use my can of Postum . . . and some cocoa . . . and kitchen knife . . . and a plate, knife and fork'.[6] The content of Mabel's letters usually varied from the highly spiritual to the lowly practicalities, but in Nebraska, most of her letters describe the material world and what she was doing in it.

On 29 October, Mabel gave her first public talk in Omaha on the 'Origin and Destiny of Man' to 17 people at the Hotel

Paxton. During the first week of November, she had interviews with the presidents of five clubs, prepared publicity and gave a second talk at the Paxton Hotel to a dozen people.[7]

While Mabel spread the teachings of Bahá'u'lláh in Nebraska, her daughter, Edris, was watching over the expenses, so Mabel sent her an accounting of what she was spending. Her room cost $4 per week and her food was $5 per week – she was eating two meals a day; breakfast was commonly fruit, cereal and canned milk in her room. She spent 30 October calling around and arranging interviews with various groups in town. In her activities, she passed the local bookstore, whose owners were very cooperative and already carried some Bahá'í books.[8]

Howard also tried to keep track of the finances, but on a bit of a hit-or-miss basis. One day he discovered that Edris was supporting them financially beyond what she was actually able to do. She continually sent funds to Mabel and also kept Howard in pocket money, but Howard discovered that supporting them had caused her to have a stack of unpaid bills amounting to $80. He insisted that Mabel not let on to Edris that they knew: 'She does not know I am writing you about it and if she did she would kill me.'[9] This financial aid for Mabel and Howard resulted in Edris being severely criticized by both her husband and her father, Theron Rice-Wray.[10]

Sylvia and Mabel took the bus to Lincoln, Nebraska, on 6 November to open it to the Faith. Upon arriving at their hotel, the Hotel Cornhusker, Mabel described the multi-pronged and energetic strategy that characterized her teaching efforts:

> sold m[anager] on letting us have a lecture room for 3 lectures free (had to explain the Cause) then dashed to both papers and had fine interviews in each one explaining the teachings and received fine cooperation – each promising to come and hear us – really interested. Had to get publicity in before deadline. Then dashed to the Radio Station and got date to see Program Director at 9:00 then phoned to our list of people to whom we had written several days before. Found the _____ were definitely not interested

– even _____ seemed pretty cool – so no chance of staying there . . . so engaged a room at the hotel . . . then rushed to the Radio again. Had wonderful interview with him – he kept us almost an hour – seemed deeply interested and said he wanted to try and come to our Sunday lecture and announced our lectures on his news broadcast and gave us 15 minutes on the air for Saturday. Then to Chamber of Commerce to meet girl Sylvia knew and phoned some more. Sylvia gave a good talk to a man there who said he was seeking for truth – then home and to rest as I hadn't slept long through the night before and Sylvia went out on several errands . . . Then we couldn't get to eat until too late to eat much so we again had small bits so as not to dull our minds . . .

Today [7 November] up early and writing feature article and report of last night to talk. Off to newspaper to see other people met at the newspaper office. Mrs Kilpatrick called up, wife of head of Uni[versity] Music School, and offered to drive us around and she took me to newspaper and then took us both to several places to interview club officers. Then back to hotel to lunch in dining rooms. Mrs R's guest, Sylvia, Mrs Roth . . . Lillian Derr, Sylvia's guest. We all ate together in state. Then I slipped off to dress for 2:30 meeting. 9 present and deeply interested opportunity. Promise to come back tomorrow and bring friends. Then took taxi on to Radio Office for interview broadcast. We wrote ahead of time the questions and the man asked us and we answered extemporaneously, all about the Cause . . . Then dashed up to interview a University Professor for a speaking date for Sylvia in their Convention – will be taken up by committee later. Forgot to mention that I have been asked to speak Dec 10 for Bus[iness] and Prof. Women Club . . .[11]

It was a whirlwind and Mabel was so busy that even her letters were rushed almost to the point of being cryptic. And the report above was just for two days.

Sylvia and Mabel returned to Omaha on Monday the 8th and made arrangements for more talks. They gave one talk to nine people, two of whom said, 'definitely that they are sure that they have found the thing they have been searching'. The next day, they visited the Florence Home for the Aged and met Mrs White, a 91-year-old woman who was on fire with the Faith. They spoke to an audience of about 30 at the Home on 'Life after Death'. On Wednesday, two women from Lincoln, Mrs Heald and Mrs Bricka, drove to Omaha and declared their Faith in Bahá'u'lláh, then returned home ready to form their own study class.[12]

November 12th was the day of a planned Peace Forum and the Birth of Bahá'u'lláh. Mabel, Sylvia and Mrs J. Sluyter all spoke to an audience of 19.[13] The next day, Friday, Mabel and Sylvia were off to Council Bluffs, across the river from Omaha, where they set up a public talk at the Chieftain Hotel for the following Tuesday. On Saturday, they hosted a pilau dinner for seven interested people and Mabel told stories about 'Abdu'l-Bahá. They returned to Omaha and went to the public forum at the Paxton Hotel, which featured Rabbi Weiss, Mrs Margaret Fisher and Mabel. Nineteen people were present. The Rabbi spoke about the contributions of the Jewish people while Mrs Fisher, President of the Women's Department of the Chamber of Commerce, talked about contributions of the 'colored race'. Mabel gave her talk on Bahá'u'lláh's contributions and greatly impressed her cospeakers.[14]

While Mabel kept up a frantic pace in Nebraska, Howard tried to make reports of her activities to the National Teaching Committee, but it was proving difficult due to her frenetic handwriting, lack of detail and her hurried, word-dropping writing. Finally, he demanded that she

> make a point every day of writing out carefully all that you and Sylvia do, so far as the work of the Cause is concerned. It is most important if any report of value is to be made to the NTC. I should have all the names and addresses of the people you contact. A legible and accurate report of meetings held and numbers attending, etc. PLEASE take time to

do this. Your letters often speak of 'rushing' here or 'dashing' there or 'hurrying' somewhere else.[15]

Mabel's subsequent letters were much more legible and she began to keep a separate record of names and numbers. She went to Council Bluffs again on 24 November, during an 'awful dust storm' that lasted all day. She had interviews with several clubs and individuals, phoned a number of people, talked with the newspaper and arranged for a display of Bahá'í books in the main bookstore. She was surprised to find that someone in Geneva, Switzerland, had sent the bookstore a subscription to *The World Order,* a Bahá'í magazine published between 1935 and 1949. For two years the owners had enjoyed it. Mabel had a meeting at a hotel with four people who had heard of the meeting through her publicity.[16]

The women spent from 25 through 27 November in Omaha giving interviews. Alma Sothman spent two hours with Mabel on the 25th. Alma was 'a fine person, 5ft 8, a Unitarian', wrote Mabel, and that they had a wonderful evening. Alma said, with tears in her eyes, that 'she did not know how to pray'. Mabel turned to Bahá'u'lláh for inspiration and 'He showed her how'. The next day, Mabel and Sylvia went to the Florence Home and visited Mrs White again.[17]

On Saturday the 29th, they returned to Council Bluffs for the day to meet with new Bahá'í Miss Heald. Back in Omaha, they gave talks to a few more small groups, then, on 2 December, addressed 250 people at a Parent-Teacher Association meeting on the topic of 'World Understanding and Peace'.[18]

For the remainder of their teaching trip, until 17 December, Mabel and Sylvia continued their meetings and interviews, spending time with those who were particularly interested in what they had heard. Her activities for December were:

7 December, talked with interested individuals then gave a talk on 'Security for a Failing World' to 10 people
8 December, visited Bahá'ís then spoke on 'Buildup for World Peace in the New Age' to about 100

9 December, worked on her radio talk and rested
10 December, spoke at the Cornhusker Hotel on 'Security for a Failing World'
11 December, spoke again at the Cornhusker Hotel, this time on 'Education in the Coming Age'
12 December, worked on her radio talk, went to the study class meeting, visited the library and sold them three books, went to a second study class session[19]

Mabel's talk on 'Security for a Failing World' (see Appendix 3) was all about the oneness of humanity and unity. She opened by saying:

> Strange as it may seem, true modernism does not consist in cocktail parties, sophistication, jazz music, crude, grotesque art, and cynicism. Rather, True Modernism consists in a World Outlook.
>
> You see, the truly modern person realizes that he is sharing this little planet of ours, called the Earth, with a great many other human beings, and he perceives that the welfare of each one of them, including himself, is dependent upon the welfare of all of them. That it is relatively unimportant into which nationality or religious system he was born, as the human race is after all just one great family and that he is part of this family.
>
> He sees the world as a whole. In fact he is consciously a citizen of the world. Now that is being modern, that is being realistic, and if he is still more modern, he will know that the attitude of self-contained nations, class-conscious classes, competitive and divided religious systems cannot be continued in an age, which, equipped with our present instruments of destruction, must achieve unity or perish.[20]

Mabel then illustrated how increasing unity led to increasing security. The first unity was the family group. This expanded through time to the tribe, the city-state and the nation. Today, she stated, 'This planet, sociologically and economically speaking, is plainly an organic unity.' She concluded with:

> Is this dream world built only of desire-images? No, it is a world toward which our planetary destiny is plainly moving. There is not an element in it, no matter how apparently idealistic, toward which social evolution and the force of events have not already shown manifest tendency. It is the type of world which modernism will inevitably produce as an alternative to planetary chaos, bankruptcy, and suicide.
>
> It is the organized aim of Bahá'ís, the world over, to speed up this evolutionary process – to accelerate the growth of favorable culture aspects in order to bring to pass this New World Order . . .[21]

The teaching efforts resulted in eight new Bahá'ís and an official group in Omaha. Mabel finished her two months of travel teaching by visiting Des Moines, Iowa, travelling with Gertrude Matteson.

Howard in Winnetka, Illinois

While Mabel continued her proclamation of the Faith in Waukegan, Howard, back in Winnetka, was having problems with his hearing. At the end of October, he wrote to Mabel saying that he had talked with someone about it, writing that the man said that 'I would gradually grow stone deaf unless I did something about it'. Howard's response was that he 'would rather trust in Baha'U'llah than in all the ear doctors who, after all, are mainly concerned in making sales. I shall certainly be in no haste . . .'[22] When Mabel expressed worry, he replied: 'As to my deafness I am far from despairing. Where did you ever get such a notion? . . . You misunderstood what I said about the instruments being of no help if I got stone deaf. Mr Allen said that it was like getting spectacles after going blind.'[23] In spite of his objections, by early November Howard had an Acousticon hearing aid. But when he went to a talk by Dorothy Baker, he said that he 'could not get a word, although I had the

Acousticon and sat on the front seat. But I saw her and that was worth a lot.'²⁴

Mabel in Waukegan, Illinois

In January 1937, the Teaching Committee wrote to Mabel saying that they had heard she and Gayle Woolson planned to open North Dakota to the Faith. They suggested that she go to Glenfield and Fargo and gave her a budget of $150.²⁵ Mabel wrote to Gayle about plans for the work and noted that since Fargo was on the way to Glenfield, they could stop at Fargo first and then continue to Glenfield. A Bahá'í from Wilmette, Marguerite Bruegger, had recently pioneered to Fargo and she could help arrange meetings.²⁶

But before Mabel could leave for North Dakota, there was a change of plans and Fargo and Glenfield were delayed while Mabel spent a month in Waukegan, north of Chicago near the Wisconsin border. On the day she left Chicago, 14 February, she and Howard were eating at a restaurant near the train station and Howard suffered from something like a fainting spell. It was a traumatic moment for Mabel: Howard was ill, but her train to Milwaukee was about to leave. Howard recovered a bit and she was able to rush off and catch the train. On board, she wrote to him an anguished letter saying, 'It just tore at my heart to leave you looking so spent . . . It has been a great lesson to me to put the most important thing first, such as my Howie.'²⁷

As Mabel wrote her distressed letter to him, he was writing a reassuring one to her, saying, 'I quickly recovered my equilibrium and nerve strength and taking everything very slowly, had a fine dinner and a fairly good appetite.' Howard then worried about her health, telling to not 'bother to write when you are so busy. A postal once in a while to let me know you are well. But not long descriptive letters. I don't want your time or strength dissipated on me. Give it all to Baha'U'llah.' He went on to say:

> I told Baha'U'llah how proud I am of you. My pride is well founded indeed. When I think of what you have

accomplished in the last 3 months, and under what great handicaps and that now you are starting off again on another great adventure in His Sublime Faith, under handicaps again that make the adventure only the more glorious, is it any wonder that I am proud and happy to be hitched up with such a courageous Pioneer.[28]

Two days later, Howard was thinking of his remaining time in the material world:

I do feel . . . that much remains to be done in the few months, days or years that remain before we are separated for a few moments, in which we must prove our worthiness of that eternal union and communion.

We must develop a silent communion and an innate and instantaneous understanding of each other. We must never descend to that low plane of argumentation and negative approach to any subject or matter. We must together learn to walk above this world if we are to prove our worthiness to walk together in all worlds.[29]

After such deep spiritual thoughts, Howard noted that he was going to get a haircut at his favorite '25¢ place'.

The Bahá'í Regional Committee of Illinois, Wisconsin, Minnesota and Iowa sponsored a series of six lectures at the Victory Memorial Nurse's Home in Waukegan from 20–27 February. After an initial talk by one woman on the 'Mysteries of the Sphinx and Great Pyramid Revealed', Mabel gave the next five lectures on the topics: 'The Universal Temple of Light at Wilmette', 'The True Origin and Destiny of Man', Education in the Coming Age', The Unfoldment of World Civilization', and 'The Seven Steps of the Soul in Its Journey from Self to God'.[30] Mabel gave more talks on 4 and 5 March, her subjects being 'The Dawnbreakers', 'A Practical Solution of the Economic Problems Based Upon the Law of God' and 'Life As It May Be Lived at the End of This Century'.[31]

The last story may be similar to one she used in a radio talk in Scranton titled 'A Prevue of the World in 2001'. Mabel obviously expected the world 64 years in the future to operate fully along Bahá'í lines by that time. She begins with a look at the world situation:

> Let us for a minute consider the present world situation: Beset on every side by the cumulative evidences of disintegration, of turmoil and bankruptcy, serious-minded men and women, in almost every walk of life, are beginning to doubt whether society, as it is now organized, can, through its own unaided efforts, extricate itself from the slough into which it is steadily sinking. Every system except the UNIFICATION OF THE HUMAN RACE, has been tried and found wanting. Sore-tried and disillusioned humanity has no doubt lost its orientation and would seem to have lost its faith and hope as well. It is hovering, unsheparded and visionless on the brink of disaster. We stand on the threshold of an age whose convulsions proclaim alike the death-pangs of an old order and the birth-pangs of a new.[32]

She then outlines the new world envisioned by Bahá'u'lláh to be up and running in the plenitude of its glory in the year 2001:

> ... the League of Nations, so feebly struggling in its early days, having now become a universal and effective institution, for supernational government. The rulers and people of the world . . . have at last actually agreed, in world conference, to simultaneously cut down national armaments . . . The world has at last disarmed . . .
> . . . A world metropolis acts as a nerve center of a world civilization. The economic resources of the planet are organized and a fair distribution to each country assured by the World Parliament and International Executive . . .
> . . . the ancient and ancestral quarrel between capital and labor will have been healed and all their joint problems solved by the far-reaching economic laws of Baha'u'llah . . . When the economists and industrialists . . . decided to

put this law of Baha'U'llah in practice, this law of dividing the profits of an industry of a business house between the people who invested their money in it AND the people who worked in it, immediately a change for the better took place . . . the workers, now part-owners . . . gave the very best they had to its success, developed unsuspected inventive genius, forgot to watch the clock, as they were building for their own future, and the more the business prospered, the more returns came to them. Of course strikes became a thing of the past. Who would want to ruin his own business?. . .

The universal auxiliary language having been taught in all the schools for several generations, unites the people in a common tongue . . .

The most important factor in world unity now being achieved is the establishment of a universal religion, based upon those eternal truths . . .

The various races will have come to see that life spiritually is one, that as there is but one universe, so there is but one God and one Truth . . . Man's higher nature, at last in the ascendancy, has made him master of things, but true servant of his brother man. And from this hilltop of development and achievement, man looks forward to great mountain tops of future progress. No longer of the generation of the half-light, man at last sees clearly, he thinks sanely, he is on his way![33]

Mabel was describing what Shoghi Effendi called the Golden Age of the Bahá'í Faith, though her time frame was a bit off.

Mabel's lectures had 14 to 16 participants and several in the group were looking forward to the Bahá'í study classes. In addition, she met with different clubs, visited nursing homes and individual people. She noted that the pace was so intense that she was out almost every night. This intensity ended up with her in hospital. In a letter to Edris, she wrote, 'I keep getting set back – then being too hungry when I started to eat . . . those cramps started, sort of colic or indigestion – anyway they were so bad during my talk Tuesday [23 February] night that finally I broke out in a cold sweat and felt as if I were going to faint or vomit so drew the talk to a close and made for the bathroom.' A nurse finally took her to hospital and put her to bed 'with hot tea to drink and hot pads'. When the doctor arrived, he pumped her stomach and the pains stopped. She stayed in the hospital until that evening and then went and gave her next talk. She also had a bad cold.[34]

On her last day in Waukegan, Mabel gave a talk to the American Business Club. The President, E.J. Wright, was so enthusiastic about it that the next day, he sent her a letter which read:

> Permit the writer to again thank you for your very wonderful lecture as presented to my club on Tuesday last.
>
> As you saw, the cross section of our American Business Club are young men who will in later years become the heads of their firms, or make advancement to an executive position, and I for one sincerely feel that your timely remarks will serve as a future goal for each and every one that had the pleasure of hear your story.
>
> We as officers of our club want you to know how grateful we are for your explanation of the Bahai House of Worship and we sincerely hope that we may all have the pleasure of a trip through your institution in the very near future.[35]

Mabel returned to Chicago the next day.

Mabel in North Dakota

Glenfield

With the Waukegan project finished, Mabel prepared for the delayed teaching trip to North Dakota. Her stay in Chicago with Howard was a brief two weeks before she departed on 23 March 1937, this time headed for Glenfield. She was joined in St Paul, Minnesota, by Gayle Woolson. Gayle was of

Syrian ancestry and had learned of the Faith from the man she later married, Dr Clement Woolson. She became a Knight of Bahá'u'lláh to the Galapagos Islands two decades later.

The two women spent six hours on a 'slow little freight and passenger train' to travel the 90 miles [145 km] to Glenfield (population 150). Mabel found the small town quite interesting:

> Talk about primitive living – there isn't a bathroom in the town. No snow except in left over drifts and patches – but wind!! But it is sunny today . . . This is an adventure! These people we are visiting are Muhamedans – sweet and simple and intelligent tho uneducated. A really thrilling experience talking to a half dozen Moslems last night.
>
> This afternoon I just finished talking to about 45 high school children and then a wonderful talk with the fine, young superintendent – a real person and broad, open-minded.[36]

Mabel gave a talk to 40 people at the town hall on 27 March. Only three or four of those who attended showed any interest. One of those was the Superintendent of the School, a farmer named Karl Ericson. Karl bought a copy of *Bahá'u'lláh and the New Era* and was later heard to be 'holding forth at [his father's general] store to a group of people on the contents of the lectures last night and saying "that woman know what she was talking about".'[37]

Carrington

While Mabel was in Glenfield, Gayle went to Carrington, a town of 2,000 population 25 miles [40 km] to the west. Gayle arranged a series of six lectures for Mabel between 30 March and 3 April in the Court Room of the Court House, 'the nicest room in town'. Mabel left Glenfield for Carrington on 28 March and joined Gayle. Their new accommodation in Carrington was an improvement over that in Glenfield: 'we are comfortably settled in a large front room in a lovely large house – twin

Harlan Ober and Howard in the early 1930s

Mabel and Howard in the late 1930s

Howard reading, sometime in the late 1930s

Portrait of Howard used on the back cover of the first edition of Portals to Freedom, *1937*

Mabel at Green Acre, August 1937

Howard lived for some time in 1937 with Muriel, her husband Reginald, a Christian Bishop, and their two children Reggie and Elizabeth, and Barbara, Muriel's daughter

© USBNA

Howard with Bahá'ís from Scranton, Pennsylvania and Binghamton, NY, 1938

beds, two closets and a bath just across the hall'. The women initially spent their time 'scurrying' around doing publicity for the talks because the newspaper only came out weekly, with the next issue not due out until halfway through the talks.[38]

Worried about Howard's increasingly fraught health, in a letter to him she commented that she was very relieved that he had gotten a typist. This was in response to his letter of the day before where he said that he had so much to tell her but that it would have to wait until his new secretary, Gladys Masters, had time to take dictation. Howard said that he kept 'her going top speed every minute'. He also had a girl who transcribed his dictation cylinders; evidently, he had acquired a dictation machine. Howard was also able to send her one of the first copies of *Portals to Freedom* that he had just received from the printer.[39] Mabel, of course, was thrilled to see his great effort finally in print: '"Portals" is superb outwardly and inwardly. The cover is truly beautiful and extremely artistic . . . A fitting garment in a literary (shall we say!) masterpiece. I can scarcely keep away from it.'[40]

After Mabel give the first of her six lectures on 30 March, in which she spoke on the 'True Origin and Destiny of Man', the local Congregational minister worryingly asked to say a few words. Surprisingly, what he said was that he 'wished that every member of all the congregations in town had been present to hear this talk. You gave a thoroughly scientific and I believe a correct explanation of evolution and man's relation to the Lord. The ideas brought out are the only ones that will solve the situations confronting humanity today.' The minister was at the second meeting, after which he again asked to speak. This time, he told the audience of about 25 'that he was giving up his pulpit to Mrs Ives next Sunday and invited them all to be present'. Mabel noted that the minister, Rev. Frederick Errington, had become her 'buddy' and that he was a 'perfect dear' who had a lovely daughter. The mayor of Carrington had also been present at the first lecture and remarked to others that 'Mrs Ives gave a remarkable lecture and she certainly was a very cultured woman and a fine speaker'.[41]

Also on the 30th, Mabel spoke to 250 students at the high school and was invited to speak to the Literary Club,[42] and to the Kiwanis Club. On 4 April, she spoke from the pulpit of Rev. Errington's church. Afterwards, she and Gayle had supper with the Errington family and Mabel wrote that 'they are simply eating the Cause up'. Howard's comment on her speaking in the church was: 'It is quite wonderful to think of you usurping your minister husband's place in occupying the pulpit of the Congregational Church.'[43]

The two travel teachers held their first discussion group meeting on 5 April with nine people present, including Rev. Errington, his wife and his daughter, Frieda. Mabel wrote that they were 'nearly Bahais'. In a letter to Howard, she said that she read to the high school literature classes from *Portals* and that the Woman's Church organization wanted her to speak. The Postmaster told some of his customers that 'Mrs Ives is right, the problems can not be solved without international co-operation and that women ought to be running the country'. She sold two copies of *Portals* in Carrington and gave one to Rev. Errington. Mabel ended up giving 13 lectures. There was never a dull moment, or even a bit of rest, for Mabel and Gayle.[44]

While Mabel's letters were full of news about lectures, study classes and speaking with individuals, Howard's letters overflowed with commentary about *Portals to Freedom*. A freight consignment of 724 copies was due at any moment, the book jackets had arrived, all 1,200 copies had been printed, the three biggest Chicago bookstores had agreed to sell them and 50 copies had been shipped to Shoghi Effendi. In his letter to Mabel of 6 April, he remarked:

> I am working on the preparation of 'Life and How to Live it', so you see, now I have three books besides the poem. One complete, Portals; the study course [The Ocean of His Utterances]; 'Life and How to Live It', and the 'Song Celestial'. That only leaves one more to complete the five 'Great Journeys in the Universe of Baha'U'llah.' 'Five in

rapid succession.' Quite a wonderful result, is it not, of that vision I had twenty years ago.⁴⁵

It isn't certain what 'Life and How to Live It' and 'Great Journeys in the Universe of Baha'U'llah' were as there are no manuscripts with these titles in the archival files.

Fargo, and John Alexander

Rev. Errington and his daughter Frieda drove Mabel and Gayle to the train station in Rockford on 10 April. From there, the two women went to Fargo and settled into the Hotel Graver, 'the most desirable place for meetings'.⁴⁶ Things started off quickly. The sole Bahá'í in Fargo, Marguerite Bruegger, and the two travel teachers hosted a tea for 'two important women' and had two others over for supper. Mabel went to the library and while she was showing the librarian some Bahá'í literature, the librarian suddenly asked, 'Wasn't there a book written by a Mr Ives just out?' She had seen it in a publisher's catalogue and was 'greatly attracted by the description'. The local bookstore did not wish to have a Bahá'í display in their window, but they did buy a copy of *Portals*, noting that they had seen reviews and been attracted to the book.⁴⁷

Mabel and Gayle kept up the pace, with only a few minor problems. On the 22nd their usual lecture room in the hotel wasn't available, so they put folding chairs in their room, which was quite large enough for the 20 people who came. Before the meeting, though, they had a visitor. Mabel wrote:

> Just as we were waking up from our naps, a knock came at the door and I peeked thru the crack (in my slip) and saw a tall, fine-looking man standing there who said he wanted to see me if he could. So I asked him to wait, we climbed into our clothes and pushed the bed up and then let him in. He was in town spending that night before a large Emergency Peace Campaign meeting at the YM[CA]. He had seen our large poster downstairs in the lobby . . . and felt that

perhaps he could get a question that was burning in his soul answered. He afterwards confessed that he thought it was destiny which took him to that poster, that it was put there for him.

Well his great dream to which he has dedicated his life since 1927 is to rebuild the League of Nations and bring about World Peace.⁴⁸

This man was John Alexander, a real-estate agent, who lived in Minneapolis. Mabel said that they had a 'marvelous talk' for two hours. John had spoken at the Presbyterian College in Jamestown, North Dakota, about his ideas for establishing peace. The president of the college, however, violently disagreed with them and 'tore him to pieces and actually shook his fist in his face . . . telling him he was all wrong'. John asked Mabel, 'Am I wrong? Can't a new world order be built upon the teachings of Christ?' Mabel and Gayle told him about the Bahá'í teachings. 'Really it was thrilling,' Mabel said.⁴⁹

After that meeting, John was, according to Mabel in a letter to Shoghi Effendi, 'forwarding the principles of Baha'U'llah which he had caught in the inner World without having ever heard of Him in the outer world'. When she introduced John to the Bahá'í Faith, 'he went away thrilled beyond words at having found that there was a great organized movement already working for the very ideals to which he had dedicated his life'. Mabel wrote that 'we had found a pearl of great price, a lover of humanity, a brilliant and forceful speaker, a successful business man, a father of four splendid children – two of them just entering college – and with a wife of rare spirituality and breadth of mind'.⁵⁰

The next day, Mabel spent an hour with 'a brilliant teacher of art'. This was Charlotte Wright. Mabel noted that they had just met by chance, 'divine chance', at a lunch counter and had a 'grand talk'. Charlotte became the first registered believer in North Dakota.⁵¹

They also met Mr Ballon, a former Unitarian minister, 'a perfectly adorable elderly man' who invited them to have tea at the hotel. When he arrived, they discovered that he had invited a group of distinguished people to meet us – a Dr and Mrs _____ from Oslo, Norway, an architect, a Professor and his wife from the University and two more, highly cultured gentlemen. And he had taken a beautiful private dining-room and a table was all set . . . for eight. The conversation was simply scintillating. Mr Ballon himself is superb and a perfect and most gracious host. From time to time he would explain something around the Teachings and all around quotations about the future life and commented so intelligently and with such [undecipherable] literary and historical allusions that it was a perfect experience to talk to them. Gayle was holding her own with a young professor and another man and I had the learned Doctor. Finally a question was asked about the basic teachings of Baha'U'llah and his historical and religious background . . . From then on I had their perfect attention and stimulated a series of delightful questions, the Cause was unfolded to them. I asked Baha'U'Lah to teach them and He did.[52]

Afterwards, the Norwegian doctor and his wife wanted a book on the Faith so they went to Mabel's room. She showed them what she had and they bought *Portals to Freedom*. Mabel evidently returned to Chicago in time for the National Convention at the end of the month.

Mabel in Minnesota and Wisconsin

Mabel's break between teaching projects, and her time with Howard, was just over a month long before she left for a month in Minneapolis/St Paul, Minnesota, on 9 June 1937. Until August, we have no further available correspondence from Howard, so this section is all from Mabel's point of view.

Gayle Woolson and her sister collected Mabel from the train station 'in her beautiful Pierce-Arrow' car. For the first two weeks of Mabel's stay in St Paul, she was able to use the apartment of a Bahá'í who had gone to Atlantic City. Mabel was delighted to have the apartment all to herself. The local

Bahá'ís kept the ice-box full and Gayle brought her dinners over at night. Gayle also organized and advertised three lectures for the first few days of her stay.[53] Mabel discovered 'a gorgeous beach in the Peninsula State Park' with 'wild beauty, wooded hills, wooded islands, Skyline golf course'.[54]

Her first talk in St Paul was to 25 people. On the 13th she had lunch with John Alexander in Minneapolis and they spent the afternoon planning a meeting to which John was inviting the members of the Board of Foreign Trade and the Civics and Commerce Association. John also introduced her to the former Governor of Minnesota, Joseph Bernquist,[55] with whom she shared Shoghi Effendi's major letters 'The Goal of a New World Order' and 'The Unfoldment of World Civilization' (both now chapters in *The World Order of Bahá'u'lláh*) and *Portals to Freedom*. Mabel noted that the Governor was very impressed with them.[56]

As she crossed back and forth between St Paul and Minneapolis and worked with the two Bahá'í communities, Mabel saw distinct problems between them. These two cities, separated only by a river but otherwise contiguous, had Bahá'í communities that had never met each other and carried out 'dull weekly old-fashioned Baha'i meetings'. Through her efforts, the two communities began to hold regular inter-assembly meetings and to deepen on how the Bahá'í Administrative Order should function. The St Paul Bahá'í community had suffered greatly when Dr Clement Woolson had passed away a year and a half before.[57] Dr Woolson was a physician who had moved to St Paul from New York in 1909 to teach the Faith and had met 'Abdu'l-Bahá in 1912. Now, his widow, Gayle Woolson, from an Arabic-speaking Muslim family who were guided to the Bahá'í Faith by Dr Woolson in the 1930s,[58] was 'completely dedicated to the Faith, active, courageous and intelligent'.[59]

While Mabel shared the Faith in Minnesota, Howard was struggling with his health. On 16 June, she emphatically told him to 'forget everything and just <u>rest</u>. That is your job now, as Baha'U'llah has some very important work ahead for you to do.' He was very preoccupied with selling and shipping his book, and that task had gotten the better of him.[60]

One day Mabel and Harriet Terry went to a Lutheran Church supper and had the opportunity to talk with the minister, 'a fine, well educated young man'. Mabel told Howard, 'I had three hours and we certainly went into things. As he and his young wife (5 children) think Christ must come "with the clouds" there was a stumbling block, but from other standpoints he was prepared and open-minded.' He was open-minded when it came to Muḥammad, but 'on matters of Christianity, he had his mind wrapped in cotton wool. He followed tradition blindly.'[61]

Busy as they were, on the night of 20 June Gayle and Mabel had nothing planned, so they went to watch a movie: 'We saw "The Last of Mrs Cheney".'[62] Two nights later, the Professor of Sociology at the university brought 22 college students and high school graduates to Mabel's apartment. She said they had a 'wonderful evening' and everyone stayed until midnight. When they left, they said they wanted to come back for more discussion.[63]

Mabel and Gayle went to Hudson, Wisconsin, a small town 18 miles [29 km] west of St Paul, on the 23rd. In spite of the intense heat, they visited a number of prominent residents and arranged for a meeting the following week.[64]

Mabel spent 28 June with eight Minneapolis Bahá'ís at a lake cottage. After a swim, the group consulted on the problems besetting the community.[65] She then went to Madison, Wisconsin, on 6 July and spent a week there before moving on to Waukegan on the 12th. John Alexander came down to Madison and took her course there, 'taking the Cause as fast as it is humanly possible'. He joined a study class and kept bringing in new people.[66] In a letter to the Guardian, Mabel also mentioned that the small group in Madison, was 'very desirous of growing into an Assembly and are eager for teachers'. She had spent three weeks in Madison in the early spring, where prior to her visit the Faith had been unknown. When she departed for Waukegan, four members of her study group were very close to the Faith.[67]

Howard had gone to Green Acre in late June and Mabel was able to join him there a month later.

Mabel asks the Guardian for guidance

With her intense travel-teaching and proclamation of the Faith, Mabel had questions and desperately wanted guidance. In a wide-ranging letter to Shoghi Effendi, Mabel opened with congratulations on the Guardian's marriage to Rúḥíyyih Khánum:

> Beloved Guardian:-
> Knowing your staggering burden of responsibility, I have refrained from writing you, but I so long to make a closer contact, to work more directly under your guidance that perhaps you will forgive me for doing so now. Also I want to express the joy of our hearts over your marriage and what it means to the world at this time. Rouhieh Khanum I have loved deeply since she was a little girl. Undoubtedly the Master planned this noble marriage before she was born and called her into the world to be the consort of the first Guardian and mother of the second Guardian. I pray Baha'u'llah that you may have the utmost personal happiness and joy in your marriage as well. No doubt the new doors which seem to be opening in Canada are one of the outer results of this glorious union.[68]

Mabel then wrote that she was concerned about the work she and Howard were doing and asked the Guardian for advice:

> Affairs have so shaped themselves during the last years that it has become possible to give almost my entire time to direct, and largely pioneer teaching. I have wanted to write of some of the more thrilling experiences and contacts, but hesitated to impose on your time. During this period the call of the Kingdom has been raised in many cities between Chicago and Green Acre, also in several cities of Nebraska and Iowa, in No. Dakota, Minnesota, Illinois and Ohio . . .
> Dear Guardian, you know that since 1920, my husband and I have been travelling from city to city, spreading the Faith of Baha'u'llah to the degree of our limited ability,

assisted by the mercy of the Beloved, who has been infinitely generous and forgiving. We earned our living as we went by selling various things. But now Howard is concentrating on writing, and as he has become quite hard-of-hearing, it seems his best way of serving at the present. So the National Teaching Committee is sending me to various places to do pioneer work. They have left the choice of places to me and I want to go exactly where Baha'u'llah wants me to go and to find the really hungry and ready hearts. It would make me so infinitely happy if you would only take over my life and send me where YOU know is the place I should go. I desire nothing except to spend every remaining hour of my life in your service. I want to make a fresh and complete dedication of my life to the Faith, and I supplicate your prayers that the dross of my being may be removed and only that which may be serviceable to my Lord remain, that the Holy Spirit alone may be heard from my lips and the Fire of the Love of God alone may flame in my heart. Please pray that that I may become a mature Bahai, and be able to attract, not a mere handful of souls to the Faith, but thousands, and people of capacity.[69]

Mabel then went on to describe the summer's events at Green Acre:

You would have been happy to see at Green Acre this summer the new motion among the Believers. In response to your passionate appeal many were arising to go out into the teaching field. Also during the Teaching Conference, the situation of lack of knowledge of the administration, similar to the condition in Minneapolis, was discussed and by the teachers who had found it in many cities, so a recommendation was made to the National Spiritual Assembly to send someone to make a survey of the Assemblies and endeavor to remedy the difficulty in these backward communities, to prepare them for the people of capacity who will undoubtedly be attracted in this wide-flung teaching

Campaign. The National Assembly have now undertaken to handle this matter.⁷⁰

Mabel concluded with another very personal request. Her son, Rouhi (commonly spelled 'Ruhi') Colston Rice-Wray, was suffering mental difficulties, and she poured out her heart to the Guardian:

> May I write of one other thing. My son, Ruhi Colston Rice-Wray, has now gone out on a ranch in South Dakota . . . to recover his mental and physical health. He is 31. The Master blessed and named him. He has a rare spiritual nature and lives half in the spiritual world, but in this world he makes unending mistakes. His life has been a series of tragic failures. He does not seem to be able to find and maintain the balance between these two worlds. A most complex and baffling situation. At one time the doctors said that he was a 'manic-depressive'. The tragedy of such souls as his is that the present psychiatrists and psycho-analysts take into consideration only the physical and mental parts of a person. The spiritual side is completely unknown to them. Then how can they understand the delicate and complex situation in a young Bahai with all his spiritual longings and inner dedication? On spiritual matters Ruhi thinks clearly, but a cloud seems to intervene when he tries to translate his ideals into actions in this world. He, himself is conscious of this cloud. His mind betrays him. In his idealism, he has again and again given up his bed that some poor man might sleep, and has himself ridden in the subway all night. He has run himself ragged securing food for the hungry and jobs for the needy. He has awakened the latent spiritual life in souls and has brought some into the Faith, but he himself is always in difficulties of some kind. Rouhieh Khanum knows him well from Green Acre days of childhood and later. I entreat you to supplicate for him that he may be healed. It would seem that he has a real contribution to make in building the new consciousness in souls if he can

be freed from his impediment. The Master held him on His knee, when he was a little boy, and said to him in English: 'Do you know what your name means, Ruhi? It means My Spirit. . . . May he become a useful soldier in the army of the Guardian!'[71]

Shoghi Effendi's response expressed his gratitude for all her teaching efforts and her report, saying that he would pray for everyone she mentioned in her letter:

> The Guardian wishes me to thank you for your welcome letter of the 24th September, and also to express his loving appreciation of your very warm references to his marriage, all of which he dearly values indeed.
>
> He has read with particular interest the detailed account of your teaching activities during the last two years, and is most delighted to realize that all through this period of uninterrupted and intense effort you have obtained most wonderful results. The thrilling experiences and contact you have had all assuredly indicate that your efforts have been guided and confirmed by Bahá'u'lláh. May the realization of this supreme bounty ever spur you on to greater service to His Cause.
>
> The Guardian wishes me to assure you of his prayers on behalf of all those individuals and groups you have come across during your teaching travels; that they may each and all become confirmed, loyal and devoted servants of the Faith.[72]

In answer to her request for guidance in where she went to teach, his suggestion was to work closely with the National Teaching Committee and ask for their advice on where she could best serve. In his own hand, Shoghi Effendi concluded writing, 'Wishing you success from all my heart.'

Howard's request to Muriel, and service to the Cause

Howard and Mabel apparently spent the remainder of the summer of 1937 in Kittery, Maine, close to Green Acre. By October, Mabel was preparing to go to Canada and Howard had to leave the Kittery house. He was then 70 and in poor health, so he wrote to his daughter, Muriel, from Kittery:

> This is just to inform you that all our plans are changed for the winter and again we are afloat in the Ocean of the Mercy of God. It is a wonderful experience to KNOW that there is no resting place save His Protection . . .
>
> Riswanea has her teaching work laid out for the next two or three months but what I shall do is still undecided.
>
> This much is certain, however, and that is that more funds will be required than would have been if I could have stayed on here. Also it is sure that Edris has all she can possibly manage, for the next two or three years at least, to make ends meet without extending her obligations.
>
> This kind of throws me on your tender mercies, doesn't it, dear. I know how willing you and Reg. [Reginald Barrow, Muriel's second husband] have always been to help but it has been all you could do . . . to keep bread and butter in your own larder.
>
> But perhaps now that Reg. has gotten back into the harness and some regular funds coming in . . . you will feel that you can do something regularly towards helping me get out this book which I am working on. Edris made Portals possible, perhaps, God willing, you can make Expanding Horizons possible.[73]

Howard continued by saying that he needed a place that would be quiet and where he could be independent. Though he and Mabel were looking for a place of their own, in the interim he asked Muriel to talk it over with her husband and pray about supporting him for a while. He noted that 'Riswanea is cared for. Between the Teacher's allowance when she is in the active field and a little business she is fostering, I think she is O.K. But my health, as you know, will not allow me to go into active business again, and besides, I have this book and other books which Baha'U'llah seems to want me to do. It is the only pathway of service, seeming, open to me.'[74]

Muriel and Reginald, who was a Christian Bishop, responded positively and Howard was soon back in Brooklyn living with them. But having to rely on others was difficult and Howard and Mabel really wanted a house of their own after so many years as transients. On 3 October, he wrote to Mabel about a house and financial self-sufficiency:

> As for having a place of our own, that will come if Baha'u'llah wills. But it certainly cannot come until we have an income sufficient to support a home and that cannot be done until the second edition of Portals is out and the new book published and successful.
>
> I am praying hard that all may be done if according to His plans for us. Now let me tell you how I am working towards this desired result.
>
> First: It will require self-sacrifice and concentrated economy for about two years . . .
>
> Secondly: In order to accomplish this result the following plan will work out, I think.[75]

Howard then writes that he had approached the Book Editor of the *New York Times* about reviewing books for the newspaper and had been given a chance to show what he could do. He then lays out a detailed financial plan involving book sales and the second edition of *Portals*. It also included Mabel's sales from her toiletries business. Totalled up, he thought that their income for seven months would be over $700, enough to pay for the second edition of *Portals to Freedom*. He went on to write, 'In the meanwhile I shall have finished my new book and it may be that by the Spring of 1939 – or only 18 months from now – our way will be clear to spend all our time in writing and teaching without having to travel around the country.'[76] When it came to financial planning, Howard was always optimistic. Unfortunately, things didn't work out as he hoped.

When Mabel wrote back, she said that 'almost every minute since your letter came yesterday afternoon, my mind and heart have been revolving around this matter'. She suggested that maybe the National Teaching Committee or Muriel and Edris could finance him in the 'pioneer field, and that means constant moving'. She promoted the idea that he become a columnist with small, country newspapers in order to build up a reputation. Howard's eyes were also troubling him and she insisted that he give them a complete rest: 'Don't read anything except my letters, bathe them faithfully, and give them a complete chance [to recover]. Because, you know, you owe them to the Faith . . . It was because you did that the last time that your sight came back. Now use your will power on this matter. You CAN meditate, instead of reading.'[77]

19
Moncton, New Brunswick, Canada
1937

Moncton, New Brunswick

On 5 April 1916, 'Abdu'l-Bahá had revealed a Tablet to the Bahá'ís of Canada and Greenland in which he charged them with the opening of all the Canadian provinces:

> Through the concerted efforts of all the friends the Standard of Unity must needs be unfurled in those states, and the divine teachings promoted, so that these states may also receive their portion of the heavenly bestowals and a share of the Most Great Guidance. Likewise in the provinces of Canada, such as Newfoundland, Prince Edward Island, Nova Scotia, New Brunswick, Quebec, Ontario, Manitoba, Saskatchewan, Alberta, British Columbia, Ungava, Keewatin, Mackenzie, Yukon, and the Franklin Islands in the Arctic Circle – the believers of God must become self-sacrificing and like unto the candles of guidance become ignited in the provinces of Canada.[1]

Mabel was still waiting for confirmation of direction on 2 October 1937 when she wrote to Howard that 'I feel that when it comes it will be Baha'u'llah's answer to what I should do. I have been wandering in the wilderness of uncertainty, waiting for clear guidance.' While waiting, she wrote that she had 'layed [sic] in the sun (in bathing suit) and read the Gleanings. Had the long daily prayer . . .' She was in contact with May Maxwell and was waiting to see if something would open up for Canada.[2] The next day, her plans began to clear and she expected to leave for Moncton, New Brunswick, within a few days.³

When she headed north, Mabel first went to Bates College in Lewiston, Maine, where she spoke on 13 October at the Women's Union to students and faculty at the school on the subject of 'The New World Order'. *The Bates Student*, the college paper, reported that the talk was about the 'unity of mankind, the establishment of universal peace, an international language, a world society of cooperation and harmony and a universal religion'.⁴

Within a couple of days after that, she was in Moncton while Howard stayed with Muriel in Brooklyn, New York. When Mabel first went to Moncton, a city of 25,000, she said she met only one person who had ever heard of the Bahá'í Faith.⁵ She told her daughter Edris of an experience she had when she entered the city for the first time:

> She said she felt like she was the apex of a triangle and that behind her and with her were marching hosts of the Concourse. Through many experiences she learned that the only way her work could be done was to get herself out of the way and let Baha'u'llah do it. Whenever through the compliments of the people and because of her successes she began to think she was pretty good and began to feel important in her own right, she said all the doors would slam shut in her face, so to speak, and her work would lose its effectiveness. She would then become aware of what she was doing. Then with the realization that she of herself could do absolutely nothing, that her effectiveness and power were in direct proportion to the degree of emptiness of her own heart (emptiness of self) so that the power of the Holy Spirit could flow thru, she would go forward again and be assisted. She used to quote Abdu'l-Baha when He said, 'The difference between me and the other Baha'is is that they think that they are doing something and I know Bahá'u'lláh is doing it all.'⁶

Getting out of the way proved to be her door-opener. As she always did, immediately on arriving in Moncton Mabel had scheduled her lectures and arranged for a short talk on the radio. On 22 October, she wrote, 'I put it all in His Hands, and <u>rested back</u> on that assurance.' On Monday the 19th, one of the 'most important women' in Moncton came to see her 'out of the blue sky'. The woman hadn't planned to visit Mabel, but felt 'impelled to'. Mabel told Howard:

> She is the moving spirit of the metaphysical study group here, and asked me to speak to her group Tuesday aft., and said she would phone several to listen to the broadcast . . . So then I knew that Baha'u'llah had taken me at my word, and had taken charge of things.
>
> You see, after days of work, the radio station had turned down the script, because it was religious and they had phoned the ministers and found out that I was not sponsored by the churches, so under some arrangement they had with the ministers they could not accept my program. Well, after much prayer and conversation with the Program director, I arranged to broadcast just what I had written (which was straight Bahai and plenty of religious content) by paying for it ($10.00) with the understanding that they give the broadcast and the lectures 6 spot-announcements over a period of three days.
>
> The response was grand and a room full of fine intelligent people turned out to the first lecture last night [21 October], an hour and a half after the broadcast. One man said: 'The reason I didn't ask any questions is because I am coming to every lecture and expect to get all my questions answered before you finish.' The pres of the University club, who was present asked me to come to have tea with the club after their meeting tonight . . . The publicity is coming out in splendid shape and I am feeling very thankful to Baha'u'llah this morning. A Jewish Rabbi stayed a long time after the lecture and talked with me. He was really interested.[7]

The result was that at her next lecture on the 22nd, so many people came that they had to bring in more chairs. The next day, 30 people came to listen to her at the University Woman's Club.

As Mabel developed her teaching skills, successes began to appear. May Maxwell wrote to the Guardian about Mabel's efforts:

> You will have no doubt heard of the astonishing work achieved in Moncton, New Brunswick by Mrs. Mabel Ives who was sent there by the National Teaching Committee and has met with a phenomenal response. Great groups of people listening eagerly to the Divine Teachings and 7 declared believers in about three months! Later I hope to follow her work by teaching the Administrative Order and in the meantime Mrs. Rosemary Sala has joined Mrs. Ives and is also achieving great results.[8]

Mabel gave lectures on six consecutive days with an average audience of 30, but some with as many as 39. There were many questions each night, most of them very thoughtful. There were a few others as well: 'Of course some Pentecostal people tried to nail me to the wall on the matter of the second coming of Christ, but Bahá'u'lláh guided me and I came out with a whole skin.' She made a second radio broadcast on the 29th, which announced a second series of lectures.[9]

Certain souls began to become apparent quite soon. Ruth Wilson attended all Mabel's lectures, took her to dinner and for tea, drove her around the area and was reading prodigiously. William Bryne bought and read *Portals to Freedom* in a day and a night and was studying the Faith on his own. One night, he asked how one joined the Bahá'í Faith and would he be acceptable. He became the first Bahá'í in Moncton. After her 29 October lecture, she wrote to Howard that when she left the hotel with William, 'who was carrying my suitcase of books, we met a group of people who had been at the lecture. They were pretty steady customers, and were deep in a discussion of the Teachings. Mr. Jarvis said: "Mrs Ives, would you speak to the Ministerial Association?" I told him that I could stand it if the ministers could.' Two other ladies who were very interested were Muriel Lutes and Mrs McEwen. Both had been coming to all the lectures.[10]

It was not all work and no play for Mabel. On 30 October, Mr Lutes, father of the 28-year-old Muriel Lutes who had been coming to the lectures, collected Mabel, Mrs McEwen and her three children and took them to his farm where

> Muriel had a real old farm supper for us, consisting of . . . Buckwheat cakes, doughnuts, sausages, maple syrup from their own sugar-maple trees, baked beans, very fresh bread and home-made ice-cream . . .
>
> Mrs. McEwen and the children returned to town about 8 o'clock . . . and then Muriel and I . . . had a wonderful talk . . . She is reading rapidly the books which I lend her. Was fascinated by Portals.
>
> The next morning, she and I walked up on the mountain – a real climb – but the air was like wine, just gobs of ozone, and when we got up to the top, walked around for an hour in their miles of sugar maple woods and went deeper into the Faith. Then we sat on some logs overlooking the great valley . . . and used the healing prayers for her mother.[11]

Many other people were deeply entranced by the Bahá'í Faith. Mabel went with Ruth Wilson and Mr Robertson to St John, a town 95 miles [153 km] to the southwest of Moncton. They looked into one hotel for possible lecture rooms, but found it insufficient, so they went to the Admiral Beatty Hotel, the best in town. When discussing where to stay, Ruth suggested they stay at the Admiral Beatty and she wanted to pay the bill. Mabel told her that she could not accept because only Bahá'ís could contribute to the teaching work. One night later on, Ruth gave her an envelope containing a poem about Mabel and three $10 bills to support her efforts. The three bills represented Ruth's acceptance of Bahá'u'lláh.[12]

Two future Knights of Bahá'u'lláh, Irving and Mabel Geary, both became Bahá'ís in Moncton through Mabel's teaching. They first attended her lectures at the Brunswick Hotel. Seeing their interest, Mabel invited the Gearys to host a study group in their home. During the following weeks, both became Bahá'ís.[13]

Moncton became Canada's third Local Spiritual Assembly when it formed at Riḍván 1938. Mabel left a vibrant community, but by 1940, there were too few Bahá'ís to reform the Assembly; Mabel explained why:

> The city is a classic example of what happens when there is not adequate follow-up work. When I left, there were four souls who I felt could be counted on to shoulder the responsibilities of the Cause. But the others, while they had accepted the Faith and had a pretty good idea of what it was all about, they did not have that type of stability that could go forward on its own steam . . . There are always some who cannot see beyond the teacher.[14]

Howard struggles on

In early November, Howard told Mabel that his epic poem, *The Song Celestial*, was being published. In her reply, she wrote about the poem, but also about the effect that his writing of *Portals to Freedom* had on one person who had been contemplating suicide:

> I can't tell you how overjoyed I am at the poem in process of being printed. Tell me all about it. Is it to be in book form and will it be possible to get it out? And what about your second edition [of Portals]? . . .
>
> [A woman] going thru a most difficult experience last summer, in NYC . . . writes that Portals, which she fairly 'lived with' was the only thing that kept her from suicide and she added 'I mean it'. She was not a Bahai, but is almost one now. She wrote: 'And the book made it possible for me to keep outwardly calm and smiling, friendly, really feeling conciliatory, if not loving, if you follow me.'[15]

Mabel wrote in one letter of how she talked to Bahá'u'lláh all the time. After one talk, she said out loud, 'Baha'u'llah, you certainly were swell tonight.' She continued that it was beyond her understanding how all the doors opened at the Missionary meeting, with the Socialists and the Metaphysical Club. 'And these blessed hungry and sincere people who come daily one after another to unburden their hearts, and ask the questions that are burning in them, how eager, how ready they are! Where have I ever found such capacity?'[16]

We don't have Howard's letters from this time, but Mabel's replies give an idea of what he was going through. One of his main problems was that he was having serious problems with his vision, so she wrote an encouraging letter on 21 November:

> Do you remember the last time this happened it was after an orgy of months of detective stories, and that when you were forced to refrain from that pastime, that a whole new world of spiritual realities opened up to you, and celestial consciousness was born with you, and a sunburst of creative expression flowed thru you in a most amazing manner and in that year or two you did the creative work of your life, and left your eternal traces in Portals, Song Celestial and your wonderful study course.
>
> Now that you have climbed another round of the ladder to the Supreme Concourse, in casting aside the distraction of smoking, and now that the outer sight may be withdrawn for a little while, perhaps the great and final step that separates you from the plane above and the exalted tree of love, may be made and you become all consciousness and find the Most great center in the Universe of God and become so polarized to that Center that nothing in the heavens or earth can ever again disturb that perfect orientation.
>
> Darling, I feel so close to my Howie in the inner world, and realize how rapidly time is passing, and what a few moments we have left to accomplish what Baha'u'llah has called us into this life to do; that nothing less than perfect spirituality and perfect connection can be our goal.[17]

Howard was also looking for a new place to stay. Living with Muriel and her husband, Bishop Reginald Barrow, and Muriel's daughter, Barbara, had its challenges. He was sleeping in the living room, and to get to the bathroom had to pass

> through Barbara's room, separated from mine only by a curtain, then through two narrow rooms used only for storage, then thru the kitchen and then through the dining-room-bedroom-living room where Reg and Muriel sleep, and where we all eat, and where they do all their work. They have a lot of company; colored ministers etc dropping in at all hours of the day and night so that I am forced to take my meals into my room which means carrying them through all those other rooms. The apt. being on the ground floor, right on the street, makes my room at the front very noisy and the gasoline fumes come in all night long from passing motors.
> I am telling you all this so that you may see how impossible it is to do any writing. I get out of the house as early as possible and come back as late as possible . . .
> Please don't preach to me. I can do all that myself. In fact my faith in Baha'u'llah and my determination to submit to His will without complaint is all that has kept me going after the first week.[18]

Howard was greatly uplifted by his wife's constant flow of letters, but needed a change. He was still giving some talks, but not many. Mabel had proposed that he join her in Canada and he enthusiastically accepted the idea, saying that he had just enough money hidden away for a bus ticket there. By 8 December, the plan was for Howard to go to Binghamton, New York, as soon as he could and Mabel would join him there in January.[19]

On 29 November, Mabel wrote a long letter to Rúhíyyih Khánum, congratulating her on her marriage to Shoghi Effendi. Then she went on to describe what she had been doing: by the end of November, she had given 22 lectures in Canada and, along with Ruth Wilson, had flown to Charlottetown on Prince

Edward Island. They had spent 42 hours in the town. During that time, they gave a talk, were on the radio twice, called on the mayor – who drove them around the town – and visited the local newspaper, which resulted in a two-column article on the Faith.[20]

In her reply, Rúhíyyih Khánum wrote: 'Your letter was a most welcome and unexpected surprise. I quite appreciate your loving desire not to bother our burdened Guardian with any details you feel unnecessary, but otherwise although I shared your letter's news with him, if ever the friends have any direct questions to ask they must ask him – because my news is of course "unofficial".' Rúhíyyih Khánum went on to say that she had heard from her mother, May Maxwell, that there were now 11 Bahá'ís in Moncton.[21]

By December, Mabel was very worried about Howard. He tried to keep his difficulties from her, but when they came out in one of his letters (which we do not have), she wrote to him, 'It rode me like a nightmare when it [news of the difficulties] did come, for days.' But things seemed to going better with the plan for Howard to go north. On the more positive side, Mabel gushed over the 'new babies of mine!' They still needed 'someone to standby as they go thru their various measles and chicken-pox – these difficulties of the new-born. But each experience brings them out stronger than ever.'[22]

Howard's proposed southern trip

Near the end of 1937, Howard was invited by his son-in-law Reg to make a trip into the American South. The Bishop had to make an organizing trip and asked if Howard would like to accompany him by automobile. Howard pondered and worried about his health – he had become very tired on a trip from Brooklyn into neighbouring New York City – but then he found a copy of a letter written to him by Shoghi Effendi in 1932 which encouraged him to teach. To Mabel, he wrote, 'This together with the conviction that came to me that here was another opportunity for self-sacrifice in the Path of God and that if I dodged it I should be forever regretful, clinched the decision.' He obtained a list of cities in the South from Horace Holley, who was 'most congratulatory on my getting back into active work'.²³ Howard was looking forward to finding out 'whether a white man and a colored man traveling together through the South will attract enmity'.²⁴

This proposal met with a very strong protest from a Florida Bahá'í who felt 'strongly that on account of the revived activities of the K.K.K. [Ku Klux Klan – a white supremacist group] in Florida your trip to that State with your son in law can do no good at this time but might bring irreparable injury to the Cause.' In a letter to the Ives, the National Spiritual Assembly wrote, 'His letter is so emphatic that the National Assembly felt strongly that your teaching plans should be discussed with a special committee of the National Assembly so that your plans can be made to confirm to the definite instructions recently given us by Shoghi Effendi concerning teaching in the southern States.'²⁵

In response, Howard wrote that he, too, had received a 'very emphatic, not to say very excited letter from him. So far as I am concerned I think I should welcome the attentions of the KKK for did not Abdul Baha say that not until persecutions began would the Faith make its greatest progress?' Howard went on to note that this Bahá'í's opinion was not universally held, for he had a letter from the Local Spiritual Assembly of Miami inviting him and Mabel to give three presentations in the city which they planned to advertise in the newspaper.²⁶

But Mabel had been none too happy with his planned trip, either, writing that 'A long trip like that would be fine for a younger and stronger man, but my darling for you, I really think it is not intelligent. More impulse than mature judgement prompted it I fear . . . Your health and strength is too precious to the Cause . . . to jeopardize it on such a wild and hasty ride.'²⁷

On 16 December, Howard wrote to the Guardian to inform him that his trip had been cancelled:

> All our plans were made, but my daughter, Muriel, suddenly developed signs pointing towards appendix trouble and her husband hesitated to leave her. Also my dear wife

became rather over-anxious about my attempting such a long and arduous trip, even telephoning long distance from Moncton, Canada, where she is teaching and confirming souls, begging me to come to Binghamton instead where they wanted me to spend a few weeks.

So here I am and having a most delightful and inspiring time with these dear friends and attracted souls.[28]

Shoghi Effendi may not have received this letter. In a letter written on his behalf the following year, the Guardian praised both Howard and Mabel for their continuous efforts and clearly didn't know that Howard's trip to the South had been cancelled:

> The Guardian has read with closest attention your letters of December 4th and February 26th regarding the teaching work which you and dear Mrs. Ives have been so ably conducting during the last few months.
>
> He hopes your trip to the South last December has been quite successful, and that your painstaking and indeed self-sacrificing efforts have been fully repaid.
>
> The news of the splendid results obtained by Mrs. Ives in Moncton has been particularly gratifying, and the Guardian wishes you specially to convey to her his warmest congratulations upon the remarkable work she has succeeded in accomplishing for the Faith in that center. It is his fervent hope that the seeds her able hands have so devotedly sown will all take root and bring forth permanent results.[29]

Shoghi Effendi added his personal note at the end: 'May the Almighty bless you and keep you and enable you and your dear wife and distinguished collaborator to extend the range of your magnificent and deeply-appreciated services to this glorious Cause, Your true and grateful brother, Shoghi'

By mid-December Mabel was being pushed to her limits, both with her workload in Moncton and Howard's desperate living conditions and desire for letters from her. In a peeved letter to Howard, she wrote:

What more can I do . . . I thought I was keeping up my end beautifully. You have no idea of the gigantic piece of work I have been doing here – and with the momentum started it just keeps me at it. This is the biggest and most concentrated piece of work I have done in my life, and the necessary correspondence – a stream of letters to Leroy, to the Pub. Com. as I continually needed more books, to the Reg. Com. [Regional Committee] in Montreal . . . ; with prospective follow-up teachers to take over after I leave . . . Then your constant demand for more letters. I have put your letters first in the days work, and since I have to sleep a little late as I rarely get to bed before 1:00 or 1:30 am . . . There are constant interruptions of phone calls . . . hungry souls who must be fed . . . Then the mail must be taken to train or PO . . . Besides that I have to have a little time to prepare my talks and for study classes, to write my 15 minute radio talks – five of which I have given – a little time for prayer and reading of the Creative Word to keep me spiritually vital so that I can give out to these many souls . . . Three night classes a week besides innumerable evenings with individuals or small groups . . .

So last night at the class, they saw I was breaking under the strain, so Ruth, my darling Ruth, whisked me off to the hospital, as the guest of the hospital and here I am, resting divinely with a special nurse and everything. I had got so stimulated lately that I had had difficulty sleeping, so last night with sedatives, I slept and slept all night and till almost noon . . . and now am bolstered up in bed writing my Howie.[30]

Both were facing severe challenges, Mabel from too much work, and Howard from too little. Mabel stayed in the hospital for three days, but was only out for a single day before Ruth took her back for another day of rest and care.[31] Leaving Moncton in January 1938, Mabel stopped off in Montreal and paid a visit to May Maxwell.[32]

20
Scranton, Pennsylvania, and Chicago
1938

On 8 January 1938, Helen Inderlied took Howard to Scranton, Pennsylvania, where he was immediately put to work sending out 350 postcards announcing a course of six lectures to be given by Mabel at the Hotel Jermyn. The next day, Howard and Helen explained the object of their coming to Scranton to five very receptive people. Howard wrote that the Binghamton Bahá'ís and Harlan Ober had everything well prepared for his arrival.[1]

Howard was finally teaching again. On 14 January, he was in Philadelphia at the request of the Local Spiritual Assembly there and spoke to 100 people. Two days later, he met with a group of 20 young people from Oslof Trigvasson's youth group.[2]

Mabel arrived in Scranton on the 16th exhausted from her long Canadian teaching trip. Howard wrote that her three months in Moncton 'just about finished her', but also noted that she left behind a dozen new Bahá'ís.[3] Having arrived in Scranton, she was however given no rest, being put to work the very next day when she began the series of six lectures in eight days at the Hotel Jermyn on the following topics:

Monday, 17 January – A Planet in Distress
Tuesday, 18 January – The Unfoldment of World Civilization
Wednesday, 19 January – The True Origin and Destiny of Man (with Chart)
Friday, 21 January – Cycles of Civilization from Adam to Present Day (with Chart)
Sunday, 22 January – A Practical Solution of our Economic Problems (based upon the Law of God)

Monday, 23 January – The World Faith of the Future and What it Means to You.[4]

The charts mentioned apparently illustrated progressive revelation and the oneness of humanity.

The teaching efforts were going well, but the Ives had a problem. The Publishing Committee had in the past kept a stock of small prayer books costing 10¢ each that could be given away to those interested. Unfortunately, the Committee, told them that the books were no longer available, but that a newer volume would soon be available at a cost of $2. Howard reported that they could have sold 50 of them in their meetings, had they been available. The cost of the new book was too high, so they planned to start their study classes the next week with mimeographed copies of selected prayers for the participants. Howard said that they were getting considerable help from the Binghamton Bahá'ís.[5] The National Assembly replied that they had been carrying on an extensive consultation with Shoghi Effendi about prayer books and that the small books would once again be made available.[6]

In February, it was Howard's turn to do the lectures at the Hotel Jermyn. His topics were quite different from Mabel's:

28 February – Is Permanent Peace Possible? Practical Methods for Removal of Causes of War. Crucial Necessity for Peace
3 March – Crashing Worlds
19 March – Marriage and Divorce. Relation of the Political and Social Problems of Modern Society
14 March – The Bahá'í Solution of the Racial Problem. How the Essential Oneness of Humanity may be Practically Exemplified in Human Relations
21 March – Religion vs Religion. The Necessity for a Simple Basis for Reconciliation between the Great Religious Systems of the World. How it may be Done
24 March – The Bahá'í Teachings Concerning Christ. How the Teachings of Bahá'u'lláh provide a Basis upon which all Religions and Sects may Reasonably Rest

28 March – Breaking through to God. How Can It Be Done? The Sun And Its Mirrors
31 March – A Blue Print of a United World. The Federation of Mankind[7]

Opposition surfaced on 6 February when a letter appeared in *The Scranton Tribune* stating that the Bahá'ís would accept 'persons of any or all religious beliefs . . .. It takes part in the War Resisters International (plainly called a "communist organization" by "The Patriot". . .) Members of the Bahai religion have recently been arrested in Turkey and will be brought to trial charged with "aiding communism and internationalism". . .' Howard refuted the letter three days later, pointing out its errors.[8]

Financial crisis

On 22 February the National Teaching Committee sent Mabel a letter which caused a serious dilemma:

> It is apparent that the Guardian is establishing a very high standard for the pioneer teachers; one more difficult than existed in previous dispensations. He is insisting that these pioneers settle in one area and firmly establish the Faith, and in doing so become self-supporting. In carrying out the teaching work, therefore, the National Assembly has felt that it has no alternative but to follow the Guardian's wishes in the matter.
>
> For this reason they felt . . . that they could not continue indefinitely a plan of support in the teaching field for any one person. I do know that the Guardian recently did not approve of an individual giving up work in order to devote all his time to the Faith, if it meant aid from the general fund or some other Bahá'í. Thus the path is clear: and although difficult no doubt it will lead us out of our present uncertainties in the pursuance of our teaching work into a clearly established and self-supporting teaching service.

The N.S.A. felt that the plan outlined in my letter of February 1st could continue only until the end of April, subject to the action of the new N.S.A.; therefore in the meantime, if something should open for you (in the way of business employment) it would be well to consider it, most seriously.[9]

This raised a very difficult subject. The Ives had been supported by Mabel's daughter Edris, Howard's daughter Muriel and the National Teaching Committee for many months. With the loss of the Committee's support, things would be much more difficult for the Ives. In response, Howard wrote a long letter to the Guardian:

Beloved Guardian:
It is with the utmost joy and thankfulness that I am writing to you, for again I am active in the field of teaching and the souls in Scranton are responding with keen interest. A study class of about fifteen has been functioning for the last two weeks and now I am beginning a second course of Lectures, combined with the Study class so as to keep the interests of the general public alive and thus attract new members to the class...

The main purpose of this letter is to ask your advice and counsel regarding our future work. Much as I hesitate to trouble you with our affairs yet I know how keenly your interest and prayers are centered in the teaching campaign in this country, and also I am told by Marion Holley that she even cabled you for advice when in doubt as to her next move.

My dear wife has been forced to take a much needed rest for several weeks and is now in Florida: being aided to do this by the generosity of that blessed May Maxwell. So Mrs. Helen Inderlied and I are carrying on in her absence...

... As the decision of the Teaching Committee is based entirely upon what they consider your explicit instructions I hope that you will make clear to us how these instructions can be made to apply to us, or whether there may never be an exception.

Please let me assure you that it is far from my desire to evade any decision of the National Spiritual Assembly or the National Teaching Committee. I simply want to get the matter clear and so be able to decide whether we shall be under the necessity of withdrawing entirely from the Teaching Service . . .

The Canadian Field is ripe for the harvest. We could undoubtedly go through the whole of that vast country establishing Assemblies in every province where there are none at present. How gladly would we do this at our own expense if we had even the barest means. For sixteen years we have been doing this at our own expense, earning our living as we went, but now our health and strength will not permit us to do this. I am in my 71st year. Mabel is eleven years younger, but her nervous energy is much weakened by the many years of work in the Cause coupled with the necessary business activities . . .

I had considerable hope that there might be an income derived from the sale of *Portals to Freedom* sufficient to support us in the field of service. Unfortunately I have not been able to save much of anything from the sale of the first edition, as we were forced to use it all to live. Now that edition is exhausted and there is no money to pay for a second printing.[10]

Shoghi Effendi replied on 30 March. He greatly sympathized, but supported the Teaching Committee's decision:

> Although he very much regrets that, owing to the Teaching Committee's inability to finance a second trip for you both to Moncton, you will not find it possible to go there again at present, he hopes and prays nevertheless that through regular correspondence with the Moncton believers you will succeed in keeping in close touch with their activities and in offering them the guidance and help they undoubtedly

require for the furtherance of their work.

The Guardian will specially pray however that you may, in a not distant future, find the necessary means that would permit you to undertake a still more extensive teaching trip to various parts of Canada, and thus attain this dear wish of your hearts.[11]

Coronado Beach, Florida

Mabel left Scranton at the 'urgent suggestions' of the National Teaching Committee [12] on 24 February. Howard and Mabel's reunion had been a short month long. On the 25th, she arrived in Coronado Beach, Florida, about 75 miles [120 km] south of Jacksonville. She had travelled by bus and stopped in St Augustine for breakfast. Mamie Seto met her there and told her to get off the bus in New Smyrna and look up the Bahá'ís in Coronado Beach. Mabel described Coronado Beach as a 'very small place, quiet and restful'.[13]

On 28 February 1939, a more relaxed Mabel told Howard about her haven:

> Here I am sitting in the shelter of sand dunes facing the vast expanse of the ocean. In front of me is a wide, hard, snow white beach so flat and solid that autos pass up and down – miles and miles of it. Behind me a few yards is my cottage – all mine – imagine! $6 a week if I stay 3 weeks (for which I have paid) and 22.50 altogether if I stay a whole month. Large living rooms, 2 bedrooms, bath (shower) and kitchen . . .
>
> I get to bed between 8 and 9 – to sleep before 10, reading the Creative Word for a while. Saw the sun rise over the ocean this morning (after 8 hours sleep) and took a long walk up the beach before breakfast . . .
>
> There is a big dune behind the house where I have dug out a seat facing the ocean, where I can sit and sun-bathe in the early part of the day . . .
>
> How wonderful it would be if you could come down

here for a week or two – no expenses except transportation.[14]

> It is miles to the nearest place to eat. Or if you can cook your meals, as I do, you have to cook on the blue flame oil stove. There is an ice box, but I don't take ice, but then I don't have meat to keep. The grocery man calls and delivers daily.[15]

While Mabel recovered from her lengthy travel teaching work, Howard was busy teaching. He sent her the mimeographed invitation for his lectures and she responded, writing, 'Your little mimeographed announcement fairly knocks my eye out – and your detailed lectures – grand. I am sure I shall not be able to measure up to your standard.' She kept pushing her invitation for him to join her, warning him, however, that he had better buy 'Swimming tights – that is all the men wear'.[16]

But by 15 March, Howard was calling for her to return and she wasn't overly happy with the idea, writing, 'Since you seem to feel that I ought to come home this week, I guess I had better to it, altho it seems foolish now that I'm down here and things paid up for the month.'[17]

Mabel in Winnetka and Howard in Scranton

It is not known just when she left Florida, but on 30 April Mabel was back in Winnetka and deeply involved in activities there. She wrote to Howard on 5 May, in shock at the passing of Grace Ober. Grace had given a report to the National Convention, then had sat down in her chair and quietly passed away:

> Have been in a daze almost what with the impact of Grace's passing and the many details I cared for concerning the funeral. Then Monday night, Harlan, Leroy, Dorothy, Edris and I met in Edris' office for a conference till midnight. Then Tuesday Harlan left for Green Acre with our blessed

> Grace's body and that noon I had lunch with Dorothy in Evanston and spoke to Edris' study class at Mary Barton's apt in Chicago . . . Edris gave a tea for me and several fine Winnetka women showed a real interest – made dates with me . . . Then to Hammond's for Convention report . . .[18]

Mabel then turned her attention to Scranton, where Howard was still working. She told him to spend whatever money he had, which came from the National Teaching Committee, and return home to resume his writing, what she called his 'greatest field of service'. She noted that 'so many delegates', at the National Convention had 'referenced Portals! What a consummate blessing it has proved to be to <u>many</u> souls!' Mabel also noted that the National Assembly wanted them to be self-supporting, if possible, suggesting that Muriel take financial responsibility for Howard and Edris for Mabel.[19] But money was a huge problem for them and she continued the financial theme in her next letter, writing:

> We might just as well face it squarely and see what we can do about it. Besides a lot of praying we have to be practical, as there will be no more money, except from time to time when I am sent out on a specific project and it has been made clear that it is for that specific thing alone. Well, so here we are. May and I have talked it over much. She suggested that we might both do things in the field of writing. You are such a good writer that if you really went after it seriously, you could make a living that way. I'm getting pretty tired of being dependent on people and we both have definite talents . . .
>
> We shall have to face being separated – you on Muriel and I on Edris or else go to it, build up a home together by our own efforts. Now let us do a lot of praying and real clear thinking about this.[20]

Mabel becomes a 'professional' lecturer

In a letter dated 21 May, Mabel wrote that her lectures in Chicago were attended by between 120 and 140 people in each session. She wrote, 'A most interesting development coming out of it. It may prove my open-door. Am praying you may find yours in writing so that together we may become independent.' What she was alluding to was the possibility that she could become a paid professional lecturer.[21]

On 23 May, Mabel wrote that she was giving her 'first professional lecture on Tuesday night . . . Then if possible I want to get in another professional lecture. This is most valuable experience and means much for the future and also it pays in dollars.' She said that a 'large absorbed audience and nearly 50 have signed up for the study class'.[22] Four days later, she wrote, 'I have had my orders in no uncertain terms to stay here for two weeks from last Wednesday, that is for 4 more meetings.' That would delay a planned move to New Brunswick (see next chapter), but Mabel thought that was all for the better.[23]

In late May, Mabel wrote to the Guardian expressing her frustrations in Chicago:

> My most dearly beloved Guardian:
> It has been such a joy and encouragement and inspiration to receive your loving and heartening letters to both my husband and me. They mean more to us than I can express. My husband is still in Scranton, Pa., where we have been teaching for the last few months, and where a lovely new group of ten believers have been brought into the Faith. As I was a month in Florida during that time and also have been in the Chicago district since before the Convention, the results in Scranton are largely due to his consecrated work, and the fine assistance of Mrs. Helen Inderlied of Binghamton. Indeed five of the ten souls are really his spiritual children – two fine young men, brilliant scientist, and another, an inventor, and a splendid and enthusiastic couple. Of the other five, one is a cultured colored woman.

It was most interesting that the group at their election of officers, elected her, the only colored person, as the chairman. This was a complete surprise to us.

Now as to Chicago: Mrs. McCullom, who is a professional lecturer something in the same category as Orcella Rexford, and attracts large audiences, is very friendly to the Cause, and will give her lists of names to certain Baha'i teachers. We met her first in Binghamton nine years ago, and it was through lecturing to her students and following with Baha'i study classes that the Binghamton Community came into being. Recently Phil Marangella followed her in Syracuse, New York, and has developed a fine study class there. She told the Binghamton friends that she would turn over her Chicago list to me if I would come here, and would introduce me to her class. So after being authorized by the National Teaching Committee and consulting with the Spiritual Assembly of Chicago, I gave a series of consecutive, nightly lectures to an average attendance of one hundred persons, though some nights it went as high as 120 or 130. This resulted in a study class, which had its first meeting last night with between 40 and 50 present. The response from these new people to the Teachings of Baha'u'llah was extraordinary, as they had only known about them 8 days. Quite a large number of them came out to the Temple on Sunday, where I happened to be the speaker.

Now the policy of the N.T.C. has always been to consult the pioneer teacher as to who shall follow up the work as it is most important that the transition from teacher to teacher be such as to carry them further along the Path to Reality in a crescendo if possible; certainly without a drop. It was such a joy and such a benefit to the Moncton Believers to have the bounty of Dorothy Baker's fragrant spirituality and skillful handling of the many personal aspects and situations which arose among so young a group. Her background of experience in Lima [Ohio] was priceless to these new souls. I am also hoping and praying that that distinguished and heavenly and mature member of your noble family, Mrs. Maxwell, my precious and lifelong friend, may also be able to pay them a visit in the not too distant future.

Following the above policy with the interests of this infant group in mind, I made certain recommendations. One of them was that Phil Marangella, who will be returning to Chicago within two weeks, be asked to give them some further lectures and take them deeper into the Faith, as he is gifted with that calming power of reaching the souls . . . To my dismay, the local Teaching Committee has taken over and has decided through the influence of its most dominant member to let this member take entire charge of this tender new group of eager souls, under the rigidity and lack of – what can I say? – which has characterized Chicago's handling of new souls. O, my beloved Guardian it looks as though the Philadelphia tragedy will be repeated in Chicago. This dear dear soul who is to teach them, I believe has never succeeded in bringing one person into the Cause, and she informed me that she did not believe in having a succession of teachers (as Abdul Baha recommended, and as Mrs. Maxwell tells us, you favor) . . . So the Assembly had turned down this wonderful chance of bringing in new blood . . . It was only when the N.T.C. asked them to cooperate in this matter that they rather reluctantly acceded. Now they are enthusiastic about it but want it handled by one of their own, whether qualified or not.

I would never have dared to write the above if Mrs. Maxwell had not insisted that it was an obligation upon me to write it. I only want to write things which will bring joy to the heart of my Guardian. Please forgive me if I should not have written it. There are at least twenty-five or thirty souls who could be brought into the Faith out of this group if they are correctly handled. But it does need a teacher who understands the art of manipulation, as the Master expressed it, and who has the power of the Holy Spirit. It isn't just following out a course of study. It takes love and friendship and intimate personal contact, and meeting 'the traveler on the way' as Abdul Baha expressed it.

Won't you please pray, O thou who art the point of God on this earth, the king of the world and the beloved of the hearts – won't you please pray that these lovely souls may not be chilled and numbed and lose interest, as they did in Philadelphia when this same thing happened; but that they may be protected and brought into the Kingdom. I shall be with them for four more meetings and do as much as I can, reinforced with the Divine Assistance. As I am helpless without that. Then, after returning to Scranton for a few days, we are expecting (Howard and I) to go to Moncton, where a cottage has already been engaged for us at a nearby beach by one of the Believers there, and which we can make a center of attraction of the summer, and do the preparatory work for establishing the Faith in one of the nearby provinces, if the doors open and means are provided. Howard and I are both trying very hard to make ourselves financially independent in some way. We hope that it may be possible for us to do this and still have time and strength left to engage in teaching. If that is your wish we want to conform to it if it is humanly possible.[24]

When the Guardian's response came through his secretary, it said:

As regards your teaching work in Chicago, it is also a matter of deep satisfaction to the Guardian to know that your suggestions and recommendations have received due consideration and approval by the National Teaching Committee. He will pray the tender new group of eager souls you have succeeded in attracting to the Cause will be handled with such wisdom, tact, and loving care as to bring about their confirmation.

May I, in closing, assure both you and Mr. Ives of his prayers for you two, that your teaching work in Moncton this summer may be blessed with abundant results, and pave the way for the gradual penetration and establishment of the Faith in the nearby provinces.[25]

In his own hand, Shoghi Effendi added: 'Assuring you and dear Mr. Ives of my deep and abiding appreciation of your excellent and historic accomplishments, and above all of the sublime spirit that so remarkably manifests itself in your persistent and unforgettable labours in the service of the Faith, Your true and grateful brother, Shoghi.'

Howard, too, wrote to Shoghi Effendi about their teaching work:

> I am writing now mainly to tell you of the ten newly confirmed souls here in Scranton and to request your prayers for their great advancement, their unity and self-consecration in this Great Faith and this wonderful Kingdom. They are all so happy, so united, so eager to spread the Glad Tidings – it warms my very soul and I know that you will rejoice with us.
>
> Also may I request your prayers in my determined efforts towards achieving independence through my writings. I am trying to make a place for myself in columnar [sic] work. The idea being to present in daily brief article of about 1,000 words, those solutions of the world and individual problems offered by the Bahá'í Teachings . . .
>
> My dear wife is still in Chicago. I am so terribly happy in the work she has done there as well as in Moncton. She is a radiant and self-sacrificing spirit. Perhaps some of the essence of our darling Grace Ober may have descended upon her. Grace seems very close to me and assisting me in my writing, as she loved to do when she was with us visibly.[26]

The spring of 1938 was a very difficult time for Howard and Mabel. Her stipend from the National Teaching Committee for travel teaching was being ended and her small toiletries business was not doing well enough to cover the loss of support. She was worried about what was to happen to those souls she had helped find the path to Bahá'u'lláh in Chicago. Howard's hoped-for income from the sales of *Portals to Freedom* was much lower than expected, in large part because the National Spiritual Assembly had decided that all his book sales had to go through the National Book Committee and they were buying his books from him at a significant discount to the regular sales price. Howard's next book, which he hoped would provide them with an income, *Expanding Horizons*, was still a year from completion.

21
Back in Canada
1938–1939

Turning to the North

Mabel dictated a letter to Howard on 31 May 1938 which was optimistic, but frustrated. She had met with Leroy Ioas, Dorothy Baker and Harlan Ober to discuss teaching plans and they wanted her to stay in Chicago until at least the middle of June and then go to Camp Christie (on Georgian Bay, a large bay on the northeast side of Lake Huron north of Toronto) in August. Between the two, she had to visit both Scranton and Binghamton. She wrote, 'This thing of being pulled in several directions is awful. I have just about made up my mind never to promise to be anywhere at anytime. Abdu'l Baha told May never to make any plans and you know that he did not and I think that I will have to do the same thing.'[1]

It was a much happier and more optimistic Howard who wrote to the Guardian on 1 June 1938. Means for them to continue their travel teaching had apparently been found, though Howard doesn't specify what they were:

Beloved Guardian:
  Your treasured letter of March 30th brought joy and renewed assurance. Matters have been so arranged, and the path opened by Bahá'u'lláh for us to go to Moncton, N.B. [New Brunswick] about the middle of this month. It is truly miraculous, by the standards of men, the way has opened and means provided so that we could transport ourselves and few belongings to Canada. Dear Ruth Wilson, one of the new believers there, and a most sincere

and dedicated soul, has even provided a cottage for us to live in this Summer.²

The Guardian's response, written by his secretary, was:

> The Guardian has learned with deep satisfaction of your plan to teach in Moncton this summer, and appreciates keenly indeed the kind invitation extended to you and Mrs. Ives by one of the new believers there, and the facilities he [sic] has offered to provide in order to render your stay as pleasant and as fruitful in its results. He will pray that your labours may, as in the past, yield such fruits as to abundantly reward you for your painstaking and highly-meritorious services.³

Mabel received a letter from the National Spiritual Assembly written on 27 June saying that her teaching expenses for May and June would be reimbursed by them. The letter continued: 'It was further voted to record the fact that at present there are no teaching projects for you and Howard, but if you later on plan to establish yourself as a pioneer for permanent settlement in some new area, the National Assembly will extend the same financial cooperations as for other pioneer teachers.'⁴

The Ives left Scranton in the middle of June and went to New Brunswick, where they lived in the cottage provided by Ruth Wilson, the second person to become a Bahá'í in Moncton. The cottage was near Shediac, about 17 miles (28 km) northwest from Moncton. When Howard wrote to Nancy Phillips in early July, he said 'You will be surprised . . . to hear from me way up here in the wilds of New Brunswick . . . We have a lovely little cottage set in the pine woods and within sight of "Northumberland Straits", rolling away towards Prince Edward island, a dim line on the horizon, and within a five minute walk of a fine beach.' Their cottage was just 'a stone's throw from . . . Mr. and Mrs. [Irving and Mabel] Geary'. The Ives were also greatly enjoying being near the Moncton Bahá'í community and were quickly involved in teaching activities. On 5

July, Mabel went with Ruth to Halifax, Nova Scotia, for several days of teaching work, and on the 8th Howard gave a deepening on the Book of Certitude.[5] In August, Mabel was still active in Halifax and had made a number of contacts in the city. She had also been invited to a three-day conference at the St Francis Xavier College in nearby Antigonish.[6]

Financially, it was a big struggle. In a letter to the National Spiritual Assembly, Mabel asked about their service to the Faith. She noted that she was relieved to no longer being supported by the Bahá'í Fund, but wasn't sure how they would support themselves, since at their ages, neither had 'the necessary energy to carry the burden of both teaching and business activities as we used to be able to do'. She went on to say, 'we are not choosing the easy road in continually travelling and teaching, being as Abdu'l Baha said "homeless and without rest". But it seems the only possible road for us. It is a drive in our souls which will never let us rest which was born at the 1919 Convention, and has grown strong with the years.'[7]

They had hoped that *Portals to Freedom* could provide an income, but the first edition was completely sold out. To reprint it in a cheaper, paperback version would involve expense, which they couldn't afford. Howard was eligible for an old-age pension, but the rules stated that a person had to have had a legal residence for five out of the previous nine years. For 15 years, he had never lived in one place for more than a few months. A friend had offered them $25 a month to help support their teaching activities and another gave them a car to use.[8]

Of their teaching work, Mabel wrote:

> The Moncton Believers are deeply interested in extending the knowledge of the Faith into the surrounding Provinces and will assist in any way that they can, both while we are in Canada and after we have left. They are progressing splendidly. Howard has been able to give them just what they needed – a deepening in the understanding of the Creative Word. His classes on the Ighan are doing wonders for them and they are most enthusiastic about them. Also

I am having a class in 'Preparation for Teaching'. We had a Bahá'í Picnic, yesterday, with thirty-odd people present. Each of the Believers gave a short talk, explaining why the Faith had attracted them and what it had come to mean to them, for the benefit of the new people present, several of whom expressed the intention of attending the study classes. Also we have been assisted to interest several fine people in the Faith from Toronto, Montreal, Winnipeg and Newfoundland.[9]

On 29 August, the National Spiritual Assembly wrote about their most recent consultations on the Ives's situation. The result was that they were going to help Howard print a second edition of *Portals to Freedom* and Allen McDaniel would look into Howard's old-age pension. The Assembly would also write to the Guardian to get permission to publish a reference to his *Song Celestial* in the *Bahá'í News*.[10]

Toronto, Canada

Howard and Mabel moved to Moncton from their Shediac cottage sometime in September, planning to spend the winter there. But things changed when Mabel wrote to a friend that 'a most interesting opening and call came from Toronto, and so suddenly, here we are, settled, we think, for the winter. The new Assembly here needed help.'[11]

On 27 October, Mabel was in Toronto while Howard was still in Moncton, though about to leave for Montreal.[12] The 700-mile drive to Montreal took Howard two and a half days. After a week's stay, he continued on to Toronto,[13] arriving on 30 October, three weeks after Mabel. Mabel wrote that she

> came here ahead of Howard (on two days notice) and spent a wonderful week up in the north woods – the real north woods. A weekend at Camp Franklin with 175 young people ... Edris was there, too. It was a marvelous experience. The 9 of [us] motored up the top of Georgian Bay near Manatuan

Island, to another camp belonging also to this Mr Christie, . . . who had been working with youth all his life. He inaugurated the idea of a co-recreational camp and has carried it on successfully for 17 years . . . Well this far north camp is called Killarny Camp and is also on an island, in Baie Fine, a superb solitude. The most beautiful spot I have ever seen. Mountains with bays and inlands lakes on all sides, dotted with wooded islands. We hiked 9 miles [14 km], and climbed two mountains and had a swim, all in one day . . .[14]

Back in Toronto, Mabel quickly found a place to live with Laura Davis and was already very busy with teaching. When Howard arrived, Mabel was speaking four times a week and had a study class of 16 people as well as a youth group. Howard wrote about their activities:

We . . . are deeply engaged again in teaching, writing, lecturing, and holding daily conversations with attracted souls. What a wonderful and thrilling experience this is. Each time we go to a new city the marvel of finding ready souls is perpetually new. Riswanea is teaching her study classes four nights a week. I do some speaking in public halls on Sundays, but most of my energy and time is spent on a new book I am engrossed with. 'The Ocean of His Utterance.' You remember I prepared 12 lessons under this title. I am recasting it in the form of a book, accompanied by daily reading compilations, 365 selections bearing on the subject matter of the 12 chapters of the book – one chapter to be read and STUDIED monthly, and one reading daily. Some job but mighty interesting.[15]

Marlene Macke described the reception and activities of the Ives in her book *Take My Love to the Friends: The Story of Laura R. Davis*:

In November 1938, the Toronto Bahá'ís eagerly welcomed Mabel and Howard Colby Ives, two veteran American believers. The Ives embodied the national teaching committee's strategy of sending experienced teachers to a goal city. Although Toronto had just formed its Local Spiritual Assembly, consolidation was needed to ensure its long-term stability . . . The Ives settled into a spare room in Laura's [Davis] house for several months.

. . . They were a perfect team, with Mabel capably organizing meetings and speaking eloquently from the stage to large audiences and with Howard working with individuals who wanted to learn more. He was especially adept at deepening new Bahá'ís . . .

Describing Howard's gift, Mabel said:

'The most priceless service which Howard rendered was the deepening of the souls as they prepared to come in and after their confirmation. Specially was that never-to-be-forgotten hour which they spent with him immediately after their acceptance by the Assembly. They each went up to his room from the council chamber, and he took them to the heights and opened their consciousness to what the Faith of Bahá'u'lláh really meant . . . He deepened them perceptibly. I have never known anyone, except May [Maxwell], who had that divine quality so naturally of lifting souls to their highest.'

Howard's gift of deepening Bahá'ís especially benefitted Laura. With daily contact for several months, Laura received an unparalleled deepening from Howard . . .

When the Ives arrived in Toronto, Howard was over 70 years old, nearly deaf and in frail health, but still fervent, even driven, in his need to share the teachings of Bahá'u'lláh. Despite failing eyesight, his penetrating brown eyes, framed by round, block-rimmed glasses, continued to attract people by their candid openness. Mabel, 60 years old, had become a Bahá'í in 1899. In 1919, she served with May Maxwell on the first Canadian teaching committee . . . Howard was often called 'Daddy Howard' and Mabel was known as 'Rizwanea'.[16]

Mabel wrote to the National Spiritual Assembly of the United States and Canada on 7 November asking that their membership be transferred from Winnetka to Toronto. She also noted that she had a 'splendid Youth group', which came from the work of her daughter Edris and Marion Rhodes at Camp Franklin during the summer.[17]

Howard told Shoghi Effendi in a letter about their teaching efforts:

> Since we have been in this home, dedicated to the service of Baha'u'llah, there has been a constant succession of blessed souls seeking Light in this Day of Light. Last evening . . . we had four for dinner, three of them young people. They stayed until almost midnight.
>
> The night before a young man spent the whole evening with Mrs. Ives. She has interested a most vital and wonderful group of youth with whom she came in contact through her daughter Edris . . . She teaches them every week and they are so inspiring and eager.[18]

One of Howard's big concerns was 'the rather cold, suspicious and unsympathetic attitude of some of our Baha'i friends'. He explained the problem, as he saw it, to the Guardian in the letter:

> One can hardly fail to draw comparisons with this attitude of an open-minded, courteous, loving heart amongst the non-Baha'is with the rather cold, suspicious and unsympathetic attitude of some of our Baha'i friends. Why is this dear Guardian? What IS the matter with us? Is this the way we are to establish the Kingdom of love and cooperation, of helpfulness and brotherhood on the earth? It is not the personal angle that distresses me so much as the obstacles thus thrown in the way of the rapid advancement of the Faith. Is the rigid adherence to the Administration rules so all-important that to it must be sacrificed to the very essence of the Teachings? What can be more important, more close to

the heart of our Beloved Master and Lord, than kindness, humility, lack of desire for leadership, the obedience to the commands against wounding any heart?

I have hesitated long before I venture to bring this whole matter to your attention. Not but that you are already aware of the prevalence of this rigidity in the high places of the Faith, but I want so much to know if there is not something I can do about it.[19]

Howard closed his letter with an optimistic postscript about a new family about to join the Faith:

Especially would we request your prayers in behalf of John and Audrey Robarts, the nephew of our blessed Grace Robarts Ober... They have three young children, all boys, aged 4, 8 and 9. We had them at our home the other evening after dining with them and taking them to one of Mabel's study classes. They are on the verge of declaring themselves. They need this Great Faith so much, and its spiritual power will inspire and assist them so greatly in bringing up their blessed children.[20]

The Guardian's response, written on his behalf, said:

Your welcome message of the 19th November addressed to our beloved Guardian has duly reached him, together with its enclosures, and he has taken great pleasure in reading their contents...

He knows full well the trying conditions under which you are working at present, but wishes you not to feel despaired or discouraged, but would urge you rather to draw renewed strength and added inspiration from such seemingly insuperable difficulties, and to persevere in your noble endeavours in service to the Faith, particularly in the field of teaching and literary activity.

The Guardian has noted the observations you had made regarding the conduct of certain administrative activities of the Cause, and wishes you to remain assured that these deficiencies, which are in part inevitable, will be gradually remedied as the Faith advances and develops.

Regarding your teaching work in Toronto, he is delighted to hear of the splendid results accomplished so far by dear Mrs. Ives, and hopes that now through your presence there, and your active and valuable collaboration, even greater and more far-reaching results will be obtained. The essential is for you both to persevere. Remain assured of his prayers on your behalf, and also for the confirmation and guidance of Mr. and Mrs. Robarts who, he trusts, will soon be enrolled as members of the Toronto community.[21]

In his own hand, the Guardian added: 'May the Beloved of our hearts pour forth His imperishable blessings upon your great work for His Cause, refresh and gladden your spirit, and enable you to render memorable services to His sacred Threshold, Your true brother, Shoghi.'

John Robarts later wrote about his and Audrey's first meeting with Howard and Mabel:

Audrey and I [had] stopped going to the Sunday afternoon [Bahá'í] meetings. Then in that Fall of 1938, one Sunday I had an urge to attend a Bahai meeting – and we went and arrived a little late. Riswanea was speaking, and we went to the front seats. I can still see and feel that radiant glorious person pouring out her message of love. I sat enthralled – not knowing she was the Mabel Ives I had heard so much about, but realizing something was going on. I could see Grace [Ober, John's aunt] in her, and I could hardly refrain from rushing up and embracing her. I did after the meeting – and that started a friendship that I can never forget ...[22]

Howard's particular teaching manner strongly affected John. He and Audrey had in fact become Bahá'ís through his aunt, Grace Ober, but had 'done nothing about it'.[23] John, who worked as an insurance salesman, began meeting Howard for lunch, and Howard would try to answer John's questions. As Barron Harper wrote in *Lights of Fortitude*, 'Confronted by John's uncertainty, Howard encouraged him to ask God for a sign. John decided to give God a sign by giving up smoking. This he did immediately and permanently, even though he smoked up to two packs a day at the time. Later, when his new telephone was installed, he was amazed to find that his telephone number was Waverly 1844.'[24] John, Audrey and their oldest son, Patrick, would all become Knights of Bahá'u'lláh for pioneering to Africa. John was also named a Hand of the Cause of God by the Guardian.

Other people who came into the Faith through the efforts of Howard and Mabel in Toronto were Lloyd Gardner and Doris Richardson. Lloyd and a friend had attended the camp at Georgian Bay and there met two staff members who were Bahá'ís. Put in touch with the Bahá'í community in Toronto, Lloyd and his friend came into contact with Howard and Mabel and attended their firesides. Lloyd later said that he was 'was loved into the Faith by "Momma Ives', whom he considered his 'spiritual mother'.[25] Doris Richardson, who later became a Knight of Bahá'u'lláh in New Brunswick, also became a Bahá'í through Howard and Mabel.[26]

Doris McKay remembered a time when she visited Howard and Mabel::

> At Chestnut Park [Toronto] I expanded under the loving concern of the four hosts: Howard and Mabel, and Laura and Victor Davis . . .
>
> On the first afternoon I was weary from standing all day at the Exposition and was glad to be back to Chestnut Park. Howard invited me to rest on the couch. Placing pillows lovingly at my head he said, 'I have just finished the last chapter of Portals to Freedom.[27] How would you like me to read it to you while you rest?' The sound of Howard's reading voice enjoyed the same effect as Willard's Washington speech. In a few minutes I was ungratefully asleep. When I awoke with a guilty start Howard was sitting beside me with

the palms of his upturned hands raised to receive heavenly blessing as he prayed earnestly that I might be refreshed.[28]

In an unsent letter to the Guardian, Mabel wrote that a youth study class begun at Camp Franklin was doing very well, but she went on to explain the effect that the meagreness of their resources was really holding them back:

> We have only scratched the surface by our present methods. There are hundreds of people in this city who are ready for the Faith. We have to have good, sustained publicity, and a hall large enough to accommodate them. We have been able to secure a small room without charge, at one of the large hotels, but we cannot get a larger room to hold the people who would respond to the type of publicity we have secured in other cities for less than $5.00 a night for eight or nine nights to put on an adequate series, which always has, and is certain here, to bring results.[29]

Mabel then laid out her vision of how effective proclamation and teaching could be done:

> It is based upon combining the different types of teaching experience in a well planned attack upon a new city, with the equipment and personnel to carry thru to and beyond the stage of establishing an Assembly and standing by until they are thoroughly integrated into the Faith and Administration. In a word, to combine trained pioneer teachers and proven teaching methods with settlement for life by other believers who are used to functioning in a Community and are capable of continuing both study classes for newly attracted souls and of holding study classes for deepening the souls . . .
> For instance:
> One experienced pioneer teacher (public lecturers).
> One who has had successful experience in teaching study classes for beginners.

One who is particularly equipped to confirm souls and who can hold classes for that purpose.
One or more who have that harmonizing gift and loving heart to enable them to work with individual souls.
One who can do the advance work in preparation for the lecture series.
And the teacher who will 'settle and live there till the end of life'.

Now, several of these divisions can be handled by one person . . .

In this way many believers could be brought into superbly productive work . . .

There is nothing new or untried about the above method, as it has been used in a haphazard fashion, proving its value even under those conditions . . .

It does seem as tho our teaching has been so haphazard and uncoordinated – so much waste motion. Lectures given in a city and no follow-up work, no coordinated teaching activity, to the end that souls can be carried right through without a hitch; not stimulated and then left to die out, as has occurred in so many cases, then a heroic effort to resuscitate them later, with great loss from every angle. The administration has gone forward with steady momentum, ever growing, ever coordination and building. But the teaching side has legged far behind, being left to uncoordinated individual initiative. Of course, I realize there has to be the self-sacrificial desire and arising, but that does not mean that we cannot have a plan and program into which the individual may fit and be immeasurably helped and augmented.[30]

Mabel may not have felt brave enough to send this particular letter to the Guardian of the Faith, but there was truth in what she wrote. Shoghi Effendi, however, had several years earlier already given an answer about teaching to Leroy Ioas:

The Bahá'í teacher should not get discouraged at the consciousness of the limitations within or without him. He should rather persevere, and be confident, that no matter how numerous and perplexing the difficulties that confront him may appear, he is continually assisted and guided through Divine confirmations. He should consider himself as a mere instrument in the hands of God, and should, therefore, cease looking at his own merits. The first and most important qualification of a Bahá'í teacher is, indeed, unqualified loyalty and attachment to the Cause. Knowledge is, of course, essential; but compared to devotion it is secondary in importance.

What the Cause now requires is not so much a group of highly-cultured and intellectual people who can adequately present its Teachings, but a number of devoted, sincere and loyal supporters who, in utter disregard of their own weaknesses and limitations, and with hearts afire with the love of God, forsake their all for the sake of spreading and establishing His Faith. In other words, what is mostly needed nowadays is a Bahá'í pioneer, and not so much a Bahá'í philosopher or scholar. For the Cause is not a system of philosophy; it is essentially a way of life, a religious faith that seeks to unite all people on a common basis of mutual understanding and love, and in a common devotion to God.[31]

On 4 January 1939, Howard wrote to Muriel describing their time in Toronto:

Our life here in Toronto is extremely active. The days just aren't long enough. We have met and come to know well many very lovely people, and the response to our work has been truly heartening. My Youth class is especially thrilling. About 15 young people, all over 21 are studying with me and we have the grandest time. We meet at the home of one of them and they sprawl on the floor in front of the fire, and we settle the affairs of the universe, to say nothing of this little world. Their minds are so clear and fresh. They can see right thru a thing, without having to clean away a lot of rubbish of preconceived ideas . . . Thank God for this new generation, who can think clearly, and who can act without fear or favor.[32]

From early January until mid-March 1939, Howard and Mabel were busy teaching in Toronto during this time, but there are no details. Howard did send another letter to the Guardian in March after receiving a letter from him (sent the previous December) in which Shoghi Effendi had enclosed six ring-stones:

> Your valued letter, with the encouraging note in your own handwriting, under the date of Dec. 31st last, with its enclosure of six ring-stones from you, came to me safely. I thank you most deeply for these great favors.
>
> Mrs. Ives is writing you at some length, so as she covers all that is in my heart also, I will make this note brief.
>
> John and Audrey Robarts, for whom your prayers were requested, and to whom you refer in your letter, joined the Group here three months ago. They are both keeping the Blessed Fast and their spiritual growth is truly remarkable. I read that part of your letter to them in which you mention their names, and they were very happy that you remembered them.[33]

In the reply, dated 22 April, the Guardian responded:

> Your valued letter of the 15th March has duly reached our beloved Guardian, and he was pleased to note that you had safely received his message, as well as the six ring-stones, which he hopes you have found satisfactory.
>
> He was also considerably rejoiced to know that Mr. and Mrs. Robarts, for whom you had asked his special prayers in your last letter, have joined the Toronto Bahá'í Community, and are progressing so well spiritually. He will continue to remember them in his prayers that they may keep on deepening in their devotion and love for the Cause, and that also

they may receive ever-widening opportunities of promoting its truth, and of extending its foundations in their centre.[34]

Hamilton, Ontario

In March, Mabel made her first teaching visit to Hamilton, Ontario, at the westernmost end of Lake Ontario. As she commonly did, Mabel wrote a newsy letter to Shoghi Effendi about her activities there:

> In the way of a brief report on the work in this locality: a series of lectures, eight in number, has just been completed in Hamilton, a city 43 miles [69 km] from Toronto. At the last meeting a study class was formed of 14 attracted souls. Mrs. Mary Barton of Winnetka, Illinois, who came over to assist in this campaign is remaining in Hamilton to consolidate the work and thereby gain experience in the teaching field, though I expect to go over weekly for a study class. The first meeting in a Toronto series has taken place and a responsive audience of 48 people gives hope of good results here. Besides this, we have had twice-weekly lectures and weekly study classes in this city. Several souls have been confirmed and there are a number of others who are apparently very close. A large Forum was held in collaboration with the Theosophical Society, who have a large hall, on the Oneness of Mankind, at which there were four speakers, one of which was a Bahai, and a Bahai chairman. Over 350 people were present and at that meeting cards announcing the coming series of Bahai lectures were given out. So a number of these people attended the opening lecture. Besides the above quite a number of lectures have been given before non-Bahai bodies, one in a church, and on next Sunday this servant is to speak before a Bible class of 60 young people.[35]

Her work resulted in the enrolment of Hamilton's first Bahá'í, Lulu Mabel Barr.[36]

In another letter to Shoghi Effendi, Mabel also listed a series of nine questions that those attracted to the Faith were asking. Seven of them were about economics in the future Baháʼí world, one was about the Baháʼí inheritance laws and one about the future Administrative Order. In his reply of 22 April 1939, Shoghi Effendi's secretary wrote:

> The Guardian wishes me to gratefully acknowledge the receipt of your detailed and welcome communication dated February 27th. He feels indeed deeply gratified and encouraged to know that you and dear Mr. Ives are being so wonderfully confirmed in your teaching work in Canada and that in Hamilton you have succeeded in forming a study class of fourteen attracted souls. He would certainly advise you not to leave this group until you ensure that after your departure the work will satisfactorily and uninterruptedly advance and progress. He will most fervently pray that you may continue to be strengthened and confirmed in your devoted endeavours, and may have the satisfaction of seeing an Assembly formed in Hamilton in the near future. You should whole-heartedly and confidently persevere, and repose your full trust in the unfailing guidance and assistance of Baháʼuʼlláh.
>
> Now with regard to your questions concerning Baháʼí economic teachings: the writings of Baháʼuʼlláh do not contain any technical teachings on the subject of economics, and on such specific financial questions as gold standardization, monetary standards and exchanges, etc. – what they provide however are certain general principles in the light of which future Baháʼí economists will have to evolve the Baháʼí Economic System of the future. These principles contribute the basis of all future economic schemes, but at present it would certainly be premature to foretell what definite economic system will be evolved and established by the Cause. The Baháʼís, therefore, cannot claim to possess at present an economic order or system which they can officially associate with the Faith, nor should they now attempt to establish any

such economic scheme, which would obviously be beyond their present-day capacity and resources . . .

No country can possible solve its economic difficulties alone, for economic interdependence is an unescapable economic reality . . .[37]

Mabel's son, Colston, married Sheila Nelson in March. Sheila had only become a Bahá'í the year before, but Mabel described her as 'beautiful both spiritually and physically and altogether lovely from every standpoint'.[38] As Sheila Rice-Wray, Mabel's daughter-in-law, was to become a powerful Bahá'í speaker and a long-time pioneer in Latin America.

Howard and Mabel were still in Toronto in late June. In a note to Horace Holley, Mabel wrote that there were three new Bahá'ís in the Toronto community.[39]

First international picnic

On 25 June 1939, the Bahá'ís of Canada and the United States gathered at Queenston, Ontario, near Niagara Falls, for an international picnic. Two cities in Canada and four in New York organized a programme under the auspices of the Toronto Local Spiritual Assembly, with Willard McKay as chairman, and with talks by Doris McKay, John Stearns, Mrs Pettibone, Elizabeth Brooks, Marguerite Firoozi, Lulu Barr, Mrs Enos Barton, Audrey and John Robarts, and Howard and Mabel Ives. Doris McKay described the event:

> We crossed the lake on a steamer. Seventy-two people . . . more than half were either new Bahá'ís or newly attracted. Howard, very feeble and greatly aged, came down from Toronto in his longing to meet his Jamestown [New York] spiritual grandchildren. It seemed as if the living Presence had moved into him, like the Friend into His house. He had lived so much with the Word in his writing of Portals to Freedom, this year and last, that, almost unconsciously, he speaks the Word instead of his own language. He took the

Jamestown people aside and poured out his love, tenderness, and counsel upon all of us. We had invited a middle-aged Syrian rug dealer, Namaan Hadbeh, to go with us. He used to live in Haifa and had met 'Abdu'l-Bahá. Howard took him in his arms, called him by his first name and questioned him tenderly. He told all the Jamestown Bahá'ís that he knew all of them by name and was eagerly interested in all of them. He said that he thought the sense of kinship he felt was because of the special closeness that he and I had between us. Howard told them that he prayed every day, for all of them. They loved him. He took down the walls of his heart and gave them his whole life in those brief moments.

The picnic was a typical Ives' idea. It was a real 'get together' in other significant ways, too. There was some consultation and it was agreed that the travel teacher circuit which included Pennsylvania and New York would be extended to include neighbouring Canadian Bahá'í communities and that we would concentrate on exchanging teachers. It was also an occasion for the Bahá'í youth of both countries to meet one another and, at this picnic, the first youth conference was planned. It would be held later in Jamestown. I think that it was at this picnic that I met the youthful Lloyd Gardner and his brother Cliff. They taught me how to make 'proper' tea. Another youth, Grace Ober's nephew, was also there – John Robarts. The picnic was truly a cross-border event signaling an increase in shared teaching activity.[40]

One participant said, 'The day was perfect and the enthusiasm of the believers and their friends knew no bound.' Four people became Bahá'ís during the picnic. With the success of this first international picnic, plans were immediately made for a similar picnic at Queenstown Heights on Sunday 13 August.[41]

In spite of all their financial difficulties and the uncertainty of the arrangements with the National Spiritual Assembly and the National Teaching Committee, Howard and Mabel received a nice boost when the Secretary of the National Spiritual

Assembly sent them a letter written on behalf of the Guardian which read, 'The Guardian deeply appreciates the very generous offer made by one of the N.S.A. members to provide the teaching expenses of Mrs. Mabel Ives for one year. Such welcome action will surely prove of immense encouragement to Mrs. Ives and cannot but evoke the deepest gratitude and admiration in all hearts.'[42] This unexpected financial support set the stage for Howard and Mabel's next great adventure.

Canadian summary

Mabel summarized what they had done in Canada in a letter to the Guardian:

> During our stay there, which was terminated in Sept. of this year, more than 150 lectures and study classes were held in Toronto, and 70 lectures and study classes in Hamilton, besides talks before outside organizations and informal evenings with new souls.
>
> As a result, 14 new believers were added to the Toronto Community, two of these were well on their way as a result of our beloved Grace Ober, the preceding fall, but had not felt ready to become formally associated with the Faith (Mr. and Mrs. John Robarts). They are now perhaps the most valuable assets of the Cause there. Also in regard to two of the youth, Elsie Beecroft, a young believer from New York, had much to do in bringing them into the Faith. She is an ardent young believer and is doing splendid work at present with the flourishing youth group of about 16. Seven of them are members and some of the others are very near. Also there are several other people who have asked for membership before I left, who for various reasons have not joined yet. Three others who had not quite come to the point of asking for membership are now, I understand, ready to take the step, and several others very near.
>
> From the frequent reports we receive from the friends there, the activity is continuing, and through the extremely

valuable monthly visits of Mrs. Doris McKay, who divides 5 days between the two cities, the friends are deepening in spiritual consciousness and their understanding of the administrative principles.

In Hamilton, the group of four new believers have asked for group status, and before we left, 3 others had written letters acknowledging their Faith in Baha'u'llah and their desire to become affiliated with the Faith, and then for family reasons asked me to hold up their letters until they could straighten out some personal matter, but affirming that their faith was unwavering. I am in frequent communication with them and also Mrs. McKay is with them as much as possible on her trips there, so that they will be ready to take the final step before long . . . There are regular meetings held there, and once a month Mr. George Spendlove lectures there. They are hoping that they may have nine members by late winter. So in the two cities are twenty-two souls added to the Faith, and about twelve more who should within the next few months. It seemed that the two cities were in too critical a condition to leave without adequate follow-up, so we strongly recommended to the National Spiritual Assembly at their Toronto meeting that Doris McKay be sent once a month for several months. We feel that she and her husband, Willard, are two of the best of our resident, or follow-up teachers.[43]

22

Memphis and Howard's Declining Health

Hamilton, Ontario to Memphis, Tennessee: An adventure

On Friday 29 September 1939, Howard and Mabel left Hamilton and began their journey to Memphis, Tennessee. They headed first for Detroit, Michigan, but didn't get far before they had a flat tyre. They arrived at the Detroit home of George and Peggy True – later to become Knights of Bahá'u'lláh – in a pouring rain at 6 p.m. and had just enough time for a quick dinner before going to a meeting at the Bahá'í Center. The meeting turned out to be the largest Bahá'í meeting ever held in the city.[1]

The next day, Howard and Mabel continued their trip. Just outside Dearborn, Michigan, 'a truck and our car tried to occupy the same place at the same time, with disastrous results for our car'. Luckily, no one was hurt, but it did mean that Howard had to stay and wait for the car to be repaired while Mabel continued to Chicago. George True came down and took Mabel to the train station, then took Howard back to Detroit.[2]

When Mabel arrived in Chicago on Tuesday, she found that Edris was very ill and in the hospital with complications from the Caesarean birth of her daughter a week earlier. For the next several days, Mabel stayed with Edris. By Sunday, when she was supposed to speak at the House of Worship, she was exhausted. Mabel wrote that it 'seemed impossible, but Bahá'u'lláh gave the strength and assistance, and to an audience filling every seat, He poured forth His Message'.[3]

Howard managed to get to Chicago after a twelve-hour

journey, 'driving with upmost care to avoid another accident'. Howard's driving skills were legendarily poor. He continued on to Waukegan, where he spent four days giving a number of talks and personal interviews.[4]

When Edris was out of danger, Mabel and Howard left Chicago for Memphis, driving the repaired car. They didn't make it very far:

> While passing Harvey, a little way out of Chicago, a man trying to pass and misjudging the speed of the approaching car, cut in too close in front of us and pushed us off the road into a telegraph pole. Poor Howard, to whom I had just turned over the wheel a little while back, was terribly shaken and his heart did handsprings. He became almost unconscious for a while on the ground. The man proved to be a minister hurrying to a wedding with his wife. He tried to get out of it, but the cops and those who had seen the accident were friendly to us, and finally we all went to the police station, where we arbitrated the matter before the judge, and we compromised by letting him off with a small payment. Otherwise it would have been a civil suit and might have dragged out for ages, and would have necessitated our presence at the hearing.
>
> Howard was taken to the hospital and the doctor said he must remain there quiet in bed for 24 hours. When I arrived there after settling the other matter at the police station, he was lying in the emergency room, but had made up his mind that he would not stay. He had been seeking help from higher worlds and felt that he was strong enough to leave. So we did, and the cop drove us back to the station where they let him rest on a cot in the 'Ladies Cell', the only place available. He put a handkerchief under his head and closed his eyes and rested, while I went to see what could be done about the car.
>
> A garage man had wanted to tow the car in for repairs from the scene of the accident, but I couldn't see it and got the cops and several of the men standing around to pull the

crumpled fenders off from the wheels so that the wheels could turn freely. The garage man had insisted that it could not be done, and also that the wheels had been forced out of alinement and it couldn't run, but I was obdurate and I managed to go to the Police Station under our own steam. Howard in the meantime had been rushed to the hospital. They thought he was going. His heart was terrible, but they didn't know about the power of Bahá'u'lláh.

Well, to go back, I took the car to another garage and got the mechanic to get the fenders entirely free of the wheels and push what was left of the running board out of the way – all for 75¢. Quite different from what the other man had wanted. Then got Howard and we went to get some supper. Later we hunted for a place to stay for the night. Finally I left H. on the porch of the only hotel (horrible place) while I went to get the car, remaining away about an hour, walking all over that town hunting for a tourist place or rooming house. None to be found. Returning, I found a new man! Howard starting to feel anxious at my delay in returning had turned to Bahá'u'lláh and completely submitted to anything that might happen, and tuned in deeply with the divine worlds so that he was completely recovered, felt fine and was better the next day and more vital than he had been before the accident. Wonderful![5]

The next day, Mabel and Howard continued to Urbana, Illinois, where they stayed with Professor Paine. They only had an hour's rest before they had to address another meeting. In the evening, they spoke to a youth group. The next day, they sold their battered and barely drivable car to a junk man. Mabel wrote that they then 'packed up all our boxes into larger boxes and tied them, and shipped them excess baggage on Howard's bus ticket'. Mabel remained a few days in Urbana and Howard went to Memphis, arriving on Tuesday 10 October 1939.[6]

Memphis, Tennessee

By the time Mabel made it to Memphis on Thursday 12 October, driving down with Mary Barton, who was also pioneering, Howard had found a house in a nice residential district at 1800 Poplar Street and an apartment for Mary a few blocks away. The next Sunday, Howard and Mabel went to the Unitarian Church and, as Mabel noted, 'the miracles began'. The minister opened the service by reading a very long passage that they recognized as being from 'Abdu'l-Bahá. He didn't identify 'Abdu'l-Bahá as the source of the quotation. He had been looking through a book and 'Abdu'l-Bahá's section was perfect for his sermon. When Howard and Mabel later asked the minister where he had found the quotation, he said that it came from a new book called 'The Bible of the World'.[7] When they asked Leroy Ioas about the book, he wrote back that it was probably a book published by Ahmad Sohrab called 'The Bible of Mankind' that contained writings from all the religions, including the Bahá'í Faith. Leroy cautioned that the Ives 'would have to proceed very cautiously with the Minister, to assure yourself that he is not actively associated with the [Ahmad's] New History Society'.[8] Sohrab, a long-time secretary for 'Abdu'l-Bahá, had become a Covenant-breaker after the appointment of Shoghi Effendi as the Guardian. Sohrab rejected Shoghi Effendi's Administrative Order and in about 1929 created the New History Society to spread his own version of the Bahá'í Faith.[9]

Several people that they met at the church, including Mrs Rugg and Johanna Zimmerman, wanted to know more about the Faith and the Ives were invited to address a variety of groups. Later the same day, Howard, Mabel and Mary went to the Fortune Restaurant for dinner. The trio took a table near the door, but Mabel was bothered by the draught caused by the constantly opening of the door, so they moved to a table near the back. Mabel

> soon noticed a most attractive girl at the next table who was eyeing me with great interest, and, as I looked at her, her

YOU ARE INVITED TO ATTEND

A Lecture Series on "THE NEW 'WORLD ORDER"
A Discussion of World Problems in the Light of the New Age

By MRS. HOWARD COLBY IVES, of Chicago, Nationally Known Lecturer

Under the Auspices of the National Assembly of the Baha'is of the United States and Canada

The Baha'i World Faith is Universal, Non-Sectarian and Non-Political. It is building a New World Order as well as new individuals in this century, based upon the **Application of the Teachings** given 2,000 years ago in Galilee, to the needs of this present age.

HOTEL CHISCA, 8:00 P. M.

(1) Wed. Nov. 1st, "World Chaos to World Rebirth"
(2) Thu. Nov. 2nd, "Dawn of a Universal Civilization"
(3) Fri. Nov. 3rd, "A Practical Solution of Our Economic Problems based upon the Laws of God"
(4) Sat. Nov. 4th, "The True Origin and Destiny of Man" (with Chart)
(5) Sun. Nov. 5th, "Recurrent Cycles of Civilization" (with Chart)
(6) Tue. Nov. 7th, "A Preview of the World in the Year, 2001"

PLAN TO ATTEND THE ENTIRE SERIES

No Collection   No Voluntary Offering   No Paid Study Classes

Announcement of talks to be given by Mabel in Memphis, Tennessee, November 1939

Mabel (left) with May Maxwell, 1940

Howard at the 32nd National Bahá'í Convention, April 1940

Howard and Mabel with friends in Waukegan, Illinois, April 1940

Howard with Alvin Blum, about 1940

Howard with Roberta Wilson in Hot Springs, Arkansas, in 1940

The first interracial Bahá'í Feast in Memphis, Tennessee, in 1941. Among those present were Howard Ives, Grace Bogan, Alvin Blum, Doris McKay, Dr and Mrs Watkins and their daughters, Professor Henderson and Johanna Zimmerman

face seemed vaguely familiar. I wondered if she could be one of Edris' college friends whom I might have met. After a bit she came over and asked if I was Mrs. Ives. She proved to be Allison Ingalls of Portsmouth, N.H. whom I had first met in connection with some educational work I was doing a number of years ago.[10]

Allison had met and admired Harlan Ober and Lorol Schopflocher. Her husband was in Honduras at that time and she was in the restaurant with her brother-in-law. She had recognized Howard because she had met him once with Harlan. Mabel wrote:

> The wonderful part was that she was just longing for a Bahá'í contact as she was in the Valley of Decision, on the point of joining her mother-in-law's church . . . but not wanting to do so until she had investigated the Bahá'í Faith, as she felt strongly drawn to it. They came over to our table and stayed a long time asking real questions. The brother-in-law was most receptive and Howard had a grand talk with him, while I talked with Allison, above the din of the music . . . This all happened on our third day in Memphis. Bahá'u'lláh must be assisting us![11]

By the end of their first week in Memphis, Howard and Mabel had been enabled to share, or at least mention, the Faith to at least a half dozen groups and had developed several strong contacts. One of those contacts was Gertrude Gewertz, 'an attractive Jewess'.[12] Gertrude would become Gertrude Blum when she married Alvin Blum in February 1942. The Blums would later become Knights of Bahá'u'lláh to the Solomon Islands during the Ten Year Crusade.

After Mabel's first report to the National Spiritual Assembly, Leroy Ioas responded for that body, 'Your initial contacts in Memphis are most remarkable, and show the guidance of the spirit, and the blessings of the Master. How wonderfully the door can be opened, when the time is ripe, and the workers ready.'[13]

Mabel complained that a big problem in Memphis was the cost of meeting rooms. The hotel everyone recommended wanted $10 per night for a room and would not budge on the price. With the expense of things like cards, posters, postage, etc., it was too much for the Ives' meagre budget. Mabel did, ultimately, find a hotel that did not initially charge her for a meeting room. She quickly organized her lecture series and published an invitation published in the newspaper.[14] By 11 November 1939, she had finished her first series of lectures to audiences of from 25 and 30 and was ready to begin her study classes. These lectures were followed up with three more. The hotel manager decided that for the second set of meeting, Mabel should pay for the room, She offered him $5, which was less than the normal rate, but he happily accepted.[15]

Mabel wrote to Shoghi Effendi that she had a study class of 25 and that 'The quality of these people is fine . . . Many of them are Unitarians. Recently the Unitarian Minister turned over his Sunday morning pulpit to me, while he was out of the city, and it was possible to speak quite directly on the Cause . . . One, a very lovely woman, whose husband is also interested, said yesterday that it was not at all difficult for her to accept Baha'u'llah as the Manifestation of God for this Day.'[16]

Thanksgiving in Gulfport, Mississippi

At Thanksgiving, Mabel, Howard and Mary Barton drove to Gulfport, Mississippi, for a five-day break and Mabel wrote to her new daughter-in-law, Sheila Rice-Wray, about the adventure. Mary drove them both ways – a full-day trip each way – and they stayed with Dr and Mrs Richard Cox at the Gulf Park College. Mabel thoroughly enjoyed those days of rest and recuperation. In the letter she wrote that she lay

> on the beach and took a real sun bath and also in the glass enclosed swimming pool. One day we drove to New Orleans, had lunch at the famous Gallitoires, and drove up St. Charles Ave. and saw the Casa Grande Apartment Hotel

where we used to live when Colston was a small boy. Also, we passed through Waveland, Miss. where he will recall that we spent a summer on the Gulf. Mrs. Cox gave several dinner parties for us and had us meeting the distinguished people from thereabouts, also she gave a reception to us before the Thanksgiving dinner . . . It was refreshing after living in the austere north, with its scarcity of good servants, to have two butlers and a maid waiting on a dinner party of a dozen people. Dr Cox drives his own plane, or should say 'pilots' his plane.[17]

Never one to pass up an opportunity to share the Faith with those as yet denied the privilege, she told the Coxs and others about the World Order of Bahá'u'lláh. She wrote:

A number of the Faculty and friends evidenced real interest and readiness, and Mrs. Cox especially was apparently in perfect sympathy . . . And then to crown it all, Mrs. Cox asked us to take over the Sunday morning Chapel, and asked Howard to give a reading from his poem, Song Celestial, and me, to speak on the Faith. So I talked on the New World Order. Following that we had a dinner party and grand questions were asked about the Faith . . .[18]

Mabel closed with a prescient note, asking if Sheila had read *The Advent of Divine Justice*. 'It certainly opens doors of opportunity to accomplish the greatest thing in history,' she wrote. In 1947, Sheila began a career as a travel teacher and pioneer in Cuba, Costa Rica, Paraguay, Bolivia and finally the Dominican Republic, where she remained until her passing in 1997. She became well known as a Bahá'í speaker.

Back in Memphis

By December 1939, the study class in Memphis was going well, but teaching efforts with the Black population of the city were struggling. They had tried to hold meetings and Feasts with refreshments, but to little avail. They had even approached the head of the LeMoyne College Arts Department, a college for Black youth, though the head was white. The professor was quite interested, but there was not much response from the students. One Black Bahá'í, Mrs Watkins, however, was described as 'very nice and a very sincere Bahá'í'.[19] Teaching of the Black population of Memphis and their integration into the larger Bahá'í community proved to be the greatest problem they were to have.

In a letter to Nancy Phillips, Howard wrote, 'There is a quite remarkable episcopalian rector here, Mr. Noe, whose sermons and prayers are full of vitality of the New Day. He is outspoken in his references to the decay of institutional Christianity and the need of new spiritual vitality. He even refers to the necessity for another Manifestation of the Eternal Christ.' Howard was trying to make an appointment to talk with him.[20]

At the end of the year, Mabel described what they had done during their two and a half months in Memphis:

> We have been having a very interesting experience here in Memphis. Following a series of nine lectures . . . a study class was organized of about twenty people, and has been going ever since twice a week. The people are charming, and we have made some lovely friends, and have had many delightful experiences. The regular Thursday night broadcast of the Town Hall of the Air was held for the first time in Memphis, instead of in New York City. George Denny, the head of it, came on to handle it here, and the President of the local club and his wife are members of our study class, so I had the pleasure of attending the big luncheon given for Mr. Denny Thursday, and of meeting him and speaking of the Cause to him . . . Be sure to tune in always on Thursday evenings at 8:30, as the programs are tending more and more towards the principles of Baha'u'llah. Indeed, at a recent one, the subject of federation was discussed almost exactly from the Baha'i viewpoint . . .[21]

Howard wrote to Nancy Phillips on 23 January 1940, describing their efforts in Memphis: 'We came to this city last Oct. and expect to be here another two months or so . . . Mabel gave nine lectures altogether and has now been conducting a semi-weekly study class for some weeks, with about twenty attendants. The interest in the Cause is most heartening.'[22]

Howard's health

Howard was struggling with his health. In a letter to Nancy Phillips he noted that he could only sit at his desk for about two hours a day. He was distinctly aware of his physical degradation and was very uncomfortable with his level of activity. The problem so worried him that in February 1940 he asked the Guardian what to do: 'Each year that passes my physical energy is, naturally, declining, but my spiritual energy seems ever to increase. I cannot bear the thought of idleness, yet I wish to use what strength I have left (bodily strength) to the greatest advantage, and who in all the world is better qualified to know how I could best use that strength than the Guardian of the Cause of God!'[23]

Howard highlighted his failing eyesight: 'Even with my glasses,' he wrote, 'anything more than 20 feet or so away was dim and the outlines blurred. Also I noted that an increasingly strong light was needed for reading.' When he went to the oculist, the diagnosis was that he had advanced cataracts in both eyes. Howard's reaction was remarkable:

> Many people have had blindness, and worse, come upon them unexpectedly. Nor is it unusual to have such calamities (so called) met with courage and cheer. That is only decent, it would seem. But my immediate reaction was quite other. In attempting to describe this spiritual-psychological experience my main intent is to clarify the experience to my own understanding, for I confess to myself a certain amazement – a questioning of the sanity (as men call sanity) of my attitude, an attitude, I again repeat, which

was not gained by philosophical reasoning, rather was it an immediate and spontaneous reaction: just as one would naturally and spontaneously react to the information that he had fallen heir to a large fortune.

For that immediate reaction to the doctor's statement that my eyesight was rapidly failing was a sort of triumphant inner shout. I wonder as I use it if 'triumph' is quite the proper word. But I can think of no more exact one.

It was as if the inner Voice spoke through the doctor's words saying: 'see how I am trusting you! You have asked for the greatest spiritual endowments. You have offered your life as a sacrifice in My Path. You have asked for renunciation, tranquility and perfect submission to My Will, and utter relinquishment of your own will. I have taken you at your word. Here is your great opportunity.' Yes: Triumph is the only word!

My first thought was that I would not distress my Riswanea by telling her of the doctor's diagnosis. But finally I decided to do so because I knew her love and courage and had confidence in her great spiritual insight. So, not long after my return home I told her. Her immediate reaction, after the first moment of astonished dismay, was a non-acceptance of the necessity of submission to the doctor's decree . . .

Such a reaction to my news was a positive shock . . . Why was it a shock? . . . Why, then, should I feel as though I had been hauled down from clear-aired Heights by dear Riswanea's suggestions of means of overcoming, of avoiding this physical disability? It cannot be because I don't want to overcome it, or that I would not accept and adopt any means to it if I were convinced that it was God's will – Baha'u'llah's will – that I should be rid of it.[24]

As noted, Mabel's reaction was quite the opposite of Howard's. She insisted that there were physical and spiritual healing cures that he had to try. Her reaction shocked Howard and he changed the subject as quickly as possible. His 'Spiritual Diary' continued with much soul-searching, but in the end he concluded that 'Abdu'l-Bahá was testing him:

> Has He not thus shown that He trusted in my sincerity? Has He not, in effect, said to me: 'I have taken from you one by one the normal use of your organs. There is scarcely a single part of your body unaffected by My Decree. Your nerves, your back, your feet, your heart, your stomach, the tumor in your vitals, your hearing, and now your sight – and you have not repined, you have not sought to evade nor have you turned away for a single moment from My Love. Nay, rather, have all this as the very evidences, signs, proofs of that Love.' I can almost hear Him saying with that divine smile – 'Congratulations!'
>
> ... No wonder it was a shock when R.[izwanea] seemed to think (only for the moment, of course) that this sublime test should be removed, that the outer sight was so valuable than the inner vision might be jeopardized. Nay! Rather, my deepest soul-longing cries out: 'I quaff the seven seas but the thirst of my heart is not allayed. Is there yet any MORE?' And when I consider how much more there is; when my spiritual vision vividly regards the ages to come and the infinite worlds to be explored; when I recognize the undoubted fact that all this life has taught me, or could ever possibly teach me, is but a sign, a token, a symbol, of what the future worlds of God shall surely teach – my whole being is lost in thanksgiving and praise to Him and of Him Who has bestowed upon me, so unworthy, so sinful and selfish, so lacking in capacity and worth – this boundless Gift and this infinite Bounty.[25]

Two days later Howard continued his 'analysis of this spiritual-psychological experience':

> It occurred to me yesterday that any act of faith is a vast gamble ... Every step we take is loaded with possibilities, with unseen and unpredictable eventualities ... So I, during

every moment of my life have been gambling with destiny. And when, 27 years ago, I was faced with the greatest of all possible chance-takings; with home, friends. profession, wife, child, income – everything valued by worldly standards as most worthful, in one scale and in the other – What? An impalpable something – or nothing; a vague chimera of the mind; a dream or spiritual intoxication! A gamble indeed!

Yet, after all, even when judged by human and purely intellectual standards, is it such a bad risk?...

So now I am attempting the all but impossible task of analyzing the reasons – the Causes – lying back of my definite acceptance of this final, or latest, or shall we say this penultimate – gamble – in which I place my outer eyesight which makes possible the vision of the material world, on the table of chance against the bare possibility securing the vision of My Beloved's Universe.

Yet when I write it thus explicitly; when it is stated thus baldly, it is seen as no gamble at all, but a certainty. For it is based upon the sincere acceptance of the Revealed Word of Bahá'u'lláh – the Word of the All-Knowing, the All-Wise God. 'The heavens of My Mercy and the Oceans of My Bounty are so vast.' 'That thou mayest soar in the Heavens of My Knowledge'; 'If ye believe in Me I will make you the friends of My soul in the Realm of My Greatness, and the companion of My Perfection in the Kingdom of My Might forever.' I could fill pages of such quoted promise from memory...

When the Divine Trumpet sounds the rallying Call do we cry aloud with the sincere believers of all ages: 'I am ready, O my God, I am ready.'?... Can the loss of physical sight be for one instant placed over against the sublime vision of those waving banners, the glimpse of the ecstatic eyes of those warriors in His Arena, the approval of their Leader's smile? No wonder that Bahá'u'lláh speaks of the 'recompense or those who speak not save by Thy permission and who give up all that they have in Thy Name and Love'...[26]

Howard's writing worries

With all his books completed, Howard was struggling to find another productive topic to write about. So, as usual, he asked Shoghi Effendi:

> I have thought of writing a book on the Seven Valleys. A kind of free translation accompanied by seven chapters on the Steps of the Soul in its Godward Journey. My contribution to the series lately published in the World Order Magazine on the Valley of Astonishment, (last Dec. number) is an illustration of what I had in mind.
>
> Yet, somehow, that does not seem exactly what would be most helpful to the spreading of the Faith. If a sequel (yet that is not the word, exactly) to Portals to Freedom could be written. Something indicating what happens, and must happen, to the soul which has entered that Divine Portal could be given to the newly confirmed souls would it be of value? Please give me a job![27]

Howard had been working on a new edition of *Portals to Freedom* and also wrestling with the extensive revisions to *Expanding Horizons* suggested by the National Assembly's Reviewing Committee the previous August.[28] He had hoped to have the book published by December 1939, so he chaffed over the Committee's suggestions and wrote to the Guardian. The Guardian responded through his secretary, 'Regarding your new book, he does not know what action the N.S.A. has taken with reference to its publication, but hopes that whatever suggestion or recommendations they may offer you will carry them out, and thereby avoid delaying unnecessarily its printing.'[29]

Howard then asked the Guardian where he could best be of use to the Faith. Shoghi Effendi's response was:

> he feels that for the present you should better concentrate on teaching the Cause, particularly in the pioneering field . . .

The teaching work in which you are now engaged in Memphis, and the considerable progress you have so far accomplished have been noted with feelings of deepest gratitude and admiration by him. It is his fervent hope that, notwithstanding the obstacles still standing in your way, and the difficulties you have experienced in contacting the coloured population, your work will steadily develop, and that soon you will succeed in establishing a local assembly in that centre.[30]

The Guardian himself added: 'May the Beloved guide every step you take and aid you to continue rendering the Cause services that will enrich its annals, and extend the range of its beneficent activities'.

Many demands on Mabel

The National Teaching Committee wanted Mabel to go to Louisville, Kentucky, but Mabel was very worried about the work in Memphis. She stressed that it would probably take another two or three months of teaching work in Memphis before the Bahá'í community would be strong enough to survive on its own. Even then, she forcefully emphasized the importance of another travel-teacher coming to continue the efforts.[31] After the beginning of 1940, the Committee agreed that Mabel should continue in Memphis, but still asked if she could at least spend a few days in Louisville. Additionally, they asked if she could also make a few short trips to Knoxville. Some of the Bahá'ís had left the city and the group's secretary had written 'a very pathetic letter simply begging' for a teacher to come.[32]

Mabel's teaching skills were in great demand. The Bahá'í community in Washington DC had sent her several letters asking her to consider the importance of the capital and to make arrangements to give her lectures there. The Bahá'ís in Utica, New York, were requesting her presence, and Miss Martin in Pine Bluff, Arkansas, and Rezsi Sunshine in Hot Springs,

Arkansas, both wrote requesting her to visit them.³³ On top of all these, she was asked to go to New Orleans at Riḍván. On 23 January, Mabel wrote to the Teaching Committee saying

> Things are getting a bit complicated with both Louisville and Knoxville to plan for. Mrs _____ reply to my letter was to the effect that they have no place for public meetings except for one night at the Andrew Johnson Hotel. Also that neither Mrs _____ nor herself are in a position to entertain anyone, that they would like whoever comes to 'take complete charge of the situation'. . .
>
> The train service between here and Knoxville is probably the worst in the country and in history (even the man at the ticket office admits it) . . . The day time trains, tho leaving early in the morning, do not get there until too late for an evening meeting. The bus has a somewhat better schedule tho taking a little longer. Any way I try to plan it, it will take a day each way, and if I stayed 3 or 4 days, that kills a week . . .
>
> Under the existing conditions, the N.T.C. had better decide which they feel is the most important of the three cities.³⁴

This was a very difficult time for Mabel. Besides all the calls for her service, Howard's health was obviously declining and the funds from the Teaching Committee were barely sufficient to cover what had to be done.

In late January 1940, the National Teaching Committee wrote to Mabel about the formation of a Local Spiritual Assembly in Memphis: 'While Feb. 1st is ordinarily the date set for the approval of establishment of Spiritual Assemblies yet at the last meeting a letter received from the Guardian in which he expressed the hope that we would be able to have 100 Spiritual Assemblies by April 21st'. The National Assembly had, therefore, extended the date for the establishment of Local Assemblies to Riḍván. The National Teaching Committee also realized that all the work they were piling up on Mabel was undoable and told her to give up any plans for Knoxville and Louisville and concentrate on Memphis. Ruth Cornell would be sent to Knoxville and Olivia Kelsey would work in Louisville.[35] Olivia would later become a Knight of Bahá'u'lláh to Monaco.

Overcoming Jim Crow in Memphis

For Mabel, electing a Local Spiritual Assembly was not really a problem and she understood the National Assembly's desire to form one that would include both Black and white Bahá'ís. The main problem was the rigidly enforced Jim Crow laws which required strict segregation of the races. People, Black or white, were very leery of anything that brought them together.[36] The Jim Crow laws were both local and state laws that strictly enforced racial segregation across the American South. Theoretically, they required separate but equal facilities for both Black and white, but in reality, Black people were treated as second-class citizens. The Jim Crow laws were well entrenched and difficult to circumvent.

Integration of the Black and white Bahá'ís was the big challenge in Memphis and it was not easily overcome. Mabel had battled this obstacle to unity from the time she arrived. In a letter written to Shoghi Effendi in January 1940, she explains the lengths they had gone to engage with the Black Bahá'ís. Professor George Henderson, who ran a Business College, was her primary contact point and she had a very difficult time arranging to meet him. As in many other communities where teachers had brought people into the Faith and then left, the Black Bahá'ís had little understanding of the Bahá'í Administrative Order. When Mabel did get in touch with Prof. Henderson, he said that most of the original Black Bahá'ís had left the city.[37]

In February, Mabel explained the difficulties in a letter to Leroy Ioas:

> Now, every letter I get from you or Horace or Allen emphasizes the matter of an Assembly here by April 1st. That too is

our earnest hope and desire. You also stress the importance of the colored friends. This is the problem. From my former letters you understand the difficulty we had in getting any interest or cooperation. However we can get some now, tho it is still very unstable . . . I'll try to make the matter clear, and then would like instruction from the Committee as to how to proceed . . .

First, Memphis has the most serious Negro problem in the South, as it is probably one half or over, Negro . . . Thus the Jim Crow Law is rigidly enforced . . . Mary and I had a long session with the Pres. of the Negro College (LeMoyne College) . . . he told us that Memphis was actually the very worst place in the entire South on inter-racial matters . . . It seems . . . that the colored political condition in this city is rotten to the core, and that there is no unity among the colored people themselves. The white people are more or less conscious of sitting on a volcano and are therefore extremely touchy on any matter of getting the races together . . .

Now the point is, shall we jeopardize the work so far and insist upon bringing the colored and white together on a social basis as we do in the North, or even to the extent that they do in Nashville, or shall we develop them as two separate groups, or shall we concentrate on the white group, at least until they are established and able to face and perhaps cope with the difficulties of the situation. I feel quite sure that if we attempted to bring any colored people into the group now, the husbands of the women in the study class and several of the women themselves would resent it to the point of dropping the whole thing . . .[38]

Leroy's response on behalf of the Teaching Committee was that they should:

1) Work mostly actively with the white group . . . until they become strong and active supporters of the Faith.
2) Do not have public Interracial meetings at this time.

Inter-racial meeting are indirect methods of teaching, having as the basis, the hope that certain liberally-minded people . . . might become interested in the Faith. It would be better to seek them out, and teach them directly.

3) Do not attempt at this specific time to hold joint meetings of the two study groups [Black and white]
4) If you stay in Memphis for a little time, then perhaps the colored group can be taught by you . . . they will come to learn that they must stand on their own feet.
5) Caution is required in establishing the Faith in the South, and it is much better to err on that side rather than on the other. The bringing of the two races together should be gradual, and without any public display . . .[39]

In a letter to Shoghi Effendi in February, Howard noted that they had been in Memphis for three months, one month more than had been their original plan. Some things were going well but others were problematic:

> Two lovely and radiant believers have become confirmed and several others are nearly so. The group that has gathered around us, due to the guidance of Bahá'u'lláh, are amongst the most cultivated and socially prominent in the city. As the Message we are giving becomes better known daily new souls are being attracted. The color question is a difficult matter here, perhaps in the whole South there is no city where the 'Jim Crow Law' (horrible term!) is more rigidly enforced. We have worked among the group of colored folk whom dear Louis Gregory attracted, but so far have not had from them a very vigorous response. We are following exactly the instructions of the N.S.A. and the N.T.C. as to how to deal with this question. Fortunately the group of white people who are becoming so deeply attracted is composed of souls more open-minded and free from prejudice than most of the southerners. We have every confidence that in the course of time the leaven of the Love of God will

have so permeated the souls who have become attracted, and those who will follow later, that that Love will burn away every atom of that prejudice which so burdens the souls of our black-skinned brothers. It is truly a tragic thing to see the patience and humility with which they bear the segregation from their white brothers.

We have twice spoken before the students of Le Moyne college, the large and influential education institution for the colored race here in Memphis, and our reception there has been most cordial and sympathetic.[40]

Teaching successes

At the end of February 1940, a whole family came into the Faith: Mr and Mrs Jemison and their four children, aged 21, 19, 17 and 12. Howard wrote that 'the whole family of six are equally interested and kept us talking on nothing else from 4:00 P.M., through dinner up to 10.30'.[41]

In March, Alvin Blum, 'an enthusiastic young Jew' who had become a Baháʼí in New York, managed to transfer his job to Memphis in order to help Mabel.[42] Alvin had arisen to serve the Cause in the Southern United States in response to the Shoghi Effendi's Seven Year Plan. 'I felt there was a need in the south,' he explained, so he found a job as a travelling salesman which enabled him to travel throughout the Southern states.[43]

During Alvin's travels he had met Howard and Mabel and was greatly influenced by them; he had been driving to their home from Nashville, Tennessee, on a regular basis. He was very impressed that Howard had 'given up his position as a Unitarian minister to be of service to the Baháʼí Faith. It has cost him his marriage and a life with his baby daughter, as well as any sense of regular income.' Mabel, 'dainty and dressed in the second-hand outfits she has remodeled, is a powerhouse. Howard, in his shiny grey suit with his neat moustache and kind eyes, has a strong, calm, centered warmth.' Alvin's daughter, Keithie, later depicted their relationship: 'Howard is unaware that he is changing the way Alvin sees being a man. Just being in the same room as Howard makes him feel different. Maybe Howard is a spiritual mentor, or a father, or a brother to Alvin. Maybe he is all three. Alvin just knows he loves the man, and Mabel. When he leaves the house he feels strong in his Faith and sure of what he is doing.'[44]

On 3 March Mabel noted that the number of those she considered to be strong Bahá'ís in Memphis had risen to eight: Mabel, Howard, Alvin, Professor Henderson, Mrs Watkins, Ruby Jenkins, Corrila Gray and Miss Glesden. But on 11 March she wrote to Leroy Ioas about a problem with a man called Jimmy Stone, who she called a 'stirrer up of trouble. A strange personality, and seems to feel that he has a perhaps (God-given) responsibility about his work in the South. He speaks about coming to Memphis to live and that he would of course have a great deal to say about how things should be run.' She went to say 'If he comes, it would be fatal.'[45] Leroy tried to reassure her that he had been working with Jimmy 'in the hope that he may change',[46] but in June, Mabel had to report that Jimmy had 'upset the colored friends' in Memphis. He had told them that Mabel had not included their meeting in the Annual Report and was demanding that she be accountable to him and the Black Bahá'ís.[47] In spite of Leroy's letter telling him to keep away from Memphis and Nashville, he was setting up meetings in both cities.

Despite these troubles, on 7 April Mabel was able to write to Leroy saying that a new couple had decided to become Bahá'ís and that Mrs Watkins said that her husband was now a Bahá'í. And in the same letter she described a short trip to Hot Springs, Arkansas made by Mary Barton and herself in mid-March. Mabel wrote:

> Our weekend in Hot Springs proved most interesting. Mary and I drove over. We found that Miss [Rezsi] Sunshine had been working very vigorously and devotedly and had one full-fledged believer and several who were very near ... and all fine people. They had arranged a public meeting at the best hotel, and the quality was good tho the quantity was

small. The personal contacts were very valuable . . . The wife of the Episcopal minister (also daughter of a Bishop in Los Angeles) is a remarkable woman, and knows the Cause is true, but hesitates on account of her husband's profession.[48]

23
Further Afield in the American South 1940–1941

Howard goes to Hot Springs, Arkansas

In early April 1940, Mabel wrote to the National Teaching Committee, 'Memphis must not be left alone now. It is just being born.'[1] But by mid-June, she had changed her mind, writing to the Committee that since there were then 'three stalwart believers to handle the study classes . . . they should be able to have a chance to try their wings at teaching.' She also noted that she had found a cottage a few miles outside Hot Springs, Arkansas, for them to move to when work in Memphis was completed.[2]

Howard went to Hot Springs in May, but when Mabel had to remain in Memphis longer to complete her work, he went to stay with Roberta (Robbie) Wilson, a new Bahá'í, since he couldn't live on his own any more. He was able to go to the National Convention in May, driven up by Alvin Blum. Mabel later wrote that 'everyone seemed to sense that it would be indeed his last Convention, and wherever he went in the grounds people were begging him to let them take his picture . . . He seemed like a patriarch at the last, venerable, noble, scarcely attached to earth at all – already straining at his moorings, and living in thought in the Worlds of Light.'[3]

Upon returning to Hot Springs, he told George Miller:

> I found it necessary to undergo a minor operation. The surgeon made some slip or other and I lost a lot of blood. Was in hospital several days, and laid up a couple of weeks. Now recuperating in this lovely spot visiting a lovely new believer and gradually recovering strength. But I always find

that when the bodily energies are at lowest ebb the forces undergo renewed and marvelous strength. Very great things are possible to the Spirit when the body is at its weakest [4]

Howard may not have said anything to Mabel about this little mishap, because she never mentions anything about it in her letters afterwards.

Mabel wrote on 31 May about her plans and a place to stay in Hot Springs. First, she said, 'My job is here' in Memphis, and goes on to say that she probably wouldn't be able to move until mid-July or August. She was also not happy with the cottage that Howard wanted to rent, insisting that

> the price is much too high, and no doubt the electricity and gas would be extra. Don't you remember that in Toronto when we paid $40 for that apartment and we could barely squeeze out under a hundred . . . You know you seem to have a lot of delicacies, such as steaks and chops and lots of fruit etc. and that makes our food come high. So that at $60 we would have nothing left for incidentals.
>
> Also if we have a cottage I was counting on having a part-time maid. Neither you nor I want to be tied down to housework . . .
>
> I would also suggest that when you feel that you have come to the end of your stay at Robbie's – that is when you feel that you might be becoming something of a burden to her, that you either arrange to board with her, or find a place nearby.[5]

Howard's response was not a happy one. He told her that the $60 for the cottage he proposed to rent would include everything, and that he had been looking elsewhere but with no success. Also, he felt that Mabel had been so busy that she had no time for him:

> I did not appreciate your engrossment in the preparation of the two courses you had to give at the Conference. But you

must confess that under any circumstances to leave me for nine days without a word was rather thick.

I was certainly flabbergasted to hear that you were planning to stay in Memphis until July 1st or 15th or even up to Aug. 1sts due considerably to the expense to have me here. To be sure I have been and am of some help to her [Roberta Wilson], and I am making a compilation book for her which she prizes very highly. And every evening we read and talk together She is growing spiritually most remarkably fast.

At the same time I fear I shall feel pretty uncomfortable to be forced to stay on another full month, or perhaps even longer . . .

Yesterday Roberta took Kay Baird and Mary Kat and a friend and myself out to the lake to look at another cottage. Only one big room with two beds in it, the kitchenette off in one corner, dining table in another, and located amongst a lot of other cottages, near but not facing the lake and cluttered up something awful. And the price was $15.00 a week, or as a great concession, $60 per mo. As for getting a boarding house at $60. – $70 per mo. I have made inquiries. There aint no such animal anywhere . . .

That $30 cottage has no running water. All water must be drawn from a tap outside the kitchen door, which would not be very convenient in rainy weather – or any kind of weather for that matter. It is about three miles [5 km] further from town and does not look very attractive for friends to come to for picnics.[6]

Mabel's reply was conciliatory: 'Whatever you do about the cottage will be alright with me, and we will simply cut our cloth to suit our pattern – that is, eat very simply. I won't mind, and you can stand it for two months.'[7] Howard and Mabel had many little contretemps like this, but always managed to overcome them quickly.

By mid-June 1940 Howard was paying board to Robbie. Others had worried about Howard accepting the hospitality of a new Bahá'í, 'but she seemed so heart-broken at the idea of his not coming, and he has been of assistance to her in so many practical as well as spiritual ways'.[8] Mabel had heard from Alvin Blum, however, that sometimes Robbie was too tired in the evenings to listen to readings, so Mabel gave Howard some advice:

> It is sometimes hard to tell just what line to follow in dealing with new souls. Lay off the evening readings from Gleanings from now on, unless Robbie specially asks for it, and you are sure she really is not too tired to listen. The child is really exhausted from her day's work and needs complete rest and relaxation in the evening. Tell her you find it a bit hard to read out loud, and let her think that is the reason you have stopped. She needs to relax and play.
>
> After I get there, she and I can have some good 'woman' talks after she is all relaxed and rested by a swim, and wants to talk. A young soul can easily get spiritual indigestion. She just adores you and always will, but the 'flesh is weak', in her present state.[9]

Special teaching project in Vogel Park, Cleveland, Georgia

With Howard ensconced in Hot Springs, Mabel moved into new, cooler quarters in Memphis. Then on 7 June 1940, Mabel, along with Johanna Zimmerman, Clare Keller, Carlotta Pitman and Tommy Rhea, a 19-year-old student and Baptist who stood 6 foot 5 inches (1.93m) tall, drove to Vogel State Park near Cleveland, Georgia, for a week-long Special Teaching Project, driving in Clare's car. As Mabel reported to the NTC, 'The experience was a great deepener to each of them. The fact that there was perfect harmony of the friends assembled at the project, with no cross-currents or desire for leadership impressed them deeply.'[10]

Mabel gave daily talks on topics such as 'Prophesies Fulfilled – The Promise of All Ages', 'Building the Spiritual Government of the Golden Age of Bahá'u'lláh' and 'Bahá'í Administration'.

Orcella Rexford spoke on 'Standards for the New Age'. Both women, along with Terah Smith, facilitated a teaching seminar on several of the days and Dr Glenn Shook gave a session on the 'New World Order'. Terah also gave a course on 'Spiritual Health and Prayer'.[11]

Mabel quite enjoyed the area of Vogel Lake – 'lovely roomy cottage, grand lake and beautiful mountains'[12] and she was very happy with the event. Two of the young people became Baháʼís and the tall Baptist youth had become highly attracted. She wrote to Nellie Roche saying, 'Perhaps the most remarkable thing to us old codgers in the Cause is that our brilliant "youth of the spirit" should have not only had the vision for this enterprise but should have had the courage, the determination and the ability – and the wisdom – to carry it forward . . . to so outstanding and successful conclusion'.[13] She also wrote that the young people

> just couldn't say enough in praise of the experience and the personnel. They admired and loved you so much and were especially impressed with Terah's course. It seemed to make a deep impression on them, and they wanted to remember it all. They also had many words of praise for Prof. Shook and Orcella. I think it was the high water mark in their experience. They came home matured and stabilized. Carlotta finally got it. It has made a new person of her . . . Johanna is just starry-eyed about it all. And Clara was specially attracted to Prof. Shook and Terah's handling of their subjects . . . And I loved just every minute of it.[14]

Mabel wrote and told the Guardian about the event:

> The first Southern Teaching Project held in the mountains of northern Georgia the first part of June was an outstanding success. No doubt Miss Roche has sent you a report of it. Five of us drove there from Memphis, and the effect on these young believers was wonderful. They came back glowing and greatly deepened and ready to work. One of

them was confirmed while there. To feel that this conference, involving no expense to the National Assembly, has set a precedent, which can well be followed over the South, as these National Parks with log cottages, well equipped, which can be rented, can be found in many places. I have been looking over the ground in this section, hoping to have some suggestions to make to our new Regional Committee, when it meets soon.[15]

Memphis, Arkansas and Mississippi

Back in Memphis from Vogel Park, Mabel brought up another problem they faced in the South besides racism – a lack of true equality between men and women. In a letter to the National Teaching Committee about Southern men not accepting the Faith from women, she wrote: 'The men of the South do not take women seriously enough – a hang over from the past. They need to meet and hear some of our business men . . . There are two fine men who could be brought in, but they need men to give them the final push.'[16] On 20 July, Mabel told Leroy Ioas that the 'group in Memphis is progressing splendidly'.[17]

Hot Springs, Arkansas

Mabel finally was able to join Howard in Hot Springs on 7 July 1940. The cottage he had found proved not to be as good they hoped, but they found another: 'Our cottage, which is roomy, is right on the lake'.[18] Robbie later described her time with Howard and Mabel:

> Riswanea was working with every interested individual we could find, giving them so freely of her time, although Daddy Howard was very ill and was writing a book. She would have us out for picnics, suppers and long evening talks. She concentrated on Kay and Lee Baird, Martha Hackett and Nan Wilson. Nan clung to her like a sick kitten . . . and monopolized a good part of her time. So did

Martha. Martha and Kay came into the Cause. So did Nan
... [Mabel] took us through the Dispensation, word for
word, as well as everything else she thought we needed.[19]

Shortly after her arrival, Mabel wrote a very long letter to Shoghi Effendi summarizing their efforts in Memphis. She concluded her letter with this:

> I implore your prayers for the work in the South. The problems are quite different from those in the North, and the people much more conservative and hidebound. Most of them are very orthodox and narrow, those who have accepted in both cities, had either already left the churches or were attending the Unitarian church, which is of course very liberal. But the percentage of such people is very small. However we feel that the world events will awaken even the most limited in time. How can they resist this Divine Call? Please pray that we may be guided and assisted to find a way to their hearts![20]

The Guardian's response was to strongly encourage he to continue her efforts to integrate the Memphis Bahá'ís:

> Your welcome and detailed communication dated July 26th was duly received by the beloved Guardian, and he was indeed greatly heartened and cheered by the perusal of its contents ...
> In regard to your teaching work in Memphis, much as the Guardian appreciates the fact that six confirmed believers have already joined the Faith, he feels that a special effort should now be made, notwithstanding any focus to the contrary, to bring together and fully integrate the white believers with the coloured ones, so that through such social intermingling and fellowship the Cause may achieve a healthy and steady growth. His prayers will be offered on behalf of the six white believers you have mentioned, that they may remain firm and steadfast, and become active,

devoted and capable Servants of Bahá'u'lláh. He will specially supplicate that through His unfailing blessings and confirmations the situation in the Memphis group may be improved, and that the teaching work among the coloured people may advance and progress.[21]

Mabel and Howard began preparing to move back to Memphis on 1 October to set things up for a visit by Dorothy Baker. It was a very stressful time for Mabel since Howard was so weak and she had both his needs and her teaching work in mind. In her diary, she wrote upliftingly to herself:

> And now a new phase of activity opens. Attend to this packing and moving with ease and joy. Be not at all oppressed with all that you have to do – just do the one thing – one at a time – and rest constantly upon God. It really does not amount to much. No regrets now about anything. One could always have done more, but what you have done has been valuable and acceptable. So be thankful and regret nothing. God has guided you thru this summer. Can not you realize that?
>
> So all is well and all will work out well. The right place will be found for Howard and you will be free to serve as God wishes – do not doubt. You have put your faith in the Glory of God. Now rest back upon that faith and be content.[22]

Almost overwhelmed with what had to be done to complete the move, on 11 October she again remonstrated with herself and told herself what she had to do:

> (O Baha'u'llah help me to do it. It is the doing that counts)
>
> (Bestow upon me the power of inner stillness!!!)
> Let go – let go! All is well. Do not be disturbed. Perfection cannot be attained in a day. Of course you will make mistakes – but when they are done, they are done. The only

way you can redeem them is by making this moment one of quiet listening and perfect happiness – KNOWING that you can be still and listen – and hold to it in the midst of whatever confusion. KNOWING that the Everlasting Arms are about you – and the light of the Face is walking before you – and that even such services as you are rendering are acceptable at the Holy Threshold and that God is assisting you.

KNOW This – know this!

Now get up quietly and feel the Presence of God within and surrounding you.²³

By 12 October 1940, Mabel and Howard were back in Memphis, though for Mabel it was a brief stop. It was a traumatic time. Her diary entry for 15 October was more self-encouragement: 'You are being guided in everything. The right place to live will be found easily. The right things will happen in connection with the group here. Rely more upon Bahá'u'lláh in everything – this is His work you are doing. He will give you time and strength ample in which to get it all done. . . . all is well.' ²⁴

Greenwood, Mississippi

On the 18th, Mabel was in Greenwood, Mississippi, where she gave a public talk:

The saddest aspect of the international situation is that it could have been avoided. If Christian nations had carried out in action in economic and national affairs the instructions of our Lord Jesus Christ, this earth would have been long before now, a Paradise. In the eighteen sixty's, Bahá'u'lláh, a prisoner of Persia and Turkey directed epistles to the heads of the various nations and peoples of the world instructing them to adjust their differences by arbitration, establish justice in their affairs. These letters were a clarion call to all mankind, and if they had been heeded, the World War and this war and the consequent suffering would have been avoided. Bahá'u'lláh revealed a plan for organizing the world, to bring about peace and maintain peace. It is interesting to know that Woodrow Wilson was a student for two years of the teachings of Baha'u'llah before he put forward his famous 'Fourteen Points', twelve of which are the same as those given in the teachings of the Baha'i Faith. But mankind was not ready . . . We need a new kind of people on earth . . . We need a spiritual power which penetrates hearts to make a new people and new institutions which will secure peace and harmony . . .

This is the age of unity . . . In no other age have people had the means to be united. Now a spiritually immature mankind is given powerful weapons by which he can destroy himself. We must grow spiritually – else destruction. Baha'u'llah opened doors, materially, intellectually, and spiritually . . . When the despotic nations are exhausted then the people will turn to God.

Civilizations do not just happen. They are man made. At each crucial point in history a great leader has been sent by God . . . The forces of destruction are organized and united. Why can not all who believe in God work in unity? To say that God has guided men, once spoke through a Divinely sent Personage, and can never do so again, is limiting the Power of God. When in all known history have we needed a God-sent Guide and Teacher of the human race more than today?

The teachings of the Glory of God, Bahá'u'lláh, is not a new sub-division, but a call to unity of religion and of the human family, fulfilling the promises of Jesus Christ.

This war is retribution for the wrongs of the nations through the centuries. It will purify and refine humanity. It is the 'Great and terrible Day of God'. It is great if we rise to our opportunities: terrible if we resist the will of God for this day.[25]

Memphis again

After returning to Hot Springs on the 19th to finish packing and round off her teaching activities there, Mabel set off for Memphis with a loaded car. She had come to Memphis to help with a visit by Dorothy Baker in early November. Dorothy arrived with Nellie Roche on 7 November. Three public meetings were set up, but when Dorothy arrived, Memphis was drenched with torrential rain which continued throughout her visit. The large crowds they had expected didn't materialize. There were 27 at the first lecture on 9 November and 35 at the second the next day: 'mostly the old standbys'.[26]

Howard spent his first week in Memphis staying with Jack and Beverly Kelley, and the two oldest Kelley children became quite attracted to the Faith. When Dorothy was there, the Kelley youth had gathered together 18 young people to hear her. After a number of meetings, the Kelley parents and one of the other young people were close to declaring their Faith. Mabel wrote that Dorothy's 'talks were brilliant and convincing'. Dorothy tried to soften the interracial difficulties and 'handled it with great skill, but had to come to the same conclusion . . . Making every effort she was able to get only one meeting with the colored group . . . However I feel that she did get very close to those sweet people [Prof. Henderson and Mrs Watkins] and made them see the importance of regular study'.[27] After a few more talks in private homes, Dorothy left on 17 November.

After all of the activity of Dorothy's visit, Mabel wrote to herself in her diary that 'You have no <u>work</u> to do – just joyous things to do.'[28] But she again had travel plans. She attended a Conference in Atlanta between 23 and 25 November and was to speak to the Federated Women's Clubs in Senatobia, Mississippi, about 35 miles (56 km) south of Memphis, on 3 January 1941.[29] She hoped to get to New Orleans and the Gulf Coast the middle of January and then go to Hot Springs and Little Rock, Arkansas, for a big project.[30]

In December, Howard sent a note to Nancy Phillips saying:

'I am rewriting my book so my time is all mapped out for a number of weeks to come. Our work for the Cause here is progressing finely. We are much gratified over the fact that a number of young people are deeply interested and more on the way.'[31]

Mabel in Hot Springs and Little Rock, Arkansas

In mid-January 1941, Mabel left Howard in the care of Doris McKay in Memphis and began her teaching campaign in both Hot Springs and Little Rock, Arkansas. Arriving in Hot Springs on 17 January, she spent her first week there giving out 500 invitations, placing 50 posters, giving three radio broadcasts and doing other publicity. Only a couple of her radio scripts have been found (see Appendix 2). This one began with a question:

> The most challenging question facing the people of America and indeed of the whole world is this: shall we build for a secure world after this war is ended, or for another war and another and another? Now is the time to decide and to begin to make our plans. When and if the Democracies win, shall we make a peace of revenge or a peace for permanent security? That is the choice which is facing the human race today. Shall we continue to let war be a breeder of more wars and more wars until man shall have annihilated his own species – this precious race of mankind, and the planet be swept clean of him? Or shall we dream a dream of some sort of collective security and make our dream come true? It is the choice we must make – now.[32]

From that point, Mabel spoke about the development of atomic weapons and how the world would benefit if those weapons were put aside and that same power put to peaceful uses. She pointed out the primary problem in the world: 'There is only one thing out of line – one little dislocation amid all this beauty, abundance and order – just one little thing – <u>man's</u>

attitude toward man.' From there, Mabel described man as a creation of God and his place on the earth. In the body of each man, all the various parts work in cooperation so that he can do amazing things. The body of humanity, however, has every part

> fighting against every other part, so innumerable diseases have taken hold of it: the disease of war, for instance, the disease of poverty, the disease or maladjustments in the individual and in its group relationships. Humanity is sick. It needs a divine physician and a divine remedy. It has alas, forgotten the remedy given two thousand years ago, or 'Love your neighbor as yourself.' It has never even attempted to apply these remedies to the relationships of one country to another country in all Christendom; or to the relationships between Capital and Labor, in any Christian country.
> It has remembered the Name of the Divine Physician but forgotten or failed to apply the remedy . . .[33]

Mabel then invited the audience to her series of nine lectures at the McGehee and Grady Manning Hotels; between 18 and 29 people responded to each session. Mabel noted that several people attended every lecture. After the lectures, she began a study class with about a dozen interested people.[34]

Then Mabel moved on to Little Rock, which she liked:

> I grow lyrical and want to speak in superlatives about this city, its capacity, its readiness, its longing and profoundly attracted souls, its friendliness and cooperation. Arriving here Feb. 8th, slightly over a week was spent in the same type of preparatory work, altho 1000 invitations were mailed or handed out and one broadcast was made. A city of 80,000 pop., the period of preparation should have been longer, but I was pushed in order to get, if possible, down to New Orleans before Convention, and possibly the Gulf Coast. Rezsi Sunshine had done some fine preparatory work, and attracted several people who have proved very valuable in bringing their friends and passing the word around and she

has proved a most able and devoted assistant, in caring for the book table, meeting and getting the names of the people who attend and by her radiant face and lovely enthusiasm making them feel welcome and at home.[35]

After a week announcing the talks, her lectures drew between 16 and 26 participants. Twenty of those continued on into the subsequent study classes. Her lectures, however, had been so well received that she ended up giving a second set for those unable to attend the first. People were particularly drawn to the fifth lecture, 'Recurrent Cycles of Civilizations – Progressive Revelation'. Because of the repetition, the first home-grown Bahá'í was found in Little Rock:

The first Little Rock believer has come to birth . . . her name is Mrs. Helene Landrom, and Sunny had been working on her before the lectures began and she was definitely attracted, and the lecture on Recurrent Cycles brought her confirmation. It is amazing how her whole character and attitudes have changed in just these few days – a real second birth. She says she feels like Jesus must have felt after His resurrection.[36]

Mabel commented, 'The loveliest stories are coming to my ears how already people's lives are being transformed and their attitudes changed just thru these evenings. . .' She attributed the successes to her ability to 'get so completely out of the way when I start to talk and pray with such passionate intensity for Bahá'u'lláh to take over'.[37]

The teaching effort continued well into February. On the 21st of that month, Mabel wrote to Howard about Mrs Garret, 'who is simple eating the Cause with rapture' and who was giving her daily massages. Mabel's nightly lectures had audiences whose faces 'were illuminated'. She was being 'pulled' to New Orleans by the Teaching Committee and strongly wished that Doris could leave Howard to help her. She asked Howard if he could come to Little Rock: 'Am thinking of you, darling and the gift you would be to these souls. What do you say to your moving over to Little Rock . . . and our settling here for a while. I feel that our work is done in Memphis. We have much larger fields for service here, in Arkansas.'[38] Howard was praying up a storm for Mabel's work, writing to her, 'If my prayers count for anything you must be a volcano of spiritual energy coupled with the calmness and tranquility and beauty of a sunset.'[39] The big teaching project was concluded on 28 February, but Mabel remained to do follow-up work. On 14 April she wrote to Horace Holley about Little Rock and Hot Springs:

> There are people ready in these cities, tho they all have a background of Fundamentalism, and many of them have been dabbling quite a bit in Metaphysical Philosophies. But they are hungry for truth and attend meetings three times a week; many of them never missing a meeting, besides personal interviews for which they are always ready. We can say that three are definitely confirmed in Little Rock and two in Hot Springs . . . There are four other who have accepted with their minds, but are waiting for that deeper confirmation in their hearts . . .
>
> There is a medical missionary of the Methodist Church, who spent a year in Persia, a Dr. Janet Miller, who told me after one of our Sunday lectures that she had met many of the Bahais in Persia and loved them . . .[40]

Altogether, 25 lectures were given in Hot Springs, mostly by Mabel, but a few by Howard who had managed to join her, and a study class of 20 formed. Rezsi Sunshine, the resident pioneer, was very helpful with the efforts. From the study group, six declared their Faith in Bahá'u'lláh, but only three, Lucy Hawkins, Jean Allen and Pauline Hanson, became registered believers.

Investigation by the FBI

Behind the scenes in Little Rock, someone was upset enough about Mabel's lectures to contact the Federal Bureau of Investigation and complain. An FBI case was opened investigating 'Baha'i Publishing Company, Mrs. Harvard Ives and Miss Reszie Sunshine' for 'conducting possible subversive activities under guise of teaching Baha'i religion'. The investigation began on 1 March 1941, when a man called the FBI to say that

> on 28 February, 1941, _____ had, at the request of a friend, attended a lecture at the McGehee Hotel in the city of Little Rock. _____ stated that this lecture was given by the Baha'i Publishing Company of Wilmette, Illinois, but he was unable to furnish the writer with the lecturer's name. However, _____ advised that the lecturer discussed the merits and advantages which would accompany the establishment of a Government in the United States that would be part of a world empire dominated by a single individual. After giving this lecture, the lecturer distributed pamphlets which were entitled 'A Pattern for Future Society'. _____ further advised the writer that while the lecture never specifically mentioned Hitler of Germany, the form of Government discussed tallied closely with the German plan of conquest.[41]

The FBI agent interviewed the complainants at their home.

> The writer was advised that _____ had attended a lecture at the McGehee Hotel on February 28, 1941. This lecture ... was supposed to have been a religious talk on a prophet which is known as Prophet BAHA'I. _____ was unable to give the writer much information in her own words, but advised that much more information could be ascertained by reading the pamphlet 'A Pattern for Future Society' which included all the principles which were expounded by the lecturer at the time she had attended the same. _____

supplied the writer with a copy of this pamphlet.

Upon examination, this pamphlet was found to be a two page affair . . . This pamphlet, in a few words, recommends the establishment of a Government by a single individual who would be the head of a 'world federal system ruling the whole earth and exercising unchallengeable authority over its unimaginably vast resources, blending and embodying the ideals of both the East and the West, liberated from the curse of war and its miseries, and bent on the exploitation of all the available sources of energy on the surface of the planet, a system in which Force is made the servant of Justice, whose life is sustained by its universal recognition of one God and by its allegiance to one common Revelation – such is the goal towards which humanity, impelled by the unifying forces of life, is moving'.

_____ advised that while she had no definite reason to suspect the lecturer of un-American activities, she is of the opinion that the principles on which this supposed religion is founded are very un-American and for that reason she did what she thought advisable and notified the Federal Bureau of Investigation . . .[42]

The agent then interviewed a person at the Little Rock Public Library, who verified that Mabel had, indeed, given lectures in the Library:

She further advised the writer that the name of the lecturer was Mrs. HARVARD IVES and that Mrs. IVES had approached her with the request that she be permitted to give a series of lectures on the Baha'i religion in the Little Rock Public Library.____ stated that at the time she did not think there was anything wrong with this woman giving these lectures.

. . . _____ stated that subsequent to Mrs. IVES giving her lectures ____ attended the one lecture which had been given at the public library and from that time on she was very doubtful as to the purpose for which Mrs. IVES was lecturing. _____ further advised that while Mrs. IVES only gave one lecture at the Little Rock Public Library, she was continuing to give lectures at the McGehee and Marion Hotels in Little Rock, Arkansas, and the Eastman Hotel in Hot Springs, Arkansas.[43]

The agent then went to the McGehee Hotel:

> _____ was unable to furnish the writer any additional information except for the fact that he recalled that at the time Mrs. IVES had given her lectures she had always been accompanied by what she called her private secretary. This private secretary went under the name of Miss RESZIE SUNSHINE. _____ stated that Miss SUNSHINE appeared to be a Russian Jewess and talks with a distinct Russian accent . . .[44]

Two months later the FBI agent made a further report, correcting Mabel's name to 'Mrs. Howard Ives'. An employee of the Eastman Hotel, where Mabel had stayed, told him that 'Mrs. IVES had registered for herself' and described her as:

Height 5' 2"
Age 45 years
Weight 100 pounds
Build Small
Dress Moderate, conservative
Hair Blondish

He stated that she had a very nervous disposition. _____ further stated that he thinks Mrs. IVES conducted several meetings at the hotel, but he is not certain of this fact, and the approximate dates are unknown except that he thinks they were held within the last year.

. . . SUNSHINE had approached _____ on several occasions in regard to the BAHA'I movement . . . At first _____ thought that SUNSHINE was engaged in some kind of a

369

book selling scheme, but later decided that SUNSHINE's interest in the BAHA'I movement was just religious. She thinks that SUNSHINE was almost fanatical on this subject, and that its main purpose seemed to be to unite the world under the BAHA'I movement.

. . . She has a slight suspicion that there is some other motive in addition to religion behind the movement but was not able to form any conclusion on that point and never gave the matter much thought because she was not interested in it . . .[45]

On 22 July 1941, the FBI agent filed a report on the results of the investigations:

Upon receipt of reference report, a letter was addressed to Cloyd C. McGuire, Chief of Police, Wilmette, Illinois requesting him to conduct the necessary investigation at Wilmette, Illinois.

In reply by letter dated April 30, 1941, Mr. McGuire reported as follows:

'Upon investigation I learned that the Baha'i is a religion founded in Persia in 1844. They are active in many countries and they take in as members all races and creeds. The Baha'i is incorporated and they are registered with the U. S. Secretary of State and U. S. Treasury Departments. Their National Headquarters is at Wilmette, Illinois, where for the past fifteen years their Temple which will cost several million dollars when completed has been under construction.

'The Baha'i have not the slightest connection with any foreign government or power.

'The Baha'i throughout the world are forbidden by their own religious teaching to engage in any movement or party politics. Their object is working for unity in life and if divided they could not carry on their universal program.

'The Baha'i is governed by an executive committee, which is composed of its members.

'The Baha'i Publishing Co.

'The Baha'i Publishing Co. is not a corporation. It is controlled by a committee composed of members of the Executive Committee. This committee views and approves all publications by that body. They have no printing presses, and the printing is done by jobbers who submit bids. Lloyd Hollister, Inc., Wilmette, Illinois, publisher of the weekly news magazine Wilmette Life, Winnetka Talk and Glencoe News has printed some of their material.

'Mrs. Howard Ives

'Mrs. Howard Ives has been a teacher for the Baha'i for the past twenty-five years. She travels about the country teaching the Baha'i faith. Their teachers receive no salary, but some allowance is made for expenses.

'Her husband was a former Unitarian Minister and after resigning from the ministry he became an Author and Lecturer. He is retired at present on account of age . . .'[46]

A final report was made on 22 August:

Investigation reveals that Baha'i Publishing Company is a religious group and properly registered with U.S. Department of State and Treasury Department. Subjects have both been religious teachers of BAHA'I religion for 15 years or more. Organization found not to be subversive in character . . .'

Inasmuch as investigation reveals that this organization is strictly religious and not subversive in character, this case is being closed upon the authority of the Special Agent in Charge.[47]

The complaints from the two people about Mabel's talks had resulted in the FBI completely exonerating her and the Bahá'í Faith of any nefarious conduct and educated the agency about the true aims and principles of the Faith.

24
The End of Howard's Physical Road
1941

Howard's health was declining rapidly as 1941 began. Mabel had a full schedule of travel teaching and was not able to give him the day-to-day care he needed, so Doris McKay took on the task of being Howard's constant companion, as well as being a teacher of the Faith. By mid-January, Mabel was off on her next teaching campaign to Little Rock and Doris was in charge of Howard. She understood Mabel's intense drive:

> I soon realized that Mabel's trip to Little Rock was an important teaching campaign and that it could not have happened without me or someone else coming here to look after Howard. Her pioneer venture in the south was just the sort of thing the Guardian would have stressed most. If I had not done another thing but just keep house so that Mabel, with a free mind, could open up the southern cities, I would have been giving Bahá'u'lláh sufficient service.[1]

It was a difficult time for Doris. Howard's health made him very dependent on others and she worried that something would happen to him. Busy as she was, after a time she became 'desperately homesick'. One day, she received a letter from her husband Willard and 'its tenderness nearly capsized my frail craft.' Since he had been her guide from the beginning, she asked Howard if she should pray to have the homesickness taken away? Howard's response was 'No', and with reflection she decided that he was right. She wrote, 'my "particles" begin to float and I sway as if on a gentle swelling tide. I feel as if a slow fire were burning in my human self. Howard is right. I will not try to extinguish that fire . . . I know what to pray for. The ME dies hard!'²

On 12 February, Howard wrote to Mabel that he was 'writing lying on my bed. I find I must keep quiet these days.'³ A few days later, after she asked if he was getting weaker, he wrote, 'No, I am not weaker than usual – since you asked – but the blasted old heart seems to kick up a bit over the least exertions. And when I try to write I soon tire and have little ambition.' As he did with most of his letters during this time, he added, 'Again I want to tell you how happy your letters made me . . . I love you, darling, somethin' fierce.'⁴

Having a lot of time with her teacher, Doris began to ask him questions, knowing that he 'has always had the ability to open new worlds to me and I know that it was written in the stars that I should have had the bounty of being with him again.' She asked 'Where does our love for people come in?' Howard responded that 'we see our Master's face' in our fellow men. Then she queried: 'Should we expect to love all people alike?' Emphatically, he said, 'Certainly not! There are as many kinds of love as there are people.' 'The quality of our love', he said, 'is determined by our loss of the consciousness of self. If we can lose ourselves in the object of our affection, be it an intermediary human spirit or the Divine Beloved, we merge or fuse ourselves with it.' Then Howard shared a story about Grace Ober's conversation with an elderly lady. During the conversation, the lady stated that 'I hear that the Bahá'ís believe in free love.' Grace said, 'We do!' The lady let out a surprised 'Oh!' to which Grace clarified, 'Do not mistake me. I said love, not lust.'⁵ At one point, Howard was given a chess set and he and Doris were 'trying it out'. He noted that 'I played many years ago but she is something of an expert.'⁶

Howard was physically very weak, but he never stopped teaching. A 21-year-old poet named Robert Miller came into the Faith after attending some of the lectures and having an 'grand epochal talk' with Howard.

On 23 February, Howard wrote to Mabel and suggested giving their one month's notice for their Memphis apartment on 1 March. He was ready to move to Little Rock and 'doing joint intensive work there'.⁷ By the end of February, the move was set. Notice had been given for the apartment and Howard was full of questions about how he could fit into the teaching work. He wrote that he was 'experimenting with walking more energetically and disregarding the physicians gloomy forecasts. Of course within limits. The point is that I am so <u>eager</u> to use my last months or years in service to the Cause. I am determined to rely upon Baha'u'llah and not upon the doctors . . . I will get the packing done slowly with the aid of the janitor and Victoria (the maid).'⁸

In early March, Mabel asked Howard to stay in Memphis until April so she could have time to find an inexpensive place for them to stay. He countered, writing that Doris had decisions to make so could Mabel come to Memphis for Naw-Rúz. That way she and Doris could talk, then he and Doris could go to Little Rock while Mabel stayed to pack and assist the friends to adjust to their departure.⁹ Mabel, however, was feeling pressured by all the places she was being asked to go – Little Rock, New Orleans, Memphis. And money problems simply exacerbated it all. Finally, she said that she could see no way she could go to Memphis. She finally wrote: 'Don't let me make any decision just now about anything further.' She then gave him detailed moving instruction. Near the end of her letter, she relented and wrote, 'Oh gosh, I suppose I ought to come over, but not for more than a couple of days.'¹⁰

At the Feast of 'Alá in March, Doris McKay proposed to host the Feast at the Ives' apartment and that all Bahá'ís, Black and white, would be invited. Horace Holley had written on 24 February on behalf of the National Spiritual Assembly about the importance of racial equality among the Bahá'ís: 'The situation in Memphis seems to be unusually important as it is part of the fundamental race work being done in the southern states, and therefore our success in Memphis is vital to the progress of the Cause.' Doris wanted to follow the direction of the National Assembly, but then she went to dinner at the home of two white Bahá'ís. The husband had missed the last Feast and when the subject came up of having all Bahá'ís, both Black and white, together, he was adamantly opposed:

> 'Out of the question!' he insisted. The 'breaking of bread' with the Blacks, he said, 'will ruin us and the Cause.' And as far as forming the Assembly went, 'we should not try it until we have 1,000 members.' And he meant White members. I began to explain some of the principles of administration that I had shared at the Feast. His wife piped in and said that she realized that she could not be a Bahá'í because she could not accept any authority other than her own self; no other authority whatsoever, even if it came from God. A third member was also present, who, although she had earlier expressed support for the spiritual principles, now stood behind the husband and wife. I was shocked by her present change of attitude and denial. A division was beginning to crystalize as these three people thought that my presentation of Bahá'í Administration was simply one of my personal interpretation. For me the situation was made even more delicate because these were people who had been taught by Mabel and were loyal to her. The situation would put Howard between two fires: Mabel and me.[11]

Checking with others, Doris soon discovered that four of the seven white Bahá'ís emphatically rejected the participation of the Black Bahá'ís. Howard was deeply upset by these highly un-Bahá'í-like views, but agreed to meet with them. The idea of an interracial Feast was dropped for the moment and Doris went to the Black Bahá'ís and told them what had happened. On 2 March, the White Bahá'ís held another Feast. Doris noted, 'We sat there bright and cordial, but as dead souls avoiding argumentative issues. The atmosphere would not lift.'[12]

Doris told both Mabel and the National Spiritual Assembly of the problem. Horace Holley reemphasized the importance of unity, quoting the Guardian's statements. Nellie Roche, who was pioneering in Nashville, sent her support and sharing her experiences in Nashville where the community had ten Black and five White Bahá'ís. There, Feasts were held for everyone in the homes of the Black Bahá'ís, but not in those of the Whites. The result of it all was that in Memphis, the number of White Bahá'ís abruptly decreased.[13]

Doris and Howard decided to host the Feast of Naw-Rúz for all Bahá'ís at Professor George Henderson's Business College. Doris visited the college and started a Bahá'í class with some of the teachers and students, several of whom soon wanted to become Bahá'ís. But before the Feast, Doris and Howard had to await the decision of Marion Little on the applications of the participants of Doris's Bahá'í class, all Black women, who wanted to become Bahá'ís. It was Marion's job to ensure that they understood the Faith and its Administration, so they faced a grilling. And Marion was a 'society woman and looking very much like one, in a very correct dark suit and stylish hat'. Both Doris and Howard were worried. Howard prepared Doris for the worst, saying 'You know that 'Abdu'l-Bahá has said that no sincere effort is ever lost. No matter what happens, you mustn't feel too badly about how things work out.' Their fears turned out to be ungrounded and all the young women were accepted as Bahá'ís. Marion said they all knew what they were getting into. Doris was tickled when the departing Marion, 'so properly and conservatively dressed danced down the street, responding to a spontaneous and ecstatic heart'.[14]

So, the Bahá'í community had lost White members, but had gained Black ones. One of the White Bahá'ís, Grace Bogan, 'was entrenched in the social values of the "old south", and had doubts about her ability to accept these new values'. Doris gave her a copy of *Bahá'í Procedure* and asked her to decide if she could accept what it meant to be a Bahá'í. On the day of the Feast, three of the white Bahá'ís, including Grace, came. There were twelve confirmed Bahá'ís in the Memphis community. The Feast began with Howard saying a prayer and then 'the silence persisted as we "broke bread" together'. The now integrated Bahá'í community of Memphis then read messages, took a group photo, read from the Bahá'í Writings and elected temporary officers for the future Local Spiritual Assembly of Memphis.[15]

Little Rock

On 19 March Howard wrote that Doris was leaving for a speaking engagement in Cincinnati on the 28th so he suggested that he go to Little Rock at that time and the friends there could take him around to find an apartment. Howard also noted that he had new glasses, saying the old ones were 'really almost worthless and it was rather dangerous to cross the streets'.[16] We do not know just when Howard moved to Little Rock, but it was before Riḍván. Mabel's letters to him from the National Convention at the end of the month have suggestions for packing: 'In moving phone be careful of that oblong box of lantern slides on top shelf of hall closet.'[17]

Howard's next letter to Mabel was written on Riḍván, 21 April, from Hot Springs. Mabel was on her way to Chicago for the National Convention. Howard wrote of his everyday life:

> I had orange juice and eggs and made the coffee and she [Helene Lancrom, his helper] waited on me nicely. The house is now all cleaned up. I am feeling fine. Quite enjoy being a hermit. But don't want it to last too long. Being able to pray aloud without disturbing anyone is fun . . .
>
> Helene is a comfort . . . I am able to control her talking proclivities. My deafness has its advantages! I will, however, from time to time, have short talks with her and try to restore her original happiness in her Faith.[18]

Continuing, he noted that the Memphis Local Spiritual Assembly would be formed that evening, the culminating event of their long tenure in that city. He sent them a telegram that read: 'Am praying you will be moved by the Holy Spirit to make one of Assembly tonight. The friends need your loving cooperation.'[19]

Mabel wrote a string of letters from the National Convention.

On 26 April, she wrote, 'Every seat is filled this afternoon and many people are standing. A grand crowd. The Temple looks simply marvelous since the gardening has seemed to raise the Temple as if it were up on a hill. It looks so majestic and awe-inspiring.' Then she warned him that she would probably have to stay in Chicago after the Convention: 'I have a special meeting with the N.S.A. on Monday and also Edris insists that I stay over long enough for her to give me a thorough physical going over (examination) and a few days rest – no work at all. Of course I say, "O I can't, I can't, I must get back to Howard" – but perhaps you would be good enough to arrange to have Helene stay overnight with you until I get back.'[20]

Mabel stayed in Chicago for two weeks at the insistence of Edris, resting from the exertions of the previous year. On the 29th, she wrote that she was 'having a grand rest, which I very much needed'. The next day she wrote, 'Am much better – voice almost normal', and on 1 May, 'I needed this rest. Took a sunbath in the yard in shorts this aft – grand. Like summer weather.' The next day, she said that she 'rested in bed and read all morning and prayed. Now after lunch am out in the yard in the bright sun. Am bravely refusing all invitations to speak, etc.'[21]

While Mabel was resting up in Chicago, Edris made 'an interesting suggestion' and she passed it on to Howard: 'That we write up an account of our teaching experiences in the last 20 years. That it would be of greatest value to future generations. Perhaps that is your next writing assignment.' Unfortunately, this suggestion was too late for Howard, and Mabel never had enough free time to do it.[22]

Howard was evidently having problems settling in to the new home, a problem compounded when Helene was not available to continue helping him. His selection of a new caretaker bothered Mabel, still up north: 'Am a bit concerned about your taking a girl off the street. <u>Please</u> either get a dependable reference or change to Mary's girl. She sounded good. You can't trust women you pick up on the street – please get someone to check up on her at once.'[23] Mabel returned to Little Rock on 10 May.

In her diary, Mabel prayed 'that Howard may truly attain

before he leaves this world and become a pure bounty of the Almighty to the world of humanity'.[24] Howard began a poem about the passage from this world to the next, illustrating his total confidence in what was to come.

> My time is almost up. I feel the beat
> Of wings about my head. There's no retreat;
> Even if I could I would not, for a breath,
> An instant. Why should I draw back from death
> Who knows – Thank God for Certitude – that Life
> is endless, and that fear and doubt and strife
> Are only here, not there. The journey's end
> Is home; a Father's arms. A loving Friend,
> The fireside chats with those gone on before
> The near approach to Him I'll love the more.
>
> Ah no! It is not this that crowds my mind.
> Of course I'll live. Of course I then shall find
> A wider field of action, freer fields of thought
> But by what light do I, whose hands have sought
> In this small world my own desire; whose soul
> Has here been fixed on dying things; whose whole
> Intent has in this world been set on that
> Which moth and rust corrupt, and treasure what
> Thieves can break through and steal; What right have I.
>
> Beyond that line imaginary – Death –
> To think, to live, to breathe a purer breath,
> Than here I sought, than here I did my deed?
> Of course there is no death: or course this little breath
> Which we call life is but the matrix fashioning
> of Baby limbs to roam in Worlds of God;
> Of baby ears and eyes to hear and see
> Such beauties as in this dark world could never be.[25]

This part of the poem was written on 13 May, but it was not completed before his time was indeed up.

On 23 May Howard began writing the letter below to his granddaughter, Barbara, who was sixteen and aspiring to be an actress. He finished it just 13 days before his death. Barbara took this letter to heart, following his wishes to 'read it often during the coming years' and its guidance inspired her life of very active service, as well as her deep study of the Writings of the Faith. Affectionately referred to as 'the dear Grandbobby letter' by the family, copies of it have passed down through the generations, and Howard's influence has proved a guiding light to the service to the succeeding generations of physical and spiritual offspring.

Dearest Grandbobby,
When I heard from Muriel that your supreme desire seemed to tend toward the stage and the life of an actress, my first reaction was disappointment. That was not at all the picture I had in my mind of your life of service in this little world. I had thought of you as marrying early to some young Baha'i, successful enough materially so that you would not have to struggle to make ends meet and could devote your time to service in the Cause and to raising a goodly family of children who would take a great part in the building of the Kingdom of God on earth.

I am not sure I have changed my mind greatly about this unless I can be assured that your service in His Cause still remains your dominant passion; you simply having altered your approach to that service. And it is in relation to this that this letter is being written. It is directed by the guidance of God. I am sure of this, and I want you to be sure of it also, and meditate upon it very deeply. I am sitting up in bed, typewriter on my knees, and in considerable pain. Nothing but the power of the Spirit enables me to write at all. This will indicate to you how deeply I feel that which I shall write. This may be the last letter I shall write to you in this passing world. I love you very – very much. Always, since your earliest babyhood we have been very close spiritually. My ambitions and expectations for you have always been simply and solely for your spiritual advancement, and with that advancement a corresponding increase in your servitude in the path of God. This is still my dominant hope and desire for you. Nothing else is of the slightest importance in comparison. It is in the hope that I may transfer to you in some measure this passionate desire for Servitude that this letter is written. Read it often during the coming years. Years that will be filled with sufferings, upheavals, famine and disease, despair, hopelessness and the dissemination of humanity. It is quite possible that you may see this country invaded, your home bombarded, your children massacred and your own life a sacrifice to the demons of man's hatred, imbecility and Godlessness. A careful study of the Guardian's latest letter to the American believers reveals that the above is not only possible but highly probable. Under these considerations anyone can see, who has come under the influence of Baha'u'llah, how absurd it is to encourage any so-called ambitions, desires and forecastings of future earthly glories. These have always been evanescent and futile. Now they are insane, or at best, childish . . .

You, my dearest, are on the verge of womanhood. I write to you, not as a child, not even as my Grandbobby. I write to you as a standard-bearer in the Army of the Lord of Hosts. You can have no part, as such, in the futile dreams of the fame-intoxicated world. You do not belong in their ranks at all. They are of those who 'crowd the earth's trough - the swine.' 'Come out from among them and be ye separate, saith the Lord of Hosts.'

The only thing about this dream of yours that causes me to regard it at all seriously is the way the opening seems to have come to you . . . But do not allow yourself to be misled by any such fiction that this door which seems to be opening to you is a way to the gratification of your longing to be an actress, or the path to fame and power. No – no! It is a test, my dear, it is the voice of 'Abdu'l-Bahá crying out to you – 'Beware!' Beware, he would say of all earthly desire, all human praise or blame, all confused thinking which tends to blind us to the inherent falsity underlying any dependence upon a civilization, a mode, a standard of comparison swiftly passing into oblivion. Beware of assuming that the stage, the drama, the 'becoming an actress' is, of itself of the slightest importance. Not 'Beware' of trying to become proficient in dramatic art, but beware of the superstition that that art is of the slightest importance in itself. Like everything else in this world, or any world, it is the use to which it is put that makes it important or unimportant. And that brings us to the real object of this letter. Your natural comeback after reading so much is to remark – 'so what?' Now I am going to try to tell you 'What.' And it is not going to be easy. But 'I take refuge in God.' As 'Abdu'l-Bahá so often said. He is the Knower, the Wise. He is the informer, the quickener of the minds of His lovers.

(It has taken me hours to write this much and I have only touched the fringe of the matter. I have had to stop and rest after only a few lines. And my eyesight (Physical only, thank God) is increasingly growing weaker. This evening Riswanea is having a group of the friends, some dozen or more, here for a buffet supper, at which she wants me to talk with them for a few moments. So let us postpone further talk together, dear Grandbobby, until tomorrow.)

June 8th

You see by the date above that the 'tomorrow' was considerably postponed . . . The pain to which I referred above turned to be rather serious. Osteopath two or three times weekly, and that proving not very helpful I am now getting X-rays and special hospital care. Today I am feeling comparatively free from serious pain so I will try to finish what was in my heart, though it must be brief.

The New World of the Kingdom which is now being built by the blood and tears of a recalcitrant humanity, as well as by the self-sacrificing devotion of the Friends of God, demands your full attention. 'This is not a matter to play on with the imagination,' declares Bahá'u'lláh, 'nor a place into which shall enter the frightened cowards. Nay, rather, it is an arena, a race course into which none shall enter save the knights of the Merciful who have renounced the worldly things. These are the assistants of God on earth, and the dawning places of power amongst the people of the world.'

These words – this trumpet call – you must take to your heart. It is a call to you. You are summoned to be in very truth an Assistant of God upon earth; a dawning place of Power in the new kingdom.

If then, it develops that the Will of God for you is the life of dramatic artistry, that life, must be entered upon in the spirit of a 'Knight of the Merciful who has renounced the worldly things.' You must regard that stage as the arena upon which the power of Bahá'u'lláh is to be manifest through, His humble servant; His selfless channel of servitude to all the peoples of the earth.

Now it is perfectly apparent that if the divine goal is to be approached by you, careful training is necessary. Just as your desire to be an actress is an empty dream unless backed by passionate self-dedication to that art, and long years of study and self-denying training, so – vastly more so – must your every thought, your every hope, your every desire be centered upon fitting yourself to be that channel for the love of God, that medium, for the expression of that love upon the boards of the stage.

You have inherited from your blessed mother and from me the background of sincere faith in the Manifestation of God in this Day. You occupy the rather unique position in this country of being of the third generation of believers. But you have also inherited certain physical and emotional characteristics from us both which have no place in your job as 'knight of the Merciful.' Emotion is one, by which I mean those physical and mental traits which find expression in decisions and acts which have not been arrived at through exhaustive thinking the thing through; the full cost has not been carefully estimated before-hand. Both Muriel and I have had this tendency to 'go off half-cocked.' I have often wondered if my life might have not been much more useful, and my many mistakes been greatly lessened, if some wise and experienced man had written to me, or talked to me somewhat as I am writing you now.

Dear Grandbobby – we are too apt to think of life as something that we face with success predestined if only our intentions are good. This is far from the truth. You might as well imagine that you can become a famous and heart-moving actress by simply passionately desiring to become such, or being willing to sacrifice yourself in that endeavor.

You must not only be willing to sacrifice you must DO IT. You must not only long to become a great actress, you must practice every detail of that art until it becomes second nature.

Just so must you practice daily, hourly, every moment, the art of saintliness – the science of uprightness – the skill of poise, of thoughtful judgement, of crushing down relentlessly every tendency toward snap-judgement, emotional outbreaks, or any slightest subservience to momentary desires and decisions based upon a passing circumstance instead of upon eternal verities.

It is plain, is it not my dear, that such a station is not to be quickly or easily attained. It is, and must be, the product of ceaseless attention, constant practice, unremitting vigilance, and steadfast courage.

You see my dear, (I repeat) I am not writing to you as a child, not even as an adolescent. I am writing to you as a woman; nay, more, I am writing to you as a woman of the future – a woman of the New Day, the New Kingdom – a Knight of the Merciful, an Assistant of God upon earth. This is why I want you to re-read this letter often during the coming years; and keep it before your children and your grandchildren – your physical and spiritual offspring.

Also, I must add: – what I have written is equally pertinent whether you decide upon a stage career or not. You are not to order your life after the model of the Christian ideal except as it is bound up with the teachings of Bahá'u'lláh;

nor are you to follow the tenets of any so-called advisor (self-appointed to direct youth in the path of 'success' . . . Your only advisor is the Manifestation of God. Your only Helper is He. Your only Name is His Name. Your only success is in clothing yourself with His attributes and characteristics.

Well – I must stop sometime, I suppose. My back cries out 'Quit,' but my heart calls 'Serve.'

All my love has gone into every word.

Upon thee, my beloved, be Glory and Peace – Ya Baha El Abha!

Uncle Grandaddy[26]

Doris McKay characterized Howard as having 'lion-like courage and often superhuman accomplishment', and alluded to his description of the secret of power:

I think it is something like this . . . The Will of God and the will of individual man . . . may, nay must, become identified, become identical . . . 'Abdu'l-Baha speaks of losing the self in the Self of God. We must accustom ourselves to the actual doing of this. . . . We cannot think of God's Will as a passive thing any more than we can think of our own will as passive, inert. God's Will is evidenced in nature, in power, in action. To identify our will with His Will is to partake of His activity, His Power, His effectiveness. To submit my will to His Will then, carries an implication of marching – creating – overcoming. But not marching alone; we march in step with Him. We throw our feeble wills in with His and so become all-conquering as He says we shall. How can the result be other than victory?[27]

Howard's passing was not unexpected. Mabel noted:

We had, many of us, premonitions that the day of his release, his ascension, was very near. Before I left Chicago, following the Convention, I knew that he would go sometime this summer . . . Indeed, as far back as last year's

Convention when Alvin [Blum] in a moment of inspiration, God guided, I believe, unexpectedly brought Howard to the convention, many, many of the friends clustered about him and begged to take pictures of him, and he was snapped again and again in the grounds of the Temple. They all said that they thought this would be his last convention. But since my return this year I knew it was very close. On Friday, June 6, at the meeting at our home, Howard said, 'I don't believe I feel able to come in. You can get along alright without me, can't you?' But later, when some rather important men arrived, I slipped into his room to tell him, and he said, 'In that case, I will come in.' So he got up in the midst of his pain, which was great, dressed, and came into the living room. I had already talked for over half an hour. Then he started, and with a voice which rang out with a deep bell-like quality, resonant and strong, he gave the most dynamic address. Everyone was spellbound. He talked for about three quarters of an hour, calling to their souls, challenging them to live in this day, declaring the majesty of God in this His Day, and the power of His Manifestation, Baha'u'llah.

As I watched him, I thought, 'This is like Grace's [Ober] farewell address. There is that same resonance of voice, that same great power, that same dynamic, ageless quality. Could this be his last? Is this his swan-song? Will he pass now into the Supreme World before our very eyes?' Afterwards, I discovered that several others present had the same thought. Sunny had felt the same way, and one of the new Bahais, who had received her spiritual confirmation thru Howard, said; 'As I watched and listened to him, I thought – Can this be his Sermon on the Mount?' And two others thought that this would be his last, his glorious farewell. Well, it was his last, indeed.[28]

Howard was weaker than usual, but as was normal, the call of the Faith again pulled Mabel to Vogel Park, where she had months before agreed to give a course. He did not like to see her go, but since she had promised, and Rezsi Sunshine and two other Bahá'í girls said that they would stay with him, Mabel left once again to teach the Faith.

Howard wrote his last letter to Mabel on 13 June:

> I went to the hospital this morning and Dr Terry told me he wanted me under observation for at least a week. So just as soon as they have a bed vacant I will go there. Have a grand rest and all meals and medicines provided. I think this is a real bounty from God. The reason for the 'observation' is that the X Rays taken in Memphis and those taken here do not agree – the location of the 'cyst' or 'tumor' seems to have changed. Me – I don't believe it for it is exactly where it was. It is much more likely that the photo missed the location. However the point is that it is nothing for you to worry about. Nothing serious.[29]

Before Mabel's departure for Vogel Park, Howard had visited a doctor who X-rayed his tumors, a large one of long standing that did not bother him, and a second new, smaller and very painful one. The doctor was puzzled by what he saw and, after Mabel had left for Vogel Park, Howard went into the hospital. Being short of funds, they put him in a ward that Mabel said was 'bedlam and horrible' and where he could not eat any of the food available. For twenty-four hours, he ate nothing, so that when Rezsi Sunshine and two other Bahá'ís came to visit, he begged them to take him home. Escaping the hospital, they took Howard to a restaurant he knew, after which he felt much better.[30]

Mabel's sojourn to Vogel Lake did not last long. Howard suffered four haemorrhages in his stomach and on 17 June Rezsi cabled Mabel to come home.[31] She made a frantic dash to get back:

> I was taking a sunbath on the beach when the wire came and with the help of the friends, was packed, dressed and off on a wild ride to the nearest railroad station 50 miles [80

km] away, in a few minutes. Mrs. Bidwell did a magnificent piece of driving and we made the train. Then another train from Atlanta to Chattanooga, and at midnight changed to the Streamline to Memphis, where changing again, I arrived in Little Rock before noon on Wednesday [18 June].[32]

When Howard discovered that Rezsi and the girls had sent Mabel a cable to come home, he became very indignant and said, 'How dare they to do this thing without consulting me. Who knows what important work for the Cause of God they have interrupted.' The next day, however, he was very thankful that they had sent the cable.[33] Arriving back in Little Rock, Mabel wrote:

> I found Howard very weak and in great pain, but smiling and happy to have me home again. I had not fully realized how he had dreaded being alone – that is, without me. A nurse was already installed and we had a doctor up to see him at once. His verdict was that there was simply nothing that could be done, except to keep him as comfortable and free from pain as possible. He said that the end might come in a few days or hours.[34]

Lying in a hospital bed or not, he was dedicated to the Faith to the end:

> In his last conscious hours he sent messages to many and endeavored to serve those around him who were intent on serving him. As a further service he permitted an autopsy as a final service to science. Every doctor agreed that it was most wonderful how he lived with all the things he had wrong with him, and more wonderful how he kept up and was cheerful and thinking of others. How he was able to live above the constant nerve-racking pressures his body was undergoing, indeed how he could behave anything like a normal human being with all the physical nerve tensions of his poor sick body. He had four things wrong with his

heart. Had hardening of the arteries, had an adhesion ever since a gall bladder operation 30 years ago, which caused difficulty in his bowels and was largely the cause of his indigestion. He had varicose veins in his stomach, an enormous aneurism (a big tumor packed hard with clotted blood) in his abdomen, and another one very recently, causing intense pain in pressing on nerves and on bladder. Suffered from frequent nausea, and was deaf, and had cataracts on both eyes. Yet, when I came home from the convention after resting a couple of weeks with Edris, hoping to get back my strength and voice (which was gone during the convention), that blessed servant of Baha'u'llah insisted that he was going to take care of all the kitchen work, and had not replaced the maid and gave me orders to keep out of the kitchen, as he was going to take care of me and also save money for the expense incident upon his passing. He was putting aside the maid's wages in a little savings account he had opened. He insisted that he felt well and plenty strong enough, and just shooed me out of the kitchen whenever I came near. Of course I reorganized things in a few days, and he realized that he could not keep on with his plans, as his poor body would not back him up. But what a gallant gesture! How self-sacrificing he always was.[35]

The pain cyclically rose and fell. When it increased, he would very quietly repeat 'Praise be to God, the Lord of all the worlds' or 'Praise be to Thee, my God and my Beloved!' He

spoke several times of pain, and each time his face would become radiant, the most heavenly smile illuminating it. It seemed to make him happy. Not one trace of resentment or self-pity, only joyful acceptance. There were four things wrong with his heart, the doctor said, and one of them, the Angina pain, was terrible. Between paroxysms, he would joke and laugh, and say divine things and be superbly entertaining and inspiring. None of us had ever imagined anything like it. He was most eager to go, as an air ship straining at its moorings. Wednesday night he sent messages to many people, thinking, it seemed, of everyone, everyone except himself. His love seemed to pour out as a great river, and then we had our wonderful moments, eternal moments, they were, together alone, talking of our life together thruout all the worlds of God. He spoke suddenly of teaching in some great university in the universe of the Placeless, and of studying there, as an experience just ahead of him. He saw writing on the wall which he could not quite decipher – some in prose and some in poetry. He saw spiritual presences in the room – sometimes speaking to them. Then in a disappointed voice, he said, 'But you know, I feel just as strong as ever. Do you think that perhaps I am not going after all?'[36]

Elizabeth Cheney later related one final story about Howard. As he lay suffering and only semi-conscious, Mabel begged God 'to allow his death and surcease of his sufferings'. A little later, Howard regained consciousness and said: ''Abdu'l-Bahá just told me that if I wished, I could go now, that my time was finished, but that if I could endure a while longer that I am going through the final stages to enable me to teach in the spiritual universities.' He told 'Abdu'l-Bahá that he was willing to suffer a bit longer for such a privilege.[37]

Howard thanked and praised God until his last conscious moment. Mabel said, 'He was steadfast even unto the end, counting his pain a great blessing, realizing indeed that it was "light and mercy, inwardly."' On 21 June, he 'attained'.[38] The nurse who was with him said that she had never witnessed such faith on any deathbed.[39] During the years of Howard's decline, Mabel had prayed for two things, that he would 'truly "attain" before he left this world, and, second, that Bahá'u'lláh would permit me to be with him at the end.' In her letter after his passing, she wrote that God had granted both her prayers.

In her journal, Mabel wrote:

June 29/41

Now he is gone – he, my beloved – gone out into the world of light. I am so glad for him that he is free from that poor sick body – and from pain. Thank God for that release. I know too that there is no separation in reality – that he is here with me even now, that he bids me to rejoice, but I miss him dreadfully, poignantly, like a refuge and infinite tenderness. He always awaited me, and always ready to extend arms of love and encouragement, was always there 100% when I needed him – never failing me when I called upon him for spiritual help, always lifting, lifting, always ready to share divine thoughts with me.

That I let the ever present thousand little things prevent me from taking time to sit down and listen to him when he was fairly bursting with those great realizations and wanting to share them with me – this is my immeasurable regret.

June 30/41

Now the 3rd period of my life opens. 1st with TC [Theron Canfield], 2nd with H. 3rd, alone, outwardly, but Howard now a part of me, are two together as one. The time for the achievement of poise has now arrived. Poise is not a first step or a cause, but an effect and a result. The two requisites are: Surrender and Stillness. Surrender opens the avenues of the spirit, frees the mind both cons[cious]and unconscious and from tensions.

Stillness prepares the mirror that it may reflect the desire and wisdom of God and makes 'listening' possible.[40]

Though physically gone, Howard's spirit continued to be active. Mabel wrote that 'He is very close to me . . . I seem to be able to contact him whenever I need him, and he advises me quite clearly . . . I knew theoretically that there was no separation, but now I know from actual experience that there is no death . . .'[41] Several others who were especially close to him had the same experience. One woman said that 'she turned to him and that he had solved a big problem for her. She said, "Daddy told me what to do and now I know."'[42]

The day following Howard's passing, the Guardian cabled: 'Profoundly deplore tremendous loss outstanding promotor Faith. Evidences his magnificent labours imperishable. Deepest sympathy, ardent prayers. Shoghi Rabbani'.[43]

In September, Mabel wrote back to the Guardian:

> Your beautiful cable about the passing of my blessed Howard was an indescribable bounty to him as well as to me. Thank you from my heart. It, indeed, crowned his earthly life. He has been very close to me since his going and has spoken to me quite clearly in the inner world on a number of occasions. He must be very happy, as, frequently when I think of him it is as if I tuned into ecstasy. It is so great I can hardly bear it. The reunion of those faithful servants of the Cause in those higher worlds must be wonderful beyond words. And now he is free from pain and limitations and can serve with so much greater power.[44]

Cables and letters flooded in. The National Teaching Committee cabled, 'Will be acclaimed in Bahai history as outstanding pioneer in teaching field. How joyous must be his reunion with the Master'.[45] Muriel and her daughter, Barbara sent: 'Sure Supreme Concourse welcoming valiant steadfast spirit'. Rúhíyyih Khánum sent a letter in which she said, 'Indeed I find it always a great and comforting thought to picture our loved ones all gathered together in the same Holy Presence! Harry Randall, Alfred Lunt, Mother, Martha [Root], Keith [Ransom-Kehler], now Howard Ives. All Faithful to the end. All rewarded now by their loving Lord'.

In the long letter Mabel wrote to friends following Howard's passing, she wrote:

> In a number of wires and letters the thought has been expressed of the certain joyous meeting between Abdul Baha and him. There was a rare bond there. And how

THE END OF HOWARD'S PHYSICAL ROAD

Howard did adore his 'Lord and Master'. The glorious majesty of Baha'u'llah was ever in Howard's consciousness, his Beloved to whom he turned in almost every hour of the day and night. Anyone who has ever occupied a room near Howard knows how often the quiet of the night, Howard's voice could be heard in ecstatic prayers. The world of Reality was ever very close to him. He lived in it more than he did in this world. And now he is completely there and the conflict with this world and its demands is over for him. Praise be to God! Now indeed, has his deepest wish come true; this is to be able to talk about God as much as he wanted to without people thinking him queer. This, he often remarked. was his idea of heaven. Ali Kuli Khan and others who were with the Master after his return to Haifa from America have often told me how often the Master spoke of Howard and what glowing tributes he paid him. How, in recounting his experiences in the west to the Family and friends He would say with glowing face: 'I have a minister in America. Mr. Ives!'[46]

Before his passing, Howard had written in his 'Spiritual Diary', 'When I recognize the undoubted fact that all this life has taught me, or could ever possibly teach me, is but a sign, a token, a symbol, of what the future worlds of God shall surely teach – my whole being is lost in thanksgiving and praise of Him Who has bestowed on me – this boundless Gift and this infinite Bounty.'[47]

On 23 June 1941, a group of about fifty friends gathered in a chapel in Little Rock, Arkansas. Mabel's daughter Edris Rice-Wray conducted the service and opened with, 'This is not a funeral. It is a Memorial gathering. This is not a death. It is the beginning of life –not a time for grieving but for rejoicing . . . Won't you join us in this spirit and rejoice with us that now our dear one has begun to live the life eternal?'[48]

Several people came forward to give personal testimonials:

An Episcopal minister said that he had never fully understood what is meant by the love for God until Howard Ives explained to him that one loves God by loving His manifestation . . .

The most striking evidence that this was in nowise a funeral was the beautiful tribute delivered by Mrs. Howard Ives. She read two of the tablets of Abdul Baha to her husband, and then told something of his life, his spiritual longings and development and his service to the Faith of Baha'u'llah through the years. She spoke of his profound grasp of the realities of existence; how he had penetrated the mysteries of being and lived in the consciousness of higher worlds. How joyously he had been awaiting his release, the beginning of his great adventure. That the other life was an ever-present reality to him; not merely a belief, or even what is usually called faith; but complete assurance – certitude. He knew. He had already experienced. She closed by saying; 'Our beloved one has ascended unto the presence of his Lord whom he so passionately loved. He is now in the Supreme World. He has been welcomed by a host of his friends and his spiritual children who will bless him throughout eternity because he was privileged to bring to them the chalice of pure light in this Day of Days. He is now with the ages; a great soul who lived greatly, loved all humanity with a yearning tenderness, served unceasingly even unto his last breath, and remained steadfast unto the end. His was a triumphant passing!'[49]

Memorial meetings were held all across the country.[50] In December, Mabel wrote a long letter to Doris McKay providing information for Howard's 'In Memoriam' article, and about their life together, ending with her own look at the man who was her husband:

> His outstanding characteristics were, I should say, his depth of spiritual consciousness, unexcelled, probably, in this country. His unique power of confirming souls. (How I miss him here in dealing with those becoming believers). The greatness and depth of his love. His faith in people. His

amazingly deep and intense emotions; his agony of remorse when he felt he had offended by his sometimes abrupt manner, and his ecstasies when, as so often happened, inner doors opened within him and heavenly mysteries were revealed to him. This became an almost daily occurrence in his later years, and almost hourly toward the last. Often his power to bring into being a spiritual atmosphere in a room when he was talking about the Faith. When he stopped talking, no one stirred and there was a beautiful silence, which no one wanted to break. Outstanding were his fearlessness and courage. He never seemed to fear anything save hurting hearts. His personal bravery was complete – most unusual. Was never afraid to attempt new things. He woke up one morning with the words ringing in his ears from one of company of lofty men with whom he had been conversing: 'Take up thy barnacled boat', five times in rapid succession 'and fly with me to the uttermost parts of the universe'. We asked Jenabi Fazel if he could tell the meaning. He said that the universe meant the universe of the teachings of Baha'u'llah, and that the five trips meant 5 teaching trips which he was to make. So we were always counting them up and after we realized 'that perhaps these were his writings; and we hurried to finish them all. Perhaps they were 1st his long years of constant traveling and teaching by word, and then his four books. 'Youth need not Die' may yet be used, that is, much of it. Or it may have referred to his sequel to Song Celestial, some of which the Guardian had put into the Baha'i World.

The Guardian was always encouraging him in his work, and wrote him so many wonderful letters. Also those ringing words of Abdul Baha to him, thrice repeated; 'Mr. Ives, expect very great things'; were always ringing in his ears and spurring him on. And – he never gave up. No matter what life did to him, and his physical sufferings thru the years were severe, he never wavered from his oath of life, his one consuming desire, his deep passion, to serve the Cause of Baha'u'llah with all that was in him and to his last breath.

This was Howard as I knew him, and who could know him better? always an entertaining and delightful companion. Never a dull moment with him, wise in his advice; his arms always a refuge when life became too difficult. My friend, my companion, my eternal beloved! His last words to me, that we would be together throughout all the worlds![51]

'Abdu'l-Bahá, in 1912, had told Howard, 'Now is the time for <u>very great things.</u>'. Howard had taken that to heart.

25
Mabel Soldiers on in the South
1941–1942

In his will, Howard unsurprisingly appointed Mabel as his executor. The will gave his daughter, Muriel, his portrait of 'Abdu'l-Bahá signed by the Master in His own hand. To his granddaughter, Barbara, he gave his signed manuscript of *Portals to Freedom*.[1]

Mabel left their apartment in Little Rock and moved in with Roberta Wilson in Hot Springs. She put all of Howard's profusely annotated books into a special suitcase and marked it the 'Howard Ives Memorial Library'.[2]

Many people had dreams of Howard coming to them and Mabel had several. In early July, she told Doris McKay about a dream in which

> he spoke to me very clearly and told me thing after thing. I have written them all down. He challenged me to a new arising to service, greater than ever before – that as I arose he could help me. That I must brush aside all limitations – that now he is free to work and assist me. I am conscious that he has passed thru three stations, that is, he is now in the third. That the first plane was one of human nearness, in which he functioned for the first few days after his release, exactly as he was before while he was here and told me things to do as he would have done before he left.
>
> Then came a time when he seemed to be withdrawn, and I was conscious that he had ascended to higher planes and was hidden by impenetrable veils of light. That he was consorting with great souls and finding his place in planes so lofty that the mind could not conceive nor follow him.

That he was occupied with entrancing experiences that I could not follow . . .

Then one night recently, I was engulfed in a heart-breaking sense of failure, following an experience in which I had seemed to do much less than my best with some souls. I touched the depths and called out to Baha'u'llah. The next morning, during my meditations, Howard came to me again, but now with power and assurance, the spiritual Howard, that I had known and so loved and revered. Now however he was clothed with a new majesty and I knew he had made his adjustment to his new life during that time of withdrawal. He had become at one and integrated with his new environment, and now was released for service, free now to function as a focus of power. That now as spirit and power he can come to me and to you, and to all who need him.[3]

With that dream, Mabel went back to serving the Faith. She wrote, 'I went downtown and arranged, without the least trouble, for weekly broadcasts, and immediately began plans and arrangements for something of which I will write later.'[4]

Howard had dreamed of having a Bahá'í summer school in the Little Rock area and on 4 July, Roberta Wilson had a dream in which she saw 200 Bahá'ís from Memphis gathered at the summer school. In the morning, she told Mabel, 'The Howard Colby Ives Bahai Summer school is a reality. It is already in existence. I saw it in action last night.' In September, Mabel wrote to the Guardian describing all the work that had been done in Arkansas and the first establishment of Bahá'í communities there. Then she wrote about the Bahá'í School she hoped to develop in the area:

A project is on hand to develop a Spring and Fall Bahai School near Hot Springs, following the pattern of the Summer Schools already established in other parts of the country, but as the weather is too hot in summer, the session would have to be when the weather is cooler. Hot Springs

Howard in 1936, the photograph used for his 'In Memoriam'

Howard's grave in Little Rock, Arkansas

Howard and Mabel, travelling teachers, in Waukegan, April 1940

is a famous Health Resort and attracts a large number of people most of the year. This would be the first regular Bahai School in the South, and would be specifically for this Region (Arkansas, The Vogel, Louisiana, Mississippi, western Tennessee and southern Alabama).[5]

She also wrote that Hot Springs had seven registered believers and that 'there is an amusing sense of rivalry between the two cities as to who shall achieve an Assembly first. Each wants to be the first to put Arkansas on the Bahá'í map. We have had several inter-city picnics this summer and so the friends have got to know each other.'[6] The Guardian's response, written by his secretary on his behalf, brought words of comfort about Howard's passing and praised her hard work:

> You have often been in his thoughts since the passing of your dear husband, and he greatly admires the manner in which you have met your separation from him, in this physical world, and continued with your very important services to the Faith, services in which hitherto he had been your devoted companion.
>
> The work which he accomplished for the Faith will never be forgotten, and he has left behind him many souls who, no doubt, will strive to follow in his footsteps and emulate the devotion and capacity with which he taught the Cause.
>
> The good news that there are now groups almost ready for Assembly status in both Little Rock and Hot Springs pleased the Guardian immensely. He thinks the best way to settle their friendly rivalry as to which goes on the Baha'i map first would be to ensure they both constitute themselves Assemblies at the same time and the earliest possible date!
>
> The way in which the believers are working these days, with such ardour and determination, to accomplish the Seven Year Plan, delights him. He feels confident that, in spite of the world conditions prevailing at present, they will let nothing prevent them from achieving their objective

and crowning their centenary with a glorious victory for the Faith.[7]

Shoghi Effendi's personal note at the end read:

> Dear and valued co-worker: The passing of your dear and distinguished husband was indeed a great loss to our beloved Faith. His many and varied services were deeply appreciated, and were in many respects unique. I will specially pray for him that his soul may receive the richest blessings from a Master Whom he served with such fervour, ability, and devotion. Persevere in your noble efforts and particularly in the teaching field. Your true and grateful brother, Shoghi

Hot Springs and Little Rock

Howard's passing barely slowed Mabel's teaching work. As the letter above written on Shoghi Effendi's behalf noted, the Guardian greatly admired how she had 'continued with [her] very important services to the Faith'. She again found herself dashing from one city to another, never with a permanent address for mail, so she set up a post office box in Little Rock.[8] For a time, she was back and forth between Hot Springs and Little Rock. In a remarkable success in Hot Springs, Reverend Baird, the Episcopal clergyman, and his wife accepted Bahá'u'lláh and left their church. In spite of having difficulties finding a new job, the new Bahá'ís were steadfast.[9]

Mabel was still remonstrating with herself in her diary, trying to make herself more spiritual and in tune with the Will of God. On 26 August 1941, she wrote: 'I dare you, Mabel Ives, to attain to a deep, mystic, spiritual consciousness, to accomplish sustained stillness, to build up a strong, cold and draft-resistant body, deep-breathing habit and a healthy, strong resonant musical, defendable voice – and the creative ability self-support and financing my work . . .'[10]

New Orleans and Baton Rouge, Louisiana

In early September, Mabel visited Marion Little in Covington, Louisiana, and in her letter to Shoghi Effendi told about their efforts:

> Marion Little and I were so grateful to receive your cable praying for the success of our winter's work. The second lecture has already been given in New Orleans and there was a fine response. The plan now is that we should leave in about a week for Jackson, Mississippi and later for Birmingham, Alabama so that with the assistance of Baha'u'llah and the intensive work on our part that an assembly can be brought into being in each of these two states. May I say that I am having considerable trouble with my health and this type of teaching work is so strenuous that it requires a great deal of strength. If it is not too much to ask would you send up a prayer that I may be supported physically as well as spiritually during this winter's teaching campaign. We so long to present you with two more states in the Baha'i fold![11]

On 15 September 1941, Mabel went to Baton Rouge and spent two weeks staying with Mr and Mrs Irving Hansen, who lived a short way outside the city. She noted that 'it is quiet and restful here – my room and bath secluded from the rest of the house and am allowed to be alone'.[12] From Baton Rouge, she travelled to New Orleans, and on 9 October began her lecture series. She stayed at the St Charles Hotel until the 17th, when she went to stay with David and Margaret Ruhe for a week (David was later to serve on the Universal House of Justice).[13] Mabel gave her course of lectures 'out of which a number of people joined a study group'.[14] In her diary, she wrote that she needed to 'give emotional, romantic, intriguing appeal to lectures – everyone is in search of love consciously or unconsciously – stress the fulfilment and happiness that comes in finding the Eternal and True Beloved – how it colors all lives and love and losses before changing into a romantic adventure...'[15]

Mabel looked at the state of the Seven Year Plan, which the American Bahá'í community was struggling to complete. On 25 September, she wrote in her diary her personal pledge to Shoghi Effendi about what she would do to aid its fulfilment:

The Pledge
Since we are facing a grave emergency in the completing of your Seven Year Plan, I pledge you, Shoghi Effendi, my Master and my King upon the earth, Guardian of God's Mighty Cause on this planet, not to accept anything less than success in pressing toward the fulfilment of the following plan and burning desire.

Goal
$1,000 by May 23, 1944 (my definite goal and plan) clear above taxes
For which I intend to give a great and enormously valuable idea and ideas thru the medium of writing – books, articles, the central theme and idea for radio scripts, moving picture scenarios and for pictorial strips for news papers – and thru lectures.

Plan
1st write one short book – large print – embodying the great idea – then follow by other books and articles, radio scripts, sermons, fictional scripts. Engage 1st class manager to book me for lectures.[16]

In her diary, Mabel sketched out an introductory chapter for her proposed book; her Introduction began with the statement that 'The sole problem of today's dislocated world is MAN. The solution, simply, is his disappearance – the liquidation of this archaic, old era, racially senile creature.' Most of the world at that moment was at war and America was soon to join in the conflagration. Mabel wrote that the only solution had to come from a spiritual source.[17] The book, however, was never finished and she was unable to even begin to save the $1,000.

Jackson, Mississippi

Mabel was on the train to Jackson, Mississippi, on 24 October[18] and spent two months in that city. Marion Little arrived there a week before she did and began making contacts and connecting with Mrs Hamilton, an 'ardent Bahá'í' and the mother of Martha Kavelin (wife of future Universal House of Justice member Borrah Kavelin). Mrs Hamilton knew everybody and belonged to everything, according to Mabel. Other Bahá'ís also came to help at different times during the campaign, including Evelyn Bivins and Lane Skelton.[19]

Mabel found Jackson to be very interesting and very different from other cities she had worked in:

> it is unique – probably the most church-minded city in the country, and these dear people take their religion, that is their church obligations very seriously. Also they are interested in prayer and believe in it, and are not afraid to talk about God, and almost every woman I have met is an active member of the Missionary Society. Of course they are very orthodox. The Baptist churches are tremendous affairs, with something going on almost every night and cars parked for blocks in front of them. Next comes the Methodists . . . The most popular evangelist, Gipsy Smith, Jr., whom Jacksonians love and fete, in fact fairly worship, started two weeks campaign at the largest church in the city the day before my opening lecture, and continued thru that whole period to capacity audiences. He took, I am told, out of Jackson a mere matter of $7,000.'[20]

Mabel wrote her goals for Jackson in her diary: 1) to have an audience averaging at least 200 people each night; 2) to have 100 people of capacity who will join the study class; 3) out of the 100, at least 33 of 'real spiritual, intellectual and financial capacity who will accept the Faith and register'; and 4) 'awaken the city to the New Day and its meaning'.[21]

But she faced a lot of spiritual competition – there was an

annual Christian Science lecture the same night as her first talk which had an 'immense audience' – only 25 people turned up to hear Mabel's lecture. Most of those who did were between the ages of 30 and 40 and one quickly became a Bahá'í. This first Jackson Bahá'í was Helen Yerger, a 33-year-old woman who had been spiritually searching for a long time, studying 'Rosicrucianism, astrology (I'm beginning to see red when they begin to talk about that; everyone seem to have gone daft on the subject).'[22] Mabel went so far as to write to the Guardian about astrology: 'In going from city to city we find an increasing number of people who are deeply interested in astrology and most of them feel that it is a definite science. As these people become attracted to the Cause, we have to deal with this matter in some way. Will you please suggest a way of handling this subject. Is there any scientific basis to astrology?'[23] His reply was that 'Astronomy is a science, astrology does not come under the same category but we should be patient with people who believe in it, and gradually wean them away from reliance on such things.'[24]

In addition to the lectures, Mabel spoke to the Lions Club, the Exchange Club, the Optimists, the BandP Woman's Club and other groups.[25] At one point, a group of theological students began attending her lectures. One was already preaching in a Baptist church and was the 'leading spirit' who brought the others. She noted that

> the thing that seemed to fascinate them was that here was someone who could answer all their questions, and who seemed to welcome questions. No doubt their professors just didn't know the answers, and these youths fairly deluged me with things which had always puzzled them. Such as: 'Is truth absolute?' And, 'what is truth?' And then many theological questions. So we had a great time. What a bounty that a Baha'i really has the answers. One night they brought one of their professors. The young preacher told Helen [Yerger] he was really interested. I wonder.[26]

Mabel discovered that the people in Jackson did not like the 'intellectual approach', but that they 'drink in the spiritual aspect'. She also discovered their deep prejudice towards Black people. She wrote, 'They love the negroes, and say "Don't take them away from us. What would we do without them?" But of course they must remain in their place. I heard a woman say, in speaking of the graduates of the negro college nearby, say, in all sincerity: "It is nice for them to go there, they make such good servants." My jaw fell. Is that all the future they have? thought I.'[27]

Mabel took her meals with a lady who attended some of her lectures and who said that she was very honoured to have Mabel there because she was such a 'good Christian'. Mabel noted, 'Their churches are crowded on Sundays. They <u>believe</u> in the church and in Christianity. A revamping of the world is out of their horizon of thought.'[28]

Mabel spent two months in Jackson, leaving three new believers and a dozen 'deeply attracted' souls.[29] One of her constant worries was the need for strong Bahá'ís to follow up her teaching campaigns. In January, Mrs Ellis was headed to Jackson to do that. Completing her work in Jackson, the National Teaching Committee told Mabel that Gertrude Gewertz (Blum) was getting things ready for her in Birmingham, Alabama, and Evelyn Bivens had prepared plans for her in Greenwood, Mississippi, north of Jackson. The Committee was very appreciative of Mabel's efforts, saying that 'While there is no question that you are expending a tremendous amount of strength and must feel very tired, never-the-less you are doubtless happy over the response which you have had in your campaigns this fall.'[30]

Edris wrote to Mabel on 8 January 1942 and told her about a dream she had just had about Howard:

> It was a Baha'i meeting, about 100 people. Everyone was milling around and suddenly I looked up and there he was just as healthy and fine looking as can be – strong and straight. He said 'I have just moved into another room.' Then 'Collie is getting along better'. 'Lynn is improved.' Then 'Mabel will be much better from now on.'

The idea he gave me was that in changing rooms he was promoted in some way. When he spoke of Collie, Lynn and you as though you were his special projects he had been working on. I was so impressed that he just seemed to radiate health and good spirits and strength and looked so meticulously groomed.

Then he was gone . . .[31]

Greenwood, Mississippi

In late January 1942, Mabel made another visit to Greenwood at the urging of Evelyn Bivins and spent a week there. She gave her series of five lectures in the evening and three in the morning to a group of 'fine and highly intelligent people' who continued their study of the Faith. One of those who attended, Mrs Cohen, accepted the Faith, but was reluctant to sign a declaration card. Finally, after being taken through the Will and Testament of 'Abdu'l-Bahá, she promised to sign if she could get her husband to do likewise.[32] Mabel noted that several new people 'were deeply attracted and a study class was formed by Mrs. Bivens to carry them on. Evelyn Bivens is an angel and serves constantly with utter devotion and steadfastness.'[33]

Birmingham, Alabama

Mabel arrived in Birmingham in early February and was supposed to have a week's rest, but she was up and out the very next morning to do her usual preparations – visiting various clubs and groups, including the Woman's Civic Club, the Woman's Chamber of Commerce, the Zonte Club and the Woman's Legion Auxiliary. This led to the President and several members of the Civic Club attending her lectures.[34]

Gertrude Gewertz was also in Birmingham and told the story of how Mabel brought an attracted soul and her husband into the Faith.[35] Gertrude had heard that Mabel was coming to Birmingham and she wanted to bring people to her talks. She had attended meetings of organizations where she thought she might find people interested in the Faith, and during the weekends she walked the streets saying the Greatest Name. One day, she noticed a sign that read: 'Dr. Juanita Johnson'. She thought it unusual to find a woman doctor, an osteopath and diet specialist, in that part of town, so she knocked on the door. The woman who answered turned out to be Dr Johnson's sister, who asked what an obviously Northern lady was doing in a Southern city. When Gertrude said that she was there to teach about the Baháʼí Faith, the sister said, 'You know, I think that my sister is going to be interested in that. She's interested in all kinds of funny things.' Gertrude made 'a mental note to visit her when Mabel Ives arrives'. When Mabel did get there, she worked

> quickly to firm up invitations . . . A hotel in the business district is booked for introductory lectures.
>
> Gertrude's hunch proves correct and Dr Juanita Johnson is in the audience. At the last lecture Mabel asks who is interested in more discussions. A number of people put up their hands. Dr Johnson is one of them. Later, Gertrude is talking with her over coffee. She is worrying about finding a place where they will be able to meet. They can no longer afford to book the hotel.
>
> Commercial places, stores and doctors' offices within the business district are the only place where black and white people are able to come together. 'Well, you can meet at my home,' offers Dr Johnson. Gertrude's coffee spills over the sides of the cup. It is not just the offer that has touched her, it is the powerful sense that there is something much bigger than her at work, helping to turn what seem to be insurmountable mountains into molehills.[36]

By 18 February, Mabel had completed her nine lectures. She wrote that there were 42 people at the final lecture and that it was a 'grand and stimulating night. Everyone was enthusiastic and the Holy Spirit flowed thru and touched the hearts.' Before the first study class, Mabel had a 'question evening' to make sure all their questions were answered. Quite a number registered for it.³⁷

Though Dr Johnson had offered her home, it may have been too small for all who wanted to participate. But then Mabel had coffee with a few of those present, including Eleanor Bridges, who owned a building downtown that had a vacant room; she gave it to the Bahá'ís to use as long as they wanted it. Mrs Bridges was an artist and her husband was a sculptor. They had dedicated their home 'over the mountain' to God, and every Sunday they held an Open House to which up to 100 people would come. Earlier, Mabel had spoken at one of the gatherings and started to hold study classes there in the afternoons 'for those women who could not come to the night series'.³⁸

Mabel was thrilled to have what she thought of as a Bahá'í Centre. She wrote:

> It is nothing less than a miracle what is happening. Here I sit in our own Center, in one of the finest office buildings in Birmingham, in the very heart of the business district, with light and heat furnished, with 25 chairs . . . a four-section bookcase with glass doors; a desk and two small tables, a lamp and other things . . . all of which has not cost us a cent . . . Our signs are up on the windows facing the hallway, announcing the lectures and classes, and curious people in nearby offices are enquiring about it and want to attend the lectures.³⁹

As Mabel finished her study classes, she noted that Martha Fettig had arranged for lectures to be given in Decatur, Alabama, north of Birmingham. She also attended the Regional Teaching Conference in Atlanta that began on 28 February.

In March, Leroy Ioas, on behalf of the National Teaching Committee, sent Mabel a letter saying how delighted they were with her work. He also told her that she was being given sufficient funds to continue her work through the end of 1942.⁴⁰

Mabel set a gruelling pace and the National Teaching Committee wanted her to take a break. But with a constant stream of requests from place after place, she didn't think she had time for a break:

> As much of this strenuous teaching work was done under great physical handicaps, the N.T.C. urged this servant to take a rest of several weeks, but there seemed to be such constant demand for teaching in many places that I was about to forgo that rest, when now both my daughter and our other Bahá'í doctor here . . . Katherine True, agree that I should have an operation which should give me a more stable condition of health so that I can carry on during this strenuous period ahead to better advantage. So I expect to enter the hospital today for ten days with a 5 weeks rest following it. It just breaks my heart to give up the teaching work planned . . .[41]

In May, Mabel sent the Guardian a letter which sympathized with the great difficulties the Guardian was having with the defection of his family, all of whom became Covenant-breakers and then went on to summarize:

> My heart has bled for you on account of the bitter experience you have been going thru in the defection of members of your family from the Covenant of Bahá'u'lláh. The whole American Community has viewed the matter with utter amazement, and it has but served to strengthen their firmness in the Faith and in loyalty to its divinely appointed Guardian. It makes us desire more than ever to bring joy to your heart. Our love for you is like an ever flowing river; and we pray that you may feel this and that it may serve to lighten your sorrow. There is only one thing that counts – that the Faith of Bahá'u'lláh may be established within the shortest possible time.[42]

The long letter also included a summary of her activities after leaving Memphis:

You will be happy to know that Jackson, Miss, in the very heart of the deep South, responded most beautifully to the Call of God, and that within two months after the first lecture was given, there was a fine study class and three registered believers. After this servant left there for Birmingham, Ala., Mrs. Ellis went there as a follow-up teacher . . . So there are today eight believers in Jackson . . .

Then in January, this servant went to Birmingham where Gertrud Gewertz had established herself as a resident pioneer, and had been making contacts and getting lists of names ready. After the nine lectures had been given, at which the largest attendance was 42, at any one lecture, about 23 wished to attend the study classes . . .

The loveliest thing about the Birmingham experience was the marvelous inner unity which we three pioneers were able to bring into being among us. We had glorious times of prayer together and perfect periods of consultation following, in which many problems were solved and questions answered. We feel that the rapid growth of that . . . Group was due in part at least to the mystic unity at its center . . .[43]

The Guardian's advice on how to teach Black Americans in the South

The problem of bringing Black people into the Faith and creating unity between them and the Whites was one that afflicted Mabel during all her years in the South. In a long letter to Shoghi Effendi in July 1942 she explained how she viewed the race problem, both within the South in general and the Bahá'í community in particular:

I would like to write at length about the whole problem of teaching in the South, which is like another country. I have been studying it now for almost three years. The conclusion that I have come to, and I find it shared by all the Southern Chairmen and teachers in the South, is that since the white race is the dominant race and the establisher of customs and the maker of laws, that it is best to get a substantial following among them before attempting to do much among the negro group, except through contacting the colored colleges and speaking in them and thus presenting the Faith to the leaders.

In the three cities where there are fixed Assemblies there has been no growth at all in the Community. And where it was forced on them as in Memphis, three of the white believers withdrew from the Community. In the South is more of a situation than a prejudice. In Memphis, for instance, the population is 45% colored, in Birmingham, 50% colored, in some parts of Mississippi, 90% colored . . . There is much more I would like to write, as for instance the difficulty involved of it being against the law to have mixed meetings in these cities. The situation in these states is much more complex than people realize. After much thought and prayer the matter resolved itself into the following steps as presenting the most logical approach to teaching in the South. Most important: Establish in the virgin states of the South by 1944. Build the kind of Communities that will grow and thus establish the Faith in the South where it is so tragically needed, thus training more and more people of the race who make the laws and build the customs, in the understanding of the principle of mankind's oneness.

At the same time present the Faith in the colleges and universities of the South both colored and white, so that the educated people of both races have at least an acquaintance with the Faith in an acceptable form.

Then after the Faith is established in a city and an Assembly formed, let these Southern believers take on as a project of their Assembly, of their own accord, and because they themselves wish to obey the spirit and the letter of the law of the teachings of the law of the teachings of Bahá'u'lláh – let them take on the project of contacting the colored university people who know the Faith and plan lectures among them and form a study group of those who are interested. Then when the crucial moment arrives when white and colored believers are to meet in a Feast together and break bread together, then they will be ready to take this (to them) perfectly tremendous step, in their stride, as a result of the situation that they have of their own accord brought into being. The tragedy in Memphis was because this situation was forced on them from without. Some of them with tears in their eyes said to me, 'If only they had given us a little more time. If only they had let us grow into it.' You see, of course, it means that in so doing, they court ostracism from society, and raiding by police, and the loss of their friends etc. Old believers can take all of this, but new souls, mere babes in the Faith, should be protected a little at first so that they can make the grade. There are very few souls like Nellie Roche, who can take it right from the beginning (though of course it was much less difficult in the college city like Nashville) but she, herself, pleads that the southern believers be left to solve this racial problem without interference from northern believers who do not understand its complexity. You see the Southern people really love and understand the negro, especially as an individual. There are a multitude of warm friendships among the two races, and if not forced prematurely they can handle it in a harmonious way so that the Faith will become acceptable in the South. If handled otherwise it will cause only rancor and strife throughout the South.

Also during the early teaching work, when there is a Bahá'í lecture given in a colored college, the new white believers and some of the near believers can be taken to hear it and thus meet those among whom they will later on form classes. This they are glad to do. So that two-fold method of opening these states to the Faith, it would seem to me (and the workers at Vogel Park [where a conference had been held]) to continue to hold lecture at public places (hotels, for instance) where the finest type of white people will come, and then carry on with those who attend. At the same time have lectures in the colored colleges. The splendid work that Dorothy Baker has been doing in this latter field, is ideal.

Your precious letter of Dec. 24th, which reached me April 9th, was a great, an inexpressible joy to this servant. O Shoghi Effendi if you only knew how utterly I long to serve you perfectly – improve especially the quality of my service. I want nothing else but this, to render ever greater and more valuable services to my last breath. Nothing else matters. Will you forgive me if I have overstepped in writing so frankly of my conclusions about the most desirable method of teaching in the South? Your kind and encouraging words in your letter are like food for the spirit. Howard is with me and at times I am very aware of him. He assists me and others who have called to him on many occasions. Will you please pray that nothing shall prevent this servant from rendering those loftier services which will be pleasing to Baha'u'llah.

Deep love and prayers for our Guardian.[44]

When Shoghi Effendi responded in a letter written on his behalf, he conveyed important principles which guided the work from then on:

> He was very happy to hear of the wonderful progress the Cause is making in the South, and shares your hope that the important Assemblies in Mississippi, Arkansas, and Alabama may be firmly established before 1944.
>
> Regarding the whole manner of teaching the Faith in the South: The Guardian feels that, although the greatest consideration should be shown the feelings of white people in the South whom we are teaching, under no circumstances should we discriminate in their favour, consider them more valuable to the Cause than their Negro fellow-Southerners, or single them out to be taught the Message first. To pursue such a policy, however necessary and even desirable it may superficially seem, would be to compromise the true spirit of our Faith, which permits us to make no such distinctions

in offering its tenets to the world. The Negro and white races should be offered, simultaneously, on a basis of equality, the message of Bahá'u'lláh. Rich or poor, known or unknown, should be permitted to hear of this Holy Faith in this, humanity's greatest hour of need.

This does not mean that we should go against the laws of the state, pursue a radical course which will stir up trouble, and cause misunderstanding. On the contrary, the Guardian feels that, where no other course is open, the two races should be taught separately until they are fully conscious of the implications of being a Bahá'í, and then be confirmed and admitted to voting membership. Once, however, this has happened they cannot shun each other's company, and feel the Cause is like other Faiths in the South, with separate Black and white compartments.

Even in places where the two races can meet together in the South, he feels it would be, in certain cases, preferable to teach them separately until they are fully confirmed and then bring them together.

Abdu'l-Baha Himself set the perfect example to the American believers in this matter – as in every other. He was tactful, but the essence of courage, and showed no favouritism to the white people as opposed to their dark-skinned compatriots. No matter how sincere and devoted the white believers of the South may be, there is no reason why they should be the ones to decide when and how the Negro Southerner shall hear of the Cause of God; both must be taught by whoever rises to spread the message in those parts.[45]

As he always did, the Guardian appended his own, personal note at the end of the letter:

> I am deeply touched by the noble sentiments you have expressed, and greatly value your activities, exertions, and above all the spirit that so powerfully animates you in His service. The work which your dear and distinguished husband has accomplished is unforgettable, and you are

now enriching the record of his past services. Persevere, be happy, and rest assured that I will continue to pray for you from the depths of my heart. Shoghi

Mabel wrote back to the Guardian almost immediately upon receipt of his letter. First, she thanked him for the 'clear exposition of the method of handling the racial situation in the South' and stated that she would 'endeavor to follow it with all its implications to the best of my ability when I return South. I can never get over the wonder and bounty of having someone in the world who really <u>knows</u> . . .'[46]

26
Mabel Joins Howard

Mabel arrived in Glenview, Illinois, on 25 April and stayed during the National Convention with her doctor daughter, Edris, who was to oversee her rest and recovery. Edris had been one of the first women to become a medical doctor when she graduated in 1927, overcoming the pioneering challenges of a male-dominated profession. (Starting in the 1950s she headed a large and ground-breaking clinical trial in Puerto Rico and used her medical and spiritual skills over the next 33 years there and in Mexico, Guatemala, Costa Rica, Panama, Chile, Uruguay and Brazil.)

Mabel spent a further week with Edris teaching in the Glenview–Rogers Park–Wilmette area. She had many things planned, including a summer school in the South, another in the virgin New England states and a return trip through Arkansas, Mississippi and Alabama.[1] But before she could begin her ambitious schedule, on 25 May Mabel found herself in the Woman's and Children's Hospital. Katherine True, her doctor, had discovered '2 fibroids and main spreadings, diseased appendix, and 2 [undecipherable] of loops of bowels'. Consequently, on the 28th, Katherine removed Mabel's uterus and appendix, as well as the fibroids. Mabel remained in the hospital until 5 June, when she moved back to Edris's home. Just five days later, Mabel was in the Evanston Hospital, where she stayed until 17 June.[2] Edris cabled Shoghi Effendi and he responded:

> He hopes that the dangers you recently encountered, owing to your operation and which your daughter cabled him about, are now all safely passed, and you are on the road to full recovery. Your valuable services can ill be spared at such a moment of historical importance to the Cause's progress

in America, and he hopes that you will follow strictly the advice of your doctors, and ensure a complete recovery of your forces.³

After a month's rest, Mabel was finally able to renew her travel teaching on 18 July, when she went to Madison, Wisconsin, and stayed with Mrs Clark. In another letter to the Guardian she detailed the teaching work planned for the rest of the summer:

> The plan now is for me to spend two weeks in the three Iowa cities where Mrs. Homer is working and has nice study classes going, to see if some of these fine people cannot be confirmed. There are 17, I understand, in the class in Cedar Rapids. Then to go on to Omaha, which is a problem Community and endeavor to bring in new blood, by putting on a Campaign. Dr. Katherine True, my surgeon, say that I should not use campaign methods for six months anyway, but can teach in ways which do not require such strenuous commitments. It is difficult to know what to do, as you told me to follow the advice of my doctors and yet the need seems so great and one is tempted to feel the request of the N.T.C. should be followed and that, if I trust Baha'u'llah and depend upon Him, that he will carry me through and strengthen this servant to do his work.
>
> After Omaha, the N.T.C. wants me to put on a campaign in Louisville in October. Please pray that I shall be guided in this matter, and that Baha'u'llah will give me adequate strength to do whatever He wishes me to do. I have written the Committee quoting your advice and the doctor's suggesting less strenuous methods for the fall anyway, but I felt under such an obligation to them to help them to carry out their plans, since they have continued my teaching allowance, through the first two months of my illness, which is enabling me to pay off, nearly, the large hospital bills incurred.⁴

Mabel stayed in Madison for six weeks, but was worried about the pending travel and her poor health. A diary entry for 17

August reads: 'Also let us put this problem of health and strength for the coming teaching trip, the baggage problem, the packing and clothes problem and the book project in His Hands – <u>trusting</u> Him to handle each one – and concentrate on building the spiritual reservoir so that work may be accomplished with ease and simplicity proceeding from the inner world with less out effort'.[5]

In September, the National Teaching Committee sent Mabel a proposed schedule of her activities up to Riḍván 1943. The schedule included:

1-15 September – Possible assistance in Iowa
15 September to 15 October – Campaign in Omaha
15 October to 15 December – Louisville
1 January to 15 March – West Virginia
15 March to 30 April – Circuit or other assistance.[6]

Cedar Rapids, Iowa

On 3 September, Mabel left Madison for Glenview. She spoke at the House of Worship on the 6th, then travelled to Davenport, Iowa, the next day. On the 8th she addressed an audience of 30, departing on the 9th for Cedar Rapids, Iowa, arriving on 10 September. Ruth Moffett had opened Cedar Rapids to the Faith previously and brought in the first believers. When Mabel arrived, she followed up on Ruth's work and had joyous success. A number of people accepted the Faith, including Mr Dunn, who accepted Bahá'u'lláh during this campaign and was 'like a force of nature'. Mabel thought that if he didn't lose 'this first fine rapture' and was deepened, he would render 'outstanding service to the Cause and it may be worth all it cost'.[7]

On 11 October, Mabel left Cedar Rapids for St. Louis to visit her son Colston and his wife Sheila. She wrote that she had a 'Beautiful time with them – got much closer'. On the 15th, she left for Louisville, Kentucky.[8]

Louisville, Kentucky

In Louisville, Mabel gave her standard six-lecture series on 'The Rebirth of Mankind' between 22 October and 9 November. In her report to the National Teaching Committee, she wrote, 'The first lecture was very well received though the attendance was unfortunately not too good, twenty-five being present. However forty came out to the second lecture and we are hoping that the audience will continue to build.'[9] Even so, Mabel was very thankful to the Concourse on High, writing in her diary: 'Thank you! Thank you! Thank you! It is so wonderful to be so conscious of the "Invisible Helpers" – and to know where to turn in one's hour of great need.'[10] Olivia Kelsey and Sara Ellen were assisting her, which was very good because Cedar Rapids had drained her strength. Mabel thought highly of Sara and expected her to become a 'campaign lecturer'. Her second lecture included an 'open-minded minister' who asked 'many excellent questions and was most friendly'.[11]

There was a constant stream of requests from places for Mabel to visit to next. In November, Nellie Roche was suggesting that she spend two weeks in Knoxville and then Birmingham before going to Texas. The National Teaching Committee proposed a busy schedule, but Mabel resisted, writing that Louisville had to be set on a solid foundation and have a strong Bahá'í guide before she could leave.[12]

On 22 December 1942, the National Teaching Committee wrote to Mabel about her reports that her health had suddenly deteriorated: 'We were all distressed to receive the news in your letter of December 15th [not in the authors' possession] that you are not well! Certainly there is no point in remaining in Louisville if the climate is detrimental to your well being.'[13] They then continued straight in to what she should do next:

> We discussed your letter in detail at our meeting Sunday and in view of the fact that Texas is not one of the virgin areas, we do not think that could be justified in developing a special project for that state, especially now when the

funds are so low. New Mexico, however, is a virgin area, and while Albuquerque has at present enough members to reconstitute the Assembly, we are not certain they will all remain. There is need for new contacts and we believe you could do some excellent work there. We have therefore, written to the member of the Regional Committee who lives in Albuquerque asking her to discuss the matter with the group and to wire us whether they would like to have you come for a month right after January 1st . . .

It is our thought that after you have spent a month in Albuquerque, you might then be able to go over to Houston, Texas and give some help there.[14]

Mabel finally left Louisville on 4 January and headed for Albuquerque.

Albuquerque, New Mexico

Mabel was in Albuquerque by 6 January 1943. The morning after her first night there was quite an experience. The room Kathryn Frankland had booked for her was a 'nice one, sunny and on the first floor' and it had a 'private bath':

> When I got there I found that the private bath meant that I had to traverse the downstairs hall, the dining room, the kitchen, the back porch . . . and then into the bathroom which connected with the couple's bedroom on the other side. When I assayed the bathroom on getting up the next morning, I had to pass thru the kitchen, as I said, where the man of the house was performing the intimate act of shaving. I had debated for quite a while whether I should just jump into my clothes and go up to Kathryn's (a block off) for my bath. However the shaving act finished me, and the dash out into the cold world. So I called Kathryn and she got Dr. Morris to come around and rescue me. I discovered signs in my rooms . . . saying what you could and could not do, with the emphasis on the 'not'. So I escaped from the

'Boarding-school', so to speak, where the woman sat in the dining room and watched you every time you came out of your room. She was a mammoth person . . .'[15]

Mabel spent the next three nights sleeping on Kathryn's couch. She ended up finding a tourist cabin at Wallace Court and was delighted: 'I see the sun rise every morning out of my east window, and sit out in the sun on warm days . . . and it's all mine and alone, which is about heaven to me . . . Also I can chant alone. It is out on the Mesa and I can walk for miles over toward the mountains.'[16]

New Mexico was a completely new kind of country for her:

Well, here I am in the Indian and Mexican country of the far west. Such color you have never seen unless you have been here. Not only the brilliant and deep blue of the sky, with the sun shining hot and bright most of the time, but also in the many brilliant colors worn by the people. Navajo rugs, Indian shawls in flaming colors – cream or light tan or gray coats with bright colored patterns in Indian design running thru them. On the streets and in the Dime stores you rub shoulder with Indians – men with yellow or green ribbons tied around their heads, women in many colored clothes, the cutest babies – some of them really beautiful and everywhere around you, you hear Mexican Spanish. There is one Movie Theatre having only plays in Spanish. We saw Tyrone Power in 'Blood and Sand'. It was not the Spanish theatre, but it is a Mexican subject – a bull fight and Tyrone is a successful Matador, so the theatre was filled with Mexicans, keeping up an undertone of conversation. When certain Spanish words were used, boys in the audience would call out in glee, repeating the word. Quite an experience. Kathryn Frankland and I were together.[17]

Though exhausted, Mabel wanted to start her usual lecture campaign. On 23 January, she was given a budget of $50 for what she thought would be the campaign. The Committee quickly let her know, however, that because of Mabel's health they were not suggesting a campaign – they were worried that the work would be too strenuous for her at that time. They suggested that she spend her time consolidating the contacts being made by Kathryn Frankland and unifying the community. The Committee wrote that they were 'really growing quite concerned about the general feeling that does exist that at the moment there are nine Bahá'ís in the place the Bahá'ís are free to move on'. They stressed that the pioneers should 'remain at their post until the Assemblies are firmly held. As a matter of fact there should be no thought whatever of their moving away at any time.'[18] In spite of the Committee's wishes, Mabel began her lecture series on 29 January, giving three lectures each week to an average of 50 people each time.[19]

In March, Rúhíyyih Khánum wrote to Mabel and included some photographs of Howard that her father, Sutherland Maxwell, had taken. She suggested one of them might be appropriate for the upcoming *Bahá'í World* 'In Memoriam' article about Howard.[20]

On 3 April 1943, five people declared their Faith in Bahá'u'lláh in Albuquerque, '2 months and 5 days from my first lecture', Mabel wrote in her journal. Three days later, struggling with her deteriorating health, Mabel awoke to a different feeling about her body:

> This morning overwhelmed and crushed by a multiplicity of things and complexity of situations – suddenly a flame of passionate anger flowed thru me and a light found and a power was released. I am master of this being . . . I am the trustee under God for this instrument which He has been training and polishing . . . thru the years. I am the trustee under God for it. It is my responsibility to hold it in line, to keep the entire mechanism functioning smoothly for His needs. He gives me the power and intelligence to do this, the power of master over this complex mechanism. He expects an integrated and usable instrument to His Hand. I have to deliver it to Him – continuously.[21]

1943 National Convention

Various people had encouraged Mabel to attend the National Convention that year, but she felt that she was too tired to go. In the end, Mabel flew out of Albuquerque on 27 April to attend the Convention. Later, Edris and Colston wrote:

> She wasn't coming to this Convention because she was too exhausted, but we persuaded her at the last minute and at the last minute she flew to Chicago from Albuquerque, getting a tremendous thrill, as she would, out of the long trip by air. This convention and was particularly wonderful to her because she saw so many of her spiritual children strong and active in the faith. She spoke of this many times. She remarked, 'How thrilling to see how they grow from year to year.'[22]

Mabel's time at the Convention was the mirror image of Howard's last Convention. Everyone wanted to see her and speak with her:

> Everywhere she turned during those few days people surrounded her, each insisting, 'But you must spend some time with me . . .' Of course that was impossible, since everywhere she looked were those who had heard about the Faith through her efforts – dozens and dozens of them. It must have been a tremendous source of inner joy to see gathered under one roof so many to whom she had given new life. She had once said to Sylvia King while teaching in Omaha, Nebraska, 'I have lived longer than you have so I will tell you this; some day you won't remember the times when you were sad, you will only remember the times when you helped the Cause of God.' This convention surely roused those memories.[23]

The end in Oklahoma City

Mabel left Wilmette on 6 May and travelled to O'Fallon, Illinois, near St Louis, Missouri, where she visited Colston and Sheila. On the 10th she continued to Kansas City and arrived in Oklahoma City the next day.[24] The friends there had been requesting her presence for months and she was finally there. Mabel had hoped to rest for a couple of weeks before starting her teaching work, but so many people seemed to need her that the time was filled with activities.

Mabel gave the first of her lectures, entitled 'A Blueprint for an Enduring World Government', on 26 May at the Biltmore Hotel. Edris later wrote: 'The friends there said it was a magnificent talk. One woman, a stranger, remarked, "Why, she's an angel." Just before this lecture she remarked that she had never felt stronger or more able to carry on.'[25]

Mabel's body, however, was struggling to keep up the pace:

> The next day she became ill (intestinal trouble) and the following lecture, which was on Sunday, had to be cancelled at the last minute after the people had gathered (she had hoped until the last minute that she could make it and was determined to do it and even called me long distance for a prescription to give her strength to go through with it.) The people were told that she would give the next one the following Tuesday. When she was told that they were expecting her and that it had been arranged she, through the power of prayer only, got up and gave it and then went back to bed. This lecture was, 'The Origin of Man and His Destiny'. One woman said she would give anything to hear every word or have a copy, it was so inspiring. The third lecture was to be Thursday. She planned on it because she was sure she would be well by then. She knew $50.00 had been spent on this campaign. The friends in this city had had a series of disappointments and setbacks and tests in their teaching efforts. She somehow managed to get up again on Thursday night and gave a lecture even though it

was obvious to the audience that she was not very strong, but the friends say that nevertheless it was a good talk.[26]

Mabel struggled to give those three lectures, each one more physically difficult then the last. After the third, she finally admitted the reality of her situation. Where Howard had eagerly looked forward to his departure from the physical world, Mabel was upset that she couldn't keep up her teaching schedule. Edris wrote:

> Following [the third] talk, she realized that she now had to give up and told the doctor she was willing to go to the hospital.
> In the hospital she grew steadily weaker and I flew down there Tuesday the 8th of June. She was tickled to death to see me and she was sure that because I was there that everything was now going to be all right, and she would get well. She said, 'Well, Edris, it's a good thing you are here to tell me I'm getting better because I'm feeling worse every day.' She remarked a number of times, 'Oh, just to sleep, sleep, sleep!' In other words, it just seemed that her whole body cried out for rest. During those first days her greatest concern was the fact that she had fallen down on her work. She kept remarking that the friends here had spent money on this and they had counted on it so, and now she had let them down. 'Why,' she said, 'I've let the Guardian down, I've let Bahá'u'lláh down.' I assured her that I would certainly carry on and finish the work here, so she outlined, in a measure, just what I should give them. She particularly stressed the Administration and the Temple that she had not touched on, even discussed various of the interested ones and how they were coming along. From then on she grew weaker and developed one severe complication after another. Her greatest joy during these days when she was awake, was to have me read the creative word and when she was very restless and uncomfortable it would have an immediate relaxing and calming effect. She kept saying, 'As

my Lord wills. If He wants me here and has work for me to do here or if He wants me there – it's all right, too.'[27]

On her last morning in this material world, 18 June, Mabel told Edris, with great difficulty,

> 'I – want – to go – home.' Several days before, I had told her I would get her some kind of place of her own where she could keep her things and where she could come back to rest when she desired. Her whole face lit up at this and she said, 'Oh, a home! Imagine having a home, a place to keep my things where I could always go and be alone. Imagine having a home!' I had not realized what it meant to have no root, to be always on the move.[28]

Colston had arrived just the previous afternoon. That final morning, Mabel kept trying to talk, but it was very difficult for her and Colston told her:

> 'You don't have to talk, Mother. I can hear you. Oh, mother, you are so beautiful – you have never been so beautiful!' and she was. She looked up at us and said, 'My children!' We said, 'Yes, Mother, we are both here.' After a pause, 'I have many children – but there is so much work to be done.' Colston replied, 'Your children will carry on the work for you, mother.' After a while she slipped into unconsciousness but was still here. Colston read the prayers for the departed over and over. I read from the Gleanings that beautiful passage on page 155, again and again. It seemed as though she somehow just couldn't get away. We wondered if it was some last step she was to take and then we wondered if it was something that we were to attain. Colston said that he felt the McHenrys were supposed to be there, so we called them and they came down. We read two prayers and in the middle of the second one, she ascended.[29]

As Edris walked down the hospital corridor,

There suddenly flashed before my inner eyes a scene that I shall never forget. Here was my mother, pretty as a picture and full of energy and happiness, walking toward a group of people who were holding out their arms to her and smiling. She was being welcomed by them. Of this group, I was able to recognize about eight people who had been close to her in this life and had passed on. Some of them, that I recall were: Howard Ives, May Maxwell, Grace Ober and Elizabeth Greenleaf.

A few seconds later the scene disappeared. I walked on. I couldn't let myself cry then because I felt that I would spoil her welcoming party in eternity.[30]

Mabel's soul had flown at 8:19 p.m. The meeting she had been supposed to address was to start just minutes later, at 8:30, and the audience was there and waiting. Colston and Edris went down and gave the lecture:

There was no other possible thing for us to do but to go directly to the hotel and carry on. To let her down now, we felt, would have marred the joy of her reunion in the realms above. (All I could think of was Howard, Grace Ober, May Maxwell, Keith Ransom-Kehler, Martha Root and many others, all with outstretched arms and beaming faces, welcoming her.)[31]

Shoghi Effendi cabled his deep sense of loss to the Cause:

Profoundly deplore loss self-sacrificing, distinguished teacher Mabel Ives. Manifold contributions before and since inception of Seven-Year Plan outstanding, memorable, highly meritorious. Assure daughter deepest loving sympathy, prayers. Abiding felicity crowning noble labors.[32]

A letter written on behalf of the Guardian to the Regional Teaching Committee said:

She was truly an outstanding servant of the Cause, and one whose example all would do well to emulate. Her self-sacrifice, devotion to the interest of the Faith, and tireless teaching activity were truly exemplary, and the Guardian hopes that her many spiritual children and admirers will arise and follow in her footsteps.

The many seeds she sowed, the new centers she helped to bring into existence, the loving and wise manner in which she handled her fellow men, are all achievements and characteristics which distinguished her Bahá'í service and won for her a high place in the ranks of the American believers.

The Guardian feels that the highest tribute the friends can pay to her memory is to do as she did and show forth the same love, devotion and enthusiasm which was hers.

He has been very encouraged this last year to see the way the friends have been striding forward with the teaching work, and truly overcoming through faith and determination, every obstacle in their path.[33]

Shoghi Effendi added in his own hand:

May the Beloved enable you to follow in the footsteps of that beloved, that indefatigable and exemplary handmaid of Bahá'u'lláh and carry on the work which she has so nobly and so energetically and so devotedly accomplished in the service of our glorious Faith. Your true brother, Shoghi[34]

At her funeral service on 20 June, 50 people came. Most were not Bahá'ís, but had been affected by Mabel. Captain McHenry conducted the service and summed up Mabel's passing, saying:

This is not a funeral. This is a Memorial Service. This is not death. This is the beginning of eternal life. Therefore, it is not a time for grieving or lamenting. This is a time for rejoicing.[35]

Letters poured in to Mabel's daughter, Edris, from all over North America. One close friend wrote:

'My eyes streamed with tears to read in your letter that she felt she had failed everyone, including Bahá'u'lláh. Oh Edie – how <u>could</u> she feel that? How could she?? With so many radiant hearts from one end of Canada and the U.S.A. to the other testifying to the contrary!! So rich a harvest for her careful planting!'[36]

Alvin Blum, later to become Knight of Bahá'u'lláh to the Solomon Islands, wrote:

I know she is reaping reward after reward for being a Martyr and Apostle of the "Blessed Perfection". Your mother was kind and lovable to everyone she came in contact with. Knowing your Mother was really one of the most beautiful experiences in my life. I have always felt that the instructions and love your Mother gave me was really the turning point in my life along spiritual lines.'[37]

Kenneth Christian, who would also go on to become a Knight of Bahá'u'lláh, wrote:

I can personally witness to so many things you have said in your account [of Mabel's passing]. It was during my college years (I think the winter of 1934–35) that Mabel and Howard were in Albany for a brief time. They had taken a little furnished apartment – were selling books at the time. They invited me to bring down one evening a group of college friends. It was a glorious evening – rich discussion of the Faith and its implications . . . . . Later, I found out that they had spent their last dollar in order to buy refreshments for that evening.

There are so many of us who will never forget how both Howard and Mabel lived the Faith.[38]

David Hofman, who had just published the English edition of *Portals to Freedom*, wrote:

Your letter arrived this morning. It was a considerable shock, especially as I had only written a joint letter to you both a few days ago, and sent copies of the book. What a wonderful thing it is to be a Bahá'í, Edie. You would never have the assurance of good and bounty, at times like this, without it. Our relationships are considerably deepened, right down to the plane of reality, and separation is that much harder, but all the other wisdom and sensitivity that hedges Bahá'í relationships more than compensate for the increased feeling.

It seems strange. I never thought of her as growing old or passing on. After leaving Montreal, only a few days old [in the Faith], she was one of the first Bahá'ís I met, and her warmth and inner strength made a deep impression on me. She, and dear Howard, were so kind and helpful and understanding. But I always remember your mother for her radiance; it came from an inner knowledge and gave the impression of competence. She has helped us all, and will continue to do so, and how wise it will be, when our time comes, to find her ready to help us again in a strange world.[39]

Laura Davis, writing for the Local Spiritual Assembly of Toronto, where Mabel had spent so much time and effort, also wrote to Edris:

We held a memorial at our last Feast for your dear mother, and each one present spoke about her friendship and love, about those wonderful things which she had left with us, remembrances which will always live in our hearts. There were many present who remembered with great joy that she was the person who first brought them into the Baha'i Faith, so the joy and happiness of their future lives will just add to the mountain of good which she has left in the world as her memorial.

You see, Toronto felt in a special way that Mable [sic] Ives was, and always would be, a part of its community.

The fact that she entered the presence of Abdul Baha and Bahaullah does not take her from us, for she is nearer now than when she was in Memphis or Little Rock. We feel her with us often . . . What a power must that teaching team be now, Daddy Howard and Rizwanea! Here they were powerful and stirring, and now that is augmented a thousand fold.[40]

Howard and Mabel, a powerful teaching team on this earthly plane, were now a powerful teaching team in the spiritual worlds.

Epilogue
Lives Well Lived

Mabel became a Bahá'í in 1899 because of an inexplicable but strong impulse to get off a streetcar at what seemed to be a random place. Howard became a Bahá'í because of an inexplicable but strong urge to meet 'Abdu'l-Bahá alone. Howard and Mabel met at a breakfast table during the National Convention in 1919. Howard's first reaction to Mabel was not to fall instantly in love, but to see the job Mabel had as a way to better teach the Faith. He therefore decided to give up a $10,000-a-year job for the travelling salesman work that Mabel was doing. Both chose their jobs so that they could teach the Faith. But that job decision brought them into further contact.

Both were married at the time of their meeting, but Mabel's husband was demanding a divorce. In deep turmoil, Mabel turned to Bahá'u'lláh and completely submitted to His desire – which led to her husband's increasing and successful demand for that divorce. Howard's wife had left him years before because he had become a Bahá'í. In what may have been one of the first times a personal problem had been taken to a Local Spiritual Assembly in America, Howard asked the Assembly for advice on what to do. Before they began their consultation on the question, the Assembly asked if Howard and Mabel would accept their decision, whatever it might be. They both immediately agreed to submit and obey. Howard was allowed his divorce and he and Mabel were married in November 1920.

Financial failure in the year after their marriage led to their momentous decision to give up house and home for a future life of travel teaching. For the next 20 years, they went wherever work or the Faith blew them, never financially stable, but growing spiritually by leaps and bounds as they continually submitted to whatever God wanted of them.

EPILOGUE: LIVES WELL LIVED

When Howard's health began to decline and he was less able to maintain the rigors of the traveling life, his ability to write came to light by bringing the couple to a monetarily disastrous visit to Knoxville, but one during which he was hired to write publicity pieces for the Tennessee Valley Authority. That led to *Portals to Freedom*.

For the last six years of their lives together, Howard focused on his writing and Mabel became the powerhouse of a travel teacher, developing a method of proclamation that proved highly successful. She became the public face of the couple, but Howard was always there to confirm and deepen those whose interest she ignited.

Howard's health declined rapidly over those last years, but he looked on it as a confirmation that Bahá'u'lláh was accepting all his sacrifices for the Cause of God. Succumbing to increasing deafness and advancing blindness, Howard sacrificed himself with delight. Mabel's health, too, became worse over those last years, but she refused to slow down and get the rest many insisted that she needed. She died 'with her boots on', never stopping until that final morning when her body could no longer arise.

During those many years, Howard and Mabel spent days, weeks and months in New York, Pennsylvania, New Jersey, Maine, New Hampshire, Illinois, Wisconsin, Minnesota, Ontario, New Brunswick, Nova Scotia, Ohio, Iowa, Nebraska, North Dakota, Kentucky, Tennessee, Alabama, Georgia, Louisiana, and Arkansas. After Howard's passing, Mabel went to Mississippi, Alabama, New Mexico and Oklahoma. All in the path of service to the Cause of God.

Howard taught the Faith to his nurse and other patients while on his death bed and Mabel travel taught literally until she dropped. Eleven future Knights of Bahá'u'lláh, one Hand of the Cause and many long-time national and international pioneers came in to the Bahá'í Faith through the selfless dedication of Howard and Mabel. They were one soul in two bodies and one of their greatest desires was that their physical union in the material world would become an eternal union in the spiritual worlds of God.

Howard and Mabel sacrificed their all for the good pleasure of 'Abdu'l-Bahá and Bahá'u'lláh. They did, indeed, accomplish 'Very Great Things'.

Appendix I
Two Talks by Howard Colby Ives

The Coming of the Promised One

Address by Howard C. Ives of New York City, delivered at the Eighth Session of the Bahá'í Congress at Hotel McAlpin, New York City, Wednesday afternoon, 30 April 1919.[1]

Did you ever stand upon a high point and see the sun rise? I have stood among the foothills of the Rocky Mountains and watched the dawn break over the hills, the morning star gradually dimming in its glory, the faint first rosy light creeping up the horizon, and then gradually, above the mountains, the first rim of the radiant glory of the orb; then lifting, and lifting, and flooding the earth with its glory. Not in all nature is there such a sight; nothing will compare with that wonderful miracle. I have heard it said that if it happened only once a year people would be on their knees for days before, longing, searching, for the first sign, hoping for that coming. Imagine, friends, if it only happened once every thousand years. Stretch the wings of your imagination and think of the legends that would be handed down from father to son, and son to son, from generation to generation and think how they would watch the constellations of the sky – for praise be to God, even in the darkest night, there are stars in the sky – and think how the traditions would have mentioned that, before the dawning, a morning star would appear, and when that morning star arose above the horizon and gradually found its way toward the zenith, think how men's hearts would leap with joy, and they would say, 'He is coming! He is coming! I have seen his sign in the sky!' And then think what a dawning that would be when the sunrise came once only every thousand years. You could not stand and wait for it. The father would see the first faint gleam upon the horizon, and the sons would see it gradually grow and grow, and the grandsons would see the first faint roseate tinge upon the mountain tops, and the great-grandsons would look and long for the orb to appear, and the great-great-grandsons would see it gradually rise above the horizon.

My friends, there is not one single thing in all this world that is not a symbol of the spiritual reality, and what I have just painted in words for you is an actual fact. The Sun of Reality rises only once every thousand years or so, the stars in the heaven precede his dawning, the hearts of men become weary through the night as they watch the stars in the sky and long for the coming of that which the stars promise. Throughout the ages it has been said that in the time of the coming of the Sun of Truth there shall be a new heaven and a new earth. What does that mean? Certainly not that this sky shall be changed and this earth beneath our feet altered. No! The sky that we see and the earth beneath our feet are but symbols again, just as the sun is a symbol and the stars are symbols. The sky is a symbol of the heaven of religion and the earth is a symbol of the hearts that are softened for the springtime.

Many thousand years ago a Sun appeared – we call his name Abraham – a Sun of Reality rose gradually according to the promise; and the star – I don't mean the material star, I mean the heart and the longing thoughts of men, longing just then as we do now – and the constellations, arose with him, thus a new heaven appeared. Abraham, Isaac, Jacob, David, Solomon, Isaiah, Jeremiah, Amos, Ezekiel were the stars of that heaven, they were the constellations appearing with that promised One.

And then Moses came, bringing with him his own group.

Then Jesus Christ came. Think of the stars that rose with him. John, Stephen, Paul, Timothy, Mary Magdalene, Mary the mother of Jesus, Mary and Martha the sisters, Luke the physician, Matthew the publican, Peter the fisherman! Ah, they are the illuminating lights that come with that promised One, they are the stars of his heaven, and they, after the sun has set, illuminate the dark sky throughout the age, then gradually dwindling in glory until the sun again rises. But when the sun appears from the horizon of the vernal equinox, on the twenty-first of March, it brings the glory of the springtime; so when the Sun of Reality rises, He brings healing on His wings, and a new springtime comes to the human heart.

Just as the farmer goes out and ploughs and harrows the hard soil, so the Spirit of God moves upon the hearts, and pain, sorrow and suffering plough the hearts. Nations tremble because of starvation, famine, agonies and tears! That is why the earth is filled with woe – woe, woe, woe – when the promised One appears. Praise be to God, for without that woe our hearts would still be hard, just as the ground is hard until with the softening of the rain and the warmth of the sun and the plough and the harrow, it is broken to pieces, in order that the seed may fall and fructify and grow and bring forth an hundred fold.

My friends, praise be to God, the promised One hath come again. We have waited long throughout the centuries: our hearts have grown into stone, our hearts have become frozen, our hearts have fallen low in woe and weeping. Praise be to God, he hath come again! He hath come again! The Sun of Reality hath risen. O that isn't all, for there is a new heaven, and there is also a new earth. What good would the sun be? What good would the crossing of the equinox be in the early spring were there not an earth to feel its rays? Of what earthly use is it, if the promised One, the Sun of Reality, dawns and there are no hearts to receive the light? Praise be to God, there are always hearts to receive the light. We are His creatures, the children of His hand, the offspring of His love. We long for Him and He longs for us. Now in this great Day of God the hearts are turning unto Him.

Was it yesterday that our dear sister, Mrs Maxwell, quoted the beautiful words from Daniel that 'the wise shall shine as the sun and they that turn many to righteousness as the stars forever and ever.' There is your perfect symbol. That is the ancient version, the old version, but the revised version has it much more beautiful. 'They that be teachers shall shine as the sun; they that turn many to righteousness as the stars, forever and ever.' Bahá'u'lláh glorified God in his wonderful Book, *The Íqhán*: 'At that time the signs of the Son of Man shall appear in the heavens.' That is, the promised Beauty and substance of life shall come from the court of the invisible into the visible world. That is the coming of the promised One; that is the coming of the Son of Man; that is the dawning of the signs in the heavens. 'The appearance', as he says again in another passage, 'when the face of the promised One and the beauty of the adored One shall descend from heaven riding upon a cloud.' That is, the divine Beauty will appear from the heavens of the Supreme Will in the human temple.

So my friends, change your point of view for a moment from thinking of the heavens above and the rising of the sun and its glory; change your point of view to the divine Beauty appearing in the human form here on earth. Imagine the divine Beauty descending from heaven 'riding on a cloud', that is the human form, the cloud hiding him from our eyes, nevertheless dwelling in the human temple, seeing with human eyes, walking with human feet, eating, drinking, suffering, longing – the divine Beauty nevertheless, the promised Beauty and substance of life! Think of those words, the promised Beauty, the very substance of life, appearing in a human temple. This is the Sun of Reality I am talking about, shining upon the human earth, the earth of human hearts.

Ah, my friends, make the picture, for his human temple is the Sun of Reality, and within that human temple, which is nothing but a cloud, the Sun is shining to those whose eyes can see it. Shall he shine in our hearts? Shall he bring forth fruits meet for repentance, as Jesus said? Shall the wheat of divine love grow? Shall the fruits of glorious perfection appear? Shall the clouds of mercy from the divine heaven pour upon ready hearts the drops of his mercy and the fire of his love? Shall there appear from this earth the great and glorious results worthy of such a Sun from such a heaven? Praise be to God, I don't even have to ask, for the new earth has come.

When the sun rises in the springtime, when the sun gradually crosses the line, what do we see? Do we see all at once the earth burst into beauty and perfection? Do we see all at once the fruits of the harvest appear? Oh, no, we see a blade of grass here and there, a little green leaf, then the rest; we see a tree just beginning to show its buds – but these are the new earth. All the cold and hard world does not exist. I don't care how many millions of dead leaves there are, the one blade of grass, the one green leaf is the new earth. And so, show me one soul responding to the new Sun; show me one life ready to lay itself down in self-abnegation and perfect renunciation; show me one martyr to the Sun of Truth; show me one who is placing heart and soul on the altar of self-sacrifice, purity and love that is the new earth! That is all the earth there is. Let the rest go, it doesn't exist. It is dark and cold, it is dead.

Does it exist? Do you say that the dead bodies in the graves exist in comparison with the people walking on the street? I tell you, my friends, all those who do not know Bahá'u'lláh, and his glory, all those who do not turn to him in this new age, simply do not exist. On the other hand, verily, they are in their graves and they know it not. Arise, arise, O earth of human hearts! Arise, burst the prison bars, come out from the cage! Be ye resurrected from the dead bodies of self and desire and ascend to that station for which ye were created! When the Sun of Reality arises in the human temple, it creates effects upon the human hearts just as the sun does upon the material earth, and results appear. He speaks, and it is done.

My friends, think, think of these last four days you and I have been listening – don't let us lose the figure – you and I have been seeing the rays of the Sun of Truth shining upon the earth and results appearing. Go ye into all the world, shine as the Sun of Truth, carry to all the world the news that rays of the Sun of Reality shining upon the world shall transform it, proclaim to them that the Prince of Peace hath come, that never again shall there be war amongst nations, never again shall there be war between creeds and classes and sects, never again shall labor and capital be arrayed against each other, never again shall there be loveless homes and divorce courts, never again shall there be strife between children in the streets, never again shall there be anything that shall mar the beauty of the love of God in the human heart. That is the proclamation – and it is done. What difference does it make if it doesn't come at once? Does that alter the fact? We who see the sun rise and cross the equinox every springtime, do we say, because the whole world does not burst into beauty and harvest at once, that it won't come? I tell you the first blade of grass is the whole thing, to anyone who sees. And so when the Word of God goes forth, the thing is done.

Arise! Arise! O ye chosen of the world, and be ye the divine helpers of God, says Bahá'u'lláh. How? Praise be to God, the command not only goes forth but the way of development is shown not only in words but in example. Bahá'u'lláh says, 'Though ye cut off my limbs, yet shall the love of God not depart out of my heart. Verily, I was created for sacrifice, therefore do I glory over the world.' Do you want then to know how you shall glory over the world, how you shall establish the Kingdom of God in hearts, how you shall carry out the teachings of these blessed Tablets that we are listening to? Here is the recipe, 'Though they cut off my limbs, yet shall the love of God not depart out of my heart. I was created for sacrifice, therefore do I glory over the world!' Those who believe in Bahá'u'lláh, those who have turned their hearts to the Center of His Covenant, those who love the Blessed Perfection, were created by the Sun of Reality in the human temple for sacrifice, and by sacrifice shall they glory over the world as He did and establish the Kingdom of the promised One in the hearts and souls.

'The blessed person of the promised One is interpreted in the holy books as the Lord of Hosts, i.e., the heavenly armies! By heavenly armies those souls are intended who are free from the human world, transformed into celestial spirits and have become divine angels.' There are your celestial armies. They who shall become divine angels, are those who have turned their backs upon the world, who were created by the love of God and His Blessed Beauty for sacrifice.

Alláh-u-Abhá!

The Underlying Unity of All Faiths

Talk given at the Bahá'í Congress and Convention of Temple Unity, Riḍván 1915.[2]

Abdul Baha, to whom several millions of people look as the inspired leader of the cause devoted to universal peace, unified government and the universal religion, has said:

> I come to America not to bring to you a new religion, but to rekindle the fading lights of your own faith, whatever its name may be. The truth behind all religions is one truth. The light within all lamps is one light.

It follows of necessity from the above simple statement, that the desires, hopes and prosperity of one man may stand as the desires, hopes and prosperity of all. The universe in which we exist is the home and origin of all; the earth we tread is the common grave of all. The materials of our bodies, our blood and skeleton, are absolutely alike. All the differences of languages, governments, colors and creeds are traceable to differences of environment, education, tradition and climate; that is to say, all the strife of man, all the warfare, in commerce, politics and society, are due to ignorance of common facts that might be well known, and to prejudice founded on misconception.

There are signs abroad that men are beginning to realize the oneness of humanity, and that this home is a universe. These signs indicate that a unified humanity is imminent . . .

There are three ways, broadly speaking, by which men express themselves in their relationship with one another and in their reaction upon experience: commerce, government and religion.

First, through commerce. It is evidenced by the signs of the times that at last men are understanding that no individual, no state, no nation can be prosperous by itself alone. Men have in vain tried to erect barriers to commerce, but the mere fact that they are dependent, for existence primarily, and for comforts and luxuries, upon the ease and freedom of commercial intercourse makes it certain that sooner or later such easy and untrammeled intercourse must be established. The reason men have not already comprehended this fact is because they have not known of the conditions under which other nations and peoples exist. Now, however, with the printing press and the widely spread newspaper, the telegraph, telephone and wireless telegraphy, in addition to extensive travel on steamships and the railroad, with increasing popular education in many countries of the world, the barrier of ignorance is being removed, and all men are being brought into intercommunication. As a consequence, commercial unification is being established, which soon or later is bound to bring about such practical results that commercial strife will disappear.

The second way by which men express their interrelation is through politics or government. Trade does not follow the flag; trade precedes it. Not trade, but war, is apt to follow it, for when the hand of the body politic says to the foot, 'I have no need of thee except to add to my well-being at thy expense', then war becomes necessary to hold the commerce that has been produced by the natural needs and development of men.

Trade between England and her American colonies was developed by the natural play of human forces. When an unnatural taxation on commerce was established, war followed, and a new flag displaced the Union Jack, representing new divisions and added possibilities of friction. Some generations later, when new lines of commerce and new ethical ideals had been accepted by the Northern states, but rejected by the South, an attempt was made by the South to establish a new division, and new national boundaries. This attempt was frustrated after tremendous expense of men and treasure, because it was realized that to permit a division of the federal state could lead only to commercial and national disintegration. The primary cause of the Civil War lay in the honest conviction of the South that the North threatened its commercial necessity, the institution of slavery. If that division of the nation had succeeded, there would have been many others, each increasing the possibility of friction; but it failed, and Northern and Southern states still form so united a group, that a hundred million persons live at peace within this great United States. The present war in Europe is demonstrating the opposite truth, that disunion means destruction. Men are learning, although still imperfectly, that in union there is strength, and that in union alone, lies the possibility of peace and prosperity. Thus does commercial unity find its only possible fruition in political unity.

The third relationship of great numbers of men is religion. Rightly understood, religion includes all other relationships. If it can be shown that religious unity among men is imminent, then we shall have the basis for a tremendous optimism, for all other unity will surely follow.

> Man must cut himself free from all prejudice and from the result of his own imagination, so that he may be able to search for truth unhindered. Truth is one in all religions, and by means of it the unity of the world can be realized.
>
> All the peoples have a fundamental belief in common. Being one, truth cannot be divided, and the differences that appear to exist among the nations only result from their attachment to prejudice. If only men would search out truth, they would find themselves united.

Abdul Baha declares that man must investigate truth independently and without bias. It is interesting to note the same sentiment in the Zend Avesta: 'It is for a decision as to religions, man and man, each individually for himself.'

And also Buddha taught his disciples: 'No doctrine is to be accepted because believed by one's father or grandfather . . . In your own mind you must judge.'

The answering impulse to make such investigation was for many of us in America first experienced during the memorable sessions of the World's Parliament of Religions at the Columbian Exposition in 1893. Swami Vivekananda, representing one of the great religions of India, in expressing appreciation of those noble souls who conceived that august assembly, said:

It was reserved for America to call, to proclaim to all quarters of the globe that the Lord is in every religion.

The Parliament of Religions has proved to the world that holiness, purity and charity are not the exclusive possessions of any church in the world, and that every system has produced men and women of the most exalted character.

It is not for me to prove the essential and underlying unity of all religious faiths, except in so far as I can do so by briefly referring to a few of their common teachings. This is not a matter for academic scholasticism. Nothing is true fundamentally that does not when uttered find a responsive sympathetic chord in the heart of the listener. 'The truth behind all religions is one truth. The light within all lamps is one light.' It is the light itself, and the light alone, that can illumine the heart and mind, not mere scholarly references to that light. However, while not urging it as proof, a useful purpose may be served and the way cleared of misconception by indicating some of the striking points of similarity that may be discovered through a sincere study of all systems of religion . . .

Because truth is one, men find by the study of comparative religion that the founders of all great religious movements have taught the same essentials. The superficial appurtenances of their teachings, however, have varied in accordance with the needs of the time and with the material and spiritual development of the people to whom they were given. In the days of Moses, for instance, when men were still elemental and there were no courts of law, the command, 'An eye for an eye, a tooth for a tooth,' was necessary and wise, but when the world had developed until the Roman law could be made operative, courts of justice were established, and this law of payment in kind was no longer necessary. With the coming of Christ the law of forgiveness was announced. This is true of many other customs which time does not permit a thorough explanation. It is more important to show that certain basic laws are common to all religions, and that the recognition of the necessity for these laws is inherent in every human being.

The similarity in the fundamental teachings of the great religions is striking. This has already been illustrated in the comparison of the Golden Rule and other moral sentiments as expressed in the various faiths of the world. It is also seen in the inculcation of the virtues of self-sacrifice, gentleness, justice, cleanliness and worship, which are universal teachings of the prophets, thus universally emphasizing the importance of a religious basis for the life of men.

Ever since Max Muller [Müller] published his famous work on the religions of the East these facts have become well known to students; but because they have not become generally diffused, or because prejudice and bigotry have prevented their acceptance, religious intolerance and sectarian strife have continued. The cooperation of ignorance and bigotry to oppose the truth is a fundamental obstacle to human progress. They are defeated only by ever new prophets coming to the world to reiterate and reemphasize these basic truths of religion, and apply them to the changing times and growing needs of the race, and to the increasing mental and spiritual vision of men.

Max Muller wrote:

> More surprising than the continuity in the growth of language is the continuity in the growth of religion. Of religion, as of language, it may be said that in it everything new is old, and everything old is new, and that there has been no entirely new religion since the beginning of the world. The elements and roots of religion were there, as far back as we can trace the history of man; the history of religion, like the history of language, shows us throughout a succession of new combinations of the same radical elements. An intuition of God, a sense of human weakness and dependence, a belief in a divine government of the world, a distinction between good and evil, and a hope of a better life, – these are some of the radical elements of all religions. Though sometimes hidden, they rise again and again to the surface. Though frequently distorted, they tend again and again to recover their perfect form. Unless they had formed a part of

the original dowry of the human soul, religion itself would have remained an impossibility, and the tongues of angels would have been to human ears but as sounding brass or a tinkling cymbal. If we once understand this clearly, the words of Saint Augustine, which have seemed startling to many of his admirers, become perfectly clear and intelligible, when he says, 'What is now called the Christian religion has existed among the ancients, and was not absent from the beginning of the human race to the time when Christ came in the flesh, from which time the true religion, which already existed, began to be called Christianity.'

And again, in a letter he once wrote to a friend:

> The true religion of the future will be the fulfilment of all the religions of the past – the true religion of humanity, that which, in the struggle of history, remains as the indestructible portion of all the so-called false religions of mankind. There never was a false god, nor was there ever really a false religion, unless you call a child a false man. All religions, so far as I know them, had the same purpose; all were links in a chain which connects heaven and earth, and which is held, and always was held, by one and the same hand. All here on earth tends toward right, and truth, and perfection; nothing here on earth can ever be quite right, quite true, quite perfect, not even Christianity – or what is now called Christianity – so long as it excludes all other religions, instead of loving and embracing what is good in each.

To spread the knowledge of facts among the people is not enough, even though this knowledge should become absolutely universal throughout the world. There must be added some liberating influence, some enfranchising ideal, that shall be of a power sufficient to free men from the chains of bigotry and prejudice which are now binding them to the dead formulae of the past. Consequently every prophet has based his teaching upon the divine authority expressed in the words, 'Thus saith the Lord.' By these words He meets a need in human nature, for he gives a food that satisfies spiritual hunger and creates a belief, a high faith, which makes it possible for the soul to go on in thought and deed to greater and greater realization of the divine principles reiterated by all the prophets.

When we remember that Zoroaster gave His message to a comparatively very small group of people occupying but a limited part of the earth's surface; that the same is true of Moses, Buddha and Muhammad; and that the exigencies of time and place limited the message of Jesus to a very few people, the unprejudiced thinker readily understands that if a universal faith is to come a great teacher must appear who will address himself to all nations, reemphasizing the ancient fundamentals, and appealing to men with, 'Thus saith the Lord'.

For the first time in history it has become possible to establish a universal religion, because men are now being brought together through commercial and political unity. The way is thus being prepared so that each member of the world's social organism may have an understanding of every other member, and soon it will be impossible for any intelligent man to say to any other man, no matter of what color or creed, 'I have no need of thee.'

The conditions existing today are such that even though we had not heard of the coming of a new prophet, with a mission to unify the faiths of men and make firm the bond of universal love and brotherhood, we might still, from our study of the great religions, expect such a prophet. These prophets have appeared at intervals in the past, and there is no question at all but that they will continue to come in future ages, restating the same basic truths, invoking the same divine authority, and fitting their teachings to the particular need of their time and age.

I quote from Baha'u'llah:[3]

> As it is said, 'We make no distinction at all between his messengers' (Koran). For all of them summon the people to the divine unity . . . All are dignified with the robe of prophethood and honored by the mantle of glory.

It is evident and certain that all the prophets are the temples of the command of God, who have appeared in different garments, . . . all of them dwelling in one Rizwan, soaring in one sky, seated upon one carpet, speaking one speech and enjoining one command. This is the unity of those essences of existence and illimitable and inseparable suns. Consequently if one of these holy manifestations says, 'I am the return of all the prophets,' it is true. Likewise in every subsequent manifestation the return of the former manifestation is realized.

. . . sanctify and purify thy gaze from outward limitations, that thou mayest behold them all in one name, one office, one essence, and one truth . . .

His knowledge must be infinite and his wisdom all-comprehensive.

The penetration of his word and the potency of his influence must be so great as to humble even his worst enemies.

Sorrows and tribulations must not vex him. His courage and conviction must be godlike. Day by day he must become firmer and more zealous.

He must be the establisher of universal civilization, the unifier of religions, the standard bearer of universal peace, and the embodiment of all the highest and noblest virtues of the world of humanity.

Wherever you find these conditions realized in a human temple turn to him for guidance and illumination.

Such a teacher and prophet was Baha'u'llah who arose only half a century ago and declared his mission to be the unification of all religions, the breaking down of the barriers of creed and sect, and the ushering in of the age of universal peace. In his coming were fulfilled those requisites necessary for such a unification. He spoke in the name of God, even as did Moses and Jesus. He did not simply present facts with convincing power, nor merely advise and warn men. He commanded with, 'Thus saith the Lord.' As a proof of His divine authority we need but point to the effect of his teachings. Wherever they have gained a foothold in the hearts of men, they have brought results that may be summed up in the words peace, unity, harmony, education, civilization. Those who investigate these results rejoice in the conviction that the tree which produces such beautiful fruits must be the tree of truth. Moreover the message of Baha'u'llah, not being limited to a particular race or religion, is making a world appeal with a power unprecedented in all history.

This is the century of light, in which the words of the divine messengers are to be translated into deeds. This is a fundamental principle of the teachings of Baha'u'llah. The time for words has passed, the time for deeds has come. According to this new standard, every true Bahai must square his life.

It is not enough merely to speak the word of God, to preach the truth, to exhort men to be good and pure and holy and just. 'Guidance hath ever been by words,' declares Baha'u'llah, 'but in this day it is by deeds.' He tells us plainly that unless the teacher is disinterested, thinking only of the kingdom of God, careless of himself, considering the interest of others in preference to his own, willing to sacrifice all that he has in the service of his fellow-man, his teaching will be of no avail, even though he speak the word of God.

Abdul Baha says, 'Irreligion is preferable to religion that leads to strife.'

It is easily demonstrable that strife and true religion – and who can speak of a 'false' religion? – are contradictory terms. Hence it follows that strife is prima facie evidence of atheism, irreligion, idolatry and polytheism. It makes no difference what profession men make if their actions give the lie to all their pious words. The day has come when by deeds alone men are to be judged.

It is to this high ideal that Baha'u'llah is calling the world, and all who follow him are committed to a passionate, unflinching, self-sacrificing service in the cause of humanity.

There is only one possible basis for world unity and peace, and that is a recognition of the essential oneness of all mankind.

One God implies one humanity. One Father signifies one human family. One divine Commander-in-chief means a unified army certain of victory; for, as expressed by Abdul Baha: 'Its banner is the love of God; its battle is that of truth; its warfare is against selfishness; its patience is its reserve; its meekness is its conquering power.'

Can such an army be conquered!

Appendix 2
Two Talks by Mabel Rice-Wray Ives[1]

Security for a Failing World

Strange as it may seem, true modernism does not consist in cocktail parties, sophistication, jazz music, crude, grotesque art, and cynicism. Rather True Modernism consists in a World Outlook.

You see, the truly modern person realizes that he is sharing this little planet of ours, called the Earth, with a great many other human beings, and he perceives that the welfare of each one of them, including himself, is dependent upon the welfare of all of them. That it is relatively unimportant into which nationality or religious system he was born, as the human race is after all just one great family and that he is part of this family.

He sees the world as a whole. In fact he is consciously a citizen of the world. Now that is being modern, that is, being realistic, and if he is still more modern, he will know that the attitude of self-contained nations, class-conscious classes, competitive and divided religious systems cannot be continued in an age, which, equipped with our present instruments of destruction, must achieve unity or perish.

Way back in the early days of the race, mankind was divided into patriarchal family groups of from 50 to 100 persons. The oldest male of the family – the grandfather or great-grandfather – was the King or Ruler of the others.

The true modernist of that day was he who saw that greater security and welfare for the family and each member thereof, lay in merging a number of these families into a tribe or clan. In this way the tribal period was born.

Later, again the spirit of modernism asserted itself when these clans further joined together to form a city state which was a much larger and more inclusive group.

Again, later, modernism expresses itself in the merging of principalities, duchies, and other smaller groups into great nations.

So the national era was born.

Today in a world so closely drawn together by commerce, travel, radio, wireless, international federations and innumerable common interests, true modernism expresses itself in the universal viewpoint and in the effort to build a <u>united world</u>, politically, culturally, and religiously.

However, with the scientific equipment to build a united world, we find ourselves further apart than ever before in our intense spirit of competitive nationalism. In reality the 19th Century made the world a neighborhood and the 20th Century has opened the door to brotherhood, yet the leaders of our political institutions, failing to perceive this logical development toward unity, which modern inventions have given to the world, and turning their entire effort toward the further widening of the breach between the various nations, races and religions of the world, have plunged it in a mad orgy of destruction.

H.G. Wells, the famous English writer and for many years an earnest searcher for ways in which to perfect the organization of humanity – states: 'Either we must make peace throughout the world, make one world State, one world-pax, with one money, one world police, one speech, one brotherhood – however hard that task may seem – or we must prepare to live with the voice of a stranger in our homes, with the knife of a stranger always at our throats, in fear and danger of death. We are confronted with two facts – one bad and one good. The first is that acts of war have become hideously immediate and far-reaching. The second is that the whole round world can be brought together into one brotherhood, one communion, one close-knit, freely communicating citizenship far more easily today than was possible with even such a little country as England a century ago.'

Stanley Baldwin has sent forth this warning: 'Many people, I fear, today fail to realize the very critical period through which the world is passing.'

Sir Oliver Lodge declared that 'Man is not yet spiritually ripe for the possession of the secret of atomic energy . . .' Technically he says that we are demi-gods, ethically still such barbarians that we would unquestionably use the energy of the atom much as we used the less terrible forces that almost destroyed civilization during the las war.

Whatever be the causes of the present chaos into which the world has fallen, many are agreed that a spiritual awakening of humanity is the first requisite for reformation and stabilization. There must come to humanity a deeper sense of brotherhood – individual, national and spiritual. Man must realize emotionally, as he already does intellectually, the actual interdependence of all people. No individual, no class, no community today can live unto itself. We are bound together by indissoluble ties.

This planet, sociologically and economically speaking, is plainly an organic unity. The prosperity of all depends upon the prosperity of one, just as the prosperity of one depends upon the prosperity of all. One nation cannot thrive while all the rest are plunged in economic disaster. Our modern industrial and technological civilization requires free and universal interchange of raw materials and commodities. The whole world as well as any part of it depends for its prosperity not only upon its ability to produce goods but also upon its ability to sell goods. When any great nation is destroyed as a consumer of world goods, the whole world suffers as well as that nation.

So it is within each country. The prosperity of the whole depends upon the prosperity of every part. Selfishness, aggressiveness, and exploitation on the part of one group not only does harm to other groups, but eventually returns like a boomerang to injure the offending group. The capitalist, taking more than his share of the profits of industry, finally harms himself by lessening the consuming power of the masses; and the masses, when usurping all power, deprive themselves of the leadership necessary for industrial organization and efficiency.

In the midst of the welter and chaos of the breakdown of our much vaunted civilization, hopelessness and despair are gripping the hearts of the informed leaders of Mankind. They realize whither the present breakdown of our various peace-pacts and efforts toward international institutions are tending. Even the body of international law which has been built up with such infinite pains was thrown into the discard at the very beginning of the last war. To what then may we look forward?

Unless some new and powerful element enters into the world situation – unless some great constructive force is released into the affairs of men, – unless a world-wide renaissance stirs the very depth of human consciousness, there is no hope of emergence from this calamitous situation.

Leaders of thought in many countries who are well aware of the gravity of the present world situation, are turning with eager attention to the program which an illustrious spiritual leader of the modern world, Baha'u'llah of Persia, has offered as a remedy for the world's ills. This program has been pictured by a well-known writer and educator, Stanwood Cobb, founder of the progressive educational movement. In an epilogue to his book, SECURITY FOR A FAILING WORLD, Mr. Cobb describes the coming world order as the Baha'is conceive it:

'A world united politically, religiously, culturally; and educated under a common universal curriculum.

'A world in which war is forever banned, and the energies of humanity are devoted solely to constructive enterprise.

'A world where language barriers are overcome by the use of a universal auxiliary language.

'A world free from customs barriers and prosperously engaged in international interchange of goods.

'A world in which the long and bitter conflict between capital and labor is changed into effective cooperation based on profit sharing and mutuality of interests.

'A world where jungle-like competition in industry and business has given place to the orderly workings of a planned economic society.

'A world of plenty in which individual wealth is limited and poverty abolished.

'A world in which science walks hand in hand with religion, and knowledge is dedicated to human progress.

'A world in which the business of government devolves upon

the fittest administrators and the best trained experts – a working aristocracy based on democratic universal foundations

'A world, above all, which knows God and seeks to follow ways of righteousness and peace.'

Is this a dream world built only of desire-images? No, it is a world toward which our planetary destiny is plainly moving. There is not an element in it, no matter how apparently idealistic, toward which social evolution and the force of events have not already shown manifest tendency. It is the type of world which modernism will inevitably produce as an alternative to planetary chaos, bankruptcy, and suicide.

It is the organized aim of Bahá'ís, the world over, to speed up this evolutionary process – to accelerate the growth of favorable culture aspects in order to bring to pass this New World Order within the present century.

A radio script written during World War II

The most challenging question facing the people of America and indeed of the whole world is this: shall we build for a secure world after this war is ended, or for another war and another and another? Now is the time to decide and to begin to make our plans. When and if the Democracies win, shall we make a peace of revenge or a peace for permanent security? That is the choice which is facing the human race today. Shall we continue to let war be a breeder of more wars and more wars until man shall have annihilated his own species – this precious race of mankind, and the planet be swept clean of him? Or shall we dream a dream of some sort of collective security and make our dream come true? It is the choice we must make – now.

With our ever more rapid development of bigger and better instruments of destruction, continent after continent could be depopulated. Science has already discovered a means of freeing the gigantic power in the atom. There is a deadly race going on at this moment between and among the scientists of the various belligerent countries, a race as to who shall first succeed in perfecting a method of producing or freeing this power in commercial quantities. Experiments have been carried on successfully for some time with a certain type of rare metal, uranium. If a ruthless and anti-social nation should discover the method first, God help the rest of the world! However so closely allied are the minds of the scientists everywhere when working on the same problem, that it would not be long until the other scientists in other countries would also discover this method or another method, and then the really titanic battle of the ages would be on – a battle which would take its toll of human beings, not a mere matter of ten millions in two months, as the present figure given for the Russian front alone, but ten times ten millions in two months.

This same power which could destroy the human race, can in a war-free world, contribute the basic power source for a great civilization. In a world where war has been discarded as a means of settling disputes between nations and the method of arbitrations, before a Supreme International Tribunal has become accepted and enforced as the new standard for international relations (the far saner and more intelligent method), this same atomic power could with safety be released to run our airplanes at many times their present speed, light and heat our houses, at a fraction of the present cost, turn the wheels of our industrial plants; in a word, provide all our power needs at a cost so small that it would scarcely need to be counted. But this can be true only in a world that has outlawed, outmoded, and outgrown war, once and for all as a method of settling its disputes between nations, between religions, between races, and between the two great pillars of our economic structure – capital and labor.

In a word, there is nothing wrong with our earth. It is bursting with abundance, prodigal with fertility. There is nothing wrong with the <u>natural</u> equipment of man, mental and physical – yes, the spiritual. There is nothing wrong with the Universe of which our planet is a part: or with the laws of the universe, or with the Creator of the universe. There is nothing wrong with God (I say it with all reverence). There is only one thing out of line – one little dislocation amid all this beauty, abundance and order – just one little thing – <u>man's attitude toward man</u>.

It is this: that he still imagines himself back in the jungle, as savage, emerging man, surrounded by animal ferocity – each individual whether animal or man, for himself alone, his back to the wall, a possible enemy behind every tree and rock – knowing nothing but the law of the jungle, the ethics of the jungle; man against man, might being the sole criterion of right, survival of the fittest, dog eat dog – in a word, FORCE.

This man, being created in the image and likeness of God, with all the powers and attributes of God latent within him, waiting for opportunity to express the power of love and understanding, for instance, the power of faith, the gift of wisdom, the power of cooperation.

Picture this being, man, in his early savage state, beginning to experiment with his newly acquired gift, the quality which lifted him above his companions, the animals – this majestic gift of free will, that is to break or conform with the laws of God in His universe – free will to become lower than the beasts or higher than the angels. Free will to choose – every moment, to choose the better way.

And man has chosen, in his long trek up through the ages, as individual man, he has chosen, often the better way, under the influence and guidance of that most lofty being – the Christ, the Son of God. But as a race, he has not yet chosen the better way. Two thousand years after the shining of that most great Light, he is still, in all his group relationships, whether it be between national, racial, religious or economic groups or divisions, he is still following the laws and ethics of the jungle.

And now this war, raging around the world, has brought him to the end of the old road. Beyond is only marsh and quicksand and extinction. As a race he must break with his savage past. He must find a new road. He must learn at long last the paramount lesson of history, the lesson which all nature teaches him as well, whether it be a mineral or a plant, a star or a sun, an animal organism or a human body, the lesson which is written so clearly that it would seem a child could read it, the lesson of <u>reciprocity</u> and <u>cooperation</u> as the price of the preservation of life.

For all nature cooperates, throughout the lesser kingdoms and the far stellar spaces. The mineral gives up of its basic elements, it precious mineral salts, to the hungry roots of the vegetable kingdom, and as a result the plant flourishes, and later at its death, returns its gift to the mineral. The plant feeds the animal and human kingdoms, and they, in turn, nourish or care for the vegetable. The vegetable kingdom throws off oxygen, a life-giving element for man and animal. The animal and man, in turn breathe out carbon dioxide, a necessity for the plant world. Even the heavenly bodies illuminate one another. Not only does the sun give light to the planets in its system, but each planet sends out reflected light to the other planets in its own and other systems. Even this little earth of ours, without light of its own, sends out also its reflected light to illumine the other heavenly bodies. So all nature reciprocates, and cooperates with one another.

Also within each kingdom and each individual thereof this same process takes place. Each atom cooperates with its brother atom to form a molecule, and in turn each molecule cooperates with its brother molecule to form a cell. Each cell again cooperates with its brother cell to form an organ, a tissue, a complete organism. Thus a plant, an animal, a human body is possible, indeed any type of organism is possible. Well, the human race constitutes a body, the body of mankind. It constitutes an organism. Yet in this body every part is fighting against every other part, so innumerable diseases have taken hold of it: the disease of war, for instance, the disease of poverty, the disease or maladjustments in the individual and in its group relationships. Humanity is sick. It needs a divine physician and a divine remedy. It has alas, forgotten the remedy give two thousand years ago, or 'Love your enemy.' 'Do good to those that despitefully use you.' Love your neighbor as yourself.' It has never even attempted to apply these remedies to the relationships of one country to another country in all Christendom; or to the relationships between Capital and Labor, in any Christian country. It has remembered the Name of the Divine Physician but forgotten or failed to apply the remedy, which is accord with the God-made laws of the universe. The time has come for a restatement of those divine laws with fresh power and urgency. It is the lesson which mankind <u>must</u> learn in this day.

My course of lectures beginning next Monday night at the Edwards Hotel will show how man may learn this lesson and apply these laws within this present century and so build a stable, a secure, a divine civilization upon this earth.

Bibliography

'Abdu'l-Bahá. *The Promulgation of Universal Peace: Talks Delivered by 'Abdu'l-Baha During His Visit to the United States and Canada in 1912* (1922, 1925). Comp. H. MacNutt. Wilmette, IL: Bahá'í Publishing Trust, 2nd ed. 1982.
— *Tablets of the Divine Plan*. Wilmette, IL: Bahá'í Publishing Trust, rev. ed. 1993.

Afrúkhtih, Yúnis Khán. 'Síyáh-Chál and Qarih-Kahar', translated by Marzieh Carpenter (Marzieh Gail), in the Bahá'í World Centre Archives.

'Bahá'í Chronicles', website. http://bahaichronicles.org/test1/.

The Bahá'í World: An International Record. Vol. VIII (1938–1940), vol. IX (1940–1944), RP Wilmette, IL: Bahá'í Publishing Trust, 1980–81; vol. XIII (1954-1963), Haifa: The Universal House of Justice, 1970; vol. XIV (1963-1968), Haifa: The Universal House of Justice, 1974; vol. XV (1968-1973), Haifa: Bahá'í World Centre, 1976; vol. XVII (1976–1979), Haifa: Bahá'í World Centre, 1981; vol. XIX (1983–1986), Haifa: Bahá'í World Centre, 1994; vol. XX (1986–1992), Haifa: Bahá'í World Centre, 1998.

The Bahá'í World. In Memoriam 1992-1997. Haifa: World Centre Publications, 2010.

Bahá'u'lláh. *Epistle to the Son of the Wolf*. Trans. Shoghi Effendi. Wilmette, IL: Bahá'í Publishing Trust, rev. ed. 1988

'The Seven Valleys and the Four Valleys', in *The Call of the Divine Beloved: Selected Mystical Works of Bahá'u'lláh*. Haifa: Bahá'í World Centre, 2018.

Bivins, Evelyn. 'The Door of Hope: A Tribute to Mr and Mrs Howard Colby Ives', radio talk, 9 July 1943. United States Bahá'í National Archives (USBNA hereafter), Ives Papers.

Gentzkow, Juliet. *The Art of Empowering Others: The Life and Times of Gayle Abas Woolson, Knight of Bahá'u'lláh*. Oxford: George Ronald, 2020.

Haney, Paul, Horace Holley and Corinne True, 'Ahmad Sohrab and the New History Society', 14 January 1958, statement by these Hands of the Cause. https://bahai-library.com/hands_sohrab_new_history.

Harper, Barron. *Lights of Fortitude*. Oxford: George Ronald, RP 2007.

Inderlied, Helen, 'My contact with Mabel Ives in Binghamton and Scranton', 13 August 1943, USBNA, Ives papers.

Ives, Howard Colby. *Expanding Horizons*. Unpublished manuscript, 1940.

— *The Oceans of His Utterances*. An advanced study course in the Revelation of Bahá'u'lláh. Typed 1963 by Muriel Ives Barrow Newhall; retyped and edited by Reginald G. Barrow, 1977; Word edition Reginald G. Barrow with the assistance of Nya Luc Leapold (1992) and the Bahá'í youth class of Douala, Cameroon, 1995.

— 'The Coming of the Promised One', talk given at the Eighth Session of the Bahá'í Congress at Hotel McAlpin, New York City, Wednesday afternoon, 30 April 1919, in *Star of the West*, vol. 11, no. 2 (9 April 1920), pp. 27–30.

— *Portals to Freedom* (1937). Oxford: George Ronald, 1943, RP many times.

— 'Senator Borah on Present World Conditions', in *Star of the West*, vol. 22, no. 11 (February 1932), pp. 328–9.

— *The Song Celestial* (1938). RP Milwaukie, Oregon: Erich P. Reich Enterprises, n.d.

— 'The Underlying Unity of All Faiths', Talk given at the Bahá'í Congress and Convention of Temple Unity, Riḍván 1915. USBNA, Ives papers.

Ives, Mabel Rice-Wray. 'A Preview of the World in the Year 2001', typescript of radio talk, 1937. USBNA, Ives Papers.

— 'Security for a Failing World', typescript of talk, undated. USBNA, Ives Papers.

Lopez, Lynn Carson. *The Life Story of Edris Rice-Wray, A Woman Doctor*. Unpublished manuscript, 1992. Much of this manuscript is in Edris Rice-Wray's own words, retyped by her daughter Lynn. George Ronald Archives.

Macke, Marlene. *Take My Love to the Friends: The Story of Laura R. Davis*. St. Mary's, Ontario: Chestnut Park Press, 2009.

McKay, Doris, in collaboration with Paul Vreeland. *Fires in Many Hearts*. Manotick, ON, Canada: Nine Pines Publishing, 1993. RP Oxford: George Ronald, 2022.

— 'In Memoriam' Howard Colby Ives, in *The Bahá'í World*, vol. IX, pp. 608–13.

Nakhjavani, Violette. *The Maxwells of Montreal*, vol. II. Oxford: George Ronald, 2015.

Newhall, Muriel Ives Barrow. *Mother's Stories* and *Stories of 'Abdu'l-Bahá as Told by Mother*. 1970/1998. https://bahai-library.com/ives_mothers_stories_abdul-baha.

Redman, Earl. *The Knights of Bahá'u'lláh*. Oxford: George Ronald, 2017.

— *Shoghi Effendi Through the Pilgrim's Eye*. 2 vols. Oxford: George Ronald, 2015, 2016.

Rice-Wray, Edris. 'To the Beloved Spiritual Children of Mabel Ives and Others Who Love Her All Over the Country and Canada, Who Hunger to Know the Details of Her Last Days in the Material World', typescript, 10 November 1943. USBNA, Ives Papers.

— and Colston Rice-Wray. 'Mabel Rice-Wray Ives'. 1943. USBNA, Ives Papers.

Saunders, Keithie. *Of Wars and Worship*. Oxford: George Ronald, 2013.

Shoghi Effendi. *Bahá'í Administration: Selected Messages 1922–1932*. Wilmette: Bahá'í Publishing Trust, RP 1995.

— *Messages to America 1932–1946*. Wilmette, IL: Bahá'í Publishing Trust, 1947. Published online by the Project Gutenberg.

— *Unfolding Destiny: The Messages from the Guardian of the Bahá'í Faith to the Bahá'í Community of the British Isles*. London: Bahá'í Publishing Trust, 1981.

Stevens, Ethel Stefana, 'The Light in the Lantern', in *Everybody's Magazine*, 1 Dec 1911, pp. 780–86. https://bahai-library.com/stevens_light_lantern.

Unitarian Universalist Association, 'The Baltimore Sermon'. https://www.uua.org/re/tapestry/adults/river/workshop9/baltimore-sermon.

van den Hoonaard, Will, C. *The Origins of the Bahá'í Community in Canada*. Waterloo, Ontario: Wilfrid Laurier University Press, 1996.

Whitehead, O. Z. *Some Early Bahá'ís of the West*. Oxford: George Ronald, 1976.

Zarqání, Mírzá Maḥmúd. *Mahmúd's Diary: The Diary of Mírzá Maḥmúd-i-Zarqání Chronicling 'Abdu'l-Bahá's Journey to America*. Trans. Mohi Sobhani with the assistance of Shirley Macias. Oxford: George Ronald, 1998.

Newspapers and periodicals

Bahá'í News. Periodical. National Spiritual Assembly of the Bahá'ís of the United States and Canada.

The Bates Student. Bates College, Lewiston, Maine.

Binghamton Press. Periodical published from 1927 to 1960. Binghamton, New York.

Boletin Bahá'í Dominicano. Periodical. National Spiritual Assembly of the Bahá'ís of the Dominican Republic.

Christian Science Monitor. Periodical published from 1908 to present. Boston, Massachusetts.

Crawford Citizen Chronicle. Periodical now defunct. Crawford, New Jersey.

Des Moines Tribune. Periodical published from 1906 to 1982. Des Moines, Iowa.

Elizabeth Journal. Periodical published from 1872 to 1922. Elizabeth, New Jersey.

Everybody's Magazine. Published in New York City, 1899 to 1929.

Frank Leslie's Popular Monthly. Frank Leslie's Publishing House, NY, 1895.

The Hagerstown Exponent. Periodical published from 1876 to 2004. Hagerstown, Indiana.

Ithaca Journal-News. Periodical published from 1914 to present. Ithaca, New York.

New York Times. Periodical published from 1851 to present. New York, NY.

The Niagara Falls Gazette. Published in Niagara Falls, New York, 1854 to present.

The Scranton Tribune. Periodical published from 1891 to 2005. Scranton, Pennsylvania.

Star of the West: The Bahai Magazine. Periodical, 25 vols. 1910–1935. Vols 1-22 RP Oxford: George Ronald, 1978. Complete CD-ROM version: Talisman Educational Software/Special Ideas, 2001.

Watertown Daily Times, 6 April 1914. Watertown, New York.

Waukegan News Sun. Periodical published from 1930 to 1971. Waukegan, Illinois.

World Order. Periodical published from 1935 to 1949 and 1966 to 2008. Washington, DC.

The World Outlook. Monthly periodical from 1934 to 1939. Nashville, TN: Department of Education and Promotion, Board of Missions, Methodist Episcopal Church, South.

Notes and References

1 Introduction

1. Ives, *Portals to Freedom*, pp. 248-49.
2. Inderlied, 'My contact with Mabel Ives in Binghamton and Scranton', 13 August 1943.
3. McKay, *Fires in Many Hearts*, p. 20.

2 Howard Colby Ives, the Early Years

1. 1870 Census, p. 70 (https://www.familysearch.org/ark:/61903/3:1:S3HY-DYJS-V5?i=69andcc=1438024); 1880 Census, p. 36 (https://www.familysearch.org/ark:/61903/3:1:33S7-9YBG-FWH?i=35andcc=1417683); https://www.familysearch.org/ark:/61903/1:1:2W7V-352.
2. *The Niagara Falls Gazette*, 2 December 1922, p. 2.
3. Whitehead, *Some Early Bahá'ís of the West*, p. 139.
4. USBNA, Ives papers.
5. ibid.
6. Ives, *Portals to Freedom*, p. 19.
7. Muriel Ives Newhall, letter to O. Z. Whitehead, in Whitehead, *Some Early Bahá'ís of the West*, pp. 139–40.
8. Erica Toussaint, personal communication.
9. *The Hagerstown Exponent*, vol. 43, no. 18 (20 September 1917), p. 1.
10. Whitehead, *Some Early Bahá'ís of the West*, p. 140.
11. Mabel Rice-Wray Ives, letter to Doris McKay dated 9 December 1941, p. 2.
12. *Frank Leslie's Popular Monthly*, vol. XL, no. 3-23 (July-December 1895), p. 353.
13. Whitehead, *Some Early Bahá'ís of the West*, p. 140.
14. Howard is incorrect about the date. Channing gave the sermon on 5 May 1819; see https://www.uua.org/re/tapestry/adults/river/workshop9/baltimore-sermon.
15. Ives, *Portals to Freedom*, p. 20.
16. Unitarian Universalist Association, 'The Baltimore Sermon'.
17. Whitehead, *Some Early Bahá'ís of the West*, p. 140.

18 ibid. pp. 140–41.
19 ibid. p. 141.
20 The Apostolic Institute, Third Annual Meeting of Directors, 10 November 1910, reported in *Watertown Daily Times*, 6 April 1914, p. 6.
21 Muriel Ives Newhall, quoted in McKay, 'In Memoriam' Howard Colby Ives, in *The Bahá'í World*, vol. IX, p. 609.
22 Ives, *Portals to Freedom*, pp. 22–3.
23 Whitehead, *Some Early Bahá'ís of the West*, pp. 140–41.
24 Ives, *Portals to Freedom*, p. 21.

3 Howard Meets the Master and Is Transformed

1 Stevens, 'The Light in the Lantern', in *Everybody's Magazine*, 1 December 1911, p. 780.
2 ibid. p. 786. See Appendix 1 for the full text of the article.
3 Ives, *Portals to Freedom*, p. 22.
4 ibid. pp. 22–3.
5 Muriel Ives Barrow Newhall, transcript of an audio recording.
6 Ives, *Portals to Freedom*, pp. 23–4.
7 *The Bahá'í World*, vol. 8, p. 666.
8 Ives, *Portals to Freedom*, p. 24.
9 ibid. pp. 24–5.
10 ibid. pp. 25–6.
11 ibid. p. 26.
12 ibid. p. 27.
13 ibid. pp. 27–8.
14 ibid. pp. 28–9.
15 ibid.
16 ibid. pp. 28–33.
17 Howard Colby Ives, letter to 'Abdu'l-Bahá dated 19 April 1912.
18 Ives, *Portals to Freedom*, p. 35.
19 Bahá'u'lláh, 'The Seven Valleys', in *The Call of the Divine Beloved*, p. 15.
20 Ives, *Portals to Freedom*, p. 37.
21 ibid. pp. 40–41.
22 ibid. pp. 42–3.
23 ibid. pp. 44–5.
24 ibid. pp. 54–6.
25 ibid. pp. 56–7.
26 ibid. pp. 58–9.
27 ibid. p. 84.
28 ibid. p. 74.

29 ibid. pp. 73–5.
30 Newhall, *Stories of 'Abdu'l-Bahá as Told by Mother*, p. 20.
31 Ives, *Portals to Freedom*, pp. 95–8.
32 Howard Colby Ives, letter to 'Abdu'l-Bahá dated 10 July 1912.
33 Howard Colby Ives, letter to 'Abdu'l-Bahá dated 7 August 1912.
34 Ives, *Portals to Freedom*, pp. 119–20.
35 Zarqání, *Maḥmúd's Diary*, pp. 189–90.
36 Ives, *Portals to Freedom*, pp. 130–31.
37 ibid. pp. 139–40.
38 ibid. pp. 140–41.
39 ibid.
40 Howard Colby Ives, letter to 'Abdu'l-Bahá dated 15 November 1912.
41 Redman, *'Abdu'l-Bahá in their Midst*, p. 264.
42 Ives, *Portals to Freedom*, p. 150.
43 ibid. pp. 152–3.
44 ibid. pp. 193–4.
45 ibid. pp. 211–12.
46 ibid. pp. 227–8.

4 Finding His Way

1 Ives, *Portals to Freedom*, p. 230.
2 Howard Colby Ives, letter to 'Abdu'l-Bahá dated 14 February 1913,
3 Howard Colby Ives, letter to Ella Cooper dated 4 April 1915.
4 Howard Colby Ives, letter to 'Abdu'l-Bahá dated 14 February 1913.
5 Howard Colby Ives, letter to 'Abdu'l-Bahá dated 20 June 1913.
6 Harlan Ober, letter to Howard Ives dated 11 October 1913.
7 Muriel Ives, letter to Howard Ives dated 22 September 1913.
8 Muriel Ives, letter to Howard Ives dated 25 September 1913.
9 Muriel Ives, letter to Howard Ives dated 26 September 1913.
10 Howard Colby Ives, letter to 'Abdu'l-Bahá dated 27 October 1913.
11 Whitehead, *Some Early Bahá'ís of the West*, p. 145.
12 Howard Colby Ives, Diary, 31 December 1913.
13 ibid.
14 'Abdu'l-Bahá, Tablet to Roy Wilhelm translated on 30 April 1914. Published by permission of the Bahá'í World Centre.
15 Ives, *Portals to Freedom*, p. 232.
16 ibid. p. 233.
17 Howard Colby Ives, letter to 'Abdu'l-Bahá dated 9 March 1914.
18 Ives, *Portals to Freedom*, p. 236.
19 ibid. pp. 239–40.
20 Green Acre Schedule, 1914.
21 Howard Colby Ives, letter to 'Abdu'l-Bahá dated 23 August 1914,

in the Bahá'í World Centre Archives. Published with permission.
22 ibid.
23 Howard Colby Ives, letter to Ella Cooper, 4 April 1915, from Wichita, Kansas.
24 Howard Colby Ives, 'The Underlying Unity of All Faiths', talk given at the Bahá'í Congress and Convention of Temple Unity, Riḍván 1915.
25 Ives, *Portals to Freedom*, pp. 248–9.
26 Howard Colby Ives, letter to Joseph Hannen dated 13 November 1916.
27 Howard Colby Ives, letter to Joseph Hannen dated 19 November 1916.
28 ibid.
29 Howard Colby Ives, letter to Joseph Hannen dated 8 January 1917.
30 Howard Colby Ives, letter to Joseph Hannen dated 1 January 1917
31 Howard Colby Ives, letter to Joseph Hannen dated 15 April 1917.
32 *New York Times*, 20 April 1918, p. 13.
33 Theodore Obrig, letter to Howard Ives dated 31 July 1917.
34 Howard Colby Ives, letter to Theodore Obrig dated 27 August 1917.
35 Howard Colby Ives, letter to Joseph Hannen dated 16 May 1918.
36 Howard Colby Ives, letter to Joseph Hannen dated 17 March 1918.
37 Howard Colby Ives, letter to Joseph Hannen dated 13 May 1918.
38 Howard Colby Ives, letter to 'Abdu'l-Bahá dated 23 October 1918, in the Bahá'í World Centre Archives. Published with permission.
39 Howard Colby Ives, letter to Joseph Hannen dated 15 November 1919.
40 *Star of the West*, vol. 11, no. 2 (9 April 1920), pp. 27–30.
41 ibid. vol. 10, no. 4 (17 May 1919), pp. 60–61.
42 ibid. vol. 11, no. 4 (17 May 1920), p. 73.
43 Howard Colby Ives, letter to Carl Scheffler dated 20 September 1919.
44 Howard Colby Ives, letter to Carl Scheffler dated 22 September 1919.

5 Mabel Rice-Wray, the Early Years

1 US Passport Applications, 1795–1925, Roll 1512, cert. no. 148250-148625; other sources indicate that Mabel was born in St Louis, Missouri.
2 Mabel's 'sister' was not recorded in either the 1880, when Mabel was two years old, or the 1900 census records. Unfortunately, a fire in 1921 destroyed almost all the 1890 census records.

3   Edris Rice-Wray and Colston Rice-Wray, "Mabel Rice-Wray Ives", p. 1.
4   Newhall, *Mother's Stories*, p. 13.
5   Mariam Haney, letter to Edris Rice-Wray dated 20 November 1943, p. 1.
6   Erica Toussaint, family recollection.
7   USBNA, Ellah Rice-Wray: correspondence Ahmad Sohrab, 8 June 1909, p. 2.
8   'Abdu'l-Bahá, Tablet to Mabel Simon and Theron Rice-Wray, translation by Ali Kuli Khan dated 11 March 1903, USBNA.
9   'Abdu'l-Bahá, Tablet to Mr and Mrs Rice Wray, translation by Ali Kuli Khan dated 2 November 1904, USBNA.
10 USBNA, Bahá'í Historical Record, Ellah Rice-Wray declaration,
11 Whitehead, *Some Early Bahá'ís of the West*, pp. 146–8.
12 Inderlied, 'My contact with Mabel Ives in Binghamton and Scranton', pp. 1–2.
13 Mariam Haney, letter to Edris Rice-Wray dated 22 November 1943.
14 Edris Rice-Wray and Colston Rice-Wray, 'Mabel Rice-Wray Ives', pp. 2–3.
15 'Abdu'l-Bahá, Tablet to Mabel Rice-Wray, translation dated 6–12 September 1906, USBNA.
16 Lopez, *The Life Story of Edris Rice-Wray, a Woman Doctor*, p. 4. (1912 folder)
17 Mariam Haney, letter to Edris Rice-Wray dated 20 November 1943, p. 3.
18 Lopez, *The Life Story of Edris Rice-Wray, a Woman Doctor*, pp. 5–6.
19 Edris Rice-Wray and Colston Rice-Wray, 'Mabel Rice-Wray Ives', p. 5.
20 'Abdu'l-Bahá, Tablet to Mabel Rice-Wray, translation dated 16 July 1913, USBNA; also (partially) in *Star of the West*, vol. 8, no. 16 (31 December 2017), p. 219.
21 Lopez, *The Life Story of Edris Rice-Wray, a Woman Doctor*, pp. 6–7.
22 Edris Rice-Wray and Colston Rice-Wray, 'Mabel Rice-Wray Ives', p. 6.
23 Mabel Rice-Wray, letters to Joseph Hannen dated 30 November 1916 and 29 January 1917.
24 Mabel Rice-Wray, letter to Joseph Hannen dated April 1916.
25 Lopez, *The Life Story of Edris Rice-Wray, a Woman Doctor*, p. 3.
26 Whitehead, *Some Early Bahá'ís of the West*, p. 146.
27 See for example *Star of the West*, vol. 8, no. 10 ((September 2017), p. 130, and no.14 (23 November 2017), p. 201.

28 ibid. vol. 9, no. 4 (17 May 1918), pp. 53–5, and no. 5 (5 June 1918), p. 58.
29 Redman, *Shoghi Effendi Through the Pilgrim's Eye*, vol. 1, p. 41.
30 Mabel Rice-Wray, letter to Joseph Hannen dated February 1918.
31 Whitehead, *Some Early Bahá'ís of the West*, p. 148.
32 'Abdu'l-Bahá, Tablet to Mabel Rice-Wray, translation by Shoghi Effendi dated 10 January 1919, USBNA.
33 *Star of the West*, vol. 10, no. 4 (17 May 1919), p. 57; no. 8, p. 160; no. 18 (7 February 1920), pp. 326, 335.
34 'Abdu'l-Bahá, Tablet to Mabel Rice-Wray, translation by Azizullah S. Bahadur dated 26 March 1920, USBNA.
35 United States Passport Applications 1795-1925, Roll 1073, 1920 Feb. cert. no. 172626-172999.
36 ibid.
37 *Star of the West*, vol. 11, no. 11 (27 September 1920), pp. 192; for her other activities see no. 4 (17 May 1920), pp. 64, 73; no. 6 (24 June 1920), p. 101.

6 Howard and Mabel Get Married

1 Mabel Rice-Wray Ives, letter to Doris McKay dated 9 December 1941, pp. 1-2.
2 'Abdu'l-Bahá, cable to Roy Wilhelm dated 14 June 1920.
3 Mabel Rice-Wray Ives, letter to Doris McKay dated 9 December 1941, p. 3.
4 ibid.
5 ibid.
6 Howard Colby and Mabel Rice-Wray Ives, letter to friends dated 7 November 1920.
7 Howard and Mabel Rice-Wray Ives, letter to 'Abdu'l-Bahá dated 19 December 1920.
8 Wedding certificate written by Howard and Mabel Rice-Wray Ives, 29 October 1920.
9 Howard Colby Ives, letter to Shoghi Effendi dated 29 January 1932.
10 Harlan Ober, letter to Edris Rice-Wray dated 9 November 1943, p. 5.
11 Newhall, *Stories of 'Abdu'l-Bahá as Told by Mother*, p. 20.
12 *The Bahá'í World*, vol. XIII, pp. 867–8.
13 Newhall, *Mother's Stories*, p.22.
14 *The Bahá'í World*, vol. XIII, p. 870.
15 Harlan Ober, letter to Edris Rice-Wray dated 9 November 1943, p. 1.
16 Ives, *Portals to Freedom*, pp. 66–7.
17 'Abdu'l-Bahá, *The Promulgation of Universal Peace*, p. 57.

18 ibid. p. 425.
19 Shoghi Effendi, *Bahá'í Administration*, p. 129.

7 A New Plan of Action and the Beginnings of a Life of Sacrifice

1. Mabel's passport application.
2. Mabel Rice-Wray Ives, letter to Doris McKay dated 9 December 1941, p. 4.
3. Howard and Mabel Ives, letter to 'Abdu'l-Bahá dated 29 September 1921.
4. Mabel Rice-Wray Ives, letter to Doris McKay dated 9 Dec 1941, p. 4.
5. Edris Rice-Wray, 'To the Beloved Spiritual Children of Mabel Ives and Others Who Love Her All Over the Country and Canada, Who Hunger to Know the Details of Her Last Days in the Material World, 10 Nov. 1943'.
6. Howard Colby Ives, letter to Doris McKay in 1934, in *The Bahá'í World*, vol. IX, p. 611.
7. National Spiritual Assembly of the United States and Canada, letter to Howard Colby Ives dated 4 Jan 1922.
8. National Spiritual Assembly of the United States and Canada, letter to Mabel Ives dated 10 October 1922.
9. Howard Colby Ives, letter to Fred D'Evelyn dated 2 January 1922.
10. 'Azízu'lláh Bahádur, letter to the Ives dated 11 August 1923.
11. 'In Memoriam for Howard Colby Ives by Doris McKay, *The Bahá'í World*, vol. IX, p. 611.
12. Edris and Colston Rice-Wray, 'Mabel Rice-Wray Ives', pp. 12-13.
13. Mabel Rice-Wray Ives, letter to Doris McKay dated 9 December 1941, pp. 4-5.
14. Howard Colby Ives, letter to Agnes Parsons dated 26 March 1923.
15. Howard Colby Ives, letter to Fred D'Evelyn dated 22 February 1923, pp. 2, 3, 5.
16. National Spiritual Assembly of the United States and Canada, letter to Howard Colby Ives dated 3 April 1923.
17. National Spiritual Assembly of the United States and Canada, letter to Howard Colby Ives dated 12 April 1923.
18. Credo Harris, letter to the Ives dated 21 May 1924.
19. Howard Colby Ives, letter to Mabel dated 13 August 1924.
20. Howard Colby Ives, letter to Mabel dated 14 August 1924.
21. Howard Colby Ives, letter to Mabel dated 7 August 1924.
22. Mabel Rice-Wray Ives, letter to Howard dated August 1924.
23. Howard Colby Ives, letter to Mabel dated 7 August 1924.
24. Howard Colby Ives, letter to Mabel dated 20 August 1924.
25. Mabel Rice-Wray Ives, letter to Howard dated 9 September 1924.

26 Howard Colby Ives, letter to Mabel dated 9 September 1924.
27 Mabel Rice-Wray Ives, letter to Howard dated 11 September 1924.
28 Howard Colby Ives, letter to Mabel dated 2 February 1925.
29 Howard Colby Ives, letter to Mabel dated 31 March 1925.
30 Howard Colby Ives, letter to Mabel dated 9 April 1925.
31 Howard Colby Ives, letter to Mabel dated 17 February 1925.
32 Howard Colby Ives, letters to Mabel dated 4 and 5 February 1925.
33 Howard Colby Ives, letter to Mabel dated 7 February 1925.
34 Howard Colby Ives, letter to Mabel dated 5 February 1925 (a).
35 Howard Colby Ives, letter to Mabel dated 10 February 1925.
36 Howard Colby Ives, letter to Mabel dated 11 February 1925.
37 Quoted in Whitehead, *Some Early Bahá'ís of the West*, p. 149.
38 Muriel Ives, undated talk, transcription of the audio recording.

8 Spiritual Struggles and Tests

1 Howard Colby Ives, letter to Mabel dated 6 February 1925.
2 Howard Colby Ives, letter to Mabel dated 3 August 1925.
3 Howard Colby Ives, letter to Mabel dated 7 April 1925.
4 Howard Colby Ives, letter to Mabel dated 9 April 1925.
5 Mabel Rice-Wray Ives, letter to Howard dated 10 May 1925.
6 Mabel Rice-Wray Ives, letter to Howard dated 4 August 1925.
7 Mabel Rice-Wray Ives, letter to Howard dated 6 August 1925.
8 ibid.
9 Howard Colby Ives, letter to Mabel 9 April 1925.
10 Howard Colby Ives, undated letter to Mabel about 10 April 1925 (Friday morning).
11 Howard Colby Ives, letter to 'Abdu'l-Bahá dated 20 June 1913.
12 Howard Colby Ives, letter to 'Abdu'l-Bahá dated 9 March 1914.
13 Howard Colby Ives, letter to 'Abdu'l-Bahá dated 29 September 1921.
14 Howard Colby Ives, letter to Shoghi Effendi dated 4 March 1931.
15 Mabel Rice-Wray Ives, letter to Shoghi Effendi dated 1935.
16 Mabel Rice-Wray Ives, letter to Shoghi Effendi dated 26 July 1937.
17 Mabel Rice-Wray Ives, letter to Shoghi Effendi dated 16 March 1939.
18 Mabel Rice-Wray Ives, letter to Shoghi Effendi dated July (?) 1942.
19 Howard Colby Ives, letter to Mabel dated 11 August 1925, pp. 1–2.
20 Howard Colby Ives, letter to Mabel dated 5 April 1925.
21 Shoghi Effendi, *Bahá'í Administration*, p. 66.
22 Howard Colby Ives, letter to Mabel dated 10 February 1925.
23 Howard Colby Ives, letter to Mabel dated 4 March 1925.
24 Howard Colby Ives, letter to Mabel dated 26 March 1925.

25 Howard Colby Ives, letter to Mabel dated 4 April 1925.
26 Howard Colby Ives, letter to Mabel dated 13 April 1925, pp. 3-4.
27 Mabel Rice-Wray Ives, letter to Howard dated 16 June 1925.
28 Mabel Rice-Wray Ives, letter to Howard 19 June 1933.
29 Mabel Rice-Wray Ives, letter to Howard 5 February 1935.
30 McKay, *Fires in Many Hearts*, p. 11.
31 ibid. p. 13.
32 ibid. pp. 13-16.
33 ibid. p. 16.
34 ibid. p. 17.
35 ibid., dedication page.
36 Howard Colby Ives, letter to Mabel dated 9 April 1925.
37 Howard Colby Ives, letter to Mabel dated 10 April 1925, p. 1.
38 Howard Colby Ives, letter to Mabel dated 19 July 1925, p. 1.
39 Howard Colby Ives, letter to Mabel dated 24 March 1925.
40 *The Elizabeth Journal*, 4 November 1925.
41 *The Cranford Citizen Chronicle*, 17 December 1925, p. 1.

9 Race Unity Work

1 Howard Colby Ives, letter to Shoghi Effendi dated 6 January 1926. Published by permission of the Bahá'í World Centre.
2 Letter written on behalf of Shoghi Effendi to Howard Colby Ives dated 6 February 1926.
3 ibid.
4 *Ithaca Journal-News*, 25 July 1926.
5 Mabel Rice-Wray Ives, letter to Doris McKay dated 9 December 1941, p. 5.
6 *Ithaca Journal-News*, 18 Mar 1927.
7 *Ithaca Journal-News*, 1 April 1927.
8 McKay, *Fires in Many Hearts*, p. 45.
9 Inderlied, 'My contact with Mabel Ives in Binghamton and Scranton', 13 August 1943.
10 Howard Colby and Mabel Rice-Wray Ives, letter to John Bosch dated 12 September 1928.
11 McKay, *Fires in Many Hearts*, p. 87.
12 ibid. p. 88.
13 Letter written on behalf of Shoghi Effendi to Howard and Mabel Ives dated 21 December 1929.
14 McKay, *Fires in Many Hearts*, p. 113.
15 *Binghamton Press*, 2 March 1929.
16 ibid.
17 ibid.

18 ibid.
19 McKay, *Fires in Many Hearts*, p. 70.
20 ibid. pp. 80, 82.
21 ibid. pp. 81, 86.
22 http://www.louhelen.org/history, *Bahá'í News*, no. 199 (Sept. 1947), p. 14.
23 Howard Colby Ives, letter to Mabel dated 24 January 1932, p. 2.
24 Howard Colby Ives, letter to Mabel dated 25 January 1932, pp. 3–4.
25 ibid. pp. 3–6.

10 Howard Breaks Down

1 Mabel Rice-Wray Ives, letter to Howard dated 23 June 1930.
2 McKay, *Fires in Many Hearts*, p. 160.
3 Howard Colby Ives, letter to Mabel dated 24 January 1932, p. 3.
4 McKay, *Fires in Many Hearts*, pp. 160–62.
5 ibid. p. 170.
6 ibid. p. 172.
7 ibid. p. 173.
8 ibid. p. 185.
9 ibid. p. 185.
10 ibid. p. 186.
11 ibid. p. 201.

11 Early 1932

1 Howard and Mabel Ives, letter to the National Spiritual Assembly dated 28 January 1932.
2 Redman, *Shoghi Effendi Through the Pilgrim's Eye*, vol. 1, p. 121.
3 Howard and Mabel Ives, letter to the National Spiritual Assembly dated 28 January 1932.
4 Howard Colby Ives, letter to Mabel dated 3 February 1932, p. 1.
5 Howard Colby Ives, 'Senator Borah on Present World Conditions', in *Star of the West*, vol. 22, no. 11 (February 1932), pp. 328–9.
6 ibid. p. 328.
7 ibid. p. 330.
8 Howard Colby Ives, letter to Mabel dated 3 February 1932, p. 4.
9 ibid. pp. 2–4.
10 ibid. pp. 4–6.
11 Howard Colby Ives, letter to Mabel dated 6 February 1932, p. 2.
12 Howard Colby Ives, letter to Mabel dated 7 February 1932, p. 1.
13 Eve (Nicklin?), letter to Howard and Mabel dated 4 February 1932.
14 Howard Colby Ives, letter to Mabel dated 10 February 1932, pp. 3–4.

15 Howard Colby Ives, letter to Mabel dated 14 February 1932, pp. 2–3.
16 Letter written on behalf of Shoghi Effendi to Mabel Ives dated 18 February 1932, in the Bahá'í World Centre Archives. Published by permission of the Bahá'í World Centre.
17 Howard Colby Ives, letter to Mabel dated 20 February 1932, p. 2.
18 Howard Colby Ives, letter to Shoghi Effendi dated 26 February 1932.
19 Howard Colby Ives, letter to Mabel dated 9 March 1932, p. 2.
20 ibid.
21 Howard Colby Ives, letter to Mabel dated 11 March 1932, pp. 1–2.
22 Howard Colby Ives, letter to Mabel dated 15 March 1932.
23 Howard Colby Ives, letter to Mabel dated 17 March 1932.
24 Howard Colby Ives, letter to Mabel dated 21 March 1932, p. 2.
25 Howard Colby Ives, letter to Mabel dated 11 April 1932.

12 Howard's Weekly 'Hakouk' Letters: January–March 1932

1 Howard Colby Ives, letter to Shoghi Effendi dated 29 January 1932.
2 Howard Colby Ives, letters to Shoghi Effendi dated 5, 12, 19 and 26 February 1932, and 4 and 18 March 1932
3 Howard Colby Ives, letter to Shoghi Effendi dated 29 January 1932.
4 Letter written on behalf of Shoghi Effendi to Howard Colby Ives dated 20 February 1932, in the Bahá'í World Centre Archives. Published by permission of the Bahá'í World Centre.
5 Howard Colby Ives, letter to Shoghi Effendi, dated 5 February 1932.
6 Letter written on behalf of Shoghi Effendi to Howard Colby Ives dated 29 February 1932, in the Bahá'í World Centre Archives. Published by permission of the Bahá'í World Centre.
7 Howard Colby Ives, letter to Shoghi Effendi dated 12 February 1932.
8 Howard Colby Ives, letter to Mabel dated 10 (?) February 1932, pp. 1–2.
9 Howard Colby Ives, letter to Shoghi Effendi dated 19 February 1932.
10 Letter written on behalf of Shoghi Effendi to Howard Colby Ives dated 17 March 1932, in the Bahá'í World Centre Archives. Published by permission of the Bahá'í World Centre.
11 ibid.
12 Howard Colby Ives, letter to Shoghi Effendi dated 26 February 1932.

13 ibid.
14 Howard Colby Ives, letter to Shoghi Effendi dated 4 March 1932.
15 ibid.
16 Howard Colby Ives, letter to Shoghi Effendi dated 11 March 1932, in the Bahá'í World Centre Archives. Published by permission of the Bahá'í World Centre.
17 Howard Colby Ives, letter to Mabel dated 17 March 1932.
18 Howard Colby Ives, letter to Shoghi Effendi dated 18 March 1932.
19 Howard Colby Ives, letter to Shoghi Effendi dated 25 March 1932, in the Bahá'í World Centre Archives. Published by permission of the Bahá'í World Centre. The interview was published as 'Secretary Wilbur on World Problems', in *Star of the West,* vol. 23, no. 1 (April 1932).
20 Letter to Howard written on behalf of Shoghi Effendi, dated 15 April 1932, in the Bahá'í World Centre Archives. Published by permission of the Bahá'í World Centre.

13 Travel Teaching and a Boarding House

1 Mabel Rice-Wray Ives, Report for the National Teaching Committee, 15 April 1932.
2 ibid.
3 Howard Colby Ives, letters to Mabel dated 2 May and 4 May 1932.
4 Howard Colby Ives, letter to Mabel dated 4 May 1932.
5 Howard Colby Ives, letter to Mabel dated 16 May 1932.
6 Howard Colby Ives, letter to Mabel dated 18 May 1932.
7 Howard Colby Ives, letter to Mabel dated 22 May 1932.
8 Howard Colby Ives, letter to Mabel dated 28 May 1932, p. 3.
9 *The Bahá'í World: In Memoriam 1992–1997,* p. 171.
10 Howard Colby Ives, letter to Shoghi Effendi dated 8 June 1933.
11 Letter written on behalf of Shoghi Effendi to Howard Colby Ives dated 25 July 1933, in the Bahá'í World Centre Archives. Published by permission of the Bahá'í World Centre.
12 Howard Colby Ives, letter to Mabel dated 28 March 1933, pp. 1–2.
13 ibid. p. 4.
14 Mabel Rice-Wray Ives, letter to Howard dated 21 May 1933.
15 Mabel Rice-Wray Ives, letter to Howard dated 19 May 1933.
16 Howard Colby Ives, letter to Shoghi Effendi dated 8 June 1933, p. 3.
17 Howard Colby Ives, letter to Mabel dated 15 June 1933, pp. 3–5.
18 Mabel Rice-Wray Ives, letter to Howard dated 16 June 1933.
19 Howard Colby Ives, letter to Mabel dated 17 June 1933, p. 4.
20 Howard Colby Ives, letter to Shoghi Effendi dated 2 December 1935.

21 Letter written on behalf of Shoghi Effendi to Howard Colby Ives dated 31 December 1935, in the Bahá'í World Centre Archives. Published by permission of the Bahá'í World Centre.
22 Howard Colby Ives, letter to Mabel dated 7 July 1933.
23 Howard Colby Ives, letter to Mabel dated 17 June 1933, p. 1.
24 Ann Reich Blair, family remembrance.
25 Howard Colby Ives, letter to Mabel dated 2 April 1925.
26 Howard Colby Ives, letter to Mabel dated 30 Mar 1925.
27 Howard Colby Ives, letter to Shoghi Effendi dated 8 June 1933.
28 Barbara Obrig, letter to Shoghi Effendi dated 9 June 1933.
29 Howard Colby Ives, letter to Shoghi Effendi dated 8 June 1933.
30 Letter written on behalf of Shoghi Effendi to Howard Colby Ives dated 25 July 1933, in the Bahá'í World Centre Archives. Published by permission of the Bahá'í World Centre.
31 Mabel Rice-Wray Ives, letter to Howard dated 4 December 1933.
32 Mabel Rice-Wray Ives, letter to Howard dated 6 December 1933.
33 Howard Colby Ives, letter to Mabel dated 7 December 1933.
34 Mabel Rice-Wray Ives, undated letter to Howard.
35 Mabel Rice-Wray Ives, letter to Howard dated 15 December 1933.
36 Mabel Rice-Wray Ives, letter to Howard dated 19 December 1933.
37 Leroy Ioas, letters to Howard Ives dated 27 December 1933 and 3 January 1934.
38 Mabel Rice-Wray Ives, letter to the National Teaching Committee dated 23 August 1935.

14 Howard Discovers His Writing Skills

1 Mabel Rice-Wray Ives, letter to Doris McKay dated 9 December 1941, pp. 7–8.
2 *Christian Science Monitor*, 4 May 1934.
3 *Christian Science Monitor*, 13 June 1934.
4 *The World Outlook*, vol. XXIV, No. 7 (July 1934), pp. 234–5.
5 Mabel Rice-Wray Ives, letter to Doris McKay dated 9 December 1941, p. 8.
6 Mabel Rice-Wray Ives, letter to Edris 28 July 1934.
7 *Bahá'í World*, vol. XX, p. 959.
8 Muriel Ives Barrow Newhall, *Mother's Stories*, pp. 18–19.
9 Howard Colby Ives, letter to Mabel dated 13 January 1935.
10 Mabel Rice-Wray Ives, letter to the National Teaching Committee dated 23 August 1935.
11 Howard Colby Ives, letter to Mabel dated 29 July 1935, p. 1.
12 Howard Colby Ives, letter to 'Lewis' dated 27 September 1935.
13 Howard Colby Ives, letter to Mabel dated 30 October 1935.

14 Howard Colby Ives, letter to Mabel dated 27 October 1935.
15 Mabel Rice-Wray Ives, letter to Howard dated 29 October 1935.
16 Howard Colby Ives, letter to Mabel dated 30 October 1935.
17 Erica Toussaint.
18 Nancy Phillips, transcription of part of an audio recording, p. 2.
19 Howard Colby Ives, letter to Nancy Phillips dated 10 October 1936.
20 Howard Colby Ives, letter to Nancy Phillips dated 24 July 1936.
21 Bahá'u'lláh, *Epistle to the Son of the Wolf*, p. 15.
22 Howard Colby Ives, letter to Nancy Phillips dated 10 September 1936.
23 Howard Colby Ives, letter to Nancy Phillips dated 3 March 1937.
24 Ives, Howard Colby Ives, letter to Mabel dated 1 November 1935.
25 Shoghi Effendi, *Unfolding Destiny*, p. 149; *Messages to the Bahá'í World 1950–1957*, p. 48.
26 Mabel Rice-Wray Ives, letter to Charlotte Linfoot dated 8 December 1935.
27 Mabel Rice-Wray Ives, letter to Howard dated 31 October 1935.
28 Mabel Rice-Wray Ives, letter to Charlotte Linfoot dated 8 December 1935.
29 ibid.
30 Mabel Rice-Wray Ives, undated letter to Howard, probably December 1935, pp. 2, 3, 6.
31 Mabel Rice-Wray Ives, letter to the Bahá'í Teaching Committee dated 13 April 1936.
32 Howard Colby Ives, letter to Mabel dated 13 April 1936.
33 Mabel Rice-Wray Ives, letter to Horace Holley dated 18 June 1936; National Spiritual Assembly of the United States and Canada, letter to Mabel dated 22 June 1936.

15 Howard Writes *Portals to Freedom*

1 *The Bahá'í World*, vol. IX, pp. 612.
2 Howard Colby Ives, letter to Shoghi Effendi dated 2 December 1935.
3 *The Bahá'í World*, vol. XX, pp. 958–9.
4 Mariam Haney, letter to Mabel dated 7 July 1941.
5 Mabel Rice-Wray Ives, letter to Doris McKay dated 9 December 1941, p. 6.
6 Howard Colby Ives, letter to Shoghi Effendi dated 12 February 1936.
7 ibid.
8 Letter written on behalf of Shoghi Effendi to Howard Colby Ives dated 8 March 1936, in the Bahá'í World Centre Archives. Published by permission of the Bahá'í World Centre.

9   Howard Colby Ives, letter to Shoghi Effendi dated 20 October 1936, p. 4.
10 Letter written on behalf of Shoghi Effendi to Howard Colby Ives dated 7 November 1936, in the Bahá'í World Centre Archives. Published by permission of the Bahá'í World Centre.
11 Howard Colby Ives, letter to Shoghi Effendi dated 31 March 1936.
12 Letter written on behalf of Shoghi Effendi to Howard Colby Ives dated 19 April 1936, in the Bahá'í World Centre Archives. Published by permission of the Bahá'í World Centre.
13 Howard Colby Ives, letter to Nancy Phillips dated 30 June 1936.
14 Stanwood Cobb, letter to Howard dated 20 August 1936.
15 Howard Colby Ives, letter to Shoghi Effendi dated 20 October 1936, in the Bahá'í World Centre Archives. Published by permission of the Bahá'í World Centre.
16 Letter written on behalf of Shoghi Effendi to Howard Colby Ives dated 7 November 1936, in the Bahá'í World Centre Archives. Published by permission of the Bahá'í World Centre.
17 ibid.
18 Howard Colby Ives, letter to Shoghi Effendi dated 26 November 1936.
19 National Spiritual Assembly of the United States and Canada letter to Siegfried Schopflocher dated 25 September 1936.
20 National Spiritual Assembly of the United States and Canada letter to Howard Colby Ives dated 25 January 1937.
21 Howard Colby Ives, letter the Bahá'í Publishing Committee dated 18 February 1937.
22 Howard Colby Ives, letter to Horace Holley dated 23 February 1937.
23 National Spiritual Assembly of the United States and Canada letter to Howard Colby Ives dated 5 March 1937.
24 Walter Guy, letter to Horace Holley dated 12 April 1937.
25 Howard Colby Ives, letter to Shoghi Effendi dated 24 March 1937.
26 National Spiritual Assembly of the United States and Canada letter to Howard Colby Ives dated 24 May 1937.
27 Mabel Rice-Wray Ives, letter to Doris McKay dated 9 December 1941, p. 9.
28 Howard Colby Ives, letter to Shoghi Effendi dated 6 April 1937. Published by permission of the Bahá'í World Centre.
29 Letter written on behalf of Shoghi Effendi to Howard Colby Ives dated 26 May 1937, in the Bahá'í World Centre Archives. Published by permission of the Bahá'í World Centre.
30 Howard Colby Ives, letter to Horace Holley dated 22 March 1938.

31 National Spiritual Assembly of the United States and Canada, letter to Howard Colby Ives dated 23 March 1938.
32 Howard Colby Ives, letter to Horace Holley dated 30 March 1938.
33 National Spiritual Assembly of the United States and Canada, letter to Howard Colby Ives dated 4 April 1938.
34 National Spiritual Assembly of the United States and Canada, letter to Howard Colby Ives dated 29 August 1938.
35 Howard Colby Ives, letter to Shoghi Effendi dated 19 November 1938, p. 3.
36 Howard Colby Ives, letter to Shoghi Effendi dated 18 February 1940.
37 Harlan Ober, letter to Howard dated 13 March 1940, p. 1.

16 *The Song Celestial*

1 Howard Colby Ives, letter to Shoghi Effendi dated 2 December 1935, p. 2.
2 Mabel Rice-Wray Ives, letter to Doris McKay dated 9 December 1941, pp. 8–9.
3 Howard Colby Ives, letter to Shoghi Effendi, 2 December 1935, p. 2.
4 *World Order Magazine*, vol. 2, no. 1, pp. 15–16.
5 ibid. no. 4, pp. 139–40.
6 ibid. pp. 157–9.
7 Howard Colby Ives, letter to Horace Holley dated 16 April 1938.
8 National Spiritual Assembly of the United States and Canada to Howard Colby Ives dated 20 April 1938.
9 Howard Colby Ives, letter to Nancy Phillips dated 9 June 1938.
10 Howard Colby Ives, circular letter, 1938.
11 Letter written on behalf of Shoghi Effendi to Howard Colby Ives dated 30 June 1938, in the Bahá'í World Centre Archives. Published by permission of the Bahá'í World Centre.
12 Howard Colby Ives, letter to Nancy Phillips dated 21 Oct 1938.
13 *The Song Celestial*, 1938 Preface.
14 Howard Colby Ives, *The Song Celestial*, pp. 2–3, 60–62.
15 Henry Crane, letter to Howard Colby Ives dated 24 October 1938.
16 National Spiritual Assembly of the United States and Canada, letter to Howard Colby Ives dated 12 July 1939.
17 Howard Colby Ives, letter to Horace Holley dated 19 July 1939.
18 Letter written on behalf of Shoghi Effendi to Howard Colby Ives dated 21 August 1939, in the Bahá'í World Centre Archives. Published by permission of the Bahá'í World Centre.
19 ibid. p. 4.
20 1939 Preface to *The Song Celestial*, unpublished.

21 Howard Colby Ives, letter to Shoghi Effendi dated 19 November 1938, p. 1.
22 Howard Colby Ives, letter to Nancy Phillips dated 23 December 1938.
23 Rúḥíyyih Khánum, letter to Howard Colby Ives dated 21 November 1939.
24 Albert Windust, letter to Mabel Ives dated 01 August 1939.
25 Howard Colby Ives, letter to Shoghi Effendi dated 2 December 1935, p. 2.
26 Letter written on behalf of Shoghi Effendi to Howard Colby Ives dated 31 December 1935, in the Bahá'í World Centre Archives. Published by permission of the Bahá'í World Centre.
27 *The Song Celestial*, Antiphony.
28 Howard Colby Ives, letter to Shoghi Effendi dated 12 February 1936.
29 Letter written on behalf of Shoghi Effendi to Howard Colby Ives dated 8 March 1936, in the Bahá'í World Centre Archives. Published by permission of the Bahá'í World Centre.
30 Letter written on behalf of Shoghi Effendi to Howard Colby Ives dated 25 July 1936, in the Bahá'í World Centre Archives. Published by permission of the Bahá'í World Centre.
31 Howard Colby Ives, letter to Shoghi Effendi dated 20 October 1936, p.1.
32 Letter written on behalf of Shoghi Effendi to Howard Colby Ives dated 15 May 1936, in the Bahá'í World Centre Archives. Published by permission of the Bahá'í World Centre.
33 Howard Colby Ives, letter to Husayn Rabbani dated 13 June 1936.
34 Dr Yúnis Khán Afrúkhtih, 'Síyáh-Chál and Qarih-Kahar', translated by Marzieh Carpenter (Marzieh Gail), in the Bahá'í World Centre Archives.

17 Howard's Other Literary Work

1 Howard Colby Ives, letter to Shoghi Effendi dated 2 December 1935.
2 Letter written on behalf of Shoghi Effendi to Howard Colby Ives dated 19 April 1936, in the Bahá'í World Centre Archives. Published by permission of the Bahá'í World Centre.
3 Howard Colby Ives, letter to Shoghi Effendi dated 19 November 1938.
4 ibid.
5 Howard Colby Ives, *The Ocean of His Utterance*, p. 4.
6 ibid. p. 5.
7 Howard Colby Ives, letter to Shoghi Effendi dated 4 December 1937, p. 2.

8 Howard Colby Ives, letter to Shoghi Effendi dated 24 June 1939.
9 Howard Colby Ives, letter to Shoghi Effendi dated 24 June 1939.
10 Letter written on behalf of Shoghi Effendi to Howard Colby Ives dated 21 August 1939, in the Bahá'í World Centre Archives. Published by permission of the Bahá'í World Centre.
11 ibid.
12 'Abdu'l-Bahá, *The Promulgation of Universal Peace*, p. 227.
13 Howard Colby Ives, *Expanding Horizons*, part 1, pp. 2–3.
14 ibid. part 2, Conclusion.
15 Howard Colby Ives, letter to Shoghi Effendi dated 24 June 1939.
16 Letter written on behalf of Shoghi Effendi to Howard Colby Ives dated 21 August 1939, in the Bahá'í World Centre Archives. Published by permission of the Bahá'í World Centre.
17 Howard Colby Ives, letter to Horace Holley dated 21 August 1939.
18 Howard Colby Ives, letter to Nancy Phillips dated 20 December 1939, p. 2.
19 Howard Colby Ives, letter to Shoghi Effendi dated 18 February 1940, in the Bahá'í World Centre Archives. Published by permission of the Bahá'í World Centre.
20 Letter written on behalf of Shoghi Effendi to Howard Colby Ives dated 17 March 1940, in the Bahá'í World Centre Archives. Published by permission of the Bahá'í World Centre.
21 'Life', privately printed.
22 'Tirzah', family collection.
23 'A best seller', draft of a letter to 'S.&S.' (Simon & Schuster?), undated and untitled manuscript.

18 Opening the Seven Year Plan: 1936–1937

1 Shoghi Effendi, *Messages to America: 1932–1946*, p. 6.
2 ibid. p. 7.
3 Howard Colby Ives, letter to Nancy Phillips dated 22 August 1936, p. 2.
4 Mabel Rice-Wray Ives, 'Digest of Teaching Campaign in Omaha, Lincoln and Council Bluffs and Neighborhood', 5 December 1936.
5 Mabel Rice-Wray Ives, letter to Howard dated 27 October 1937.
6 Mabel Rice-Wray Ives, letter to Howard dated 30 October 1937, pp. 3–4.
7 Mabel Rice-Wray Ives, 'Digest of Teaching Campaign . . .'.
8 Mabel Rice-Wray Ives, letter to Howard dated 30 October 1936, pp. 1–3.
9 Howard Colby Ives, letter to Mabel dated 7 December 1936.
10 Lopez, *The Life Story of Edris Rice-Wray, a Woman Doctor*, p. 78–9.

11 Mabel Rice-Wray Ives, letter to Howard dated 7 November 1936, pp. 2–6.
12 Mabel Rice-Wray Ives, 'Digest of Teaching Campaign . . .', p. 2.
13 ibid.
14 Mabel Rice-Wray Ives, letter to Howard dated 20 November 1936.
15 Howard Colby Ives, letter to Mabel dated 17 November 1936.
16 Mabel Rice-Wray Ives, letter to Howard dated 26 November 1936, p. 2.
17 ibid. p. 1.
18 Mabel Rice-Wray Ives, 'Digest of Teaching Campaign . . .', p. 4.
19 Mabel Rice-Wray Ives, letter to Howard dated 12 December 1936.
20 Mabel Rice-Wray Ives, 'Security for a Failing World', typescript of undated radio talk, p. 1.
21 ibid. p. 5.
22 Howard Colby Ives, letter to Mabel dated 29 October 1936.
23 Howard Colby Ives, letter to Mabel dated 31 October 1936.
24 Howard Colby Ives, letter to Mabel dated 8 November 1936, p. 2.
25 Bahá'í Teaching Committee, letters to Mabel dated 17 January 1937 and 4 February 1937.
26 Mabel Rice-Wray Ives, letter to Gayle Woolson dated 22 January 1937.
27 Mabel Rice-Wray Ives, letter to Howard dated 14 February 1937.
28 Howard Colby Ives, letter to Mabel dated 14 February 1937.
29 Howard Colby Ives, letter to Mabel dated 16 February 1937, p. 1.
30 *Waukegan News-Sun*, 17 February 1937.
31 ibid. 4 and 5 March 1937.
32 Mabel Rice-Wray Ives, 'A Prevue of the World in the Year 2001', radio talk, p. 1.
33 ibid. pp. 2–6.
34 Mabel Rice-Wray Ives, letter to Edris Rice-Wray dated 25 February 1937.
35 E. J. Wright, letter to Mabel dated 10 March 1937.
36 Ives, Mabel Rice-Wray Ives, letter to Howard dated 27 March 1937, pp. 1–2.
37 ibid. p. 4.
38 Mabel Rice-Wray Ives, letter to Howard dated 28 March 1937.
39 Howard Colby Ives, letter to Mabel dated 27 March 1937, pp. 1–2.
40 Mabel Rice-Wray Ives, letter to Howard dated 31 March 1937.
41 ibid. pp. 4–5, 8–10.
42 ibid. p. 9.
43 Howard Colby Ives, letter to Mabel dated 6 April 1937, p. 1.
44 Mabel Rice-Wray Ives, letters to Howard dated 6 April and 11 April 1937.

45 Howard Colby Ives, letter to Mabel dated 6 April 1937, pp. 1–2.
46 Mabel Rice-Wray Ives, letter to Howard dated 11 April 1937, pp. 1–2.
47 Mabel Rice-Wray Ives, letter to Howard dated 20 April 1937, p. 2.
48 Mabel Rice-Wray Ives, letter to Howard dated 24 April 1937, pp. 2–4.
49 ibid. pp. 5–7.
50 Mabel Rice-Wray Ives, undated letter to Shoghi Effendi, p. 1.
51 Mabel Rice-Wray Ives, letter to Howard dated 24 April 1937, pp. 7–8.
52 ibid. p. 12.
53 Mabel Rice-Wray Ives, letter to Howard dated 14 June 1937, pp. 1–2.
54 Mabel Rice-Wray Ives, letter to Howard dated 17 June 1937, pp. 1–2.
55 Mabel Rice-Wray Ives, letter to Howard dated 14 June 1937, pp. 2–3.
56 Mabel Rice-Wray Ives, letter to Shoghi Effendi dated 26 July 1937.
57 ibid. pp. 2–3.
58 'Bahá'í Chronicles', http://bahaichronicles.org/test1/. See also Gentzkow, *The Art of Empowering Others*, a biography of Gayle Woolson.
59 Mabel Rice-Wray Ives, letter to Shoghi Effendi dated 26 July 1937, p. 2.
60 Mabel Rice-Wray Ives, letter to Howard dated 16 June 1937, p. 2.
61 Mabel Rice-Wray Ives, letter to Howard dated 17 June 1937, pp. 5–6.
62 Mabel Rice-Wray Ives, letter to Howard dated 21 June 1937, p. 2.
63 Mabel Rice-Wray Ives, letter to Howard dated 23 June 1937, p. 1.
64 ibid.
65 Mabel Rice-Wray Ives, letter to Howard dated 28 June 1937, p. 2.
66 Mabel Rice-Wray Ives, letter to Howard dated 12 July 1937, p. 1.
67 Mabel Rice-Wray Ives, undated letter to Shoghi Effendi, p. 2.
68 Mabel Rice-Wray Ives, letter to Shoghi Effendi dated 26 July 1937.
69 ibid.
70 ibid.
71 ibid.
72 Letter written on behalf of Shoghi Effendi to Mabel Rice-Wray Ives dated 27 October 1937.
73 Howard Colby Ives, letter to Muriel Barrow dated 15 September 1937.
74 ibid.
75 Howard Colby Ives, letter to Mabel dated 3 October 1937.

76 ibid.
77 Mabel Rice-Wray Ives, letter to Howard dated 27 October 1937.

19 Moncton, New Brunswick, Canada: 1937

1. 'Abdu'l-Bahá, *Tablets of the Divine Plan*, p. 27.
2. Mabel Rice-Wray Ives, letter to Howard dated 2 October 1937.
3. ibid.
4. *The Bates Student*, vol. 65, no. 11 (13 October 1937).
5. Mabel Rice-Wray Ives, letter to Rúhíyyih Khánum dated 29 November 1937, p. 1.
6. Edris Rice-Wray, 'To the Beloved Spiritual Children of Mabel Ives and Others Who Love Her All Over the Country and Canada, Who Hunger to Know the Details of Her Last Days in the Material World', 10 November 1943, pp. 3–4.
7. Mabel Rice-Wray Ives, letter to Howard dated 22 October 1937, p. 1.
8. Quoted in Nakhjavani, *The Maxwells of Montreal*, vol. 2, p. 301.
9. Mabel Rice-Wray Ives, letter to Howard dated 30 October 1937, p. 1.
10. ibid. pp. 1–2.
11. ibid. p. 2.
12. ibid. p. 3.
13. *The Bahá'í World*, vol. XIX, p. 652, and vol. XIV, p. 310.
14. van den Hoonaard, *The Origins of the Bahá'í Community in Canada*, pp. 216–17.
15. Mabel Rice-Wray Ives, letter to Howard dated 4 November 1937.
16. Mabel Rice-Wray Ives, letter to Howard dated 10 November 1937.
17. Mabel Rice-Wray Ives, letter to Howard dated 21 November 1937.
18. Howard Colby Ives, letter to Mabel dated 24 November 1937, pp. 1–2.
19. Mabel Rice-Wray Ives, letters to Howard dated 6 December 1937 and 9 December 1937, p. 6.
20. Mabel Rice-Wray Ives, letter to Rúhíyyih Khánum dated 29 November 1937, pp. 1–2.
21. Rúhíyyih Khánum, letter to Mabel dated 22 January 1938, pp. 1–3.
22. Mabel Rice-Wray Ives, letter to Howard dated 2 December 1937.
23. Howard Colby Ives, letter to Mabel dated 3 December 1937.
24. Howard Colby Ives, letter to Shoghi Effendi dated 4 December 1937.
25. National Spiritual Assembly of the United States and Canada, letter to Howard dated 20 December 1937.
26. Howard Colby Ives, letter to Horace Holley dated 22 December 1937.

27 Mabel Rice-Wray Ives, letter to Howard dated 7 December 1937.
28 Howard Colby Ives, letter to Shoghi Effendi dated 16 December 1937.
29 Letter written on behalf of Shoghi Effendi to Howard Colby Ives dated 30 March 1938, in the Bahá'í World Centre Archives. Published by permission of the Bahá'í World Centre.
30 Mabel Rice-Wray Ives, letter to Howard dated 9 December 1937, pp. 1–3, 5.
31 Mabel Rice-Wray Ives, letter to Howard dated 17 December 1937.
32 Rúḥíyyih Khánum, letter to Mabel dated 22 January 1938, p. 3.

20 Scranton, Pennsylvania, and Chicago: 1938
1 Howard Colby Ives, letter to Horace Holley dated 10 January 1938.
2 Howard Colby Ives, letter to Horace Holley dated 16 January 1938.
3 Howard Colby Ives, letter to Nancy Phillips dated 11 March 1938.
4 From Mabel's lecture card, 17 January 1938.
5 Howard Colby Ives, letter to Horace Holley dated 29 January 1938.
6 National Spiritual Assembly of the United States and Canada, letter to Howard dated 4 February 1938.
7 From Howard's lecture card, 28 February 1938.
8 *The Scranton Tribune*, 6 and 9 February 1938.
9 Leroy Ioas, letter on behalf of the National Teaching Committee to Mabel Ives dated 22 February 1938.
10 Howard Colby Ives, letter to Shoghi Effendi dated 26 February 1938, in the Bahá'í World Centre Archives. Published by permission of the Bahá'í World Centre.
11 Letter written on behalf of Shoghi Effendi to Howard Colby Ives dated 30 March 1938, in the Bahá'í World Centre Archives. Published by permission of the Bahá'í World Centre.
12 Howard Colby Ives, letter to Nancy Phillips dated 12 February 1938, p. 2.
13 Mabel Rice-Wray Ives, letter to Howard dated 25 February 1938.
14 Mabel Rice-Wray Ives, letter to Howard dated 28 February 1938, pp. 1-3.
15 Mabel Rice-Wray Ives, letter to Howard dated 7 March 1938, p. 4.
16 Mabel Rice-Wray Ives, letter to Howard dated 11 March 1938, pp. 1, 3.
17 Mabel Rice-Wray Ives, letter to Howard dated 15 March 1938.
18 Mabel Rice-Wray Ives, letter to Howard dated 5 May 1938, pp. 1–2.
19 ibid. pp. 2–3.
20 Mabel Rice-Wray Ives, letter to Howard dated 8 May 1938, p. 2.

21 Mabel Rice-Wray Ives, letter to Howard dated 21 May 1938.
22 Mabel Rice-Wray Ives, letter to Howard dated 23 May 1938, pp. 1–2.
23 Mabel Rice-Wray Ives, letter to Howard dated 27 May 1938, p. 1.
24 Mabel Rice-Wray Ives, undated letter to Shoghi Effendi written in late May 1938.
25 Letter written on behalf of Shoghi Effendi to Mabel Ives dated 21 June 1938, in the Bahá'í World Centre Archives. Published by permission of the Bahá'í World Centre.
26 Howard Colby Ives, letter to Shoghi Effendi dated 1 June 1938, in the Bahá'í World Centre Archives. Published by permission of the Bahá'í World Centre.

21 Back in Canada: 1938–1939

1 Mabel Rice-Wray Ives, letter to Howard dated 31 May 1938.
2 Howard Colby Ives, letter to Shoghi Effendi dated 1 June 1938.
3 Letter written on behalf of Shoghi Effendi to Howard Colby Ives dated 30 June 1938, in the Bahá'í World Centre Archives. Published by permission of the Bahá'í World Centre.
4 National Spiritual Assembly of the United States and Canada, letter to Mabel Ives dated 27 June 1938.
5 Howard Colby Ives, letter to Nancy Phillips dated 9 July 1938.
6 Mabel Rice-Wray Ives, letter to Horace Holley dated 8 Aug 1938, p. 1.
7 ibid. pp. 1–2.
8 ibid. p. 3.
9 ibid. p. 3.
10 National Spiritual Assembly of the United States and Canada, letter to Howard Colby Ives dated 29 August 1938.
11 Mabel Rice-Wray Ives, undated letter to a friend from November 1938.
12 Howard Colby Ives, letter to Nancy Phillips dated 21 October 1938.
13 Howard Colby Ives, letter to Nancy Phillips dated 23 October 1938.
14 Mabel Rice-Wray Ives, undated letter to a friend from November 1938.
15 Howard Colby Ives, letter to Nancy Phillips dated 11 November 1938, p. 2.
16 Macke, *Take My Love to the Friends: The Story of Laura R. Davis*, pp. 62–3.
17 Mabel Rice-Wray Ives, letter to Horace Holley dated 7 November 1938.

18 Howard Colby Ives, letter to Shoghi Effendi dated 19 November 1938, p. 1. In the Bahá'í World Centre Archives. Published by permission of the Bahá'í World Centre.
19 ibid. p. 2.
20 ibid. p. 3.
21 Letter written on behalf of Shoghi Effendi to Howard Colby Ives dated 31 December 1938, in the Bahá'í World Centre Archives. Published by permission of the Bahá'í World Centre.
22 John Robarts, letter to Edris Rice-Wray dated 30 August 1943.
23 Mabel Rice-Wray Ives, letter to Shoghi Effendi dated 23 November 1938, p. 1.
24 Harper, *Lights of Fortitude*, p. 478.
25 *The Bahá'í World*, vol. XIX, p. 663.
26 Redman, *The Knights of Bahá'u'lláh*, p. 277.
27 Presumably for the second edition.
28 McKay, *Fires in Many Heart*, p. 279.
29 Mabel Rice-Wray Ives, letter to Shoghi Effendi dated 23 November 1938, p. 1.
30 ibid. pp. 2–4.
31 Letter written on behalf of Shoghi Effendi to Leroy Ioas dated 14 November 1935.
32 Howard Colby Ives, letter to Muriel dated 4 January 1939, p. 1.
33 Howard Colby Ives, letter to Shoghi Effendi dated 15 March 1939.
34 Letter written on behalf of Shoghi Effendi to Howard Colby Ives dated 22 April 1939, in the Bahá'í World Centre Archives. Published by permission of the Bahá'í World Centre.
35 Mabel Rice-Wray Ives, letter to Shoghi Effendi dated 16 March 1939.
36 van den Hoonaard, *The Origins of the Bahá'í Community in Canada*, p. 179.
37 Letter written on behalf of Shoghi Effendi to Mabel Ives dated 22 April 1939, in the Bahá'í World Centre Archives. Published by permission of the Bahá'í World Centre.
38 Mabel Rice-Wray Ives, letter to Colston Rice-Wray dated 20 March 1939.
39 Mabel Rice-Wray Ives, letter to Horace Holley dated 21 July 1939.
40 McKay, *Fires in Many Hearts*, p. 277.
41 *Bahá'í News*, no. 128 (August 1939), p. 7.
42 National Spiritual Assembly of the United States and Canada, letter to Mabel Ives dated 21 September 1939.
43 Mabel Rice-Wray Ives, letter to Shoghi Effendi dated 10 December 1939.

22 Memphis and Howard's Declining Health

1. Mabel Rice-Wray Ives, letter to Leroy Ioas dated 5 October 1939, p. 1.
2. Mabel Rice-Wray Ives, letter to friends dated 19 October 1939, p. 1.
3. ibid. pp. 2–3.
4. ibid. p. 2.
5. ibid. p. 2–3.
6. ibid. p. 3.
7. ibid. p. 4.
8. Leroy Ioas, letter to Mabel dated 21 October 1939.
9. See Paul Haney, Horace Holley and Corinne True, 'Ahmad Sohrab and the New History Society'.
10. Mabel Rice-Wray Ives, letter to friends dated 19 October 1939, p. 4.
11. ibid.
12. ibid. p. 5.
13. Leroy Ioas, letter to Mabel dated 21 October 1939.
14. From Mabel's Memphis talks card, November 1939.
15. Mabel Rice-Wray Ives, letter to Leroy Ioas dated 8 November 1939.
16. Mabel Rice-Wray Ives, letter to Shoghi Effendi dated 10 December 1939, p. 2.
17. Mabel Rice-Wray Ives, letter to Sheila Rice-Wray dated 14 Dec 1939.
18. ibid.
19. Mabel Rice-Wray Ives, letter to Leroy Ioas dated 18 January 1940, pp. 1–2.
20. Howard Colby Ives, letter to Nancy Phillips dated 23 January 1940.
21. Mabel Rice-Wray Ives, letter to 'Clair' dated 30 December 1939.
22. Howard Colby Ives, letter to Nancy Phillips dated 23 January 1940.
23. Howard Colby Ives, letter to Shoghi Effendi, 18 February 1940, p. 2.
24. Howard Colby Ives, 'Spiritual Diary', 2 April 1940, pp. 1–2.
25. ibid. pp. 6–7.
26. ibid. 4 April 1940, pp. 8-11.
27. Howard Colby Ives, letter to Shoghi Effendi, 18 February 1940, p. 2.
28. Howard Colby Ives, letter to Nancy Phillips, 20 December 1939.
29. Letter written on behalf of Shoghi Effendi to Howard Colby Ives dated 26 November 1939, in the Bahá'í World Centre Archives. Published by permission of the Bahá'í World Centre.
30. Letter written on behalf of Shoghi Effendi to Howard Colby Ives dated 17 March 1940, in the Bahá'í World Centre Archives. Published by permission of the Bahá'í World Centre.
31. National Teaching Committee, letter to Mabel dated 8 December 1939; Mabel Rice-Wray Ives, letter to the National Teaching Committee dated 18 December 1939.

32 National Teaching Committee, letter to Mabel dated 10 January 1940.
33 Mabel Rice-Wray Ives, letter to the National Teaching Committee dated 12 January 1940.
34 Mabel Rice-Wray Ives, letter to Charlotte Linfoot, 23 January 1940.
35 National Teaching Committee, letter to Mabel dated 25 January 1940; cable dated 25 January 1940; letter to Mabel dated 4 February 1940.
36 Mabel Rice-Wray Ives, letter to Leroy Ioas dated 8 February 1940, p. 1.
37 Mabel Rice-Wray Ives, letter to Shoghi Effendi dated 18 January 1940.
38 Mabel Rice-Wray Ives, letter to Leroy Ioas dated 8 February 1940.
39 National Teaching Committee, letter to Mabel dated 13 February 1940.
40 Howard Colby Ives, letter to Shoghi Effendi 18 February 1940.
41 Howard Colby Ives, letter to Nancy Phillips dated 29 February 1940, p. 2.
42 Mabel Rice-Wray Ives, letter to Leroy Ioas dated 11 March 1940.
43 *The Bahá'í World*, vol. XV, p. 439.
44 Saunders, *Of Wars and Worship*, pp. 72, 74.
45 Mabel Rice-Wray Ives, letter to the National Teaching Committee dated 11 March 1940, pp. 1–2.
46 Leroy Ioas, letter to Mabel dated 31 March 1940.
47 Mabel Rice-Wray Ives, letter to the National Teaching Committee dated 19 June 1940, p. 3.
48 Mabel Rice-Wray Ives, letter to the National Teaching Committee dated 7 April 1940, p.1.

23 Further Afield in the American South

1 Mabel Rice-Wray Ives, letter to the National Teaching Committee dated 7 April 1940.
2 Mabel Rice-Wray Ives, letter to the National Teaching Committee dated 19 June 1940.
3 Mabel Rice-Wray Ives, letter to Doris McKay dated 9 December 1941.
4 Howard Colby Ives, letter to George Miller dated 27 May 1940.
5 Mabel Rice-Wray Ives, letter to Howard dated 31 May 1940.
6 Howard Colby Ives, letter to Mabel dated 1 June 1940.
7 Mabel Rice-Wray Ives, letter to Howard dated 2 June 1940.
8 Mabel Rice-Wray Ives, letter to the National Teaching Committee dated 19 June 1940.

9   Mabel Rice-Wray Ives, letter to Howard dated 25 June 1940, p. 2.
10 Mabel Rice-Wray Ives, letter to the National Teaching Committee dated 19 June 1940, p. 1.
11 Vogel Park Special Teaching Project schedule.
12 Mabel Rice-Wray Ives, letter to Howard dated 9 June 1940.
13 Mabel Rice-Wray Ives, letter to Nellie Roche dated 20 July 1940.
14 ibid.
15 Mabel Rice-Wray Ives, letter to Shoghi Effendi dated 26 July 1940, p. 4.
16 Mabel Rice-Wray Ives, letter to the National Teaching Committee dated 19 June 1940, p. 2.
17 Mabel Rice-Wray Ives, letter to Leroy Ioas dated 20 July 1940, p. 1.
18 Mabel Rice-Wray Ives, letter to Nellie Roche dated 20 July 1940, p. 1.
19 Roberta Wilson, letter to Edris Rice-Wray dated 15 December 1943, p. 1.
20 Mabel Rice-Wray Ives, letter to Shoghi Effendi dated 26 July 1940, p. 4.
21 Letter written on behalf of Shoghi Effendi to Mabel Ives dated 10 November 1940, in the Bahá'í World Centre Archives. Published by permission of the Bahá'í World Centre.
22 Mabel Rice-Wray Ives, diary entry for 1 October 1940.
23 Mabel Rice-Wray Ives, diary entry for 11 October 1940.
24 Mabel Rice-Wray Ives, diary entry for 15 October 1940.
25 Bivins, 'The Door of Hope: A Tribute to Mr and Mrs Howard Colby Ives', transcript of radio talk, 9 July 1943, quoting talk by Mabel Ives as reported in the *Greenwood Commonwealth*, 18 October 1940.
26 Mabel Rice-Wray Ives, letter to Marion (Little?) dated 20 December 1940, p. 2; Mabel Rice-Wray Ives, diary entries for 7 and 9 November 1940.
27 Mabel Rice-Wray Ives, letter to Marion dated 20 December 1940, p. 2.
28 Mabel Rice-Wray Ives, diary entry for 19 November 1940.
29 Mabel Rice-Wray Ives, letter to 'Mario' dated 20 December 1940, p. 1; Mabel's diary entry sidenote, last page.
30 Mabel Rice-Wray Ives, letter to Marion dated 4 January 1941.
31 Howard Colby Ives, letter to Nancy Phillips dated 11 December 1940.
32 Mabel Rice-Wray Ives, radio script, undated, p. 1.
33 ibid.
34 Mabel Rice-Wray Ives, report to the National Teaching Committee dated 1 March 1941, p. 1.
35 ibid.

36 ibid. p. 2.
37 ibid. p. 3.
38 Mabel Rice-Wray Ives, letter to Howard dated 21 February 1941.
39 Howard Colby Ives, letter to Mabel dated 22 February 1941.
40 Mabel Rice-Wray Ives, letter to Horace Holley dated 14 April 1941.
41 FBI, report of 9 April 1941, p. 1, in USBNA, Brent Poirier Papers.
42 ibid. p. 2.
43 ibid. p. 3.
44 ibid.
45 FBI, report of 6 June 1941, p. 2, ibid.
46 FBI, report of 22 July 1941, ibid.
47 FBI, report of 22 August 1941, ibid.

24 The End of Howard's Physical Road

1 McKay, *Fires in Many Hearts*, pp. 293–4.
2 ibid. p. 294.
3 Howard Colby Ives, letter to Mabel dated 12 February 1941.
4 Howard Colby Ives, letter to Mabel dated 17 February 1941, pp. 4, 6.
5 McKay, *Fires in Many Hearts*, pp. 300–01.
6 Howard Colby Ives, letter to Mabel dated 22 February 1941, p. 2.
7 Howard Colby Ives, letter to Mabel dated 23 February 1941.
8 Howard Colby Ives, letter to Mabel dated 27 February 1941, pp. 3–4.
9 Howard Colby Ives, letter to Mabel dated 7 March 1941, p. 2.
10 Mabel Rice-Wray Ives, letter to Howard dated 12 March 1941, pp. 6, 10.
11 McKay, *Fires in Many Hearts*, pp. 301–2.
12 ibid. pp. 303–04.
13 ibid. p. 304.
14 ibid. p. 307.
15 ibid. p. 307.
16 Howard Colby Ives, letter to Mabel dated 19 March 1941, p. 1.
17 Mabel Rice Wray Ives, letter to Howard dated 24 April 1941, p. 2.
18 Howard Colby Ives, letter to Mabel dated 21 April 1941, pp. 1–2.
19 Howard Colby Ives, letter to Mabel dated 21 April 1941, p. 4.
20 Mabel Rice Wray Ives, letter to Howard dated 26 April 1941, pp. 1–2.
21 Mabel Rice Wray Ives, letters to Howard dated 29 and 30 April, and 1 and 2 May 1941.
22 Mabel Rice Wray Ives, letter to Howard dated 2 May 1941, pp. 3–4.
23 ibid. pp. 7–8.
24 Mabel Rice Wray Ives, diary entry for 1 May 1941, p. 5.

25 Howard Colby Ives, last poem written on 13 May 1941.
26 Howard Colby Ives, letter to Barbara dated 23 May 1941.
27 McKay, 'Howard Colby Ives', In Memoriam, in *The Bahá'í World*, vol. IX, pp. 611–12.
28 Mabel Rice Wray Ives, letter to friends dated 27 June 1941, pp. 5–6.
29 Howard Colby Ives, letter to Mabel dated 13 June 1941.
30 Mabel Rice Wray Ives, letter to friends dated 27 June 1941, pp. 5–6.
31 ibid. p. 1.
32 ibid.
33 ibid. p. 8.
34 ibid. p. 1.
35 ibid. p. 9.
36 ibid. p. 2.
37 Elizabeth Cheney, story told at Louhelen on 30 August 1953 and shared with the authors by Jack McCants in an email dated 4 March 2014.
38 Mabel Rice-Wray Ives, letter to friends dated 27 June 1941, p. 3.
39 'Howard Colby Ives Memorial Gathering', 23 June 1941, Little Rock, p. 1.
40 Mabel Rice-Wray Ives, diary entries for 29 and 30 June 1941.
41 Mabel Rice Wray Ives, letter to Florence Aten dated 2 July 1941, p. 1.
42 Mabel Rice-Wray Ives, letter to friends dated 27 June 1941, p. 3.
43 Shoghi Effendi, cable to Mabel Ives dated 21 June 1941, ibid., also printed in *The Bahá'í World*, vol. IX, p. 613.
44 Mabel Rice-Wray Ives, letter to Shoghi Effendi dated 16 September 1941, p. 1.
45 National Teaching Committee, cable to Mabel dated 29 June 1941.
46 Mabel Rice-Wray Ives, letter to friends dated 27 June 1941, pp. 4–5.
47 McKay, 'Howard Colby Ives', In Memoriam, in *The Bahá'í World*, vol. IX, p. 613.
48 'Howard Colby Ives Memorial Gathering', 23 June 1941, Little Rock, p. 1.
49 ibid. pp. 1–2.
50 Mabel Rice-Wray Ives, letter to Florence Aten dated 2 July 1941, p. 1.
51 Mabel Rice-Wray Ives, letter to Doris McKay dated 9 December 1941, p. 10.

25 Mabel Soldiers on in the South

1 Mabel Rice-Wray Ives, letter to Muriel dated 1 July 1941.

2 Mabel Rice-Wray Ives, letter to Johanna Zimmerman and Claire Keller dated 5 July 1941, p. 2.
3 Mabel Rice-Wray Ives, letter to Doris McKay dated 5? July 1941, p. 1.
4 ibid.
5 Mabel Rice-Wray Ives, letter to Shoghi Effendi dated 16 September 1941, p. 3.
6 Mabel Rice-Wray Ives, letter to Shoghi Effendi dated 16 September 1941.
7 Letter written on behalf of Shoghi Effendi to Mabel Ives dated 24 December 1941, in the Bahá'í World Centre Archives. Published by permission of the Bahá'í World Centre.
8 Mabel Rice-Wray Ives, letter to Johanna Zimmerman and Claire Keller dated 5 July 1941, p. 1.
9 Mabel Rice-Wray Ives, letter to the National Teaching Committee dated 18 February 1942.
10 Mabel Rice-Wray Ives, diary entry for 26 August 1941.
11 Mabel Rice-Wray Ives, letter to Shoghi Effendi dated 16 September 1941, p. 3.
12 Mabel Rice-Wray Ives, diary entry for 15 September 1941.
13 Mabel Rice-Wray Ives, diary entries for 9 and 10 August 1941; Margaret Ruhe, letter to Edris Rice-Wray dated 3 December 1943.
14 Mabel Rice-Wray Ives, letter to Shoghi Effendi dated 24 May 1942, p. 2.
15 Mabel Rice-Wray Ives, diary entry for 21 October 1941.
16 Mabel Rice-Wray Ives, diary entry for 25 September 1941.
17 ibid.
18 Mabel Rice-Wray Ives, diary entry for 24 October 1941.
19 Mabel Rice-Wray Ives, letter to the National Teaching Committee dated 10 December 1941, pp. 4–5.
20 ibid. p. 1.
21 Mabel Rice-Wray Ives, diary entry for 26 October 1941.
22 Mabel Rice-Wray Ives, letter to the National Teaching Committee dated 10 December 1941, p. 1.
23 Mabel Rice-Wray Ives, letter to Shoghi Effendi dated 16 September 1941, pp. 3–4.
24 Letter written on behalf of Shoghi Effendi to Mabel Ives dated 24 December 1941, in the Bahá'í World Centre Archives. Published by permission of the Bahá'í World Centre.
25 Mabel Rice-Wray Ives, letter to the National Teaching Committee dated 10 December 1941, p. 2.
26 ibid.

27 ibid. p. 4.
28 ibid.
29 Mabel Rice-Wray Ives,, letter to the National Teaching Committee dated 18 February 1942, p.1.
30 National Teaching Committee, letter to Mabel Ives dated 2 January 1942.
31 Edris Rice-Wray, letter to Mabel dated 8 January 1942, pp. 1–2.
32 Mabel Rice-Wray Ives, letter to the National Teaching Committee dated 18 February 1942, p. 1.
33 Mabel Rice-Wray Ives, letter to Shoghi Effendi dated 24 May 1942, p. 2.
34 Mabel Rice-Wray Ives, letter to the National Teaching Committee dated 18 February 1942, p. 2.
35 *The Bahá'í World: In Memoriam 1992–1997*, p. 67.
36 Saunders, *Of Wars and Worship*, pp. 90–92.
37 Mabel Rice-Wray Ives, letter to the National Teaching Committee dated 18 February 1942, pp. 1–2.
38 ibid. p. 2.
39 ibid.
40 Leroy Ioas on behalf of the National Teaching Committee, letter to Mabel dated 5 March 1942.
41 Mabel Rice-Wray Ives, letter to Shoghi Effendi dated 24 May 1942, p. 2.
42 ibid. p. 1.
43 ibid. pp. 1–2.
44 ibid.
45 Letter written on behalf of Shoghi Effendi to Mabel Ives dated 5 July 1942, in the Bahá'í World Centre Archives. Published by permission of the Bahá'í World Centre.
46 Mabel Rice-Wray Ives, letter to Shoghi Effendi, undated but probably late July 1942, pp. 1–2.

26 Mabel Joins Howard

1 Mabel Rice-Wray Ives, letter to Shoghi Effendi dated 24 May 1942, p. 3.
2 Mabel Rice-Wray Ives, diary entry for 2 June 1942, p. 1.
3 Letter written on behalf of Shoghi Effendi to Mabel Ives dated 5 July 1942, in the Bahá'í World Centre Archives. Published by permission of the Bahá'í World Centre.
4 Mabel Rice-Wray Ives, letter to Shoghi Effendi, undated but probably late July 1942, p. 1.

5 Mabel Rice-Wray Ives, diary entry for 17 August 1942, p. 3.
6 National Teaching Committee, letter to Mabel Ives dated 21 September 1942, p. 2.
7 Mabel Rice-Wray Ives, letter to the National Teaching Committee dated 28 October 1942, pp. 1-2.
8 Mabel Rice-Wray Ives, diary entry for 11 October 1942, p. 7.
9 Mabel Rice-Wray Ives, letter to the National Teaching Committee dated 28 October 1942, p. 1.
10 Mabel Rice-Wray Ives, diary entry for 23 October 1942, p. 7.
11 Mabel Rice-Wray Ives, letter to the National Teaching Committee dated 28 October 1942, pp. 1-2.
12 Mabel Rice-Wray Ives, letter to the National Teaching Committee dated 28 November 1942; NTC to Mabel, letter dated 17 Nov 1942.
13 National Teaching Committee, letter to Mabel dated 22 December 1942, p. 1.
14 ibid.
15 Mabel Rice-Wray Ives, letter to Olivia Kelsey (?) dated 21 January 1943, p. 1.
16 ibid. p. 2.
17 ibid. p. 1.
18 National Teaching Committee letters to Mabel Ives dated 23 and 31 January 1943.
19 Mabel Rice-Wray Ives, diary entry for 28 January 1943.
20 Rúḥíyyih Khánum, letter to Mabel Ives dated 19 March 1943.
21 Mabel Rice-Wray Ives, diary entry for 6 April, 1943.
22 Edris and Colston Rice-Wray, 'Mabel Rice-Wray Ives', p. 24.
23 ibid.
24 Mabel Rice-Wray Ives, diary entries for 27 April to 11 May 1943.
25 Edris Rice-Wray, 'To the Beloved Spiritual Children of Mabel Ives and Others Who Love Her All Over the Country and Canada, Who Hunger to Know the Details of Her Last Days in the Material World', 10 November 1943, p. 1.
26 ibid.
27 ibid. pp. 2-3.
28 ibid. p. 4.
29 ibid. p. 5.
30 Edris Rice-Wray, *The Life Story of Edris Rice-Wray, a Woman Doctor*, p. 81.
31 Edris Rice-Wray, 'To the Beloved Spiritual Children of Mabel Ives...', p. 5.
32 Cable from Shoghi Effendi, quoted ibid. p. 7.

33 Letter written on behalf of Shoghi Effendi to the Regional Teaching Committee of Alabama, East and Middle Tennessee dated 10 November 1943, quoted ibid. p. 9.
34 ibid. p. 9.
35 Edris Rice-Wray, 'To the Beloved Spiritual Children of Mabel Ives...', p. 6.
36 Letter from a Bahá'í in Toronto to Edris Rice-Wray dated 19 June 1943, p. 3.
37 Alvin Blum, letter to Edris Rice-Wray dated 26 July 1943.
38 Kenneth Christian, letter to Edris Rice-Wray dated 31 July 1943.
39 David Hofman, undated letter to Edris Rice-Wray (in 1943).
40 Local Spiritual Assembly of Toronto, letter to Edris Rice-Wray dated 3 August 1943.

Two Talks by Howard Colby Ives

1 *Star of the West*, vol. 11, no. 2 (9 April 1920), pp. 27–30.
2 USBNA, Howard Colby Ives Papers.
3 These quotations are from the translations available at the time, now superseded by authoritative translations.

Two Talks by Mabel Rice-Wray Ives

1 Both the talks given here are from undated and unpublished transcriptions in USBNA, Ives Papers.

Index

Note: Place names of cities and towns in the United States and Canada are listed under the name of the state.

'Abdu'l-Bahá ix, x, xi, xiv, 2, 18-9, 22-39, 47, 51, 54, 64, 69, 71-4, 77, 83, 85-7, 89, 91, 92, 96, 98, 100, 105, 109, 121, 123-4, 126, 129, 137-8, 147, 149, 161, 164, 169, 178, 196-7, 205, 216, 228, 231, 256, 261, 276, 235-6, 294, 307, 311, 328, 334, 341, 381-82, 385, 390, 392, 395, 397, 406, 414, 431, 432, 441, 443, 449
  described by Howard Colby Ives xiv, 38-9, 85-6, 207, 209-10, 216-17, 226, 229, 231, 238, 240
  Tablets
    to Barbara Ives 180
    of the Divine Plan 54, 77, 256-7, 285
    to Howard Ives xi-xii, 2, 5-6, 31-2, 36-7, 40-44, 46-51, 53, 61-2, 76-7, 80, 82, 88-9, 110, 196-7, 394
    to Mabel Rice-Wray Ives 67-68, 70, 72, 74-75, 76, 82, 88-9
    to Roy Wilhelm 46
    to Theron Rice-Wray 67, 68
  Will and Testament 69, 73, 91-2, 166, 466
Adams, president 10
Afnan, Ruhi 124, 126, 200-01
Africa 32
Afrúkhtih, Dr Yúnis Khán 232-5
Alabama 258, 399, 413, 416, 433
  Birmingham 401, 405, 406-11, 419
  Decatur 408

Alexander, John 273-7
Alexander Hamilton Institute (Business Course) 44-5, 79
Allen, Jean 366
Allen, Mr 95-6
Apostolic Institute, The 16, 41
Arizona
  Jerome 193
Arkansas 258, 366, 398, 399, 413, 416, 433
  Hot Springs 344-5, 350, 352-3, 357, 362-4, 366, 369, 377, 397-400
  Little Rock 362, 363-9, 372, 374, 377-8, 393, 397, 398, 399, 400, 431
  Pine Bluff 344

Báb, the 92, 109, 117, 161, 228, 229, 231
Baghdadi, Zia 171
Bahádur, 'Azizu'lláh 93
Bahá'í Administrative Order 81, 168, 256, 276, 288, 326, 334, 336
Bahá'í News 210, 212, 225, 314
Bahá'í Procedure 376
Bahá'í World, The 204, 207, 395, 422
Bahá'u'lláh x, 5, 23, 32, 34, 36, 44, 72, 80, 97, 109, 111, 115-16, 119, 123, 130, 137, 140, 142, 147, 149, 156, 164-6, 176, 181-2, 185-88, 200, 204-5, 217, 220-21, 225, 228, 231, 236, 246, 249, 258-9, 264-5, 272, 274, 276, 279, 281, 283,

501

285-8, 291-2, 306, 309, 311, 317, 326, 331, 333, 338, 340, 348, 359-60, 365, 372, 374, 381, 386, 390, 393, 395, 398, 401, 413-14, 417, 425, 428-29, 431, 433, 439, 454
  belief in/acceptance of 28, 37-8, 42, 46, 64, 75, 104, 112, 261, 289, 330, 336, 366, 400, 418, 422
  Faith of ix, 35, 256-7, 278, 394, 409
  imprisonment 198, 229, 232, 234, 360
  life 112, 196, 216
  Revelation of 127, 177, 191, 238, 244, 342
  teachings 38, 40, 47, 60, 81, 91, 113, 117, 125, 146, 153, 197, 227, 267-8, 275, 298, 316, 361, 384, 411, 449
  Writings x-xi, 52-3, 141, 161, 191-5, 210, 226, 242, 382-3, 438, 440, 447-8
    Epistle to the Son of the Wolf 194
    Gleanings from the Writings of Bahá'u'lláh x-xi, 285, 355, 426
    Hidden Words 43, 134
    Kitáb-i-Aqdas 153
    Kitáb-i-Íqán 313, 437
    Seven Valleys 22, 27, 31-2, 43, 119-20, 238, 343
    Tablet of Ahmad 198
    Tablet to the Christians 199
Bahá'u'lláh and the New Era 116, 270
Baird, Kay (Lee) 354, 307-8
Baird, Rev. and Mrs 400
Baker, Dorothy 134, 201-2, 264, 303-4, 306, 311, 350, 359, 362, 413
Baker, Frank 201-2
Ballon, Mr 274-5
Barr, Lulu Mabel 325, 327
Barrow, Muriel *see* Ives, Muriel,
Barrow, Reginald 282-3, 292, 293-4, 462
Barton, Mrs Enos 327
Barton, Mary 304, 325, 334, 336, 350

Beecher, Ellen 69
Beecroft, Elsie 329
Bellegarde, Mons. 135
Bernquist, Joseph 276
Bidwell, Mrs 388
Bivens, Evelyn 403, 405, 406
Blum, Alvin 335, 349-50, 352, 355, 356, 429
Blum, Gertrude (Gewertz) 335, 386, 405, 406-7, 410
Blum, Keithie (Saunders) 349
Bogan, Grace 376
Borah, Senator William 145-6, 157-8
Bosch, John 128
Breakwell, Thomas 4
Bricka, Mrs 261
Bridges, Eleanor 408
Brooks, Elizabeth 327
Brotherhood Church 16, 19-22, 27, 30, 35, 40, 41
Bruegger, Marguerite 265, 273
Bryne, William 288

California 64
  Geyserville 128
  Los Angeles 70-71, 351
  San Francisco 51
  Tropico 70, 73
Canada 85, 292, 301, 327-8, 329
  see also Manitoba, New Brunswick, Newfoundland, Nova Scotia, Ontario, Prince Edward Island, Quebec
Capper, Senator Arthur 151-2
Carson, Edris Rice-Wray *see* Rice-Wray, Edris
Channing, William Ellery 15, 467
Cheney, Elizabeth 390
Childs, William 7
Christian, Kenneth 429
Christian Science Monitor 185
Christie, Mr 315
Clark, Mrs 417
Cobb, Stanwood 135, 208, 211, 214, 454
Cohen, Mrs 406

Coleman, Mrs 120
Collison, Mary and Rex 116-19, 128
Connecticut
  Hartford 156
  New London 16, 50
Connecticut Universalist Convention 17
Cooper, Ella 41, 51
Cornell, Ruth 346
Cornell Cosmopolitan Club
Cornell University 126
Cox, Dr and Mrs Richard 336-7
Crane, Henry 225

Dante 229
D'Evelyn, Dr Frederick 77, 92
Davis, Laura 315-16, 320, 430-31
Davis, Mr & Mrs 135
Davis, Victor 320
Denny, George 338
Derr, Lillian 260
Doty, Pearl Battee 66
Drury, Miss 156
Dunbar, Hooper 192
Dunn, Mr 418

Eggleston, Lewis (Lou) and Helen 134
Ellen, Sara 419
Ellis, Mrs 405, 410
Elizabeth Journal 121
Ericson, Karl 270
Errington, Frieda 271-3
Errington, Rev. Frederick, and Mrs 271-3
Everybody's Magazine 18, 21

FBI (Federal Bureau of Investigation) 367-71
Fettig, Martha 408
Fisher, Mrs 261
Firoozi, Marguerite 327
Florida 215, 294, 300, 303, 305
  Coronado Beach 302
  Miami 294
Ford, Henry 73
Frankland, Kathryn 70, 420-22

Gardner, Cliff 328
Gardner, Lloyd 320, 328
Garret, Mrs 365
Geary, Irving and Mabel 290, 312
Geneva, Switzerland 145, 262
Georgia 258, 356, 433
  Atlanta 362, 388, 408
  Vogel State Park, Cleveland 355-7, 386-7, 399, 412
Georgian Bay, Lake Huron 311, 314, 320
Getsinger, Lua 32
Gewertz, Gertrude *see* Blum, Gertrude
Glesden, Miss 350
Gray, Corrila 350
Greenland 285
Greenleaf, Mrs (Elizabeth) 121
Gregory, Louis 34, 84-5, 95, 133, 151, 163-4, 348
Gulf Park College 336

Hackett, Martha 357-8
Hadbeh, Namaan 328
Hamilton, Mrs 403
Hancock, John 10
Haney, Mariam 65-6, 69, 70-71, 184, 205
Haney, Paul 69, 71
Hannen, Joseph 54, 61, 73, 74
Hansen, Mr & Mrs Irving 401
Hansen, Pauline, 366
Haquelenburg, Major 101
Harper, Barron 320
Harris, Hooper 69
Hawkins, Lucy 366
Hayes, Bill 203
Heald, Mrs or Miss 261, 262
Heist, Dr Albert 99-100
Henderson Professor George 346, 350, 362, 376
Hofman, David 429-30
Holley, Horace 152, 165, 217-18, 246, 294, 327, 366, 374, 375
Holley, Marion (Hofman) 300

Homer, Mrs 417
Hooker, Dr Donald 159
Hoover, President 165
Hopper, Bessie 135
Hoyt, Elizabeth (Ives) 10, 44, 178
Hoyt, William 43-4
Hubert, James 133

Idaho 158
Illinois 203, 258, 266, 278, 433
  Chicago 64, 74, 79, 189, 193, 228, 265, 269, 272, 275, 278, 304, 305-9, 311, 331-2, 377-8, 385, 423
  Glenview 416, 418
  O'Fallon 425
  Rogers Park 416
  Urbana 189, 202, 333
  Waukegan 265, 266-9, 277, 332
  Wilmette 171, 189, 201, 202, 265, 266, 367, 370-71, 416
  Winnetka 189, 193, 202-3, 204, 236, 258, 264, 303-4, 317, 325
Inderlied, Helen 3-4, 69, 126-8, 297, 300, 305
Ingalls, Allison 335
Ioas, Leroy 246, 311, 322-3, 334, 335, 346, 347-8, 350, 357, 408
Iowa 266, 278, 417, 418, 433
  Cedar Rapids 417, 418, 419
  Davenport 418
  Des Moines 264
Irani, Dr 135
Ives, Barbara (Obrig, Reich) ix, 61, 106, 180-81, 228, 252, 292, 380-85, 392, 397
Ives, Charles 7
Ives, Douglas 14
Ives, Elizabeth Hoyt 10, 14, 15, 17, 44-5, 80, 178
Ives, Florence 7, 113
Ives, Gertrude 7
Ives, Howard Colby
  early life and family 7, 9-11, 14-17
  correspondence with
    'Abdu'l-Bahá 26-7, 33-5, 37, 40-42, 44, 47-8, 50, 61-2, 76, 82, 88-90, 110
  Tablets and messages from
    'Abdu'l-Bahá xi, xii, 2, 5-6, 31-2, 35-7, 46-50, 53-4, 80, 196-7, 394
Joseph Hannen 54, 61
Horace Holley 217-18, 246-47
Barbara Ives 380-85
Mabel Ives xii-xiv, 97-9, 101-2, 104-5, 107-10, 112, 114-15, 120, 147-51, 169, 170-71, 173-74, 175-81, 189-90, 200, 202-3, 261-2, 264, 265-6, 272-3, 283, 353-5, 373-4, 377, 387
Muriel Ives 282, 323-4
Doris McKay 130-31
National Spiritual Assembly of the United States and Canada 4, 5, 91, 95-6, 143-5, 206, 208-10, 212-19, 220-21, 225-7, 246, 248, 294, 298, 301, 304, 310, 314, 328, 343, 374
Theodore Obrig 55-61
Agnes Parsons 95
Nancy Phillips 191, 193-8, 312, 338-9, 362-3
Rúḥíyyih Khánum 227
Shoghi Effendi 5-6, 93, 111, 123, 129, 153-64, 171-3, 176-7, 180-81, 205-6, 208, 209, 210-12, 215, 218, 220-21, 228-9, 231-2, 236-7, 239-40, 246, 248, 293-95, 300-01, 309, 311-12, 317-18, 324, 339, 343-4, 348-9
literary work
  Portals to Freedom ix, xii, xiv, 1, 2, 4, 5, 9, 17, 32, 85-6, 203, 204-19, 220, 239, 248, 271-3, 275-6, 283, 288, 290, 301, 309-10, 313-14, 320, 327, 343, 397, 429, 433
  The Song Celestial 202, 204, 205,

220-35, 239, 247, 272, 290, 291, 314, 337, 395
The Ocean of His Utterances/Expanding Horizons 236-48, 272, 310, 315, 343
stories, poems, articles 7-9, 11-14, 184-6, 189-90, 190-98, 248-54, 379
meeting and relationship with 'Abdu'l-Bahá ix, 3, 23-6, 27-30, 31-4, 38-9, 205, 341, 392-3
travels and talks *see* individual place entries
Ives, Hoyt 10
Ives, Julius 7
Ives, Mabel Rice-Wray
description of Howard Ives 394-6
early life and family 3-4, 51-2, 65-74
correspondence with
'Abdu'l-Bahá 70, 82, 88-90
Tablets from 'Abdu'l-Bahá 5-6, 67, 68, 70, 72, 74-6
Joseph Hannen 73, 74
Horace Holley 327, 366, 37-75
Leroy Ioas 311, 344, 445, 346-8, 357, 408
Howard Ives 2, 5, 98, 100, 102, 108-09, 115, 136-38, 174-75, 176, 180-81, 191, 202, 258, 255, 272, 273-74, 276, 277, 284, 285, 287, 289, 291, 293-94, 295-96, 302-03, 304, 321-22, 325, 329-30, 353-55, 365-66, 374, 377-78
National Spiritual Assembly of the United States and Canada 4, 92, 143-5, 203, 279-80, 294, 299, 304, 312, 313, 314, 317, 328, 330, 335, 374
National Teaching Committee 168, 261, 299-300, 343, 345, 352, 355, 357, 392, 405, 408, 418-19
Edris Rice-Wray 187, 286, 405
Rúḥíyyih <u>Kh</u>ánum 292-3, 422

Shoghi Effendi 5-6, 93, 111-12, 123, 129, 148, 205, 274, 277, 278-81, 305-8, 321, 325-7, 329-30, 336, 338, 346, 356-8, 398-9, 401, 404, 409-15, 417
Federal Bureau of Investigation 367-71
meeting with 'Abdu'l-Bahá 71
travels and talks *see* individual place entries
Ives, Muriel ix, 10, 20, 65-6, 97, 105, 175, 179, 187, 252, 284, 294, 383, 392, 397
becoming a Bahá'í 43-4, 45, 178-80
childhood and youth 10, 14-16
meeting 'Abdu'l-Bahá 44, 178-80
correspondence with
Howard Ives 282, 323, 380, Shoghi Effendi 180
marriages 55, 61, 282-83,
support of Howard and Mabel Ives 284, 286, 292, 294, 300, 304
Ives, Theodore 7, 113
Ives, Waldo Rolfe 10
Ives, Whitney Thayer 10
Ives, William 7, 113

Jarvis, Mr 288
Jemison family 349
Jenkins, Ruby 350
Jesus Christ 9, 15, 27, 57, 58-60, 68, 94-5, 112, 117-18, 132, 133, 159, 196, 197, 198, 238, 274, 277, 288, 298, 338, 360, 361, 365, 436, 438, 444, 446, 449, 457
Jináb-i-Fáḍil (Mázindarání) 82, 93, 95, 395
Johnson, Juanita Dr 407-8
Jond, Dr & Mrs, 159

Kat, Mary 354
Kavelin, Borrah 403
Kavelin, Martha 403
Keller, Clare 355, 356
Kelley, Beverly and Jack 362
Kelsey, Olivia 346, 419

Kendrich, Dr 171
Kentucky 433
  Louisville 85, 96, 344-6, 417-18, 419-20
Khan, Ali-Kuli 69, 393
Kidder, Elizabeth 85
Kilpatrick, Mrs 260
King, Sylvia *see* Mattheson, Sylvia
Kinney, Carrie 23, 44, 81, 82, 84
Kinney, Edward (Saffa) 23, 81, 82, 83, 84
Kirchner, Luella 74
Knobloch, Fanny 134
Kuen, Dr C.B. 45

Landrom, Helene 365, 377
Langrall, Hazel 169
Latin America (various countries) 327, 337, 416
Little, Marion 376, 401, 403
London, England 22
Louisiana 258, 399, 433
  Baton Rouge 401
  Covington 401
  New Orleans 70, 336, 345, 362, 364, 365, 374, 401
Lunt, Alfred 92, 96, 392
Lutes, Mr 289
Lutes, Muriel 289

Macke, Marlene 315-16
Maine 258, 433
  Green Acre 50-51, 143, 175, 181, 277-80, 282, 303
  Kittery 258
  Lewiston 181-2, 286
  Portland 181-2
  Portsmouth 183
Manitoba, Canada
  Winnipeg 314
Mann, Amelia 146
Mann, Charles & Mrs 146-7
Mann, Grace 146-7
Mann, Jessie 146
Mann, Roland 146
Marangella, Philip 306, 307

Martin, Miss 344-5
Maryland 258
  Baltimore 15, 54, 61, 65-7, 135, 146-7, 150-51, 157-64, 169
  Chevy Chase 134
Mason, Dr and Mrs Joe 150, 162
Massachusetts
  Brewster 15
  Springfield 120
  Williamstown 10
Masters, Gladys 271
Matteson, Gladys 271
Mattheson, Sylvia (King) 258-62, 423
Maxwell, May 80-81, 104, 133, 285, 288, 293, 296, 300, 304, 307, 316, 427, 437
Maxwell, Sutherland 422
McCullom, Harriet 126, 306
McDaniel, Allen 165, 314
McEwen, Mrs 289
McHenry, Elizabeth 171, 426
McHenry, John S. 171, 246, 426, 428
McKay, Doris 4, 81, 84, 116, 119-20, 126, 129, 130, 133, 138-42, 155, 204, 320, 327-8, 330, 363, 365, 372-7, 385, 394, 397
McKay, Willard 84, 116, 126, 138-42, 155, 327, 330, 372
McMichaels, Mrs, 197
Michigan
  Davison 134
  Dearborn 331
  Detroit 51, 73-6, 79, 124, 189, 331
  Louhelen 134
Miller, George 352
Miller, Janet 366
Miller, Robert 373
Mills, Mountfort 22, 31, 81, 83
Minnesota 266, 276, 278, 433
  Minneapolis 274, 276, 277, 279
  St Paul 274, 276
Mississippi 258, 399, 411, 413, 416, 433
  Greenwood 360-61, 405, 406
  Gulfport 336
  Jackson 401, 403-6, 410

Senatobia 362
Missouri
  St Louis 67-8, 413, 424, 470
  Versailles 67
Moffett, Ruth 5, 413
Moore, Clarence 20-21, 41
Moore, Marie (Mrs Clarence) 41, 51
Morgan, Arthur 184
Morris, Dr 420
Müller, Max 445-6

National Convention 52, 63, 64, 74, 76, 77, 78, 79, 85, 95, 144, 216, 256, 275, 303-4, 305, 313, 352, 364, 377-8, 385-6, 389, 416, 423, 432, 441
National Spiritual Assembly of the Bahá'ís of the United States and Canada 4, 84-5, 96, 134, 212, 215, 227, 256, 279, 298, 299, 345, 346, 374-5
  correspondence with
    Howard Ives 4, 5, 91, 95-6, 143-5, 206, 208-10, 212-19, 220-21, 225-7, 246, 248, 294, 298, 301, 304, 310, 314, 328, 343, 374
    Mabel Ives 4, 92, 143-5, 203, 279-80, 294, 299, 304, 312, 313, 314, 317, 328, 330, 335, 374
  Plan of Unified Action 144-5
  see also Seven Year Plan
National Teaching Committee xiii, 4, 76, 77-8, 100, 112, 129, 146, 168, 218, 236, 261, 265, 279, 281, 284, 288, 299, 300-01, 302, 304, 306, 308, 309, 316, 328, 343, 344-5, 347, 352, 355, 357, 365, 392, 405, 408, 418, 419, 427-8
Nebraska 258, 278, 433
  Council Bluffs 261-2
  Lincoln 258-61
  Omaha 258-64, 417-18, 423
Nelson, Sheila *see* Rice-Wray, Sheila
New Brunswick, Canada 285, 305, 312, 320, 433
  Moncton 286-90, 293, 295-6, 297, 301, 306, 308-9, 311-15
  Shediac 312, 314
  St John 289
Newfoundland, Canada 285, 314
New Hampshire 258, 433
  Dublin 33-4, 51
  Manchester 169-71
New Jersey 172, 433
  Cranford 121-2
  Elizabeth 121
  Jersey City 16, 17, 63
  Keyport 124
  Montclair 37-8, 65
  Newark 67, 69, 175
  Summit 16, 41, 55, 121
  Vineland 45
New Mexico 258, 420-21, 433
  Albuquerque 420-23
New York 90, 126, 258, 327, 328, 433
  Albany 105, 183, 258, 429
  Binghamton 126-9, 133, 155, 156, 170, 183, 292, 295, 297-8, 305-6, 311
  Brooklyn 7, 171-2, 175, 177, 283, 286, 293
  Brooklyn Bridge 10
  Buffalo 93, 119, 129
  Fredonia 97
  Geneva 7, 99, 116, 124, 126, 127, 129, 133, 155, 170
  Ithaca 124, 126
  Jamestown 101, 327-8
  Kings 10
  Niagara 7
  New York 9, 10, 21-3, 27, 32, 63, 77, 80-81, 83-4, 85-6, 90, 92, 123-4, 132, 175, 181, 240-41, 276, 329, 338, 349, 435
  Pottersville 112
  Rochester 93, 95-6, 101, 108, 124, 133
  Schenectady 258
  Scranton 3, 311-12

Syracuse 93, 131-3, 306
Utica 102, 105, 258, 344
New York Times 283
Nicklin, Eve 147, 156
Noe, Mr 338
North Dakota 258, 265, 269, 274
  Carrington 270-72
  Fargo 265, 273-5
  Glenfield 265, 269-70
  Jamestown 274
Nova Scotia 285, 433
  Halifax 313

Ober, Grace Robarts 32, 43-4, 51, 79, 81, 83, 84-5, 98-9, 119, 127, 129, 133, 134, 137, 139-40, 142, 151, 155, 303-4, 309, 318, 319, 323, 328, 329, 373, 386, 427
Ober, Harlan 32, 43-4, 51, 69, 79, 81, 83, 84-5, 98-9, 119, 125, 127, 129, 133, 137, 138-9, 141, 151, 155, 218, 297, 303, 311, 335
Ober, Mary 139, 142
Obrig, Barbara *see* Ives, Barbara
Obrig, Muriel *see* Ives, Muriel
Obrig, Theodore (Ted) 55-61
Ohio 73, 168, 171, 258, 278, 433
  Akton 73
  Birmingham 94
  Cincinnati 183, 201, 377
  Cleveland 73, 183
  Columbus 93, 95-6, 168-9
  Dayton 201-2
  Lima 201-2, 306
  Sandusky 73
  Youngstown 93
Oklahoma 258, 433
  Oklahoma City 424
Ontario, Canada 285, 433
  Hamilton 325-6, 329-30, 331
  Queenston 327
  Toronto 311, 314-30, 353, 430
Oregon ix
  Portland 1
  Ontario 192
Oslo, Norway 275

Paine, Professor 333
Parsons, Agnes 34, 51, 95, 121, 135
Pennsylvania 328, 433
  Allentown 54
  Eire 97
  Mansfield 170
  Meadville 15
  New Castle 138, 148, 150, 155-6
  Philadelphia 14, 45, 120, 132, 297, 307-8
  Pittsburgh 45, 90, 92, 93, 127, 139, 149-50, 155-6, 162, 169
  Scranton 218, 267, 297-9, 300, 302, 304-5, 308-9
Pettibone, Mrs 327
Phillips, Nancy xi, 192-200, 208, 312, 338-9, 362-3
Pitman, Carlotta 355
Portals to Freedom, see Ives, Howard
Prince Edward Island 285, 312
  Charlottetown 292

Quebec, Canada
  Montreal 296, 314, 430

Randall, Albert 51, 81
Randall, Harry 51, 95, 392
Ransom-Kehler, Keith 392, 427
Redman, Earl xv
Reed, Congressman 101
Reich, Eric 228
Remey, Mason 74
Rexford, Orcella 5, 135, 306, 356
Rhea, Tommy 355
Rhodes, Marion 317
Rice-Wray, Colston (Ruhi) 65, 69, 105-6, 280, 327, 337, 418, 423, 424, 426-7
  meeting with 'Abdu'l-Bahá 71
Rice-Wray, Edris 65, 69-73, 90, 177, 189, 200, 202, 205, 212, 214, 303, 304, 314, 317, 331-2, 335, 378, 389, 393, 416, 423-8, 430
  correspondence with
    Mabel Ives 187, 268, 286, 405

Shoghi Effendi 416
  meeting with 'Abdu'l-Bahá 71
  support of Howard and Mabel Ives
    176-7, 187, 191, 214-15, 259,
    282, 284, 300, 302
Rice-Wray, Ella 68-9
Rice-Wray, Ellah 67, 68-9
Rice-Wray, James 67
Rice-Wray, Landon Carter 69
Rice-Wray, Sheila Nelson 327, 336-7, 418, 424
Rice-Wray, Theron 67-9, 73-4, 80, 259, 391
  Tablet from 'Abdu'l-Bahá 67, 68
Richardson, Doris 320
Rieger, Dr 101
Robarts, Grace see Ober, Grace
Robarts, John and Audrey 318, 319-20, 324, 327, 328, 329
Robarts, Patrick 320
Robertson, Mr 289
Roche, Nellie 356, 362, 375, 412, 419
Root, Martha 4, 392, 427
Roth, Mrs 260
Rugg, Mrs 334
Ruhe, David and Margaret 401
Ruhi courses 242
Rúḥíyyih Khánum 227, 278, 280, 292-3, 392, 422

Sala, Rosemary 288
Scheffler, Carl 64
Schopflocher, Lorol 335
Schopflocher, Siegfried 212, 335
Scranton Tribune, The 239
Seker, Henry and Bessy 140
Seto, Mamie, 302
Seven Year Plan 5, 230, 256-8, 349, 399, 402, 427
Shoghi Effendi 85, 87, 92, 96, 108-110, 113, 124, 142-3, 148-9, 195, 199, 200-01, 256, 258, 274, 276, 298, 334, 392, 402, 427
  correspondence with
    Leroy Ioas 323

Howard Ives 93, 111, 123-4, 129-30, 153, 157-60, 165-7, 171-2, 176-7, 180-81, 205-8, 210-11, 214, 216-17, 221, 226-32, 236-7, 239-40, 246, 248, 256, 272, 293-5, 300-302, 309, 311-12, 317-19, 324-5, 343-4, 348, 349, 392
Mabel Rice-Wray Ives 93, 111, 123-4, 129-30, 148-9, 278-81, 305-9, 325, 326-7, 336, 346, 358-9, 399-400, 401, 404, 410-15, 417-18, 427-8
National Convention (American) 256
Regional Teaching Committee 427-8
Edris Rice-Wray 416-17
writings 143, 152, 153, 161, 165, 276, 337
  The Advent of Divine Justice 337
  The Goal of a New World Order 143, 154, 161, 165, 276
  The Unfoldment of World Civilization 276
  The World Order of Bahá'u'lláh 276
Shook, Dr Glenn 356
Síyáh-Chál 231, 232
Simon, Albert G. 65, 74-5
Simon, Albert Jr. 65
Simon, Caroline McGrew 65
Simon, Mabel see Ives, Mabel Rice-Wray
Skelton, Lane 403
Sluyter, Mrs J. 261
Smith, Gipsy Jr. 403
Smith, Terah 356
Sohrab, Ahmad 53, 64, 201, 334
Solomon Islands 335
Sothman, Alma 262
South Africa 85
Sparks, Jared 15
Spendlove, George 330
Stearns, John 327
Stevens, Ethel Stefana 18

509

Stewart, Mrs 135
Stone, Jimmy 350
Storch, Juanita 64, 83
Sulaymán Khán 230
Sunshine, Rezsi 344-5, 350, 364-6, 367, 369-70, 387-8

Tennessee 258, 399, 433
  Kingsport 246
  Knoxville 184-6, 204, 344-6, 419, 433
  Memphis 331-9, 344-51, 352-60, 362-6, 373-7, 387-8, 398, 411-12, 431
  Nashville, 202, 347, 349, 350, 375-6, 412
  Norris 185-6
Ten Year Crusade 116, 256, 335
Terry, Harriet 277
Texas 419-20
Thompson, Juliet 51, 61, 82, 84
Trigvasson, Oslof 297
True, George and Peggy 331
True, Katherine 409, 416-17

Underhill, Eyelyn 127
Unitarian Church 15-17, 40-41, 121, 262, 274, 334, 336, 349, 358, 371
Universal House of Justice, The 192, 256, 401, 403

Vail, Albert 41

Ward, Forsyth 126, 258
Ward, Janet 258
Washington DC 54, 61, 67, 73, 86, 132, 134-5, 142, 147, 151, 155, 161, 163, 344
Watkins, Mrs 338, 350, 362

Wattson, Francis 50
Weiss, Rabbi 261
White, Mrs 261-2
Whitehead, O. Z. 7
Wilbur, Roy Lyman 164-5
Wilhelm, Roy 54, 63, 77, 150
  Tablet from 'Abdu'l-Bahá 46
Wilson, Nan 357-8
Wilson, Roberta (Robbie) 352, 353, 354-5, 357, 397-8
Wilson, Ruth 288-9, 292-3, 296, 311-13
Wilson, Woodrow 361
Windust, Albert 228, 246
Wisconsin 258, 265, 266, 433
  Hudson 277
  Kenosha 189, 202
  Madison 202, 277, 417-18
  Milwaukee 189, 202
  Racine 189, 202
Wood, Clara 213
Woolson, Dr Clement 270, 276
Woolson, Gayle 265, 269-70, 275-7, 276
World Order magazine 220, 262, 343
World Outlook, The 186
World War
  First 54, 55, 360
  Second 255, 360, 402
Wright, Charlotte 274
Wright, E. J. 269
Wyoming 7
Yerger, Helen 404

Zimmerman, Johanna 334, 355, 356

www.ingramcontent.com/pod-product-compliance
Lightning Source LLC
Chambersburg PA
CBHW060511230426
43665CB00013B/1480